Windows NT SNMP

Windows NT SNMP

James D. Murray

O'REILLY™

Cambridge · Köln · Paris · Sebastopol · Tokyo

Windows NT SNMP

by James D. Murray

Copyright © 1998 O'Reilly & Associates, Inc. All rights reserved.
Printed in the United States of America.

Published by O'Reilly & Associates, Inc., 101 Morris Street, Sebastopol, CA 95472.

Editor: Deborah Russell

Production Editor: John Files

Printing History:

    January 1998:   First Edition

ISBN: 1-56592-338-3

This book is dedicated to:

All of the members, past and present, of the PairGain Technologies network management group;

P.J. Mead Books & Coffee Gallery, Orange, California;

Fe, my love.

—James D. Murray

Table of Contents

Preface

The Simple Network Management Protocol (SNMP) is one of many protocols that are collectively known as the Internet Protocol (IP) suite.* IP protocols are used to convey specific types of information across an IP network, such as the Internet. SNMP is the protocol recommended specifically for the exchange of management information between the hosts residing on all IP networks.

Most SNMP books are filled with the theories and philosophies behind SNMP and network management, but contain precious little practical knowledge on the actual application and implementation of SNMP. This lack of practical information is very frustrating, especially when you find yourself asking real-world questions such as:

- Should I use static or dynamically allocated memory for tables?
- What kind of data structures should an agent use to store MIB data?
- How do I reinitialize an agent when restarting the operating system?
- What if my management program times out waiting for a response?
- Where should I store the data my management application retrieves?
- How do I get a hex dump of an SNMP message and interpret the data?
- Can I implement SNMP in Visual Basic, Java, or Perl?

Unfortunately, the answers to virtually all of these implementation-dependent questions are: "It depends on the system," "Whatever works best," and "Any way you want, as long as you follow the RFCs."† In your effort to discover for yourself what works best, you may waste hours writing code, then end up throwing it

---

* Also commonly called the TCP/IP Protocol suite, named after its two core protocols.

† Requests For Comments are Internet standards documents.

away.* Because SNMP can be implemented on any device that contains an operating system and at least a rudimentary network protocol stack, it is nearly impossible to write a book comprehensive enough to cover all of the problems and decisions you might encounter while attempting to implement SNMP on every type of system. This book tackles SNMP from the very narrow viewpoint of the SNMP service included with Microsoft Windows NT, so the implementation details I describe are very specific and, I hope, very useful.

Windows NT and the Win32 operating system make an excellent support platform for SNMP. NT's support of TCP/IP networking and its graphical user interface allow the development and support of both SNMP management systems and agents. Windows NT also supports application services: special Windows applications that run in the background and that may be started, stopped, added, and removed without rebooting the system. SNMP under Windows NT (and Windows 95) is implemented as the SNMP service.

The heart of the SNMP service is the SNMP extendible agent. As a programmer, you will use Management Information Base (MIB, sounds like "rib") modules and the SNMP RFCs as the functional specifications for writing "extension agents," and a dynamic link library (DLL). These, along with the Microsoft SNMP API (Application Program Interface), allow the SNMP extendible agent to process SNMPv1 requests and send SNMPv1 traps. The extendible agent and extension agents exchange information using the SNMP API. (If you don't know all this terminology, don't worry. That's what this book is for.)

The SNMP API also allows Win32 programmers to experience writing code for both SNMPv1 management applications and SNMPv1 agents, and to test this code using tools commonly available to the SNMP community. The service also supplies several common implementation details for you (such as ASN.1 and BER parsing) and allows you to concentrate on supporting the specific objects defined in your MIB modules.

Although SNMP is about "network" management, you don't actually need a network to develop SNMP management applications and extension agents; management applications and agents residing on the same system can easily talk to each other.† If you are interested only in monitoring the status of individual computers or other networked devices, but not the network itself, you'll find that SNMP is also quite capable of supporting system management operations.

---

* This will rarely be a pleasing prospect to a programmer, especially one whose progress is being measured against a schedule drafted by a project manager who lives by the theory that "if I don't understand it, it must be easy."

† Although I greatly encourage you to develop using at least a simple two-node, peer-to-peer network. We're talking two Win32 machines and less than $100 (U.S.) of networking equipment here.

Audience for This Book

This book is intended primarily for Win32 programmers who need to implement SNMP management on a Windows NT or Windows 95 system and need to learn a little bit about IP network management along the way. This book contains detailed explanations of the code you will need to write to implement your MIBs under the Microsoft SNMP service. The working code examples on the CD-ROM provided with the book are intended to be used as the base of your own projects. This book should also be of use to system administrators and network administrators.

Part I of this book contains a considerable amount of introductory material on TCP/IP networks, network management, and SNMP in general. If you are already experienced in network management, you can skip over these chapters and dig right into the SNMP service. But if you could use a little help in reading SNMP MIB modules, remembering how UDP works, or even revisiting what network management is all about, then please take the time to read the first few chapters.

This book focuses primarily on the Intel system architecture and Microsoft software products. This is the reality of the marketplace. There are many more Windows NT systems running on Intel platforms than on DEC Alpha or MIPS platforms. And, there are probably more Windows NT developers using Microsoft development tools than the tools from any other vendor (and possibly from all other vendors combined).

Organization of This Book

This book is organized into ten chapters and four appendixes, as listed below. All code examples are taken from the working example projects on the CD-ROM.

Part I: SNMP Basics

Chapter 1, *Introduction to SNMP*, contains a simple overview of network management, the implementation of SNMP under Windows 95 and NT, and the history of SNMP.

Chapter 2, *Network Basics*, summarizes the basic components of computer networks, the OSI Reference Model, the TCP/IP network packets used by SNMP, and some of the history of TCP/IP.

Chapter 3, *Network Management and SNMP*, discusses the basic aspects of network and system management, management information, SNMP configuration parameters, and why you should—or should not—consider using SNMP for system and network management.

Chapter 4, *Inside SNMP*, provides extensive coverage of the internal operation and structure of the SNMP protocol and messages, the objects and data types, and the ASN.1 language used to write MIB modules.

Part II: SNMP Details

Chapter 5, *Getting Started with the SNMP Service*, describes the installation, operation, and removal of the Microsoft SNMP service and its components under Windows 95 and Windows NT. It also examines the SNMP service configuration parameters and how to modify them using both the policy editor and the registry.

Chapter 6, *Using the Extension and Utility APIs*, is an in-depth look at the Microsoft SNMP Extension and Utility APIs. It includes working code examples that demonstrate the operation of each API call, along with a walk-through of the *SNMP.H* header file.

Chapter 7, *Writing Extension Agents*, discusses how to write an extension agent. It includes many working code examples that show you how to implement each SNMP Extension API call and use it in an extension agent, as well as how to collect management data stored in both process memory and the registry. It also covers how to build, install, test, debug, and remove extension agents.

Chapter 8, *Implementing Traps*, explains how to write an extension agent DLL that is capable of sending SNMP traps. It examines methods for collecting management information and detecting trappable events, and it provides recommendations for how, when, and where to send traps.

Chapter 9, *Using the Management API*, is an in-depth look at the Microsoft SNMP Management API. This API is used to write simple SNMPv1 management applications that run under Windows NT (and, with a bit of fudging, under Windows 95 as well). It includes many working code examples that demonstrate the operation of each API call, as well as a walk-through of the *MGMTAPI.H* header file.

Chapter 10, *Writing Network Management Applications*, discusses how to design an SNMP management application that uses the SNMP Management API to send, receive, and process SNMPv1 request messages and to receive SNMPv1 traps. It also discusses the problems of performing SNMP management.

Part III: Appendixes and Glossary

Appendix A, *References*, contains many book and Internet references for SNMP, TCP/IP, WinSock, and network management information and software.

Appendix B, *Microsoft Knowledge Base*, lists all Microsoft Knowledge Base articles through October 1997 that refer to the SNMP service and APIs.

Appendix C, *RFCs*, lists all of the RFCs (Requests for Comments) referenced in this book.

Appendix D, *What's on the CD-ROM?*, describes the book's accompanying CD-ROM. The *README.HTM* and *README.TXT* files in the CD's root directory contain detailed information about the example programs, documents, and demo and trial software packages it contains.

The *Glossary* defines the terms used in this book and in the world of NT SNMP.

About the Code and the CD-ROM

The CD-ROM contains entire working examples that are discussed in this book and used to derive the code in many of the book's figures and examples. It also contains quite a few RFCs and MIB modules relevant to the discussion of SNMP in this book. As an added bonus, we've included many SNMP and TCP/IP software packages, trial applications, and demos; all of these operate under Windows NT, and many under Windows 95 as well.

All of the code examples in this book and on the accompanying CD-ROM are written in Standard C or Visual Basic, have been built using Microsoft C++ version 5.0 or Visual Basic 4.0a, and have been tested using Windows NT 4.0. You should have no problems porting these examples to other C compilers or to C++ if you should wish to do so, and many should also run under Windows 95. Updates of the example projects may be available via FTP from the O'Reilly Web server. (See Appendix D and the CD-ROM for details.)

Conventions Used in This Book

The following typographical conventions are used in this book:

Italic is used for URLs (ftp, telnet, http, news, etc.), directory names, filenames, and registry keys. It is also used for emphasis and for the first use of a technical term.

UPPERCASE is used for MS-DOS and Windows file and directory names.

`Courier` is used to show the contents of files, source code, and the output of commands.

Comments and Questions

SNMP may be simple, but writing a book certainly isn't. I have examined and tested the contents of this tome for technical correctness and usability. But if you should find any errors, or have suggestions for future editions, please pass them along. You may contact O'Reilly at:

> O'Reilly & Associates
> 101 Morris Street
> Sebastopol, CA 95472 USA
> 1-800-998-9938 (in the USA or Canada)
> 1-707-829-0515 (international or local)
> 1-707-829-0104 (FAX)

You may also send us messages electronically. See the ads in this book for information about all of O'Reilly & Associates' online services.

Acknowledgments

My primary thanks go to my illustrious O'Reilly editor, Deborah Russell, mistress of time, space, and dimension, without whom I would just be another unfortunate distributor of dangling participles and split infinitives.

Many thanks to the people who performed a technical review on early drafts of this book: David T. Perkins, SNMPinfo; Bob Natale, ACE*COMM; Thomas Cikoski, Panther Digital Corporation; David Reid, SNMP Research International, Inc.; Mickey Williams, Codev Technologies; Mary Quinn, FTP Software, Inc.; Dr. Robert Krupczak, Empire Technologies, Inc.; Dr. Russell J. Clark, Empire Technologies, Inc.; Matjaz Vrecko, MG-SOFT Corporation; and Gregor Vrecko, MG-SOFT Corporation.

Many thanks to the companies that contributed software for inclusion on the CD-ROM that accompanies this book: ACE*COMM Corporation; Cinco Networks, Inc.; Dart Communications; DMH Software; Empire Technologies, Inc.; MG-SOFT Corporation; Network Computing Technologies, Inc.; RedPoint Software Corporation; The SNMP WorkShop; and Visual Edge Software Ltd.

My gratitude to all the people at O'Reilly & Associates who made this book a reality, especially to Edie Freedman, the O'Reilly graphics artist whose intuitive cogitation resulted in a Nutshell animal with a beard almost as long as my own; to John Files, the production manager and copyeditor for the book; to Seth Maislin, the indexer; to Jane Ellin, the proofreader; to Sheryl Avruch and Claire Cloutier LeBlanc, who ensured quality control; to Nancy Priest, the designer; and to Elissa Haney, who provided production support.

Special thanks are also bestowed upon PairGain Technologies for providing me with the experience of dabbling for years in system and network management from the telco perspective, and to the many hundreds of people who have made SNMP a reality and who continue to keep it alive and growing.

I

SNMP Basics

This part of the book introduces the Simple Network Management Protocol, its implementation on the Microsoft Windows platforms, and the networking concepts that underlie the protocol.

Chapter 1, *Introduction to SNMP*, contains a simple overview of SNMP, its implementation under Windows NT and Windows 95, and the history of SNMP.

Chapter 2, *Network Basics*, summarizes the basic components of computer networks, the OSI Reference Model, the TCP/IP network packets used by SNMP, and some of the history of TCP/IP.

Chapter 3, *Network Management and SNMP*, discusses the basic aspects of network and system management, management information, SNMP configuration parameters, and why you should—or should not—consider using SNMP for system and network management.

Chapter 4, *Inside SNMP*, provides extensive coverage of the internal operation and structure of the SNMP protocol and messages, the objects and data types, and the ASN.1 language used to write MIB modules.

In this chapter:
• Why SNMP?
• What Is SNMP?
• SNMP and Microsoft
• SNMP History

1

Introduction to SNMP

SNMP, the Simple Network Management Protocol, is a protocol used to remotely manage the nodes on a TCP/IP network. The Internet Engineering Task Force (IETF)* recommends that all nodes residing on a TCP/IP network have the capability of being managed remotely over the network. The Internet-standard Networking Management Framework is used to manage TCP/IP networks, and SNMP version 1 is the recommended standard network management protocol for this framework.

This chapter briefly describes what SNMP is and how it works. It discusses some of the history of SNMP and its implementation on Microsoft platforms. It also looks briefly at the topic of network management, which SNMP is intended to simplify.

Why SNMP?

Before I describe SNMP itself in any detail, let's look at why we need such a protocol. What does it mean to manage a network, and how can a protocol like SNMP help in that management?

Network management allows you to monitor and control network devices remotely using conventional computer network technology. Using SNMP, one workstation running one or more management software applications can monitor management information collected by thousands of network devices (e.g., servers, workstations, routers). You can then use this information to determine the current

---

* The IETF is an organization that is chartered to create and revise standards for the Internet, most notably TCP/IP. Therefore, many organizations using TCP/IP networks have a standing requirement that all networked devices must directly, or by proxy, support SNMP.

The Simple Protocol

Why is SNMP considered to be a "simple" protocol? The design of the protocol itself is simple because it requires only four operations to be able to perform all network management tasks. All SNMP messages contain only a few header fields and are typically very small in size. And the management information defined by SNMP is a set of very simple objects. Alas, the use of the word "simple" does not imply that SNMP makes network management simple, or that SNMP itself is always simple to implement. (If, after reading this book, you don't think SNMP is really simple, then you should try comparing it to the other system and network management protocols used by your favorite telco and telecom communities. For me, CMIP and TL1 come to mind.)

---

health and level of performance of the network. You can also use it to determine where problems on the network are located and how best to fix them.

To manage a device that's connected to a network, you need to either manipulate it directly (*local management*) or manipulate it via some centralized process (*remote management*). Obviously, the more devices that are connected to a network, the harder it will be to manage them locally.

Most devices let you manage them locally through the use of switches, gauges, and displays on an instrument panel, or a terminal interface with menus rendered using a Character User Interface (CUI). But local management requires that a human manager be physically present at the location of the managed device to press buttons, watch LEDs flicker, interpret data as it is displayed on a dumb terminal plugged into the device's serial port, and so on. This is a very inconvenient way to manage hundreds or thousands of devices that are spread out over a large geographical distance. Even if the thousands of devices are located in the same building (such as in a telephone company's central office), it would still take a small army of people to configure and monitor all of the devices. That's why the ability to manage nodes remotely is so important. SNMP provides that ability.

Figure 1-1 shows a device that supports SNMP management over a local serial connection, a remote modem link, and a network connection. The device also has a front panel that can be used to perform many of the management functions, but the disadvantage is that you must have physical access to the device. The local connection has the advantage of being fast because it does not have to share its dedicated channel with other management devices, but having only one management port (often called a *craft port*), means that the local console must be in the local proximity of the device. The remote management console allows management access from thousands of miles away via modem, but you still have the problem of having only one management port. The network connection allows a virtually unlimited number of managed nodes to be accessed by one or more management stations.

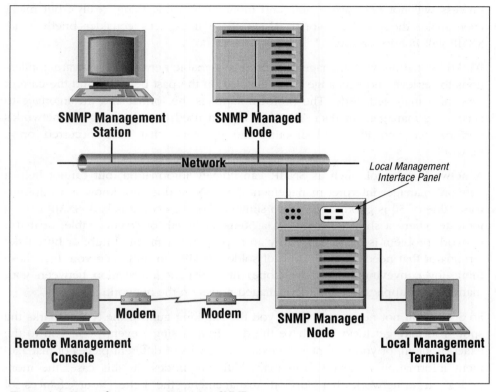

Figure 1-1. Network management using SNMP

After you read about the way SNMP operates, you may begin to believe that SNMP is capable of any type of control operation on any type of network device. You may have even read articles on SNMP that proclaim it to be the perfect protocol, capable of the remote control of power stations and utility plants, the control of navigation systems, and the maintenance of huge information data-bases. While the simplicity of SNMP does theoretically give it unlimited capabilities, SNMP also has some potential drawbacks; in certain ways it is quite fragile, unsecure, and non-real-time. These drawbacks will probably lead you to use SNMP only for mundane, low-priority network management tasks. You are likely to choose other, more robust network protocols for use with applications that require time-critical remote control.

Why Not SNMP?

The phrase "the right tool for the right job" applies to everything from wire cutters to workstations. It also applies to software tools and maintenance and management practices. Trying to fix a problem using the wrong tool or the wrong process will not only waste time and money (the same thing, really), but might even make the problem worse. Along these lines, let's consider briefly what SNMP will *not* do for you.

We know that network management protocols enable networked software applications to retrieve and exchange data collected on the past behavior and the current state of a managed node. The protocol supplies the format and the interface to access the management data. The data is then used in monitoring the network's performance and in troubleshooting the problems that have occurred on a network.

A network protocol, such as SNMP, can convey information, but cannot help a network manager interpret management data. SNMP does not know if a udpInErrors value of 50 is good, or if a zero snmpOutTooBigs count is bad. SNMP cannot indicate where a short is located in a 50-meter length of coaxial cable, or that a network problem is being caused by an improperly segmented hub, or by a flaky terminator that needs another drop of solder. SNMP can only help you infer these things by conveying (useful, we hope) management information between your management application and the managed nodes on the network.

So SNMP will not necessarily show you the smoking gun, or the X that marks the spot. You may get lucky and have the data from a single event point you to the exact problem, or you may need to examine dozens of different pieces of management information retrieved from many different nodes. In this case, the more nodes on a network that support management, the better your chances of isolating any problems that may occur.

Often, a single network problem will generate many different alarms and notifications. It takes an experienced network manager to figure out that all of those "link down," "loss of sync word," and "power feed open" messages mean that someone has unplugged the router, tripped over the server's power cord, or core-sampled your T1 line. It would take a truly sophisticated (and expensive) network management system to correctly interpret the exact cause of such problematic situations and display a single "Coffee was spilled on the console keyboard (again)" alarm message.

So don't believe that marketing glossy that promises a network filled with devices that support network management will make all your network problems easy to solve, or just go away. Having a garage filled with tools won't keep your car from eventually breaking down. Network management—and SNMP—is only a tool, and one tool of many. You will do best if the tools you use have useful features, are well-oiled, and are being used by the people who know how to use them.

What Is Network Management?

When you perform network management, what exactly are you managing? That's not as easy a question as you might think, as we'll see in Chapter 3, *Network Management and SNMP*. But here are some simple tasks you might perform under the umbrella of network management:

- Collecting information from devices connected to the network—such devices include routers, servers, and workstations. Information includes how the devices are functioning and how they fit together. Sometimes this aspect of network management is known as *configuration management.*

- Observing how the network is working and being able to detect when something goes wrong (e.g., a router stops routing data, a device loses power and disappears from the network). This aspect of network management is known as *fault management.*

- Monitoring how well the network is functioning—whether it is able to keep up with the current or expected workload, and what is the present working condition of the device. This aspect of network management is known as *performance management.*

Network management is a cooperative union formed by managers and agents. A *manager* is a person or department of people responsible for maintaining the health of a computer network and the tools that they use to do so. An *agent* is a hardware device or software process that collects and distributes statistical information on the operation of a network device.[*]

Managers gather information from agents to check periodically on how well a network is performing and to diagnose any problems that are occurring or that may occur. A manager's job is more complicated than that of the utility person who comes around every so often to read your gas and electricity meters, but it's basically the same thing. Unlike the utility person, a manager is responsible for not only fixing a faulty network, but also for changing its configuration when necessary.

---

[*] Network management systems are sometimes called "managers." However, to keep the terminology as clear as possible, this book refers to such nodes as "management systems" and reserves the term "manager" for the human operator who must inevitably interpret the management data collected by the management system, and who must employ corrective courses of action.

What Is SNMP?

SNMP is one of the many protocols found in the Internet Protocol suite. The management framework in the IP suite is the Internet-standard Networking Management Framework. SNMP is the primary protocol in this framework used in the transfer of network management information between two or more network entities or nodes (for example, workstations, routers, etc.).

Network management information includes any data that is used to monitor and control the state of a network node. Such data may include the past performance history of the communication links currently established by the node, a command to reset a node or cause it to download new firmware, and the current number and type of faults present on the node.

What Does SNMP Offer?

Why use SNMP? There are other network management protocols available. The IETF does strongly recommend—but does not require—the implementation of the SNMP protocol on all devices residing on an IP network. The IETF neither obliges you to support SNMP nor discourages you from using it on a non-IP network.

You may have the choice of supporting several different network management protocols, and even the possibility of ignoring the currently available standardized offerings and creating a protocol of your own. (However, as someone who was once hired to do just this, I don't recommend this laissez-faire solution).

You may not have the choice of which protocol to use. Some authority may be dictating the management protocol you will implement, such as the need to interface with the product from a vendor that only uses SNMP. You may also have a customer that demands SNMP support, whether they actually use SNMP or not. (Silly, yes, but it happens . . .)

Assuming that you have a choice, here are some advantages of using SNMP:

SNMP is standardized

SNMP is the standard network management protocol for TCP/IP networks. Like TCP and IP, SNMP is also a component of the Internet Protocol suite. The Internet community develops, standardizes, and implements Internet protocols specifically for the transportation and management of data on Internet technology-based networks.

Internet protocols themselves are open, nonproprietary standards developed through voluntary efforts by the Internet community. SNMP is actively maintained, and all future enhancements to SNMP are based on existing protocol standards. And you will never pay a royalty for the use of SNMP itself.

SNMP is universally supported

Because SNMP is defined as an Internet standard, you can expect all SNMP-managed devices, from communications satellites to coffee makers, to use the same type of management interface and to support a common set of network management information. SNMP is supported by all major vendors of IP and IPX network devices, and is compatible with more complex network management frameworks, such as the Telecommunication Management Network (TMN).

SNMP is extendible

SNMP was designed with the capability of supporting any type of information on any type of device that may be part of any type of computer network. This is primarily accomplished by SNMP's definition of a core set of operations that remain the same on all managed devices. SNMP leaves to the device designers the details of how to represent and store device-specific management information to be decided by the device's designers.

SNMP is portable

SNMP is implemented entirely in software and is independent of operating systems and programming languages. And although SNMP was originally based on the TCP/IP network model, SNMP has been ported to many other network addressing and transport mechanisms, including IPX/SPX and AppleTalk.

The functional design of SNMP is also portable. SNMP defines a core set of operations that must function identically on all devices that support SNMP.

Many network devices are capable of supporting SNMP as an upgradable option. A network administrator obtains the SNMP agent firmware and MIBs from the vendor and uploads them to the network device. In some cases, SNMP is contained in a separate management assembly that is attached to a hardware port on the device.

SNMP gives distributed management access

SNMP enables the management of distributed network nodes from any point on a network. A TCP/IP network, such as the Internet, typically does not have a single control center. Entities that control and maintain the network are instead distributed over great physical and logical distances. SNMP allows such distributed network elements to be managed from a central point, or from a group of points using multiple network management systems.

SNMP is lightweight

A primary goal of SNMP is to add a network management capability to a device without impacting the operation of the device or its performance. What good would a thermometer and stethoscope be to a doctor if their use threatened the life of a patient?

SNMP management may be added to a network device with very little increase in workload and demand on system resources. In most cases, the central processes controlling the network device are not even aware of the SNMP agent. In some cases, a device might support a separate processor used specifically for system and network management. This is a very nice feature that increases both the capability and the cost of the device, but it is not required by SNMP.

About the SNMP Protocol

SNMP itself is a protocol, rather than a language or a product. Essentially, a protocol is a set of rules that are created by negotiation and that are followed so specific information may be exchanged without confusion or misinterpretation (in this case, between the network nodes). The rules for SNMP define the following:

- The structure of data used to manage a device on a network
- The policies for accessing that data
- The format the data takes before being transported to other devices across a network
- The operations used to manipulate the management data

When management systems and agents exchange management information using the SNMP protocol, they are actually sending SNMP messages. Each message is a separate packet of binary information that is sent discretely over a network, in much the same way that letters are transported through the postal system. The packet-switched design of TCP/IP networks requires that all types of data be sent using several different types of protocol messages.

About SNMP Messages

Each SNMP operation has its own type of message. Each of these messages is used by a management system to request that an operation be performed on managed variables maintained by an SNMP agent. There are three request-and-response operations: Get, GetNext, and Set. The corresponding messages used to request these operations are named GetRequest, GetNextRequest, and SetRequest.

The response message returned by an agent as a reply to a request is called a GetResponse. And despite its name, a GetResponse message is returned in reply to GetNextRequest and SetRequest messages as well. A fourth operation, Trap, is sent by an agent using the trap message. Trap messages are unsolicited and therefore do not have a corresponding request message.

All by itself, an SNMP message does not contain all of the information necessary to convey the message from one network node to another. An SNMP message only contains management information and some authentication data. If you were to write a note to a friend and drop it into a mail box without first sealing it in an envelope with an address and stamp, the post office would be unable to deliver it. Same idea with SNMP messages. You need an envelope, address, and stamp for each message.

In many ways, the method SNMP uses to exchange messages on the network can be compared to the process of writing and mailing a letter. SNMP defines the contents of the letter (which takes the form of a set of orders or a status report), the format of the information on the written page, and the requirements of the type of envelope, how it is addressed, and where you put the stamp.

Once you have the letter sealed and addressed, SNMP's job is complete. The process of how or where to mail the letter and how the letter is to arrive at its destination and then be delivered to the recipient is of no concern to SNMP. These aspects of letter sending and delivery are defined by other network protocols. (We'll describe the protocols used to convey SNMP messages briefly in Chapter 2, *Network Basics.*) And because SNMP doesn't care how your letter gets there—or if it gets there at all—your letter is free to travel any way that the postal protocol in use determines to be suitable (truck, ship, aircraft, etc.).

Terminology

SNMP, and network management in general, is fraught with terms and lingo used to convey information. Of course, just knowing the definitions of a few terms won't get you very far. You need to know how they are used and feel comfortable using them.

From the start, let me say that you cannot possibly hope to share exactly the same terminology with every other computer networking aficionado that you meet. Great conflicts usually arise when discussing the differences between a "node" and an "element," when it is appropriate to refer to something as "an entity," and just what a "host" is. Often the best policy is not to immediately join in a conversation, but to listen to the terminology being used instead.[*]

Much of the terminology used in this book involves the SNMP management model. In this model there are management nodes and managed nodes. A *management node* is typically a workstation or server on a network that is running one or more network management processes. These processes are software applications used to collect management information from the "managed nodes," and they organize and display the information for the human managers.

---

[*] Many years ago in my model rocketry days, a bead of glue used to strengthen the bond between a fin and the body tube of a model rocket was called a "filet." Depending on the rocketry group, this was pronounced either "FILL-it" or "fil-LAY." If you used the pronunciation not used by the people around you, you were laughed off the field. This distinction became unimportant to me later in life when I began to date women who cared nothing for model rocketry.

They are commonly described as management stations, management consoles, or management applications. They are also described using the more abstract terms of management systems, management elements, or management entities.

A *managed node* is any network device that is capable of being managed, including management nodes themselves. A node is "managed" or "under management" when it is actively monitored by an SNMP agent. Every managed node is a member of one or more *management communities*; each community is identified by a human-readable name called a *community name*, or a *community string* when it is encoded in an SNMP message. A node that does not belong to one or more specific communities is said to belong to all management communities.

An *agent* is software or firmware that runs as one or more processes on a node.* The agent provides management services by collecting and returning management information that is requested by a management node (this process is also referred to as "remote management"). The agent may also send unrequested notifications as an indication that specific events have occurred (*traps*).

If the agent processes are running on the node it is actively managing, the node is said to "support SNMP management." If the agent is not running on the node that it is managing, then the agent is described as a *proxy agent* because it is managing a node that cannot locally support SNMP management or perhaps network connectivity itself.

SNMP network management itself is composed of three parts:

SNMP protocol
> Specifies the behavior of the Get, GetNext, Set, and Trap operations, and defines the format of the SNMP messages exchanged by management systems and agents.

Structure of Management Information (SMI)
> The set of rules used to specify the format used for defining managed objects that are accessed via the SNMP protocol.

Management Information Base (MIB)
> The map of the hierarchical order of all managed objects and how they are accessed.

All management operations are performed on managed objects (also called *MIB objects*). They are referred to as "objects" because they are data with a specific set of attributes, and are all commonly manipulated using the Get, GetNext, and Set

---

* Software resides in volatile memory (RAM) and must be loaded before it is executed. Firmware resides in non-volatile memory (NVRAM or ROM) and stays in memory even if you shut the power off. Aside from this difference, they are the same thing.

operations (or methods) defined by SNMP. (The Trap operation is merely an event report.)

They are also described as *MIB variables* because each object has zero or more separate instances that are maintained by the agent, just as all variables in a program are created as separate instances. Most MIB variables are static and exist for as long as the agent is running. Some variables are dynamic, and their instance may be created and destroyed at run-time as needed by the agent. The phrase *MIB database* is often used when referring to a logical collection of management data, and *MIB data* when referring to the management data itself.

As you can see, *MIB* is perhaps the most overloaded term used in SNMP. All managed objects are arranged hierarchically in a *MIB tree*; a *MIB branch* is a logical grouping of MIB objects under one location in the tree; a *MIB segment* is a logical grouping of one or more MIB branches; and any addressable point in the MIB is a *MIB node*. A *MIB view* is a set of managed objects (also called *MIB variables*) that are locally accessible by an agent and visible to a management system; a *MIB module* is the definitions of the objects residing in one or more branches of the MIB tree; each object is registered in the *MIB name space*; and a *MIB file* is the physical disk file that contains the source code for one or more MIB modules. The contents of a MIB module is typically viewed using a special type of tool called a *MIB walker* or *MIB browser.* And *MIB compilers* are used to convert the MIB code into a format suitable for input to a C compiler, or for parsing by a database engine.

NOTE   The most important thing you must realize about MIBs is that a MIB is not a database. A MIB is simply a pattern for the organization of management data. It provides a road map of how to access management data, but it does not specify how or where the data is physically stored, in what format it exists, or if it exists at all. A MIB is therefore best thought of as a logical schema rather than a physical database.

There is also a conceptual difference between "a MIB" and "the MIB," just as a difference exists between "an internet" and "the Internet." "The MIB" is the sum of all information defined in the MIB tree, including all of the areas where objects are yet to be defined. "A MIB" is just one of the MIB modules that specifies the managed objects residing in one or more subtrees of "the MIB" tree.

All MIB modules and the SMI are expressed using a text-based data description notation known as *Abstract Syntax Notation One* (ASN.1). ASN.1 notation is capable of describing any type of data with complete independence from hardware architectures, religious persuasion, or political partisanship. MIB data is conveyed across a network using SNMP messages that are encoded using the

Basic Encoding Rules (BER). While ASN.1 provides an unambiguous description of data in an ASCII text format, BER provides the same function, but encodes the messages in a binary format suitable for transmission across a network. Both ASN.1 and BER are necessary for the implementation of SNMP, which must remain completely independent of the type of hardware and software that it is managing.

SNMP and Microsoft

SNMP was originally developed for TCP/IP network management in 1990 (see the section called "SNMP History" later in this chapter). At that time, Microsoft itself did not have a standard network management protocol for its Win16 operating platforms. And neither Microsoft's first 32-bit platform, OS/2 (1991), nor its eventual successor, Windows NT 3.1 (1993), specified a standard network management protocol.

Today, Microsoft has standardized on the use of the Remote Procedure Call (RPC) protocol and the Microsoft System Management Server (SMS) for the management of all Windows-based networks. However, many TCP/IP network policies require that their nodes be manageable using SNMP. If a Windows NT workstation or server is to operate as a host on such a TCP/IP network, it must support SNMP.

Such requirements have made it essential that SNMP support be included with Microsoft's TCP/IP-32 protocol suite. SNMP is therefore included as an optional Win32 service that can be easily installed if a Windows NT workstation or server is required to support SNMP. A second SNMP service used to receive traps is also included as part of the Microsoft SNMP Management API.

By providing the SNMP services and a TCP/IP protocol stack, Windows NT is able to respond to SNMP requests and both send and receive SNMP traps. These capabilities do not require any intervention from the user and require only minimal configuration by the system administrator. The SNMP service also provides the programmer with an API that he or she may use to write dynamic link libraries (DLLs) to define which managed objects are supported by the SNMP service.

The SNMP Service

Windows NT supports both SNMPv1 management and agent capabilities, including the ability to send and receive traps. The SNMP service is also fully integrated into the Windows NT system and is included as part of its distribution. Under Windows NT, the SNMP service is quite easy to install, configure, and control.

Windows 95 only supports the SNMP agent functions. The SNMP management capability is not included. Microsoft apparently views Windows 95 only as a thing to be managed, not as a thing to provide management (although Windows 95 is capable of using part of the NT management capabilities, as you will read in later chapters). The SNMP service was also not included with the original Windows 95 standard distribution, but is instead included as a CD-ROM extra.*

A service is a special type of Win32 software application that interfaces with the Windows NT Service Control Manager (SCM) using the Win32 API. Services are used to monitor hardware devices and system processes, and supply access to ancillary operating system functions and to peripheral devices.† The Windows NT SNMP service is a Win32 software application that supports the Microsoft extendible SNMP agent. It is the *extendible agent* that implements the sending, receiving, encoding, and decoding of SNMP messages.

The SNMP service isolates you, the programmer, from many of the implementation details associated with an SNMP agent. The decoding, parsing, and encoding of SNMP messages, and the interface to the network and operating system services used for communication, are all handled transparently for you by the SNMP service and extendible agent. You only need to be concerned with the design and implementation of the code specific to the objects in your own private MIBs. The MIB-independent details (ASN.1 parsing, BER encoding and decoding, etc.) are all handled by the extendible agent.

MIB-specific details are handled by the SNMP service in the form of DLLs called *extension agents*. Each extension agent (also called a subagent) implements a set of registered managed objects defined in a MIB module and communicates with the SNMP service using the SNMP API. When the SNMP service receives an SNMP request message, it passes the message data (called *variable bindings*, or *varbinds* for short) on to the extension agent that implements the MIB variables specified in the request. The extension agent is then responsible for applying the rules of SNMP to the varbinds and for constructing the data for a GetResponse message. The extension agents are also used to send traps.

It is the extension agent DLLs that give the SNMP service its extendible quality. Extension agent DLLs are loaded when the SNMP service is started, and they may be enabled or disabled at run-time to control which managed objects are supported by the extendible agent; the main goal of this book is to describe how to write these agents.

Chapter 5, *Getting Started with the SNMP Service*, describes both SNMP services in greater detail—how to start and stop them, how to tell what services are installed, and how the Windows NT and Windows 95 implementations differ.

---

* This may reflect an initial view by Microsoft that Windows 95 is more of an end-user than an administrative tool, and that very few consumers would require SNMP management capability.

† Windows 95 does not have a Service Control Manager, and instead automatically loads services only at startup as it would any driver.

Extendible vs. Monolithic Agents

There are two basic designs of agents:

Monolithic agents

>These agents are closely coupled to the management data that they maintain and to the operating system of the device in which they reside. Monolithic designs tend to be closed architectures and may not be readily adaptable to new environments, although not necessarily so. Perhaps the best definition of monolithic is "not extendible."

Extendible agents

>These agents are an open, modular design that is able to adapt to new management data and operational requirements. Extendible designs tend to be as independent of the node's operating system and the type of CPU as is practical. The words "extendible" and "extensible" are often used interchangeably.

Each of these designs has its benefits and drawbacks. The monolithic designs are optimized for a specific operating system and CPU, so they tend to run faster than the more generic, extendible agents. The "hard coded" monolithic designs also tend to consume less memory and resources than their extendible counterparts and they do not use dynamic memory allocation, which can be very slow on many systems. Network devices with smaller processors and a very limited amount of memory usually benefit from using an agent with a monolithic design.

Extendible agents, however, can be easily modified to support new MIB objects, and usually without recompiling the agent code itself. They are often portable across a wide variety of systems and may be stopped, started, and debugged just like any other process.

The Microsoft SNMP service is, of course, an extendible SNMP agent. The common SNMP functions and network interface are handled by the extendible agent, and the customized processing of private MIB data is handled by the extension agent DLLs. It is the use of DLLs that allow software components to be added and removed as required without needing to modify and recompile any code.

SNMP Under Windows NT 5.0

What new features and modifications might be in store for the SNMP service in the releases of NT 5.0? As of the publication of this book, the release of NT5 is probably a year away. But the information made available at the first NT5 beta release indicates that the new NT5 SNMP agent will include the following:

- Full bilingual support for SNMPv1 and SNMPv2c (the section "Versions of SNMP" later in this chapter describes these versions)

- The ability to map SNMPv2c requests to SNMPv1 for processing by extension agents

- Multiphase commits used to synchronize the setting of MIB variables by multiple extension agents

- A new extension agent framework that is backward-compatible with the original framework

- A code generator to create extension agents

- MIB-II, LAN Manager 2, IP Forwarding MIB (RFC 1354), and Host Resources MIB (RFC 1514) extension agents included

- All MIB modules included with SNMP service installation

The major enhancement is the addition of support for SNMPv2c (SNMPv2 without security) for both the extendible agent and the extension agent framework. The extension agent code generator reads SMIv1 and SMIv2 MIB modules and creates an extension agent framework in standard C. All you need to do is write the custom code for the methods that perform the actual manipulation of the management data; all other processing code is written for you.

The new SNMP management features of NT5 will include the following:

- Full support for WinSNMP 1.1a and SNMPv2c; WinSNMP is a standard that promotes the development of SNMP-based network management applications running under the Microsoft Windows operating systems.

- Backward compatibility with the existing Microsoft Management API

- An IP helper API that allows the retrieval of TCP, IP, ARP, and other data without the need to use SNMP

- Full support for NT5's Web-based management infrastructure

The most dramatic change to SNMP in NT5 is the integration of the WinSNMP API and full support for SNMPv2c. All code written using WinSNMP is portable to all operating systems that support WinSNMP, including Win16, Win32, Solaris, AIX, HP-UX, and DEC Alpha.

The original Microsoft Management API (MGMTAPI) will be a wrapper that sits on top of WinSNMP and translates all MGMTAPI calls to WinSNMP API calls. You may use MGMTAPI to support your current MGMTAPI application under NT5, and even continue to use MGMTAPI to implement management applications (however, there will be some performance penalties due to the extra overhead). You are advised and encouraged by Microsoft to use the WinSNMP API for writing all SNMP management applications. WinSNMP also allows SNMP sessions to be controlled asynchronously using event-driven response reporting (non-blocking mode), and eliminates problems with multiple processes attempting to connect to the trap port.

The initial release of NT5 will most likely not support AgentX (described later in this chapter), but it may be added if consumers and developers ask for it.*

None of the new NT5 SNMP features will be included in the initial release of Windows 98. The new agent features might be available as updates to both NT4 and Windows 98 in a future Service Pack release.

SNMP History

Few concepts in telecommunications spring up overnight. The latest telecom and telco concepts that you are reading about in this week's trade papers are all developed based on "a priori" technology. To use a commonly pitched phrase, telecommunications is "evolutionary, not revolutionary."

Development and standardization is often an long and slow process, and the adoption of new technology by industry even slower. How many people really know the complete story of how the current revision of a particular technology was developed? And yet, a detailed knowledge of history is important to understanding any technology, modern or ancient.

Whenever I start to delve into a corner of technology that's new to me, I do take the time to realize that there is probably a long history of development that's worth exploring. For the Internet, you'll go back at least to 1969; for computer networking itself, you'll find yourself back in the 1950s; and for telecommunications, don't stop until you've read about the works of Nikola Tesla dating from the late 1880s, and the invention of the telephone in 1876. Or go all the way back to where modern telecom started, with the creation of Morse code and the telegraph in 1837.

Fortunately for the readers of this book, SNMP has a much shorter history. But understanding how SNMP came to be what it is today will ultimately give you a better appreciation of SNMP itself.

NOTE   For a detailed recounting of the events that occurred in the development of SNMP from 1987 to 1990, please refer to the preface of *The Simple Book*, First Edition, by Marshall T. Rose (Prentice Hall, 1990). The preface of Dr. Rose's revised Second Edition continues the history of SNMP from 1990 to 1995, but does purposely omit the earlier and very interesting historical material found in the first edition.

---

* If AgentX support is important to you, then let Microsoft know at *manageit@microsoft.com.*

SNMP Milestones

In 1983, TCP/IP became the standard network protocol suite used by the United States Department of Defense; its adoption officially marked the obsolescence of the ARPANET and the birth of the Internet. By the mid-1980s, the Internet was growing rapidly in size and without any standardized form of network management to maintain it. Every group responsible for managing a section of the Internet was using different tools, equipment, and policies. By the late 1980s, several independent groups of developers were researching network management models that could be used to standardize the concept of how the Internet was managed.

The earliest model was the High-level Entity Management System (HEMS). Although HEMS proved quite successful on experimental networks, it never saw active distribution and use across the Internet. (Today HEMS remains in limited experimental use and is defined in RFCs 1021, 1022, 1024, and 1076.*)

In 1987, another model was proposed by the Open Systems Interconnection (OSI) group of the International Standards Organization (ISO). The OSI proposed using its Common Management Information Protocol (CMIP) as the network management framework to manage the Internet. CMIP was already used to manage OSI-based networks, and the OSI proposal involved the creation of CMOT (CMIP over TCP) as the actual network management protocol to be used for the Internet. For many reasons, however, CMOT (see RFCs 1095 and 1189) failed to fully evolve and today is only sparsely used.

In March of 1987, yet a third group of network developers began work on the Simple Gateway Monitoring Protocol (SGMP). SGMP was very simple in design and easy to implement. By August of that same year, SGMP was ported to several different operating platforms and was being increasingly used by other groups and vendors on the Internet. And in November 1987, the draft standard RFC 1028 describing SGMP was published.

In February 1988, the then Internet Activities Board (IAB)† convened an ad hoc committee to determine which of these three network management models should be used for the Internet. The resulting decision was that CMOT, although not ready for distribution, was the natural choice for an Internet network management framework. SGMP, because of its current acceptance and wide deployment in the Internet community, was to be the current, but short-term, network management solution for the Internet; it would eventually be completely replaced by

---

* References for all RFCs relevant to SNMP are listed in Appendix C, *RFCs*.

† The IAB was renamed the Internet Architecture Board in 1992.

CMOT.* And HEMS, because it lacked the acceptance and distribution of SGMP and the backing of a major standards body, was dropped from consideration.

To allow the future transition of systems from SGMP to CMOT, a common network management framework was to be developed that would be used by both models. This framework was named the Simple Network Management Protocol (SNMP), and the chair of the SNMP working group was Marshall T. Rose. By August 1988, the "Internet-standard Network Management Framework" had been created (RFCs 1065, 1066, and 1067), and in April 1989 SNMP was promoted by the IAB to *recommended* status as the de facto TCP/IP network management framework (RFC 1098). By this time there were problems and disagreements growing between the CMOT and SNMP groups on many details of the network management framework. One other important factor also existed at this time: SNMP was both a stable and widely accepted standard, but CMOT was neither.

In June 1989, the IAB convened the ad hoc Internet network management committee again, but this time discarded the idea of a common management framework, and instead allowed CMOT and SNMP to develop independently. The SNMP camp began a working draft of the SNMP standard in August 1989, reached consensus the following December, and in May 1990 saw the IAB promote SNMP to a *standard* protocol with a *recommended* protocol status (RFC 1157). This action firmly cemented SNMP as the network management protocol and the framework recommended for use on the Internet and on all TCP/IP networks.

In March 1991, documents defining the format of MIBs and traps were published (RFCs 1212 and 1215), and the TCP/IP MIB definition was revised (RFC 1213) to create what is known today as SNMP version 1 (SNMPv1).

IAB Protocols

The IAB has established two official categorizations for protocols: the state of the categorization (*standard, draft standard,* and *proposed*), and the status of the protocol (*required, recommended, elective,* and *not recommended*). Several unofficial states (*obsolete, experimental,* and *historic*) are used to identify protocols that are off the formal standards track. All of these categories are defined in "Internet Official Protocol Standards," which is currently RFC 2200. In this categorization, SNMPv1 is a recommended standard protocol.

---

* Similarly, BASIC and Pascal were originally conceived as practical models for teaching the fundamentals of computer programming only, and weren't really supposed to move beyond the classroom—an example of two other short-term solutions that "got away."

Versions of SNMP

There are presently two major versions of the Simple Network Management Protocol: SNMPv1 and SNMPv2. SNMPv1 is a "recommended standard" protocol and part of the Internet Management Framework. SNMPv2 is intended to be an update of SNMPv1, adding several features purposely omitted from SNMPv1 to expedite its acceptance and release.

The maintainers of SNMP sought to expand the framework by adding security and administration mechanisms and performance improvements to SNMPv1. In July 1992, three RFCs (1351, 1352, and 1352) defining "Secure SNMP" (SNMPsec) were published, and work on SNMPv2 was also begun. Secure SNMP never saw wide implementation, mostly due to vendors preferring to make the transition directly from SNMPv1 to SNMPv2 with security.

In April 1993, the twelve documents created by the SNMPv2 Working Group defining SNMPv2 were promoted to "proposed standard" by the IETF. This next revision (SNMPv2p) replaced the community-based administrative framework of SNMPv1 with a party-based framework, and also attempted to add security (RFCs 1441, 1445, 1446, 1448, and 1449). Although work continued on SNMPv2, it saw little industry acceptance. The complexity of its administrative and security framework was the major deterrent to both vendors and consumers of its adoption.

In 1994, the SNMPv2 Working Group met to decide what changes would be necessary for SNMPv2 to gain industry acceptance. Most of the original SNMPv2 RFC documents were revised and five new ones added. It was finally decided that there would be no major changes to the framework. The new and revised SNMPv2 RFCs were published in early 1996.

Disagreements based on the security and administrative aspects of the new Internet Management Framework have caused SNMPv2 to become fragmented into several camps, each differing on how they implement security:

- SNMPv2 with user-based security (SNMPv2u)
- SNMPv2 with user-based security and additional features (SNMPv2*)[*]
- SNMPv2 without security (SNMPv2c)

SNMPv2u (also SNMPv2usec) is an experimental, user-based SNMPv2 that provides security based on user names and the protocol operations of SNMPv2. SNMPv2u is defined by RFCs 1905, 1906, 1909, and 1910. SNMPv2 (also SNMPv2star) is an experimental attempt to combine the most desirable features of SNMPv2p and SNMPv2u. No RFCs have yet been published that specifically describe SNMPv2.

---

[*] SNMPv2*, pronounced "SNMPv2 star," is a combination of SNMPv2p and SNMPv2u.

SNMPv2c combines the community-based approach of SNMPv1 with the protocol operation of SNMPv2, and omits all SNMPv2 security features. SNMPv2c is also experimental and is defined by RFCs 1901, 1905, and 1906.

The original SNMPv2 (SNMPv2p, party-based SNMPv2, SNMPv2-Classic, etc.) and Secure SNMP are no longer used and are now considered historic. SNMPv2c is widely accepted and supported by every major management-side product and by a small, but growing, number of agent-side products as well. Work also continues on both SNMPv2u and SNMPv2*. (See Appendix A, *References* for a listing of Web sites that report their progress.) Only SNMPv1 is a full Internet standard and in wide use.

There is also an SNMPv3 development effort currently underway. The creation of SNMPv3 resulted from the Internet Engineering Steering Group (IESG) mandating the formation of an SNMP advisory group to unify the concepts and mechanisms of SNMPv2u and SNMPv2* into a single protocol with strong security (SNMPv3 uses SNMPv2u security). Appendix A lists the URLs where you can find the latest information on the development of SNMPv3.

Table 1-1 summarizes all of the RFCs defining SNMP as of October 1997. No RFCs for SNMPv3 exist at this time.

Table 1-1. Historical Record of the RFCs Defining SNMP

RFC	Description	Published	Current Status
1065	SMIv1	August 1988	Obsoleted by 1155
1066	SNMPv1 MIB	August 1988	Obsoleted by 1156
1067	SNMPv1	August 1988	Obsoleted by 1098
1098	SNMPv1	April 1989	Obsoleted by 1157
1155	SMIv1	May 1990	Standard
1156	SNMPv1 MIB	May 1990	Historic
1157	SNMPv1	May 1990	Standard
1158	SNMPv1 MIB-II	May 1990	Obsoleted by RFC 1213
1212	SNMPv1 MIB definitions	March 1991	Standard
1213	SNMPv1 MIB-II	March 1991	Standard
1215	SNMPv1 traps	March 1991	Informational
1351	Secure SNMP administrative model	July 1992	Proposed Standard
1352	Secure SNMP managed objects	July 1992	Proposed Standard
1353	Secure SNMP security protocols	July 1992	Proposed Standard
1441	Introduction to SNMPv2	April 1993	Proposed Standard
1442	SMIv2	April 1993	Obsoleted by 1902
1443	Textual convention for SNMPv2	April 1993	Obsoleted by 1903
1444	Conformance statements for SNMPv2	April 1993	Obsoleted by 1904
1445	SNMPv2 administrative model	April 1993	Historic

Table 1-1. Historical Record of the RFCs Defining SNMP (continued)

RFC	Description	Published	Current Status
1446	SNMPv2 security protocols	April 1993	Historic
1447	SNMPv2 party MIB	April 1993	Historic
1448	SNMPv2 protocol operations	April 1993	Obsoleted by RFC 1905
1449	SNMPv2 transport mapping	April 1993	Obsoleted by RFC 1906
1450	SNMPv2 MIB	April 1993	Obsoleted by RFC 1907
1451	Manager-to-manager MIB	April 1993	Historic
1452	Coexistence of SNMPv1 and SNMPv2	April 1993	Obsoleted by RFC 1908
1901	Community-based SNMPv2	January 1996	Experimental
1902	SMIv2	January 1996	Draft Standard
1903	Textual conventions for SNMPv2	January 1996	Draft Standard
1904	Conformance statements for SNMPv2	January 1996	Draft Standard
1905	Protocol operations for SNMPv2	January 1996	Draft Standard
1906	Transport mapping for SNMPv2	January 1996	Draft Standard
1907	SNMPv2 MIB	January 1996	Draft Standard
1908	Coexistence of SNMPv1 and SNMPv2	January 1996	Draft Standard
1909	Administrative infrastructure for SNMPv2	February 1996	Experimental
1910	User-based security for SNMPv2	February 1996	Experimental

Another SNMP standardization effort that is underway is *SNMP Agent Extensibility* (AgentX). The AgentX Working Group was chartered to define standards-track technology for SNMP agent extensibility. The result will be an interface specification that allows independently developed sub-agents to communicate with a master agent running on a networked device. The acceptance of this specification will allow developers to create sub-agents that conform to a single model and are portable to a wide variety of operating systems.

Appendix A lists the URLs where you can find the latest information on the development of AgentX.

2

Network Basics

SNMP is a high-level protocol. It is so high-level, in fact, that it is most often implemented by application processes rather than by low-level system drivers. What is easy to overlook from SNMP's lofty cloud is that it relies on many layers of foundation software and hardware to convey management information between management systems and agents across a network.

This chapter presents a very basic overview of the bedrock of SNMP: the OSI Reference Model, the TCP/IP protocol stack, the network messages used to exchange information, and the basic devices that are the network itself. If you are already quite familiar with network concepts, you can skip this chapter.

What Is a Network?

A *network* is a definite path, or set of paths, that conveys information transmitted between two separate entities. More simply, it is a set of connections that allows two or more computers—or people, for that matter—to exchange information.

Humans and computers who need to exchange information via a network must use a common transmission medium, channel of communication, and information transport mechanism. For humans, we might describe the common medium as "the air," the channel as "the audible range of the human voice," and the mechanism as the human languages and cultural protocols used to encode the data, such as "Standard English" and Robert's Rules of Order. For computers, the medium is copper wire or optical fiber, the channel is a range of voltage levels or frequencies, and the transport mechanisms are network protocols.

There are even networks that require both humans and computers as essential devices. I'm sure that you are familiar with the concept of using a floppy disk to copy information from one PC to another ("SneakerNet," as it is often called).

Although not efficient for large amounts of data, this "bucket brigade" process of using a floppy disk transmission medium, floppy drive communications channel, and human information transport mechanism, does qualify as a network.

Many people associate computer networks with long distance communications (the "tele-" in "telecommunications"). However, this is not necessarily the case. The longest communications networks are several light-hours in size (thanks to the Voyager and Galileo deep space probes). But networks may also be as small as the conductive paths etched onto an integrated circuit, or the nervous system of a single-celled animal.

Networks are not necessarily very complex. In terms of both nodes and users, the most complex computer network by far is the Internet. The Internet is a global interconnection of millions of devices that is used by millions of users—both human and computer. However, my three home computers and the two, 25-foot lengths of RG-58/U coaxial cable connecting them (a very simple network indeed) qualifies as a network just the same as the Internet.

There are many concepts common to all communications networks regardless of their size and complexity. A network may be made up of hundreds or thousands of addressable devices each called by the generic term *node, element,* or *host.* Network nodes include routers, bridges, hubs, workstations, printers, modems, and file servers. The devices on any network can be divided into two groups: those that both create and consume network information, and those that direct the flow of network traffic.

If the specific purpose of a device is to direct the flow of network information, we call this device a *router, bridge,* or *hub.* These devices direct network traffic across a network, or from one network to another, and they make up the foundation of all but the simplest computer networks. Devices that don't direct network traffic, but instead create and consume it, are all lumped into the category of *end-systems* or *end-hosts* because they reside at the ending (and beginning) points of a network. And both routers and hosts may act as *proxies,* allowing foreign or non-network capable devices to access, and be accessed by, the network. Let's look at these definitions in a little more detail in the following sections.

Routers

Routers are specialized network devices whose primary purpose is to direct the flow of network data in a timely and efficient manner. This is accomplished using data stored in the network traffic itself.

Each packet of information on a network contains the address of the device that created the packet (the source address) and the address of the device that is intended to receive the packet (the destination address). A router will read these addresses and determine where to send the packet. The destination may be on the same network segment as the router, in which case the packet is sent directly to its specified destination. But the destination may be a segment of the network that is a considerable logical distance away, and in this case, the packet will have to be forwarded to other routers before it can reach its destination.

Every router contains information about all hosts and other routers in a network. If a router supports management, then it will supply routing information for each network addressing protocol Management Information Base (MIB) that it supports. (Chapter 1, *Introduction to SNMP*, introduced the concept of a MIB, and I'll describe MIBs in more detail in Chapter 4, *Inside SNMP*.) For example, a router that supports RFC 1156 (MIB-I) or RFC 1213 (MIB-II) can provide information on all IP-capable routers, support for Novell MIBs provides IPX routing information, support for RFC 1742 provides AppleTalk routing information, and so forth.

Bridges

Bridges provide a function similar to that of routers, but there is one important difference. A bridge routes packets from one network to another. Bridges read the source and destination addresses of each packet that they receive and build tables of the hardware addresses of the nodes on each network. If the bridge receives a packet from network A that has a destination address of a node on network B, the bridge removes the packet from network A and retransmits it on to network B. A bridge therefore allows two separate networks to operate as a single network.

A bridge that supports standard MIBs (such as RFC 1493 and RFC 1525) can provide information on their configuration and current performance to a management system. Two important performance measurements used to determine the maximum network traffic capacity of a bridge are the filtering rate and the forwarding rate. The *filtering rate* is the rate at which the addresses of packets are examined. The *forwarding rate* is the speed at which the packets are forwarded from one network to another. Both of these performance statistics are measured in frames per second.

Hubs

A *hub* is used to connect a group of hosts to a local area network (LAN) at a single point. Multiple end-hosts, such as printers and workstations, may all connect to a single hub that is connected to the network. The hub directs all network traffic to the end-hosts and places all of the end-host traffic on the network.

The basic hub (also called a *concentrator*) does not perform any routing or error-checking functions. It simply receives a packet from the network, duplicates the packet, and forwards one duplicate to each node attached to the hub. Packets transmitted by each node attached to the hub are transmitted out on to the network, even if their destination is only another node attached to the same hub.

Switching hubs provide more routing intelligence between packets and nodes by examining the destination address of a packet and transmitting the packet to the proper port (or back out on to the network if the destination address is not local to the hub). Switching hubs may also first store the entire packet in RAM and then perform a CRC check to determine whether the packet has been damaged during transmission. Undamaged packets are routed to the proper port; erroneous packets are discarded.

An intelligent hub that can support a management agent can provide statistics on the network traffic for each node. Switching hubs can also connect different segments of a LAN and be configured to directly route packets from a specific source to a specific destination.

End-hosts

End-host is a name typically given to all addressable network devices that produce and consume network traffic. Hosts include commonly networked devices such as servers, printers, and workstations, and more exotic devices such as channel banks and PBXs. The majority of nodes on any network qualify as hosts, and their need to exchange information is the reason computer networks exist in the first place.

Hosts are also called *end-systems* because they reside at the end points in a network topology map. Bridges, routers, and hubs are called *intermediate systems* because they direct network traffic rather than create and consume it. They are also typically referred to as *multi-homed hosts* when they have more than one network connection or interface.

Proxies

A *proxy* is a logical designation for a device that acts as a moderator or translator on behalf of another device. A proxy allows networked devices using dissimilar protocols and transmission media to communicate. Both routers and hosts are capable of acting as proxies. A proxy may function as an active management server or as a passive translation gateway.

An *active management proxy* is responsible for actively polling the device, collecting management information, and making this information available to management systems. For example, a modem attached locally to a workstation via a serial port knows nothing about network management and nothing about how to actually communicate using a network. If a network management system (NMS) elsewhere on the network needs information on the workstation's modem, the workstation must act on behalf of the modem as an active proxy agent by receiving the management request, collecting the requested management information from the modem, translating the information to a suitable format, and then sending it to the NMS.

A *passive proxy gateway*, on the other hand, simply translates management requests from one management protocol to another. The proxy does not actually perform management operations, but only acts as an intermediary between a management system and the devices that use incompatible network management protocols. For example, a gateway can be used to translate SNMPv2 messages to the SNMPv1 message format and back again for an agent that only speaks SNMPv1.

About TCP/IP

TCP/IP is a suite (or "toolkit," if you prefer the terminology) of protocols used to convey data from one part of a network to another. There have been many other protocol suites invented for the same purpose, but TCP/IP is special in that it is literally the life's blood of the Internet.

NOTE   TCP/IP is an enormous topic, and this discussion is only a brief summary. There is much more to learn; check out the references in Appendix A, *References*, for additional sources and information.

While TCP/IP was vital to the development of the Internet, let me mention in passing that there would be no Internet without other important technologies, including Ethernet LAN technology and T1 communications services.

The Internet was created in 1969 with funding from the U.S. Department of Defense (DoD) Advanced Research Projects Agency (ARPA).* The purpose of the ARPANET project was to find a way to successfully transport electronic information anywhere in a geographical area under sub-optimal conditions. This would be necessary if, say, that part of your network had been destroyed by somebody dropping nuclear warheads on it using InterContinental Ballistics Missiles, or from an orbiting space platform (the 1960s, the Cold War, Lyndon B. Johnson, Fidel Castro, Nikita Khrushchev—you remember it from history class).

---

* ARPA was founded in 1957, supposedly in response to the USSR's successful launch of Sputnik. ARPA was renamed DARPA (Defense Advanced Research Projects Agency) in 1972.

The first formal protocol used by ARPANET was the Network Control Protocol (NCP), which was adopted in 1970.* NCP was simple, rather hardware-dependent, and not very extensible, but it served the early ARPANET community. Work began in 1973 on the Transmission Control Protocol (TCP) by groups from DARPA and Stanford University. TCP was a higher-level protocol than NCP and promised greater independence from the network hardware. The publication of a paper on TCP the following year marks the first use of the term "internet." In 1976 DARPA began to experiment with the use of TCP/IP on an internet. And by 1977 other networks were beginning to link into ARPANET using TCP/IP.

The TCP/IP protocol suite was officially established in 1982 by the Defense Communications Agency (DCA)† and DARPA. These agencies described a TCP/IP network as an *internet*, and an interconnected set of TCP/IP networks as an *Internet*. At the same time, the DoD officially adopted TCP/IP as its standard networking protocol (MIL-STD-1778). TCP is described in RFC 793 and IP is described in RFC 791.

In 1983, the DoD split off from ARPANET, forming MILNET, an unclassified segment of the Defense Data Network (DDN), formed only the year before. DARPA continued to support both networks. ARPANET, which had used NCP since 1970, officially crossed over to TCP/IP on January 1, 1983, and thus marked the birth of the Internet.

The Internet was now considered to be the sum of both MILNET and ARPANET. The government funding for ARPANET was eventually discontinued and in 1990, ARPANET itself was decommissioned. Its function as an Internet backbone was passed on to the National Science Foundation's NFSNET.

Why did TCP/IP beat out all other contenders for control of the Internet? And why is TCP/IP sometimes described as the single greatest contributing factor to the growth and popularity of the Internet? There are many historical factors, but the primary answers reside within the functionality of TCP/IP itself.

TCP/IP is an open standard, existing in the public domain, and freely available for use by anyone. The TCP/IP standard is maintained by the Internet Engineering Task Force (IETF) with the help of private, commercial, government, and military members worldwide. The TCP/IP protocol suite offers a standardized collection of services used for transporting information across an internet. These services are widely available and may be implemented on any node in a network. New protocols are proposed and are occasionally included in the suite. (SNMP was included

---

* Not to be confused with the IBM Network Control Program, used to control IBM 37xx Front End Processors.

† DCA changed its name to Defense Information Systems Agency (DISA) on June 25, 1991.

in 1989.) The design of TCP/IP is independent of any specific hardware, operating platforms, network configuration, or transmission media. TCP/IP is found on token ring, Ethernet, FDDI, and X.25 networks, and may be used across serial links (SLIP) and dial-up connections.

Although TCP/IP itself is arcane and complex, a TCP/IP network is completely decentralized (one of the original requirements of the Internet), and the IP addressing scheme allows hosts to hook up anywhere they like, and on a worldwide scale. Every TCP/IP host is its own separate island linked to the greater mind (similar to the idea of televisions in every home—except for the "greater mind" part).

The OSI Reference Model

Many models can be used to describe the physical and abstract components needed to implement a computer network. Many models are required because no single model can represent all systems. And rarely does everybody agree on a particular model to use. A very common and popular model for describing data communications protocols is the Open Systems Interconnect (OSI) Reference Model.

The International Standards Organization (ISO) began development of the OSI model in 1977, and adopted it in 1983 for use as a common reference for the discussion and development of data communication standards, and a common description of the interconnection between systems. The OSI Reference Model divides the functions of data communications into seven sections or "layers." Each layer represents an action or service provided by software or hardware when data is transferred between two electronic devices.

Figure 2-1 depicts the OSI Reference Model using both the names and numbers of each layer. The layers are organized vertically as a stack. Each layer receives data from the layer above it, processes the data, and passes it on to the next lower layer. This is accomplished using the protocols that reside at each layer.

When an application sends data across a network, the data is conceptually passed down the stack starting at the application layer, and it leaves the host at the physical layer. When the host receives data, the data arrives at the physical layer and is passed back up the stack and out at the application layer to the system applications.

The OSI Layers

In the OSI Reference Model, SNMP resides high up in the application layer. Therefore, SNMP messages must be processed by all of the layers below it before they

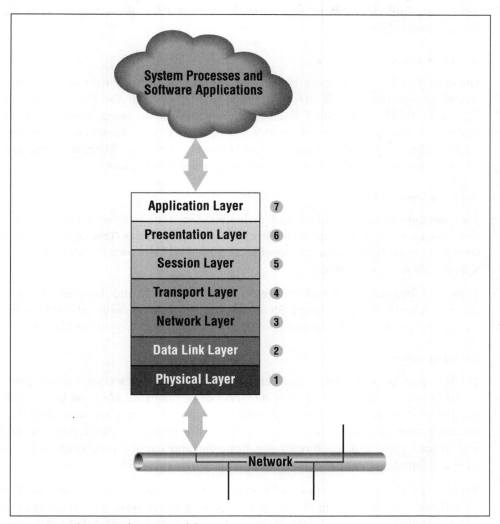

Figure 2-1. The OSI Reference Model

may hit the wire (or the fiber, or the air). Let's have a brief look at look at the type of protocol service that each OSI layer provides.

Physical layer

The physical layer defines the electrical, mechanical, functional, and procedural characteristics used to access and send a stream of bits over a physical medium. This layer includes the medium (coax, optical fiber, copper wire, radio waves, etc.), the physical connections (DB-25, C50, V.35, etc.), and the modulation and framing techniques (HDSL, ADSL, IEEE 802.3, FDDI, etc.). When you speak of serial ports, 10BASE-T cables, and Network Interface Controllers, you are referring to the physical layer.

Data link layer

The data link layer is responsible for the reliable delivery of data at the lowest levels. Its services include error detection and correction, the framing of data (e.g., LLC, HDLC, SDLC, IEEE 802.2), and synchronization using hardware handshaking (Media Access Control, or MAC). This layer is also the home of Ethernet, a LAN technology used to transmit data between computers. Many networks use Ethernet, and it is the most popular LAN technology in use today.

Network layer

The network layer establishes and maintains connections over a network, and provides addressing, routing, and delivery of packets to hosts. This layer also insulates the upper layers from the specific details of the network. IP, PPP, IPX, and X.25 are found in this layer.

SNMP was originally designed for use on TCP/IP networks and therefore favors IP network addressing in its design. SNMP has, however, been easily adapted for use on networks using other addressing schemes, most notably Novell NetWare IPX.

Transport layer

The transport layer provides error detection, correction, and software flow control of data between networks. Most of the services in this layer are used by connection-oriented protocols that require reliable, end-to-end error recovery and flow control. Connectionless transport protocols do not guarantee the delivery of data and instead must gain their reliability from the application layer. Both TCP and UDP are found in this layer.

SNMP uses the connectionless UDP transport protocol. Because UDP itself is "unreliable," SNMP management applications must provide the reliability by keeping track of all messages that they send.

Session layer

The session layer is responsible for establishing and managing sessions (connections) between applications and the network. This layer also provides synchronization points in the data stream that allow the application layer to recover from transmission errors. RPC, SAP, and NetBIOS are all in this layer.

An SNMP agent must establish "connectionless" sessions to listen for SNMP request messages and send responses. Under Windows NT, the WinSock API is used to establish a management session by dynamically creating a socket (an end-point in a network connection) using the specific protocol port reserved for SNMP.

Presentation layer

The presentation layer performs data and protocol negotiation and conversion. Services in this layer convert data to a format that is exchangeable between hosts and is transportable across a network. The data representation format used must be agreed upon by the hosts exchanging the data. Data compression and encryption are also performed at this layer.

As we mentioned in Chapter 1, SNMP uses the Abstract Syntax Notation One (ASN.1) and Basic Encoding Rules (BER) data representation standards to encode SNMP messages using a format that can be unambiguously interpreted by all SNMP management systems and SNMP managed hosts.

Application layer

The application layer is used by software applications to prepare data for use by the other six OSI layers. This layer is also the only interface an application has to the network itself. FTP, Telnet, SMTP, and the X Window System Protocol are all found in this layer.

Although application layer services are implemented as software applications (e.g., an FTP client) or processes (e.g., an NNTP daemon), not all applications that use the network are part of the application layer. Only those applications and processes that provide other applications access to the network are part of this layer.

The concept of an Application Program Interface (API) is derived from the application layer. A Windows application, for example, does not interface directly to the Win32 operating system, but instead interacts with it using the Windows application layer—the Win32 API. The Microsoft SNMP APIs allow your applications to communicate over the network using the SNMP management protocol.

SNMP and the OSI Model

SNMP itself is independent of the transport, network addressing, and data link mechanisms used on a network. Although SNMP was originally designed for use with TCP/IP over Ethernet networks, you are as likely to find SNMP implemented to support such network transports such as Novell IPX/SPX and AppleTalk DDP, and many data link technologies, including ARCNET, ATM, and FDDI.

Figure 2-2 shows the location of SNMP and its associated protocols within the OSI network layer model. SNMP itself is implemented by software applications residing in the application layer. SNMP requires the services of the presentation layer (ASN.1 and BER) to render management data in a form that is suitable for transportation across a network, and allows it to be correctly interpreted regardless of the type of network device that receives it. UDP/IP encompasses the transport and network layer services used with SNMP.

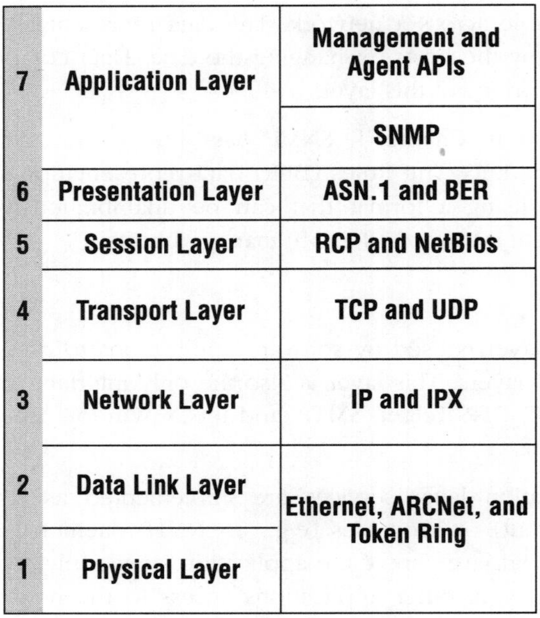

		Management and Agent APIs
7	Application Layer	
		SNMP
6	Presentation Layer	ASN.1 and BER
5	Session Layer	RCP and NetBios
4	Transport Layer	TCP and UDP
3	Network Layer	IP and IPX
2	Data Link Layer	Ethernet, ARCNet, and Token Ring
1	Physical Layer	

Figure 2-2. SNMP and the OSI model

Now that you have a general idea of what goes on in each OSI layer, the next step to cover is what happens to the data between the time it is passed to the application layer and the time it is sent out on the network.

Protocol Data Units

Data is passed from one OSI layer to another in discrete blocks called *protocol data units* (PDUs). A PDU is actually a logical designation for the data in a packet that is used by a specific OSI layer or protocol. For example, an IP packet may be referred to generically as a Network PDU (NPDU), a UDP datagram as a Transport PDU (TPDU), and an SNMP message as an Application PDU (APDU).

Before data can be transported across a network, it must be passed down the network stack and "encapsulated" or "multiplexed" using the PDU formats defined at each layer. Each PDU is placed in the envelope of the next PDU until it reaches the physical layer, where it is sent out to the network.

When the message reaches its destination, the message must be "decapsulated" or "demultiplexed" before the data in the message can be used. As the data is passed up the OSI stack, each PDU is stripped away; the information it contains is used to perform error checking and message routing, and to indicate what protocol services should be used to process the message.

Figure 2-3 shows an SNMP message encapsulated in the envelopes it would need to be transported across an Ethernet network using UDP/IP. The outermost envelope is used to identify the data link layer mechanism, which is Ethernet. The next envelope, IP, handles the actual routing of the message from node to node across the network. The UDP envelope indicates which protocol port on the receiving host should be used to receive the message. And the SNMP message itself is recognized not only by the port at which it is received, but also by the information it contains. (I'll describe the cyclical redundancy checksum (CRC) shown here in the next section.)

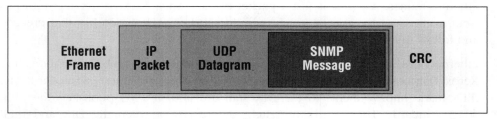

Figure 2-3. An SNMP message and its network envelopes

In most cases, a PDU is simply a header block, or "preamble," containing some identifying information, followed by a payload of data. The payload is a PDU received from the next layer up. PDUs therefore grow in size the further down the OSI stack they go, as more headers are added on during the process of encapsulation (see Figure 2-4).

So realize that when you use a network to send the message "Lunch?" to your friend in the next cubicle, you aren't just sending six bytes of data. A lot of network control information (also known as "overhead") must be tacked on to your message for it to be conveyed across the network and be presented properly.

To really get an idea of what goes on to get an SNMP message from host to host, we need to dig into the PDUs themselves. We'll cover the data link, network, and transport layer PDUs here and we'll detail the presentation and application layer PDUs in Chapter 4 when we cover ASN.1 and SNMP messages.

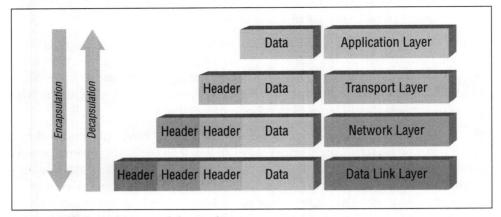

Figure 2-4. Encapsulation and decapsulation

The Ethernet Frame

All information conveyed across an Ethernet network is encapsulated inside of Ethernet frames. A *frame* is just a packet of data. Such packets are referred to as "frames" because the special synchronization and error detection bits that precede and follow the transmission block are said to "frame" the data.

Ethernet was created by Digital Equipment Corporation, Intel Corporation, and Xerox Corporation in 1973 in what is known as the DIX Ethernet Standard. The IEEE made improvements to the DIX standard and in 1983 published the IEEE 802.3 standard.* There are some slight differences between the DIX and IEEE 802.3 frame formats, but these specifications are essentially the same network interface protocol.

Both frame formats use a specific sequence of bits in the preamble that is used by the receiver to synchronize the reading of the data. This preamble is eight octets in length in the DIX format and seven octets in the 802.3 format. The 802.3 preamble is followed by a one-octet bit sequence, called the Start of Frame Delimiter (SFD), which identifies the beginning of each transmitted packet.† A 32-bit postamble, called the Frame Check Sequence (FCS), contains a CRC-32 value calculated from the data contained within the frame. The internal format of both DIX and IEEE 802.3 Ethernet frames is illustrated in Figure 2-5

---

* Specifically, Working Group 6.4 of the International Federation for Information Processing (IFIP) became IEEE Project 802.3.

† Despite the organizational semantics, the pattern of the bits in the first eight octets of both a DIX Ethernet frame and an 802.3 Ethernet frame are identical.

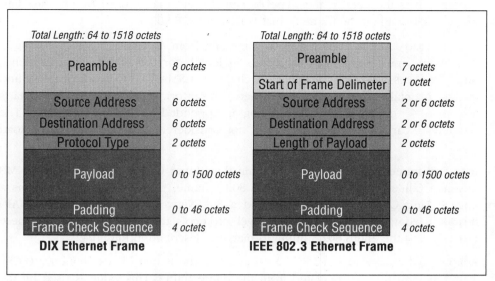

Figure 2-5. Format of the DIX and IEEE 802.3 Ethernet frames

The source and destination address fields contain the Media Access Control (MAC) layer address of the source and destination hosts.[*] These fields are commonly six octets in length, but IEEE 802.3 also allows two-octet address fields.

A MAC address is the physical hardware address of a Network Interface Controller (NIC) installed in a network node. Every NIC has assigned a unique, 48-bit MAC address. The first 24 bits of the MAC address are known as an *organizationally unique identifier* or OUI. Each manufacturer of Ethernet interfaces is assigned a block of unique OUIs by the IEEE. Each manufacturer uses an OUI and a 24-bit number that it creates to form the unique 48-bit MAC address of each interface device manufactured. No two devices on an Ethernet network should have identical MAC addresses.

Following the address fields, the DIX frame contains a protocol type value used to indicate which network service should be used to process the frame's payload data. For IP, this value is 0x0800; for Novell NetWare it is 0x8138. A listing of all protocols supported by Ethernet is contained in the Assigned Numbers RFC (which is currently RFC 1700).

The 802.3 frame, however, does not use this same field to store the protocol type, as the protocol type can be easily read from the 802.3 payload data. Instead, this field stores the length of the entire payload (excluding any padding that is

---

[*] Also called a physical node address, hardware address, node number, station address, or Ethernet address.

present). It is the data in the Type or Length field that is used by the data link layer to determine if the frame format is DIX or IEEE 802.3.

The payload itself is a chunk of data ranging from 46 to 1500 octets in length. Each frame must be at least 64 octets in length for the Ethernet Carrier Sense Multiple Access/Collision Detection mechanism (CSMA/CD) to work properly and to help maintain a minimum level of network performance. If the payload data is less than 46 octets in length, padding is appended to the payload data. The padding is part of the payload, but is not considered to be part of the payload data.

In a DIX frame, the payload will contain the IP and UDP headers and the SNMP message (all explained below). In an 802.3 frame, the payload also contains a Logical Link Control (LLC) header and a Sub-Network Access Protocol (SNAP) header used to identify the higher-level protocols that created the data. These headers, and the entire 802.3 frame format, are described in RFC 1042.

Following the payload is a CRC-32 value called the Frame Check Sequence (FCS). This CRC-32 value is calculated from the entire frame. This value is used by the packet receiver to detect whether the frame was damaged en route. Damaged frames are always discarded by the device performing the calculation (usually a bridge or a router). The frame's preamble and CRC value are stripped before the payload information is passed on to the network addressing layer for processing.

The IP Packet

Each device on a network is assigned one or more logical network addresses. The address is a description of the location of the device on a network. An IP address is a logical address assigned to a network device interface on an IP network. Every NIC and network connection point (or "node") is assigned a network address.

Whereas a MAC address is literally written in stone in the firmware of a NIC, an IP address is written only in persistent, nonvolatile memory; it may be changed quickly with only a few keystrokes and perhaps a system restart. The management of network addresses on a large LAN or WAN is an art unto itself.

The maximum length of an *IP packet*, including the header, is 65535 octets. The IP header does contain a 16-bit checksum value. This checksum is calculated only for the IP header itself and not for the IP packet's payload data. The checksum header field is always set to zero before the checksum calculation is made.

The IP header contains quite a bit of data and varies in length (see Figure 2-6). We won't go into detail here about the information stored in the IP header (every TCP/IP book already does this). The fields you will be the most interested in are the Source Address (also called the Source IP Address or SIP) and the Destination Address (also called the Target IP Address or TIP).

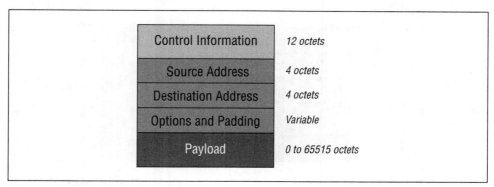

Figure 2-6. Format of the Internet Protocol packet

IP is only used as an envelope to provide logical addressing for a packet of data. IP itself is not a reliable protocol. What that means is that IP does not guarantee the delivery of the packet and does not report any errors it detects in the IP packet.

The Internet Protocol version 4 (IPv4) was released in 1981 and is described in RFC 791.* IPv4 is currently the most widely used network addressing protocol on the Internet; it will eventually be fully replaced by IPv6, also known as Internet Protocol Next Generation (IPNG).

User Datagram Protocol

The User Datagram Protocol (UDP) is a connectionless transport protocol included in the TCP/IP suite and described in RFC 768. UDP is specifically used to route messages at the host level. What this means is that the information stored in the UDP envelope is only of interest to the network host that sent the message, and to the network host that received the message. The network nodes in between the hosts (routers, hubs, and bridges) don't use the UDP transport information. UDP itself has no concept of network addressing or connections, and relies completely on IP for moving datagrams between network hosts.

The UDP header is 8 octets in length and contains the source and destination port addresses, the total length of the datagram, and a 16-bit checksum value (see Figure 2-7). The port addresses (also called port numbers) are used to identify the

---

* For additional information regarding IP, see RFCs 1108, 1191, 1349, 1358, 1393, and 1455.

network port on the host that sent the message, and the network port on the destination host that is to receive the message.

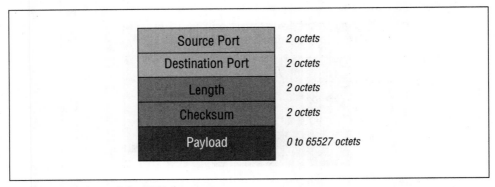

Figure 2-7. Format of the UDP datagram

The length of a UDP datagram may range from 8 to 65535 octets depending on the size of the payload. The checksum value is used to determine whether the datagram has been damaged during transport. If the checksum value is set to zero, the error checking mechanism is turned off, and the responsibility of detecting errors in the datagram payload is left only to the data link layer (in this case, the CRC value in the Ethernet frame).

If a nonzero checksum value is present in the header, and UDP detects that damage to the datagram has occurred, UDP will notify the application layer service specified by the target port number that an error has been detected. If a UDP error is indicated in an SNMP message received by a management system, the datagram is discarded and a "retry" request message is sent to the agent. If the UDP error is detected by an SNMP agent, the datagram is discarded and the agent will silently remain idle, waiting for the management system to send a "retry" request message.

The destination port number is the key to how the data in the UDP datagram payload will be processed. Each port number is assigned to a specific process layer service, such as Telnet, TFTP, or SNMP. The UDP transport layer passes the UDP payload data to a specific service based on the protocol port number. Both the IP network address and the UDP protocol port number must match that of a host on a network for an SNMP message to be delivered successfully (more on this later in the chapter).

If it's unreliable, why bother?

UDP is often described as an unreliable protocol. The term "unreliable" implies that UDP is unstable and poorly designed, but this is not the case. *Unreliable* is a term used to describe all connectionless protocols because they cannot reliably guarantee the error-free delivery of each packet that they convey.

Using a *connectionless transport protocol*, packets are routed across a network in a half-organized/half-panicked bucket brigade. Every packet is treated independently from all other packets, and a dedicated circuit or path to route the packets is not established. Each packet is a hot potato that is literally thrown from node to node. What's more, there is no acknowledgment that each packet has been received. Because of this, there is no guarantee that a packet will arrive at its intended destination, arrive in the order it was sent, not be duplicated, or arrive anywhere at all.

Compare this to a *connection-oriented transport protocol*, such as TCP. TCP keeps track of each packet sent using a protocol handshaking mechanism. If a packet does not arrive at its intended destination, the packet is re-sent until an acknowledgment of its reception is received by the sender or until the send times out.

The packets also travel along a specific route from source to destination, in much the same way that a telephone call is a dedicated connection between two callers. A connectionless transport protocol is more like the post office, where you drop your letters in a box and they are not guaranteed to arrive in any specific order, arrive at a specific time, all be transported via the same route, or arrive at their destination at all.

Before you give up on connectionless transport protocols forever, realize that the Internet suite of protocols is designed to make every possible attempt to deliver data. Packets are not just thrown away at the first sign of discrepancy. In fact, the only time a network is truly unreliable is when there are failures of physical network devices, or when the network's resources are exhausted. In such cases, there are so many damaged packets present on the network that even a reliable TCP connection will fail.

UDP is often used to send small packets of data on local area networks where the instance of packet corruption is extremely low. If 99.9% of all packets arrive at their destination in an undamaged state, then you might begin to wonder why you'd bother wasting time and bandwidth on connection management and handshaking. UDP allows a greater utilization of bandwidth for transporting data at a sacrifice of error correction. However, you must realize that the busier a network, the more likely UDP and IP are to fail.

Using UDP also allows you to use a protocol error checking and correcting mechanism of your own design. Under SNMP, it is the responsibility of the network management system to correlate each SNMP request message sent with an SNMP response message received. If confirmation from an agent of the arrival of an SNMP message is not received, the management system must decide whether to send out a "retry" request or to give up and report a "no response from host" error.

UDP is also a lightweight, easy to implement transport protocol. In terms of your processing dollar, TCP is very expensive. To make any mechanism robust and reliable, it will end up requiring a lot more code. So TCP's connection establishment, transmission handshaking, and data buffer management mechanisms come at the cost of higher overhead, slower operation, and greater consumption of system resources than the more svelte UDP.

When you send packets via UDP/IP, imagine your data as part of the almost 100% delivery rate achieved by the U.S. Postal Service in its connectionless delivery of letters and packages—not as a note adrift on the ocean in a bottle. Yes, there is a chance that something will be lost, but it is not very likely to happen. And if something does get lost, your network application can take steps to recover.

Protocols, Ports, and Sockets

When a packet travels across a network, it is examined by the network layer of each node that receives it. If the destination address of the packet does not match the local address of the node, the packet is forwarded to the proper host or to the next router. If the addresses match, this indicates that the packet has arrived at its destination and is processed by the higher layers in the protocol stack.

Previous sections have discussed the information in the PDU headers used to indicate which protocols and services process a message. Now let's take a look at how that same information is used.

Protocol Numbers

The header of each network layer PDU contains an 8-bit value used to indicate which transport layer protocol should be used to process the PDU's payload. This value is called the *protocol number.*

On a Windows NT system, the transport protocols are defined in the *%System-Root%\SYSTEM32\DRIVERS\ETC\PROTOCOL* file. This file contains a table that associates a name and a number with each protocol that may be supported by the host's network stack. The *PROTOCOL* file on an NT4 workstation appears in Example 2-1.

Example 2-1. PROTOCOL file

```
# Copyright (c) 1993-1995 Microsoft Corp.
#
# This file contains the Internet protocols as defined by RFC 1060
# (Assigned Numbers).
#
# Format:
#
```

Example 2-1. PROTOCOL file (continued)

```
# <protocol name> <assigned number> [aliases...] [#<comment>]

ip        0     IP        # Internet protocol
icmp      1     ICMP      # Internet control message protocol
ggp       3     GGP       # Gateway-gateway protocol
tcp       6     TCP       # Transmission control protocol
egp       8     EGP       # Exterior gateway protocol
pup       12    PUP       # PARC universal packet protocol
udp       17    UDP       # User datagram protocol
hmp       20    HMP       # Host monitoring protocol
xns-idp   22    XNS-IDP   # Xerox NS IDP
rdp       27    RDP       # "reliable datagram" protocol
rvd       66    RVD       # MIT remote virtual disk
```

If you look through the Assigned Numbers RFC (currently RFC 1700), you will see that many more protocol numbers exist than are listed in this table. But most network hosts only require the use of a few protocols, and the *PROTOCOL* file typically (and harmlessly) lists more protocols than are actually used by the host.

The network layer compares the protocol number in the network PDU with those listed in the *PROTOCOL* file to determine on which transport service to pass the PDU. For example, a protocol number of 6 indicates TCP, while an SNMP message will contain a protocol number of 17, indicating UDP.

Port Numbers

After the PDU is processed by the transport layer, it is then passed to an application layer for final processing. Application layer processes that handle PDUs are called "network services," and are identified by their assigned *port numbers*. Each transport layer PDU contains two 16-bit port numbers identifying the source port that sent the message and the destination port that is to process the PDU. These ports are usually on two different hosts, but a host may certainly send any network message to itself.

On a Windows NT system, the network services are defined in the *%System-Root%\SYSTEM32\DRIVERS\ETC\SERVICES* file. This file is very similar in structure to the *PROTOCOL* file. Each line contains the name of a network service followed by the port number and the associated transport protocol name. The *SERVICES* file on an NT4 workstation is nearly 6K in size, so we'll just look at a few entries in Example 2-2.

Example 2-2. Partial SERVICES file

```
# Copyright (c) 1993-1995 Microsoft Corp.
#
# This file contains port numbers for well-known services as defined by
# RFC 1060 (Assigned Numbers).
#
```

Example 2-2. Partial SERVICES file (continued)

```
# Format:
#
# <service name> <port number>/<protocol> [aliases...] [#<comment>]
#

echo              7/tcp
echo              7/udp
systat            11/tcp
systat            11/tcp      users
daytime           13/tcp
daytime           13/udp
netstat           15/tcp
qotd              17/tcp      quote
qotd              17/udp      quote
ftp-data          20/tcp
ftp               21/tcp
telnet            23/tcp
smtp              25/tcp      mail
time              37/tcp      timserver
NeWS              144/tcp     news
sgmp              153/udp     sgmp
tcprepo           158/tcp     repository    # PCMAIL
snmp              161/udp     snmp
snmp-trap         162/udp     snmp
print-srv         170/tcp                   # network PostScript
biff              512/udp     comsat
exec              512/tcp
login             513/tcp
who               513/udp     whod
shell             514/tcp     cmd           # no passwords used
syslog            514/udp
printer           515/tcp     spooler       # line printer spooler
```

Many of the ports listed in the *SERVICES* files are "well-known" ports that are defined in the Assigned Numbers RFC. A well-known port is permanently assigned to a specific network service, and is identified by the same port number on all network hosts. This allows applications to know in advance which port to use when communicating using a specific protocol. All well-known port numbers are in the range 1 to 1023.

SNMP uses two well-known ports: 161 and 162. Port 161 receives all SNMP request messages. If a management system wants to send an SNMP request message to an agent, it specifies port 161 as the destination port in the UDP header. The SNMP response message is sent by the agent to the same port used by the management system to send the request message.

Port 162 is the SNMP trap port. When an SNMP agent needs to send a trap to a management system, it specifies the destination as port 162 in the UDP header. The management system understands that all messages arriving via port 162 are SNMP Trap messages.

Sockets

Well-known port numbers are preassigned and might be described by a programmer as being "statically allocated." The connections made to the ports, however, are "dynamically allocated" using a *socket*. A socket is the logical combination of a port number, a protocol number, and a network address that forms an end-point in a network connection. To create a socket, a network address and transport service is specified, a port number is assigned, and a handle or descriptor to the socket is returned. All dynamically allocated ports are assigned numbers ranging from 1024 to 65535.

For example, if you wanted to send an SNMP message to a host with an IP address of 127.65.11.1, you would create a socket using the parameters 127.65.11.1, 17, and 161. All data sent to the network using that socket would be sent to the destination port 161 on the host at address 127.65.11.1 using the UDP transport protocol.

Under Windows, sockets are created using the WinSock API. Both the SNMP service and the SNMP trap service use WinSock to send and receive SNMP messages. You don't need to know anything about WinSock to use the SNMP API (but it never hurts to improve your education).

Figure 2-8 shows an example of three sockets opened by SNMP management and agent processes running on two different network hosts.

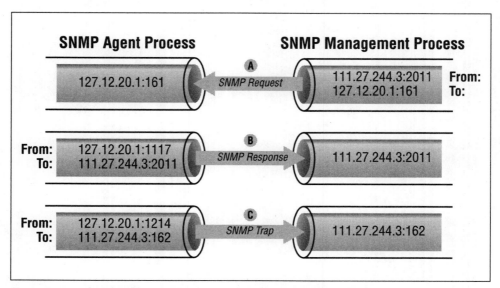

Figure 2-8. Sockets used by an SNMP management system and agent

Socket pair A shows the management process sending an SNMP request message to the agent. The sending socket identifies the source address and port of the message and specifies the address and well-known port destination of the message. Socket pair B shows the response message sent back by the agent to the sending port on the management host. Socket pair C shows the agent sending a trap to the well-known SNMP trap port on the management host.

Revisiting the post office analogy, you can think of a network address as the street address of an apartment building, a port number as the number assigned to each apartment, and a protocol number as the method used to deliver the mail. All mail sent to the apartments arrives at the same address and is then delivered to each tenant based on the apartment number appearing in the address and the type of packaging (letters are dropped through a mail slot, packages are left on a door step, etc.).

3

Network Management and SNMP

In this chapter we look at the concept that inspired the creation of SNMP: network management. We've talked briefly about network management, but what do we really mean by this term?

What Is Network Management?

Ask ten different people what "network management" is and you will receive ten different answers. This isn't so bad if the ten people you ask are just walking around the local shopping mall (and if you count each "I don't know" as a separate answer). But when the ten people are in your company's network engineering group or the Management Information Systems department, you may begin to suspect that something is amiss. Now throw in another ten different answers from the salesmen and marketing types. You've now realized that with all these different definitions of network management, probably very few people know what it really is.

This is really nobody's fault. A network can be managed on several different levels. At the lowest level is *network maintenance*. The technicians at this level use crimpers, wire cutters, soldering irons, digital multimeters, and network analyzers to manage the network's "physical plant." They argue about the benefits of 10BaseT over 10Base2 cables and remark on how much better the network is operating now that they replaced those 75 ohm terminators with the 50 ohm'ers. Network maintenance people may also talk fondly of the time they "pinned some lid's coax," but that shouldn't concern you (unless you are operating an amateur radio obnoxiously and without a license).

At the next level are the folks in a group we might call *configuration management*. This is where decisions are made involving the planning of the physical and logical construction of the network. The configuration is defined by the devices connected to the network, how they are connected, and what is used to connect them. Configuration decisions include how to segment the routers, what kind of system management software to use on the hosts, whether to provide fixed IP addresses or use a DHCP server, and how we convince the people in finance that we need T1 service for our Internet connection. Anger one of these people, and they'll configure the router on your segment to swallow all packets originating from your workstation—and then claim for days that they are "working on the problem."

At the next higher level are the *network administrators*. Once the network's configuration is stable (but is it ever, really?), the netadmins sit atop their management-given thrones and reign supreme over the network. It is their task to perform logical configuration and service operations, such as monitoring the number of available ports on hubs and routers, adding the 300th user to a server licensed for only 256, finding the Network Interface Controller that's abandoned the concept of CSMA/CD, noting how little bandwidth is available on the company's Internet connection between the hours of 9:00 a.m. and 6:00 p.m., and answering—or ignoring—all email sent to "helpdesk." A netadmin is either chasing or being chased, sort of like Harrison Ford in *Bladerunner* or *The Fugitive*.

Management or Administration?

The terms *management* and *administration* are often used synonymously, but they are actually two different aspects of the same concern. Administration is concerned with forming policies, performing accounting and cost analysis, and maintaining facility, equipment, and personnel records. Management is concerned with the execution of administrative policies, delegating responsibility, and making sure that all is running smoothly. You could say that administration is mostly strategic, while management tends to be more tactical and logistical. Both also require a fair amount of diplomatic skill.

And at the highest level are the *network users* themselves—the most helpless "managers" of any network. For a user, performing network management is usually no more than logging in and out of servers, deleting old files, and occasionally changing a password or a default printer queue. From a user's point of view, access to the network should be fast and the network itself should provide most of the services the user will need. The real network managers just want to keep the users from accidentally (or purposely) screwing up the network.

So, a fair answer to our original question is that network management is a collection of processes and policies used for maintaining the health and efficiency of a computer network, regardless of the network's size or the type of work performed upon it.

System and Network Management

We've talked about network management. Another term that you probably have heard is *system management.* Although these terms are often used as if they refer to the same concepts, they are not interchangeable. They do, however, have some overlap in their definitions, and that is usually the source of confusion. Both types of management involve collecting data from devices, such as routers, servers, and workstations; however, they differ in how the data is used.

System management is the process of monitoring and maintaining individual devices, either configured as stand-alone units or connected to other devices as a network. System management activities include installing new and updated software, making backups, monitoring free disk space and power levels, configuring user accounts, and installing and removing system services.

Network management, which we've looked at briefly, includes the collective functions used to monitor and maintain the health of a network at the device level. How the network is performing is based on the capacity and current level of operation of its devices. Functions performed by a device that do not impact the performance of the network, such as communicating with a local peripheral device, are typically of no concern to network management.

Both system and network management focus on the monitoring and control of devices. But system management is concerned with a device as an independent entity, or as a member within a logical group of related systems. Network management is concerned with a device as only a small part of the anatomy of a network. Another way to look at it is this: is your concern for the health of only a set of specific devices, or is it for the health of an entire network?

The overlap in these concepts is where one leaves off and the other begins. You should be able to see how performing system management functions, such as backing up a large amount of data on a server or updating a router with buggy firmware, can affect a network. And network management functions, such as restricting the amount of network traffic that can be routed, can certainly affect individual systems on a network.

To get a basic idea of how, why, where, and when network management is performed, we need to have a look at one possible model of managing a computer network.

Types of Nodes

The basic model of network management groups all nodes on a network in the following categories:

- Managed nodes—any network device that is currently collecting and supplying management information.

- Management nodes—any network device that is capable of retrieving management information from managed nodes.

- Nodes that are not manageable—such a node either does not support network management (although a network management proxy for the device may exist) or supports an incompatible network management protocol.

Each *managed node* will run an agent process that services requests for management information made to the managed node by management nodes. When a request is received, it is checked to see if the sender is authorized to make the request. If so, the agent collects the request information from the node and returns the information to the management node in the form of a response.

A *management node* is typically a workstation operating a network management system in the form of a software application with an interactive menu-driven or graphical user interface. Management nodes may also be automated software processes called remote monitoring (RMON) probes, whose only purpose is to collect management information from managed nodes.

A node can be both a managed node and a management node at the same time—for example, a workstation that is running both an agent process and a network management system. Such a node is referred to as a *bilevel entity*.

The picture of distributed management becomes clearer if you imagine that most devices on a network are capable of collecting information on their performance and operational status, and then presenting that information in a standardized way. The management information is collected and processed using network management software and is organized into a useful picture of the overall state and health of the network.

Local vs. Remote Management

Manufacturers typically design network devices so that they may operate without any form of network management; however, usually some form of local management, such as a front panel or dumb terminal interface, is required to configure the device. Network management may be added later on as an upgrade of the device's firmware, or as an additional hardware assembly that is attached to the device.

SNMP's Own Terminology

At this point, you have probably recognized SNMP's parallel to the client/server information systems model. SNMP does not use overloaded and overused terms such as "client," "server," and "database," and instead either defines its own terms or uses those existing terms defined by OSI network management practices. Using specific terminology helps avoid the misinterpretation of SNMP concepts by people who have differing views and opinions of precisely what things "client" or "database" represent.

Not all network elements contain useful information about their physical or logical corner of the network. In fact, many network devices do not use the network to perform their primary functions at all, and many are not even aware that they are attached to any kind of a network. Consider a device that converts data signals from one format to another. Let's say you attach an optical fiber to the device's input interface, and a pair of copper wires to its output interface. The device is only aware of a few things: the signals it receives from the fiber, the process it uses to convert the signals from one data format to another, and the converted signals it transmits on the copper lines. Such a device will probably have a front panel with a few lights to indicate its present state, a few buttons used to enter data, a digital readout to display information, and possibly a simple menu. A serial interface might also be supported that is used to attach an asynchronous serial (dumb) terminal to access local device management information in the form of character-based menus. Controlling a device using its physical interface is called *local management.*

Now imagine that you had thousands of these devices spread out all over a city, state, or continent. As we discussed briefly in Chapter 1, *Introduction to SNMP*, you would find it very costly, in terms of both time and money, to travel to the location of each device to modify its configuration and monitor its performance. You would need some form of *remote management* that would allow you to access all of the devices in the field from a single point.

How would such remote management work? Working with the device you currently have, you could easily attach a modem to the device's serial port and allow administration personnel to call in remotely to monitor the device. The only problem with this plan is that you must have one modem per device; you would therefore tie up one phone line for as long as you were connected to the device. An expensive prospect, especially if you have hundreds of devices and you need to monitor them all constantly!

Let's see if we can improve this plan. The next thing to consider is some type of management proxy server. This would be a computer that contains specialized software designed to allow the remote management of your devices. The server would have a direct serial connection to each device and would support several dial-up modem connections. All a manager would need to do is dial up and connect to the server and then request management information from a specific device. The server would then either collect the device information that you requested (and format it nicely for you to browse) or simply pass on the management menus already present in the device's firmware.

This is a better solution in that you do not require one modem per device, although you do need a server that can handle many serial connections. There is also the added expense of the server itself and the cost to write and maintain the server's specialized management software.

An alternative to the centralized management server is a distributed form of management, where each device exists as a peer on a network, and can be queried by management systems that have network access (sound familiar?). The network could be based on the data that is being processed by the device. Special management commands could be included in the actual data being processed (in-band management), or the device could support some other type of network that is only used to convey management information (out-of-band management).

Functional Areas of Network Management

Network management is both a framework and a set of processes for planning, implementing, and maintaining computer networks (a network management paradigm, if you will). There are many different network management standards groups, each with its own concept of how networks should be managed, and even what the definition of the term "network management" is.

All models of network management have the same central themes, such as security and configuration, performance, and fault monitoring. The more complex network management models also include network administration functions, such as planning, support, asset records, and accounting and cost management.

Many people believe that network protocols themselves are network management frameworks; they think that if a device supports a management protocol, then it must therefore support a management framework. However, this is certainly not the case. Although many system and network management protocols do contain specific information on device configuration and provisioning, performance monitoring, and alarm reporting, the protocol itself is only a tool used to provide a structure for interpreting the management information. The protocol is not the management framework itself.

Rather than discuss a specific network management paradigm (there are many books written on the topic of network management that already do this), this section briefly presents some functional areas that are commonly found in most network management philosophies. Each of these areas is applicable to platforms ranging from the largest and most complex network to the simplest, non-networked workstation.

Configuration Management

The configuration of a network is determined by the types of devices that populate the network and their current operational parameters. *Configuration management* is therefore primarily concerned with the physical and logical connections of routers, bridges, hubs, and hosts, and with how each of these types of devices is configured to operate. There are actually three separate aspects of configuration management:

- *Inventory* is the set of devices on a network, or the set of hardware and software components installed in a network device, and their associated static information.

- *Configuration* is the map of how the inventory components are connected.

- *Provisioning* is the changeable operational parameters that specify how each component is to function.

You can see all three of these aspects of configuration management in the CMOS setup program of a typical PC. The inventory of all hardware components includes disk drives, video and storage adapters, peripheral ports, and network interface controllers. The read-only data associated with each device, such as manufacturer's name, model and serial number, and firmware revision, is all part of the inventory information.

The configuration is a map of how all items in the inventory are connected together. For a network configuration, this map shows how each network node is physically and logically connected to all other nodes on the network. For device configuration in a network, this map indicates which drives are controlled by which adapter and which cards are plugged into which type of bus. The configuration will also indicate whether features such as Advanced Power Management (APM) and Desktop Management Interface (DMI) are present and active.

The provisioning is all the variable parameters that indicate how the node is to functionally perform. Provisioning items for a workstation include the time and date, capacity of the floppy and hard disk drives, memory cache settings, hard disk addressing features, and settings of all hardware peripheral ports. The controlling parameters for the APM and DMI features are also provisioned information.

A system or network management framework provides a single interface that may be used to read, compare, and change the configuration, inventory, and provisioning of many networked devices. This framework includes a database of all possible settings in the form of manuals, online help files, or successive calls to technical support. Unfortunately, there is no single management application that can manage the configuration of all devices. This makes a typical network management system a collection of many different software applications for managing many different types of devices.

Fault Management

When something unexpected happens on a network, some sort of signal might be raised, or you might observe a change in the operational condition of a device. Both of these events may indicate that the network has experienced a problem. If the problem has a negative effect on the service of the network, then it is considered a "fault." The detection, identification, isolation, reporting, and correction of both problems and faults is the concern of fault management.

Fault management is the most important form of system or network management. The ability to quickly detect a service-affecting problem, report it to a management device, and possibly apply corrective action is a mechanism that typically takes precedence over all other forms of management.

Network faults may be detected reactively or proactively. *Reactive* fault detection occurs when a fault is already present in the network. For example, a router detects that a network device has stopped responding, or that two devices are using the same network address. The router will then send out a reactive notification (called an alarm or alert), which signals that a fault has been detected. Much reactive management occurs in the form of users calling the network administrator with problem reports.

Proactive fault detection involves identifying an existing condition as the source or symptom of a problem that may eventually affect the service of the network. A server with a hard disk that has filled to more than 90% of its capacity may be an indication of a potential fault (the fault actually occurs if the disk is filled to 100% of its capacity). A network device that is reporting that more than 5% of the packets it has received are damaged may not be considered a fault at the moment, but it is an indication that a problem currently exists and a fault is likely to occur.

Just what is considered to be a problem? Usually, any event that is unintentional and service-affecting is a problem that requires immediate attention. Devices that have lost power and broken network connections are the most common, immediate, and service-affecting types of faults. Problems created by bugs in software or firmware, or a device provisioned with incorrect information, are also common sources of problems.

To predict when and where a fault might occur requires the added expense of extra monitoring equipment, detailed information of the operation of the network, and the additional network bandwidth required by the proactive fault detection processes. Because of the added development time and costs involved, you are likely to find significant proactive fault detection built into the management systems for only the largest types of networks.

Performance Management

A network is said to be performing well if there is at least a minimal acceptable level of available bandwidth present, and if the nodes are able to process network traffic within their workload capacity—in other words, there is lots of room to move around and nobody is overworked or overloaded.

Performance management involves monitoring network performance and tuning the network as necessary. What type of data provides a measure of performance depends upon the type of network. The most common type of performance data is usually at the packet level, and includes the following:

- Number of bad packets (CRC or checksum errors) received
- Number of response timeouts or packet resends
- Number of packets that failed to be delivered

A significant number of bad packets or bad packet transmissions usually indicates some type of problem. Devices or communications links that are unexpectedly removed from service and routers that have insufficient memory to handle their work load are also factors that hurt performance.

Some network devices are able to gather statistics about the network at the signal level. The attenuation (decrease in power of a signal) or margin loss of the electromagnetic signal itself may indicate that a specific segment of a network requires a repeater, or perhaps that a section of cable is damaged or degrading.

Performance monitoring involves observing not only a device's current statistics, but also a history of its performance. Observing the history of a performance indicator will give an idea of what has been happening with the device in the past few hours or days, and helps to determine if the system has been, or will be, experiencing problems. For example:

- If an alarm on a server has sounded, indicating that one of its drives has reached 90% of its capacity, you would look at a history of the drive's usage to see if this is an infrequent occurrence; if the capacity is normally around 90%, it may indicate that you need to upgrade to a larger drive.

- Noting the history of margin and attenuation values of a communications line recorded over the past 30 days will give an idea of whether the line is slowly degrading, possibly due to environmental contamination, or has suffered recent damage.

- A history report indicating that a channel was out of service for a few hours should prompt you to look at the alarm and fault management logs to see exactly what the problem was and how it was corrected.

Other Functional Areas

Many other forms of management may be in use in a particular network management framework, including the following types:

- *Security management*—Includes all actions used to prevent access, use, and alteration of a network by unauthorized personnel. This includes physical security, such as the isolation of key network components, and logical security, including system passwords and the encryption of network data.

- *Accounting management*—Used to determine the cost of operating and maintaining the network (cost management) and to monitor its usage so charges for its use may be assessed (chargeback management).

- *Asset management*—Involves the statistical record keeping of the equipment, facility, and personnel used to maintain the network.

- *Planning management*—Involves analysis of trends that indicate the potential future need to increase the network's size (number of nodes), upgrade the network's capacity (adopt higher-bandwidth network technology), or downsize the network.

To Network or Not To Network . . .

By now you may be asking, "Why isn't network management a part of every device?" Network management is a common option on most network routing devices. And thanks to popular operating systems, such as UNIX, Novell NetWare, and Microsoft Windows, and protocol suites such as IPX/SPX and TCP/IP, it is fairly easy to add network management to most file servers and workstations that are network hosts.

But there are still many devices that do not directly support network management, or even a standard form of management by a proxy. For a manufacturer to even consider the expense of adding network management to a device, the following criteria must be met:

The management interface must be standardized and extensible

The management interface is the presentation of management data to other devices on the network. Obviously, all devices sharing a common form of management must have the same management interface. And when such an interface has been ratified as an international standard by one or more standards organizations and widely adopted by industry, then the credibility of the management interface is greatly increased.

The management interface must be extensible

Networks rarely contain only devices that are completely homogeneous and compatible. In fact, anything from a supercomputer to a kitchen appliance may be directly attached to a network, or indirectly attached using a proxy. For this reason, a management interface must be extensible enough to be able to support any type of information necessary to monitor and control any networked device.

The management interface must be portable

If you manufacture many different types of network devices, or if you support a wide variety of network technologies, then cost considerations are very important. You must try to reuse as many of the hardware and software components that you develop as possible. Be sure to use a network management protocol that can be supported by a wide variety of devices and that can be implemented as a single software package that has been ported to many different operating systems.

The management mechanism must be inexpensive

While a perfect, all-purpose, drop-in, plug-and-play network management solution does not exist, nor will ever exist, the fundamental management mechanism can be generic enough to be included in an unmodified state in a wide variety of devices. If this is the case, then only the specific code needed to manage a particular device needs to be developed, integrated, and supported by the device's manufacturer.

The management mechanism must be implemented as software only

If a management system requires that a specific management hardware device be integrated into every managed system, then a manufacturer is not likely to adopt it, citing a poor cost versus benefit ratio as the reason. And there are so many types of network devices that can be managed that constructing common management hardware devices for all of them would be an enormous design and standardization effort that would require many years to complete. Such an effort would likely end up being cost-prohibitive.

Other manufacturers must support the management mechanism

> A standard management system is of no interest if no one is using it. On the other hand, if manufacturers within an industry look around and realize that most of their competitors' products support a popular form of network management, then you can bet that they'll be rushing to include it as well.

Customers must want and even demand the management mechanism

> Above all, give the customers what they want, but also give them what they need. Network management is often present on a customer's "must have" list of features when purchasing a network system or device, but few customers will have a network management framework in place, or even a plan for deploying a system of network management. The network management solution you offer must be standardized, useful, and, above all, simple.

Network Management Using SNMP

SNMP fits perfectly into the model of network management that we have just discussed. SNMP is designed around a distributed network management framework. Each network node collects management information that describes its past and present state, and makes this data available to management systems also residing on the network.

The SNMP Management Model

SNMP defines two types of management entities: managers and agents. You may also think of these entities as "those who manage" and "those who are managed." You probably already have personal experience with this model (but note that SNMP has yet to incorporate cubicles, status reports, and 9:00 a.m. Monday morning staff meetings as part of its managerial requirements).

A network management station (NMS) is typically a computer that is used to run one or more network management system (also, confusingly, NMS) applications. Medium- to large-scale network management systems are usually built on top of a third-party software platform called a network management suite (you guessed it—NMS), such as HP OpenView and IBM NetView. The management station is used by the human manager to issue requests for management information from managed nodes. The station receives the requested information and then displays the management data in a useful way.

The role of a management agent is to monitor one or more network nodes, collect data on their operation (management information), and report this data to the management system when it is requested. Most of the work in SNMP management is performed by the management applications running on a management station. Why? Because a manager's computer and its resources are typically dedicated to the task of management, while a managed node usually has more important things to do.

A node is typically a host to either a management system or a management agent; if this were always the case, the SNMP management model could be simple indeed. But SNMP entities may also have one or more operational variations:

- Nodes that both manage and are manageable (bilevel entities)
- Nodes that understand multiple versions of the SNMP protocol (bilingual entities)
- Nodes that act as proxy agents for other devices (gateways or mid-level managers)
- Nodes that are managed by mechanisms other than SNMP
- Nodes that are not manageable at all

It is possible for a node to contain both a network management system and a management agent. A very good example is a Windows NT workstation running the SNMP service and an SNMP network management application. In fact, it is likely that all SNMP management nodes will also contain an SNMP management agent so they may be recognized and identified by other management systems.

Remember there may be at least two versions and several flavors of SNMP in use on a network. A node that supports both SNMPv1 and SNMPv2 is said to be "bilingual," and it is more likely that the management systems will be the bilingual nodes on a network.

An SNMP proxy agent is a network node that performs management services on behalf of another device that does not (or can not) support an SNMP agent. Peripherals and test equipment that may not actually reside on the network can be proxied, as can processes running in an operating system.

Many other system and network management protocols exist. If a node supporting a non-SNMP management protocol can be proxied by a multi-lingual SNMP agent that is able to translate requests into a form the node can process, then the node may reside within the SNMP management model.

Devices that cannot supply any form of management data at all are not part of the SNMP model.

Community Names

SNMPv1 defines a community-based administration framework used to manage SNMP elements. Each SNMP community is a group that contains at least one agent and one management system. The logical name assigned to such a group is called the *community name*. The community name is physically encoded into the SNMP messages sent by each member of the group, and in this form it is referred to as a "community string." The community string is used by the message receiver to identify the community for which the message intended.

A managed node indicates that it belongs to a specific community by accepting or rejecting requests containing a specific community string. For example, if an SNMP agent accepts all requests containing the community string "public," then the agent is asserting that it belongs to the "public" SNMP community. If the same agent rejects SNMP requests containing the community string "private," then the agent does not consider itself to be a member of the "private" community. All management nodes belong to SNMP communities for the purpose of interacting with managed nodes. A management node belongs to a particular SNMP community if it sends SNMP messages that contain the name of the community.

The assignment of acceptable community names to managed nodes is performed by the human network managers, and may be on many things, such as function (the PRINTER community), location (the "Engineering Lab" community), user (the "Software Group" community), or device manufacturer (the "PairGain Technologies" community). And community names will usually not be modified unless there is a significant change in the administrative configuration of the network.

If an SNMP agent is not provisioned with any community names, then it will typically accept and process SNMP requests containing any community string. Such a node effectively belongs to all SNMP communities on a network.

Figure 3-1 shows a map of several SNMP communities in a local area network. All of the nodes depicted support an SNMP management agent. Most nodes exist in only one community, but some exist in two or three. For example, the router is assigned to both the "Engineering Lab" and "campus" communities. And the printer server belongs to the "campus," "PRINTER," and "public" communities. The community labeled "All Communities" includes all of the SNMP-managed nodes that are currently not assigned a community name, so they effectively belong to all SNMP communities. And because a network management application may typically send SNMP messages to any community with a known community name, most management nodes will fit into the "All Communities" community as well.

SNMP Proxy Agents

I mentioned earlier in this chapter that a proxy agent, or simply "a proxy," is a network node that performs management services on behalf of another device.

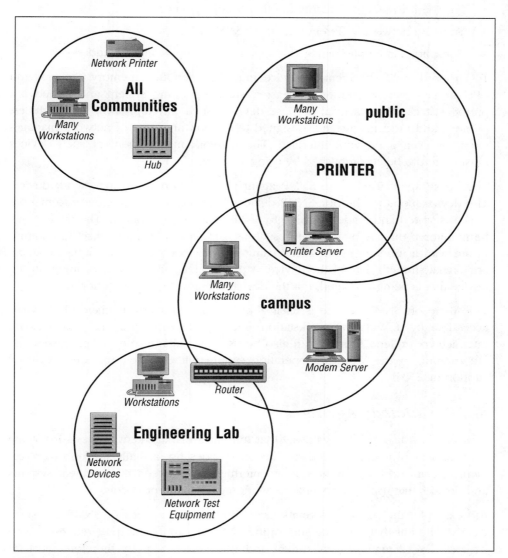

Figure 3-1. SNMP communities

An SNMP proxy allows a device that does not support SNMP protocol requests (or even network communication itself) to be monitored and controlled using SNMP.

A proxy agent allows SNMP to be used to do the following things:

- Manage a device that cannot support an SNMP agent
- Manage a device that supports a non-SNMP management agent
- Allow a non-SNMP management system to access an SNMP agent

- Provide firewall-type security to other SNMP agents

- Translate between different formats of SNMP messages

- Consolidate multiple managed nodes under a single network address

To support an SNMP agent, a device must have enough memory capacity and CPU horsepower to support at least a small operating system and a network protocol stack. Many special-purpose devices, such as telephones, fax machines, printers, and modems, are not designed to support any type of network management, or even a network interface. The network management of such devices must therefore be accomplished by using a proxy.

The proxy agent itself is an SNMP agent process running on a network device. The device monitors the non-SNMP devices for specific management information, which is stored and made available to SNMP management nodes. The device may be monitored directly by the agent, such as using the AT command set to communicate with a modem, or indirectly using sensors to collect temperature, voltage, and signal strength data of the device. A proxy agent may also be running on the device that is being managed, but the device is unaware of the agent process.

The Microsoft SNMP service is itself a proxy agent for any manageable devices accessible by a Windows workstation, such as modems, printers, and network interface controllers. A proxy can also be used to manage software processes that are running in the Windows operating system without the processes explicitly supporting SNMP.

SNMP Gateway Agents

A proxy may also act as a gateway that translates management requests from one management protocol to another. The proxy does not actually perform management operations, but only acts as an intermediary between management systems and devices that use incompatible network management protocols.

For example, the message formats used by the two versions of SNMP are sufficiently different that a device supporting SNMPv1 cannot interpret requests made by an SNMPv2 management system and vice versa. A proxy therefore must be used to translate the SNMPv2 requests to SMNPv1 for the managed device to process, and the SNMPv1 responses from the device must be translated to the equivalent SNMPv2 messages for the management system to correctly interpret.[*]

The device that is being proxied may reside on the same network as the proxy agent (such as a group of workstations) or be physically attached to the proxy (such as a bank of modem cards plugged into a motherboard) or be remotely

---

[*] Note that in this case, using bilingual management systems or agents would remove the need for the proxy.

attached (such as a cable or infrared connection to a printer). It is only important that intelligible management information somehow be conveyed between the managed device and the proxy.

A proxy may be designed as a gateway to allow several SNMP-manageable devices to be accessed using a single network address. Requests for management information would be made by SNMP to the proxy, and the proxy would pass the request on to the appropriate managed device. The response would then be returned from the device to the proxy and then passed on to the NMS. The proxy gateway could also function as a single trap destination for multiple agents, with the proxy being responsible for forwarding the traps to their proper final destinations.

A proxy gateway may also act as a firewall and provide a single point that performs all UDP validation (packet filtering) and PDU authentication (application filtering). Address checks could be made to verify that an SNMP message originated at an address listed as authorized to make Get or Set requests. Invalid and unauthentic requests are discarded by the gateway.

Proxy agents may seem to solve a number of problems. However, in some cases, the use of a proxy agent is only a short-term, stopgap measure. All too often, it is tempting to write a proxy "translator" rather than building full management support into a device that is capable of supporting a management agent. Table 3-1 summarizes the pros and cons of proxies.

Table 3-1. Pros and Cons of Management Proxy Agents

Proxy Pros	Proxy Cons
Adds pseudo-SNMP management to devices that would not otherwise be SNMP-accessible.	Often difficult to design and implement.
	May not make use of available full management capabilities of device.
Isolates proprietary and arcane management protocols from the public network.	Requires additional network elements or processes.
Allows network elements to support multiple protocols. Consolidates multiple agents to a central access address.	Adds an extra level of complexity to debugging.
Potentially quicker implementation than a full protocol stack and SNMP agent.	Design may make troubleshooting of network more difficult.
Used as a (possibly) quick way to make a non-SNMP node accessible via SNMP.	Implementers may believe (dangerously) that a short-term, stopgap proxy measure is a good, long-term solution.

4

In this chapter:
- *The Basics*
- *The Languages of SNMP*
- *Managed Objects*
- *Scalar and Columnar MIB Variables*
- *The SNMP Message*
- *SNMPv1 Traps*
- *Using a Protocol Analyzer*

Inside SNMP

This chapter looks at the operational characteristics of SNMP and how management information is logically organized. You need to have a good grasp of the internal structures and operations of SNMP if you're going to be able to perform timely and successful troubleshooting of network management problems.

Most of what you need to know about SNMP is the definition and the operation of the protocol itself and the structure of the managed data that is collected. Once you understand how the SNMP messages are properly constructed and interpreted, you have a good foundation in SNMP. Information after this point will focus on how the SNMP messages are actually used, and the specific details of the network devices that support SNMP.

If you are already an "expert" on SNMP, then you may wish to only skim this chapter. The information here is presented mainly for Win32 programmers who suddenly find themselves needing to know something about SNMP, or those who are just interested in learning all they can about yet another Windows NT network service.

The Basics

A network node that makes management data available using the SNMP protocol is said to be "SNMP manageable." The management data itself is a collection of integer, string, and MIB address variables that contain all of the information necessary to manage the node. This includes administrative and security policies used to access the node; the inventory, configuration, and provisioning information of the node's hardware and software; and the data which indicates the present and past operational status of the node. As I've mentioned, these variables are often called by the generic term "managed objects," but are referred to as "MIB variables" in SNMP vernacular.

MIB variables contain the actual management data used to determine the state and configuration of a managed node, and to effect changes in its behavior. SNMP defines the structure of management data and provides the operations used by a management system for manipulating the data stored in MIB variables. When an SNMP management system is in the act of "managing a node," it is in reality using SNMP to read and write the data contained in the node's MIB variables.

The managed objects themselves and their data are maintained by a managed node's SNMP agent process. The agent is the gatekeeper of the managed objects and performs the actual reads and writes based on requests made by the management system. The agent is also responsible for implementing the SNMP protocol in the managed node.

It is this basic concept of simply reading and writing data stored in variables that is the heart of the operation of SNMP.

Four Simple Operations

SNMP defines four operations used by SNMP management systems to manipulate the managed objects that are maintained by an SNMP agent. These operations are named Get, GetNext, Set, and Trap. Requiring only four operations to perform all network management functions is part of SNMP's "simple" design.

The *Get* operation retrieves the value of a specific instance of a managed object. An "instance" is the physical incarnation of a MIB variable as it exists in memory or in persistent storage. A variable may contain an integer or string value, or the address of another variable defined in the MIB.

The Get operation is very straightforward. For example, assume that an agent maintains three managed objects with the following names and values:

Name	Value
erroredSeconds	17
mostSevereAlarm	24
shelfID	"Sebastopol"

If we perform a Get operation on erroredSeconds, the value returned would be 17, which is the current value stored by this object. We then say that we "performed a get on erroredSeconds." It might be more proper to say that we "retrieved" or "fetched" the value of erroredSeconds, but why deprive SNMP of its own lingo?

The second operation is *GetNext*. This operation gets the value of the next lexical managed object instance from the object specified. If we perform a GetNext on erroredSeconds, the value 24 is returned; this is the value stored by mostSevere-Alarm, the next managed object instance after erroredSeconds. The usefulness of this operation may not be immediately apparent to you, but it's invaluable for retrieving the data stored in the rows of tables and from MIB variables that cannot be specifically named.

The third operation, *Set*, changes the value of a managed object. Most managed objects have a "power-on default" value with which they are initialized when the SNMP agent starts up. This value may then be modified by the SNMP agent in response to specific events (the reception of a bad packet, the ticking of the system clock, and so forth). But occasionally a management system will also need to change the value of a managed object, and it uses the Set operation to do so.

The fourth operation, *Trap*, is an unsolicited notification sent to one or more management systems by an agent as an indication that a specific event has occurred. Traps are examined in detail later in this chapter and in Chapter 8, *Implementing Traps*.

The Message Is the Management

SNMP is a request-and-response protocol. A management system sends a request to an agent in the form of a Get, GetNext, or Set operation. The agent replies to the call with a response that indicates if the operation was performed successfully or if an error occurred.

Both management systems and agents must send all SNMP messages to specific network addresses. For each SNMP request that is sent by a management system, only one SNMP response will be returned by each agent that receives it. If a management system sends a single SNMP request to a broadcast address, it may receive many responses in return. And finally, SNMPv1 agents do not send management operation requests and SNMPv1 management systems do not send management operation responses.

A special type of unsolicited response called a *trap* may be sent by an agent to a management system without first receiving a request. A trap is nothing more than an event report, and is usually an indication that the agent has detected the occurrence of something unexpected. Windows programmers will come to realize the amazing similarity between the reception and reporting of a trap response by a management system and the sudden, stomach-sinking appearance of the Win32 message box reporting that a GPF (General Protection Fault) has occurred. The reception of an SNMP trap, however, is not necessarily an indication that a fault has occurred.

Client Pull and Server Push

The transaction of SNMP request and response is sometimes described by the *client pull* model, which depicts the management system client as pulling the data it needs from the agent server. Traps are described by the *server push* model, where a server agent pushes unrequested data to a client management system.

The Languages of SNMP

SNMP is a very specialized protocol. It was created specifically to transfer network management information between two or more network entities. We defined network management information as any data that is used to monitor, configure, and control the state of a network node. An SNMP-managed node is any device on a network that makes its management information available using SNMP.

SNMP itself is a protocol rather than a language. A good definition of *protocol* is "a set of rules that are created by negotiation, and are followed so that information may be exchanged without misinterpretation." Language is an encoding mechanism used to describe the data contained within a protocol. And the protocol is the set of rules for conveying the data between entities.

There are three separate languages used by SNMP to convey management information:

Structure of Management Information (SMI)
   specifies the format used for defining managed objects that are accessed via the SNMP protocol.

Abstract Syntax Notation One (ASN.1)
   used to define the format of SNMP messages and managed objects (MIB modules) using an unambiguous data description format.

Basic Encoding Rules (BER)
   used to encode the SNMP messages into a format suitable to transmission across a network.

Each of these languages supports the other two by adhering to strict rules governing its format and interpretation.

Chapter 1, *Introduction to SNMP*, explained how important the Management Information Base (MIB) is to SNMP. Without the MIB there is no information to communicate using SNMP. You might as well create a language with a grammar and a syntax, but not have a vocabulary to provide its content.

To write any extension agent, you will always begin with a MIB. You must be very familiar with both the SMI and ASN.1. Because the conversion of MIB data to and from BER is handled transparently for you by the Microsoft extendible agent, you don't need to work with BER directly when writing an extension agent. For that reason, BER is covered here in very little detail. However, if you plan to use a network data monitoring utility, such as Microsoft Network Monitor, Cinco Networks NetXRay, LANalyzer for Windows, or Packet Sniffer, you may want to learn BER to interpret the data in the SNMP messages.

SMI: Structure of Management Information

MIBs are very highly structured representations of data. As we've mentioned, the rules for defining managed objects and creating the structure of an SNMP MIB is called the Structure of Management Information (SMI). The SMI defines the rules for defining managed objects within a MIB, and specifies the structure of the MIB used for network management.

SMIv1 is described in RFCs 1155, 1212, and 1215, and specifies:

- The requirement that MIB modules and the managed objects that they define are to be described using the CCITT X.208 ASN.1 data description language

- A listing of the subset of the ASN.1 language components and features used to describe a MIB

- The definition of new ASN.1 APPLICATION data types specifically for use in SNMP MIBs

- The assertion that all ASN.1 constructs are to be serialized using the CCITT X.209 BER prior to transmission across a channel of communication

- The definition of the high-level structure of the Internet branch (iso(1).org(3).dod(6).intenet(1)) of the MIB naming tree

- The definition and description of an SNMP managed object

The SMI is primarily concerned with the organization and administration of managed objects on the Internet. It describes a naming structure, called the MIB naming tree, that is used to identify managed objects, and defines the branch of the MIB tree where SNMP managed objects reside. The SMI also describes the basic format used to define a managed object, although the SMI itself does not actually define any managed objects.

When a network node supports SNMP management, it must not only support the SNMP protocol, but also implement one or more managed objects defined in the MIB tree. The objects specifically implemented by a node are part of the node's MIB view.

The SMI also specifies that all MIB modules are to be written using a subset of the ASN.1 notation for describing the structure of management data. Because writing an extension agent always begins with using one or more MIB modules as a functional specification, make sure that you can at least read ASN.1 notation.

SMIv1 and SMIv2

There are two versions of the Structure of Management Information: SMIv1 and SMIv2. MIB modules written using either version may be used to implement extension agents. SMIv2 (defined in RFCs 1442, 1443, and 1444) is a backward compatible update of SMIv1, so it is possible to convert an SMIv2 MIB to SMIv1. The only exception is the Counter64 type defined by SMIv2, an equivalent of which cannot be created using SMIv1. (Refer to RFC 2089 for information on how conforming bilingual SNMP agents handle the Counter64 type.)

The IETF requires that new and revised RFCs specify MIB modules using the SMIv2 format. This policy has lead to a widespread use of both versions of the SMI.

Abstract Syntax Notation One

ASN.1 (pronounced A-S-N dot one) is a language created by the ISO for the description of data independent of any specific implementation. ASN.1 allows any data to be represented in an unambiguous, textual form that is used as a template or schema. The implementation details of how the template is realized and the data stored is left to the requirements of the specific systems.

The entire ASN.1 language is originally described in the CCITT X.208 specification, but the SMI limits SNMP to using only a small subset of the ASN.1 language for describing management data. And this subset is described thoroughly in many SNMP books. So unless you really like reading dry, academic specifications, you need not bother obtaining a copy of X.208.

After looking over the syntax of ASN.1 you might consider it to be not only complex, but also complicated. Keep in mind that ASN.1 was designed to represent any type of data in an unambiguous, machine-independent form. The data represented by ASN.1 shares the same context and interpretation on all machines. This is, in fact, the "abstract" part of ASN.1.

It is the generality and flexibility of ASN.1 that make it a truly universal tool for defining the structure of data. And realize that data is all that ASN.1 is capable of representing. ASN.1 does not support code in the form of logical decisions, branching, or mathematical operations. Only data structures, simple and complex, may be rendered. Any decisions or operations that are to be performed on raw MIB data must be determined and performed by the SNMP entities accessing the data.

The remaining part of this section covers only the basic parts of ASN.1 that you'll use when reading a MIB and implementing its structure and data in an extension agent.*

Syntax

ASN.1, like any other language, has a grammar, syntax, and set of stylistic conventions. This section briefly summarizes the basics of ASN.1 syntax. I'll elaborate on it more later in this chapter.

Because ASN.1 is all about data, most of the constructs in the language are concerned with the definition of data types and the assignment of data values. In ASN.1, a data type is defined using the following syntax:

```
<Datatype Name> ::= <Datatype Definition>
```

For example, you can define a data type named "MostSevereAlarm" that is based on the ASN.1 INTEGER type:

```
MostSevereAlarm ::= INTEGER
```

The MostSevereAlarm type can now be used in place of INTEGER when creating an instance of a variable:

```
circuitAlarms MostSevereAlarm ::= 3
```

The variable "circuitAlarms" is of the type "MostSevereAlarm" and is currently assigned the value of 3. Of course you could write the same thing in C as:

```
typedef MostSevereAlarm int; MostSevereAlarm circuitAlarms = 3;
```

What's the big deal about ASN.1? Well, for defining the structure and content of data, ASN.1 has a few more bells and whistles than C. For example, in ASN.1 we can assign a restricted range to MostSevereAlarm:

```
MostSevereAlarm ::= INTEGER (1..5)
```

MostSevereAlarm is now defined as being allowed to contain only INTEGER values in the range 1 to 5. You can't imply this restriction in C using only a single typedef statement. You would also need to use code to check the value assigned to MostSevereAlarm to determine if it were in the proper range. ASN.1 only defines the accepted range of a variable; the agent implementing the access to the variable must perform the actual range checking.

---

* For an agonizingly detailed, but well-written, must-have tome on SNMP MIBs, pick up a copy of *Understanding SNMP MIBs* by David Perkins and Evan McGinnis, Prentice Hall, 1997.

We can also assign a label to each possible value of MostSevereAlarm. This is very similar to an enumeration found in both Pascal and C:

```
MostSevereAlarm ::= INTEGER { critical(1), major(2), minor(3), warning(4),
                             informational(5)}
```

Now we can use not only INTEGER values in assignments to variables based on the MostSevereAlarm type, but also a textual label:

```
circuitAlarms MostSevereAlarm ::= 3
unitAlarms MostSevereAlarm ::= minor
```

Data structures in the form of ordered lists are created using the SEQUENCE keyword. The following is an example of an ordered list:

```
ErrorCounts ::= SEQUENCE {
  circuitId           OCTET STRING,
  erroredSeconds      INTEGER,
  unavailableSeconds  INTEGER
}
```

We can now instantiate a list variable base on the ErrorCounts data type and initialize its members as follows:

```
circuitPerformance ::= ErrorCounts {
  "",                 "Unassigned",
  erroredSeconds      0,
  unavailableSeconds  0
}
```

Stylistic conventions

A set of stylistic conventions exists for creating labels for ASN.1 values, macros, identifiers, and data types in SNMP. All labels are case-sensitive, may contain alphanumeric characters and hyphens, and are typically human-readable. The following conventions are used for creating item labels:

Item	Convention	Example
ASN.1 data types	Initial uppercase	DisplayString
Data values	Initial lowercase	true
Data identifiers	Initial lowercase	sysDescr
ASN.1 keywords	All uppercase	INTEGER
ASN.1 macros	All uppercase	OBJECT-TYPE
Module names	Initial uppercase	OReilly-MIB

ASN.1 keywords that are commonly used in SNMP MIBs include the following:

BEGIN	EXPORTS	OBJECT
CHOICE	IDENTIFIER	OCTET

DEFINED	IMPORTS	OF
DEFINITIONS	INTEGER	SEQUENCE
END	NULL	STRING

Comments

ASN.1 defines comments that may be embedded directly within ASN.1 code. Comments usually contain human-readable text that describe the code and are ignored by compilers by simply converting the comments to whitespace. Comments are always created per line; block comments spanning multiple lines using a single set of comment delimiters are not supported by ASN.1.

ASN.1 defines a comment as starting with two hyphens (--) and ending with either two hyphens or an end-of-line character, whichever comes first. Here are a few examples of ASN.1 comments:

```
-- This is a comment --
-- This is a comment too
-- This is a comment----And this as well
```

Comments may seem very simple, but there are at least two major causes of syntax errors created by comments. First, commenting out a comment often exposes the comment text to the parser. Consider the following:

```
-- A local MIB definition
myTimeStamp ::= OCTET STRING (SIZE(6))   -- 6-octet time stamp definition
```

The first line contains a single comment. The second line contains an ASN.1 construct followed by a comment. The comments on both lines are terminated by the end-of-line, and this code compiles without error.

Now let's modify the code to comment out the construct:

```
-- A local MIB definition
-- myTimeStamp ::= OCTET STRING (SIZE(6))   -- 6-octet time stamp definition
```

This looks perfectly fine, but remember that comments are also terminated by the double hyphens. This code now compiles with a syntax error because the ASN.1 compiler considers the character string "6-octet time stamp definition" to be outside of the comment and attempts to compile it as valid ASN.1 code.

Another ASN.1 comment gotcha is when a sequence of hyphens is used to start comments, or as dividers to separate logical sections within a MIB module. If the number of hyphens in the line is not a multiple of four, then a syntax error will result:

```
-------- --Good. Two sets of hyphen pairs
-------Neither the last three hyphens nor this text are commented out
```

The Basic Encoding Rules

The relationship between ASN.1 and BER is that of source code and machine code. ASN.1 is a text-based, human-readable notation that is compiled into BER data. Before a network node sends an SNMP message, it must convert (or more correctly, "serialize") the ASN.1 data to a smaller, binary representation that unambiguously retains the intellectual content of the management information.* The resulting serialized data is BER.

After an SNMP message is received, it must first be converted from BER and into a data format that the receiving system can use. BER therefore is used only to render the SNMP message in a format suitable for transport across a network. If you look at an SNMP conversation using a protocol analyzer, the payload of each UDP datagram is a BER-encoded SNMP message.

The process of BER data parsing and conversion is transparently handled for you by the SNMP service. It is therefore not necessary for you to understand the conversion rules of BER before writing an extension agent, and this is why BER is not covered in this book. However, it is necessary to understand BER if you will be reading hex dumps of SNMP messages, such as those created by simple network monitoring tools. Also, knowing BER will give you a deeper understanding of SNMP.

Most of the SNMP books listed in Appendix A, *References*, give tutorials and overviews of BER and use examples of encoded SNMP messages. The actual BER specification, CCITT X.209, is very dry and academic, and is not very helpful when first learning BER.

Managed Objects

Managed objects are always defined and referenced within the context of a MIB. A MIB itself is only a collection of managed object definitions, also called MIB objects, MIB items, or MIB variables. As a programmer, you may think of a MIB as an API, or a collection of global variables maintained by an agent, that gives management systems access to the management data of the node.

Each managed object is defined in a MIB module using the OBJECT-TYPE macro as defined by SMIv1. An ASN.1 macro is very similar to a class in that it describes the format and attributes of a managed object. The object may be scalar and have only a single instance, or it may be columnar and have zero or more instances.

---

* Unfortunately, BER does not completely live up to this requirement. BER-encoded data may contain ambiguities that make its correct interpretation difficult.

The following is the sysContact object defined in MIB-II, and is a typical definition of a scalar MIB variable:

```
sysContact OBJECT-TYPE
    SYNTAX  DisplayString (SIZE (0..255))
    ACCESS  read-write
    STATUS  mandatory
    DESCRIPTION
      "The textual identification of the contact person
      for this managed node, together with information
      on how to contact this person."
    ::= { system 4 }
```

The "sysContact" label is the name or object descriptor of the variable and OBJECT-TYPE is the macro. The attributes of the object are described by the four clauses defined by OBJECT-TYPE and defined in RFC 1155.

SYNTAX is the data type of the object and includes any range restrictions. (ASN.1 data types are explained in the following sections.) ACCESS describes the current access mode of the object. Access modes defined by SMIv1 are read-only, read-write, write-only, or not-accessible.

STATUS describes the current need and validity of the object. The possible values are the following:

Mandatory
> Objects that are mandatory must be implemented by an agent, and the values that they contain are valid for use.

Optional
> Objects that are optional may or may not be implemented by an agent. (Popular preference in the SNMP community is to discourage the use of "optional" as a STATUS value.)

Deprecated
> Deprecated objects are in transition to the obsolete STATUS. They have been replaced by newer objects, but the data contained by a deprecated object may at times still be valid.*

Obsolete
> An obsolete object is no longer supported by the MIB and should not be implemented by an agent. It is not necessary that an object be replaced with another object before receiving a status of obsolete; nor is it necessary for an object to be deprecated before it is rendered obsolete.

DESCRIPTION is a human-readable string that describes the purpose of the object and how it is to be used. The range of values that may be assigned to the object

---

* Deprecated was added to the SMI by RFC 1213.

should be described, along with any significant relationship it has to other managed objects within the same MIB. Documentation for many of the MIB modules currently in existence can only be found in the DESCRIPTION strings for their objects.

Managed Objects Aren't Necessarily Object-Oriented

The phrase *managed objects* is used to describe the management data defined in a MIB, maintained by an agent, and accessed using SNMP. The term *object* implies a collection of data, a set of associated attributes, and the code that is used to operate on the data. The actual managed objects supported by an agent contain only data and attributes, but do not provide any methods used for accessing or performing operations on the data they contain (nor are they polymorphic or inheritable), as would be the case if they were truly object-oriented. This is because all SNMP-managed objects are operated upon identically using the rules of SNMP. The SNMP protocol therefore defines the only methods that may be used to operate upon all SNMP managed objects.

MIB-II Managed Objects

RFC 1213 contains the definition (you can call it the source code) of the RFC1213-MIB, also known as MIB-II. (MIB-I is defined in RFC 1156 and has been superseded by MIB-II.) In the MIB tree, MIB-II is located at the following: iso(1).organization(3).dod(6).internet(1).mgmt(2).mib(1). MIB-II contains 171 managed objects organized into eleven functional groups. All SNMP-managed nodes that reside on a TCP/IP network are required to implement these groups as needed to make available a standard body of managed objects for network management operations.

Since the publication of MIB-II in March 1991, many other functional groups have been added to the mib(1) branch for the support of non-Ethernet data link interface (frame relay, ATM, FDDI, SONET) and non-TCP/IP transport mechanisms (AppleTalk, X.500, IPX). Each new group is described as a MIB module and is published in the form of an RFC.

There are also many MIB modules that have been published that define the management objects supported by many different types of network devices and interfaces, such as routers, bridges, repeaters, RS-232 serial ports, modems, printers and printer interfaces, and uninterruptible power supplies (UPSs). These private MIBs are located at the iso(1).organization(3).dod(6).internet(1).private (4).enterprises(1) branch of the MIB tree. And most, if not all, of the extension agents that you write will be to support private, device-specific MIBs.

MIB-II is the consummate example of a MIB and is described in detail by almost every book currently published on the subject of SNMP. For this reason, we will focus here on the objects defined by the system group of MIB-II. These objects are used as recurring examples throughout this book, and you will use them quite a bit for testing your management system code and increasing your understanding of SNMP.

All devices that support SNMP management are required to implement the system group of the RFC1213-MIB MIB. The management information in the system group identifies the node to a network management system. The system group is located in the internet branch (1.3.6.1.2.1.1) of the MIB naming tree, and the seven managed objects in this group are listed in Table 4-1.

Table 4-1. The MIB-II System Group

Object Identifier	Object Descriptor	Access	MIB-I	MIB-II
system.1	sysDescr	read-only	*	*
system.2	sysObjectID	read-only	*	*
system.3	sysUpTime	read-only	*	*
system.4	sysContact	read-write		*
system.5	sysName	read-write		*
system.6	sysLocation	read-write		*
system.7	sysServices	read-only		*

Objects have the following meanings:

sysDescr

A description of the node that includes the name and version of the hardware, operating system, and networking software. This string is most often displayed by management stations to identify a specific managed node. This string is usually identical among nodes produced by the same manufacturer and of the same product family, and may contain information such as hardware and software version and processor type.

sysObjectID

The registration OID (Object Identifier—OID is pronounced "oh-eye-dee") of the node. Each type of device that is described in a vendor's private enterprise MIB reserves an OID in its MIB that is used to identify the device to management systems.

sysUpTime

The interval of time that has elapsed since the SNMP agent process was reinitialized. The agent process is typically reinitialized each time a warm or cold boot is performed, so this interval should not be interpreted as the duration that the node itself has been up. This value is measured in hundredths of a second.

sysUpTime

Included as a time stamp in each trap message sent by an agent. The time stamp may be used by a management system to accurately log the arrival of traps based on the time of the agent, and to determine whether any trap messages received are duplicates. An agent may also use the value of sysUp-Time to set the value of other managed objects, such as a lastConfigChanged object. And a management system that is polling an agent may also poll the sysUpTime value to determine if the agent has been reinitialized between polling intervals.

sysContact

The name of the person, group, or organization responsible for maintaining the node. Contact information, such as telephone number or email address, may be present as well.

sysName

The name of the node itself. This is typically the host and domain name of the node, or a simple, dry explanation of the node's purposes (e.g., "Internet router"). Depending upon the humor level of the node's manager, the name may also be something inventive, such as the name of a Chinese philosopher or Babylonian demon, or even quite comical, such as "Spiff's Spaceport," or "HDSL to Pooh's House."

sysLocation

A description of the physical location of the node. This description may be as general or specific as you like, but should always be useful, such as "Telephone closet, 3rd floor," or "James' Cubicle x2864." Whimsical descriptions, such as "Behind the hot water pipes, third washroom along, Victoria Station," are also prevalent.

sysServices

An INTEGER value whose first seven bits are flags indicating what system services are supported by the node. This value stored by sysServices is created by OR'ing the following bits together:

Bit Field	Functionality	OSI Layer
0x01	Physical	1
0x02	Datalink/Subnetwork	2
0x04	Internet	3
0x08	End-to-end	4
0x10	End-to-end interface	5
0x20	Applications interface	6
0x40	Applications	7

Of these seven objects, only sysContact, sysName, and sysLocation are writable. What this means is that you cannot change the values of the read-only variables using SNMP. These values may be initialized when the agent process is created (sysDescr and sysObjectID), modified only by the operation of the agent (sysUp-Time), or hard-coded in the agent itself (sysServices).

The only object requiring further explanation is sysObjectID. The value of sysObjectID provides a unique registration value used by management systems to specifically identify the type of network device, usually by manufacturer, product family, and model. This allows the management system to display a more useful identification description of the node, such as "O'Reilly & Associates, Frammis Series, Frotis 9000," rather than the default description "SNMP Generic Device."

Each registration value is an OBJECT IDENTIFIER. And each product will have its own registration OID in its manufacturer's private enterprise MIB. Example 4-1 shows the definitions of several mythical O'Reilly network devices and their MIB registrations.

Example 4-1. MIB registrations

```
--O'Reilly enterprise MIBs
ora              OBJECT IDENTIFIER ::= { enterprises 2035 }
                                                          -- 1.3.6.1.4.1.2035


--Product group
products         OBJECT IDENTIFIER ::= { ora 1 }           -- 2035


--Product registration OID
registration     OBJECT IDENTIFIER ::= { ora 3 }           -- 2035.3


--Product MIBs
oraBeedle        OBJECT IDENTIFIER ::= { products 1}        -- 2035.1.1
oraFrammis       OBJECT IDENTIFIER ::= { products 2}        -- 2035.1.2
oraWhammy        OBJECT IDENTIFIER ::= { products 3}        -- 2035.1.3


--MIBs for individual Frammis models
oraFrotis        OBJECT IDENTIFIER ::= { oraFrammis 1 }     -- 2035.1.2.1
oraFrammis97     OBJECT IDENTIFIER ::= { oraFrammis 2 }     -- 2035.1.2.2
oraFramLite      OBJECT IDENTIFIER ::= { oraFrammis 3 }     -- 2035.1.2.3


--Registration objects for sysObjectID
orareg-Beedle    OBJECT IDENTIFIER ::= { registration 1 }   -- 2035.3.1
orareg-Frammis   OBJECT IDENTIFIER ::= { registration 2 }   -- 2035.3.2
orareg-Whammy    OBJECT IDENTIFIER ::= { registration 3 }   -- 2035.3.3


--Registration objects for sysObjectID of all Frammis models
orareg-Frotis    OBJECT IDENTIFIER ::= { orareg-Frammis 1}  -- 2035.3.2.1
orareg-Frammis97 OBJECT IDENTIFIER ::= { orareg-Frammis 2 } -- 2035.3.2.2
orareg-FramLite  OBJECT IDENTIFIER ::= { orareg-Frammis 3 } -- 2035.3.2.3
```

This MIB defines the branches for three product families: Beedle, Frammis, and Whammy. Each MIB is located in the 2035.1 branch of the O'Reilly private enterprise MIB. Each product family has a corresponding registration OID in the 2035.3 branch. The Frammis product family has three models, which are each registered under the Frammis MIB, and each model has its own MIB and separate registration OIDs as well.

If you request the sysObjectID value of a Whammy on any network, the OID value 1.3.6.1.4.1.2035.3.3 would be returned. A management system would then look this OID up in its registration database. If it found a match, then the management system could display additional information on the O'Reilly Whammy device stored in its local database.

A node is typically registered with a management system by the manager when the vendor's product MIBs are loaded. The registration might also be performed automatically by an installation program. In any case, once a product or any object has been registered in a MIB, its registration (name and OID) should not be changed or removed.

NOTE   Registration OIDs are simply placeholders used as unique vendor
           identifiers for each product. They are not actual objects implement-
           ed by an SNMP agent, or defined in the vendor MIBs using the OB-
           JECT-TYPE macro. If you were to perform a Get operation on a
           registration OID, you would receive a genErr in response. Why? Al-
           though the OID does exist, it has no associated object implemented
           in the agent's MIB database and a genErr therefore results.

SNMP Data Types

Many different data types are available in ASN.1, but SMIv1 restricts SNMPv1 MIBs to using only the ASN.1 UNIVERSAL types; all managed objects defined under SNMPv1 are based on these three types:

INTEGER

A signed whole number. ASN.1 does not assign a specific size limit to INTE-GERs, although most SNMP implementations define INTEGERs to be 32 bits in size with a range of -2147483648 to 2147483647.

OCTET STRING

A sequence of octets.* The sequence may be printable ASCII characters or arbitrary binary data.

---

* The size of an octet is system-independent and is always eight bits in length. The size of a byte is system-dependent and contains the number of bits needed to represent a single character used by the system.

OBJECT IDENTIFIER (OID)

Stores the location of a variable (managed object) within a MIB. The location is stored as an array of 16-bit unsigned integers called subidentifiers. The MIB naming tree is described as a collection of Bids. The OBJECT IDENTIFIER may be thought of as identical in concept to pointer variables in C, which store the address of a location in memory.

ASN.1 NULL is not actually a data type, but is instead a data value. It is used to indicate that a MIB variable is municipalized, or does not contain valid data. You will typically see ASN.1 NULL used in an assignment as follows:

Value::= NULL

There are also five ASN.1 APPLICATION data types defined for use in SNMP MIBs. These types are defined by RFC 1155 and not by ASN.1:

```
IpAddress ::=
[APPLICATION 0]
IMPLICIT OCTET STRING (SIZE(4))

Counter ::=
[APPLICATION 1]
IMPLICIT INTEGER (0..4294967295)

Gauge ::=
[APPLICATION 2]
IMPLICIT INTEGER (0..4294967295)

TimeTicks ::=
[APPLICATION 3]
IMPLICIT INTEGER (0..4294967295)

Opaque ::=
[APPLICATION 4]
IMPLICIT OCTET STRING
```

As you can see by their definitions, these five APPLICATION types are all derived from the universal types INTEGER and OCTET STRING. In fact, the definitions of Counter, Gauge, and TimeTicks are all identical. They differ only in how the data that they store is manipulated by the agent and interpreted by the management system. The IMPLICIT ASN.1 keyword is used when deriving a data type from another type.

Each of these complex data types has a specific behavior, but does not define how to use the MIB variable they are used to create. A MIB variable defined using any APPLICATION type must therefore include a DESCRIPTION of how the value it contains is to be interpreted. This is usually a good rule for all MIB variables.

IpAddress

IpAddress is simply an OCTET STRING with a SIZE of exactly four octets stored in network (big-endian) byte order. MIB variables of this type are expected to contain a four-byte network address, specifically those defined by the Internet Protocol (IPv4).

Counter

Counter is an unsigned 32-bit integer variable used to store an incrementing count in the fixed range of 0 to 4294967295. Once reaching its maximum value, the Counter will wrap to 0. A Counter variable acts much like the trip odometer in an automobile in that it may be reset and may never be decremented. Unlike an odometer, however, a Counter may be temporarily disabled and be reinitialized to a value other than zero.

Gauge

Gauge is an unsigned 32-bit integer variable used to store an incrementing and decrementing count in a variable range within 0 to 4294967295. Once reaching its minimum or maximum specified range value, the Gauge value will "latch" (stay topped out or bottomed out) until the value moves back into the range specified for the Gauge.

As an example, imagine a temperature sensor with a range of -40 to 400, and a Gauge variable used to store the current value of this sensor, restricted to the range of values 0 to 255. If the sensor value exceeds 255, the value stored in the Gauge will stay latched at 255 until the sensor reading falls below this value. The same is true if the sensor value is below 0, at which point the Gauge will remain bottomed out at 0 until the sensor value rises up above this value. To accommodate the full range of this sensor, the range of the Gauge variable should be redefined to be 0 to 440 and the actual sensor value accordingly remapped to this range.

TimeTicks

TimeTicks is an unsigned 32-bit value that contains an interval of time. This value is always stored in hundredths of a second. If a TimeTicks variable is used as an incrementing time counter, it will roll over after 497 days.

Opaque

Opaque is a type primarily for use by the SMI to create new data types not defined for use by SNMPv1. The data stored in an Opaque variable are always BER-encoded values.

Textual Conventions

A textual convention is a form of ASN.1 subtyping that allows the redefinition of an existing ASN.1 data type. The redefined type is not actually a new ASN.1 data type, but instead is a restricted version of an existing data type. For example, you can make a new, pseudo data type in C using the following statements:

```
#define BOOL     int
#define FALSE    0
#define TRUE     !FALSE
```

We can do about the same thing in ASN.1 using this textual convention:

```
Bool ::= INTEGER { true(1), false(2) }
```

In both examples, a new data type is not actually created. Instead, a new name based on an existing data type is defined. The new name may be used to declare variables:

```
Bool JobIsComplete ::= false
```

RFC 1213 defines two textual conventions to be used with SNMPv1. The first is DisplayString, which is really an OCTET STRING, 0 to 255 octets in length, containing only the printable ASCII characters (32 through 126) defined in RFC 854. The other, PhysAddress, is an OCTET STRING with no SIZE clause, used for storing media-level or physical-level hardware addresses.

Many other textual conventions have found their way into common usage thanks to the wide use of SNMPv1 and the development of SNMPv2. Table 4-2 lists some of the conventions you might encounter in SNMPv1 MIBs. When creating textual conventions in your own MIBs, you should be careful not to accidentally redefine any conventions already in common use.

Table 4-2. Well-Known Textual Conventions Found in SNMPv1 MIBs

Name	Syntax	Description
DateAndTime	OCTET STRING(SIZE(8|11))	Date and time with optional time zone offset
DisplayString	OCTET STRING(SIZE(0..255))	Printable ASCII characters
MacAddress	OCTET STRING(SIZE(6))	IEEE 802 hardware address
PhysAddress	OCTET STRING	Hardware address
TimeInterval	INTEGER(0..2147483647)	Time interval measured in hundredths of a second
TimeStamp	TimeTicks	sysUpTime value
TruthValue	INTEGER	{ true(1), false(2) } Boolean
VariablePointer	OBJECT IDENTIFIER	MIB variable identity

Subtyping

In the previous examples, most of the textual conventions contained explicit restrictions on the range of the values that they may be assigned. This is accomplished using ASN.1 subtyping. In SNMPv1, variables declared using the

INTEGER, OCTET STRING, Gauge, and Opaque types may have their range of assigned values restricted by using subtyping.*

Table 4-3 lists several examples of INTEGER textual conventions and the subtyping of their ranges. A subtype may be assigned to a label as a textual convention, or directly to the SYNTAX clause in an OBJECT-TYPE macro. The range of an INTEGER is expressed as a decimal or hexadecimal integer values. Multiple ranges and fixed values may be specified and need not be contiguous.

Table 4-3. Examples of INTEGER Subtyping

Example	Description
INTEGER	Range unspecified
INTEGER(-127..128)	Signed 8-bit
INTEGER(0..255)	Unsigned 8-bit
INTEGER(1..10)	Only the values 1 through 10
INTEGER(0|2|4|6|8)	Only the values 0, 2, 4, 6, 8
INTEGER(0..2|20)	Only the values 0 through 2 and 20
INTEGER(-32768..32767)	Signed 16-bit
INTEGER(-32768..-1|1..32767)	Signed 16-bit, excluding 0
INTEGER(0..'ffff'h)	Unsigned 16-bit
INTEGER(0..'7fffffff'H)	Signed 32-bit
INTEGER(1)	Only 1

INTEGERs may also be used to form enumerated integer textual conventions. Enumerated INTEGERs are a form of ASN.1 subtyping, but with a textual label assigned to each possible value. Enumerated INTEGER values may be in the range 1 to 2147483647 (0 is an acceptable value in ASN.1, but not with SMIv1). The labels are only used to reference the enumerated values within a MIB module. The actual INTEGER values of an enumeration are used in the SNMP messages themselves.

SMIv1 defines that each label must be 1 to 64 characters in length and be composed of only letters, digits, or hyphens. The first character must be a lower-case letter, the last character may not be a hyphen, and each hyphen may not be immediately followed by another hyphen (or it will be mistaken for a comment). Each label must be unique within an enumeration, but not necessarily within the MIB module itself.

---

* Not all MIB compilers fully support subtyping. For example, the Microsoft MIB compiler, MIBCC, does not support INTEGER and OCTET STRING types declared with multiple, fixed subtypes, such as INTEGER(2\|4\|8\|16).

The following example lists several examples of enumerated INTEGER textual conventions. These examples show how enumerated integers may be used to create a new label, or be assigned directly to the SYNTAX clause in an OBJECT-TYPE macro.

```
Boolean ::= INTEGER { true(1), false(2) }
    SYNTAX INTEGER { true(1), false(2) }
Alarm-level ::= INTEGER { critical(1), major(2), minor(3), warning(4),
                          informational(5)}
Day ::= INTEGER { sun(1), mon(2), tue(3), wed(4), thu(5), fri(6), sat(7) }
DayRange ::= INTEGER { first(1), last(7) }
Bps ::= INTEGER { bps-96(9600), bps-192(19200), bps-384(38400), bps-567(56700) }
    SYNTAX INTEGER ( reset(1) }
MyInteger ::= INTEGER           -- Range unspecified
```

SMIv1 also allows an OCTET STRING to be declared using a textual convention. For OCTET STRINGs these range restrictions are declared using the SIZE clause. The size (or length) of an OCTET STRING is expressed as a decimal or hexadecimal value and may be fixed or variable in length. Multiple sizes and size ranges may also be specified. Table 4-4 lists several examples of OCTET STRING textual conventions.

Table 4-4. Examples of OCTET STRING Textual Conventions

Example	Description
SystemName ::= OCTET STRING	Length unspecified
DisplayString ::= OCTET STRING (SIZE (0..255))	0 to 255 octets
MacAddress ::= OCTET STRING (SIZE(6))	Exactly 6 octets
DateAndTime ::= OCTET STRING (SIZE (8 | 11))	8 or 11 octets
SYNTAX OCTET STRING (0..2|20)	0 to 2 or 20 octets
UnicodeChar ::= OCTET STRING (SIZE(2))	Exactly 16-bits
MyUnicodeString ::= UnicodeChar (SIZE(10..12))	Error! Cannot reSIZE
MyUnicodeString ::= UnicodeChar	Good. 2 octet string

Subtypes of the Opaque data type are also specified using the SIZE clause (see Table 4-5). An Opaque is just an OCTET STRING in sheep's clothing, so it is subtyped in the same way.

Table 4-5. Examples of Opaque Subtypes

Example	Description
Opaque	0 to 65535 octets
Opaque(SIZE(0..240))	0 to 240 octets
Opaque(SIZE(12))	12 octets exactly
Opaque(SIZE(0|14|24))	0, 14, or 24 octets

Table 4-5. Examples of Opaque Subtypes (continued)

Example	Description
Opaque(SIZE(0 | 2..8 | 24..36))	0, 2 to 8, or 24 to 36 octets only
Opaque(SIZE(0..6))	0 to 6 octets
Opaque(SIZE(0 | 1 | 2 | 3 | 4 | 5 | 6))	0 to 6 octets

The subtyping for the Gauge data type is specified the same as for INTEGERs. But the behavior of a Gauge with a restricted range of values, or even multiple ranges of values, is not immediately obvious. Table 4-6 lists several examples of Gauge subtyping.

Table 4-6. Examples of Gauge Subtypes

Example	Description
Gauge	0 to 4294967295
Gauge(0..110)	0 to 110
Gauge(40..400)	40 to 400
Gauge(20..100 | 110..120)	20 to 100 and 110 to 120
Gauge(0 | 2 | 4 | 6 | 8 | 10)	0, 2, 4, 6, 8, and 10 only
Gauge(0 | 5..10)	0 or 5 to 10
Gauge(12)	12 only

As we previously noted, a gauge will "latch" at its minimum and maximum range value if the actual data measurement exceeds the gauge's subtyped range. But the range of a Gauge need not be a set of contiguous values, such as 0 through 10. The total range of a Gauge may be fragmented among several fixed or contiguous range values. In all cases, a Gauge variable will never store a value that is not specified by its range subtype.

Scalar and Columnar MIB Variables

The occurrence of a variable in a MIB is called the "instance" of that variable. A scalar variable may have only one instance in a MIB. Columnar variables may have zero or more instances and are always arranged in the form of a one-dimensional list or a two-dimensional table.

Each scalar MIB variable is referenced by both its OID and its instance identifier. An instance identifier is a non-negative INTEGER, OCTET STRING, or OBJECT IDENTIFIER value, and is appended to the end of an OID. For example:

```
<OBJECT IDENTIFIER>.<instance identifier>
```

The instance identifier is used to unambiguously identify the specific instance of a MIB variable. Each scalar variable defined in a MIB may only have one instance. A scalar variable is specified by appending a ".0" to its OID, indicating that there is at most (and at least) one instance of the variable.

For example, if we want to perform a GetRequest operation on the value of the managed object located at OID 1.3.6.1.2.1.4.1, we need to specify 1.3.6.1.2.1.4.1.0 to "get" the object's instance value. If we perform the GetRequest operation without appending the ".0" instance identifier to the OID, the agent will not be able to match the OID to any known managed object in its MIB namespace, and will therefore return a noSuchName error.

Columnar objects declared in an ordered list always have an instance identifier of ".1". Columnar objects residing in a table may have one or more instance identifiers referred to as the table entry index values.

Lists and Tables

In addition to the simple data types, the SMI defines structured data types in the form of ordered lists and tables. A list is a one-dimensional collection of MIB variables grouped into an ordered list. Each variable declared in a list must be of the INTEGER, OCTET STRING, OBJECT IDENTIFIER, or any of the APPLICATION data types, and there may be one or more variables (or "members") in the list. A list is very similar to a struct in C.

A table is a two-dimensional collection of lists or, more simply, a "list of ordered lists." Each list in a table is a "row" and there may be zero or more rows in a table. A table may be defined using only one list, so every row in a table is identical in format to all other rows in the table. A table is similar in many ways to an array of structs in C.

In most MIB definitions, lists and tables are used much like spreadsheets. They may be used to contain a report of the current alarms on a node, a listing of the entries recorded in a system event log, performance history information collected in 15-minute intervals over the previous 24 hours, or the statistics of all active TCP connections and UDP ports. Tables store and reference data using the same model as a relational database.

More creative uses of these structured types include the construction of linked lists, hash tables, floating-point numbers, binary trees, and multi-dimensional arrays.

You declare list objects using the ASN.1 SEQUENCE type. The SEQUENCE is used to declare the MIB variables contained in the list. You can think of a SEQUENCE as a record in a database, with each declared MIB variable being a field in the record:

```
Employee ::= SEQUENCE {
   id          INTEGER,
   level       INTEGER,
   fullName    DisplayString,
   address     DisplayString
}
```

The list begins with a SEQUENCE identifier, which by convention must begin with an uppercase letter. Each member in the list is declared using a member identifier and a data type. The member identifiers always begin with a lowercase letter. Each member is an independently addressable columnar variable that must be defined using an OBJECT-TYPE macro. List members are described by a variety of names, including list objects, entry members, and list or aggregate variables.

Example 4-2 shows a list that contains two INTEGER variables.

Example 4-2. A list with two INTEGER variables

```
intList OBJECT-TYPE
    SYNTAX      IntList
    ACCESS      not-accessible
    STATUS      mandatory
    DESCRIPTION
      "A list containing two INTEGER values."
    ::= { myMib 1 }

IntList ::= SEQUENCE {
  intValue1    INTEGER,
  intValue2    INTEGER
}

intValue1 OBJECT-TYPE
    SYNTAX      INTEGER
    ACCESS      read-write
    STATUS      mandatory
    DESCRIPTION
      "An INTEGER value."
    ::= { intList 1 }

intValue2 OBJECT-TYPE
    SYNTAX      INTEGER
    ACCESS      read-write
    STATUS      mandatory
    DESCRIPTION
      "Another INTEGER value."
    ::= { intList 2 }
```

The intList object is the definition of the list. This object declares itself to be based on the IntList type. The ACCESS mode is declared as not-accessible because structured types are not scalar variables, and therefore are not directly accessible. The

IntList SEQUENCE contains the declarations of the variables that are in the list. The intValue1 and intValue2 OBJECT-TYPE macros are the actual definitions of the scalar variables in the list.

A list therefore organizes a collection of scalar MIB variables into an ordered list. Here's the equivalent of the intList list in C:

```
struct {
    long intValue1;
    long intValue2;
} intList;
```

If we were to illustrate intList, we'd see a table with only one row:

intValue1	intValue2

You use a table to store more than one row of data. You declare a table object using the ASN.1 SEQUENCE OF type. A SEQUENCE is used to declare the objects in an ordered list, and SEQUENCE OF is used to define an object that is a table, an ordered list of ordered lists. If you think of a list as a one-dimensional array, then a table is an array of arrays.

A SEQUENCE may be used with only one table. If a MIB requires multiple identical tables to be defined, then each table must have its own SEQUENCE declared, even though all of the SEQUENCEs are identical. The same restriction is true of all members in the table. A single variable definition may not be split among multiple SEQUENCE definitions. Each entry member (or columnar variable) declared in a SEQUENCE must have its own OBJECT-TYPE definition. Table members are also described by a variety of names, including aggregate or columnar variables, entry members, and table variables.

Let's modify the intList example to make it a table (see Example 4-3).

Example 4-3. A table object

```
intTable  OBJECT-TYPE
    SYNTAX     SEQUENCE OF intTableEntry
    ACCESS     not-accessible
    STATUS     mandatory
    DESCRIPTION
      "A table of INTEGER values."
    ::= { myMib 1 }

intTableEntry OBJECT-TYPE
    SYNTAX     IntList
    ACCESS     not-accessible
    STATUS     mandatory
    DESCRIPTION
      "Entry in the intTable table. Each entry contains
      an index (intEntryId), and two INTEGER values."
    INDEX
```

Example 4-3. A table object (continued)

```
        { intEntryId }
     ::= { intTable 1 }

IntList ::= SEQUENCE {
    intEntryId   INTEGER,
    intValue1    INTEGER,
    intValue2    INTEGER
}

intEntryId OBJECT-TYPE
    SYNTAX     INTEGER
    ACCESS     read-only
    STATUS     mandatory
    DESCRIPTION
      "Table entry index value."
    ::= { intTableEntry 1 }

intValue1 OBJECT-TYPE
    SYNTAX     INTEGER
    ACCESS     read-write
    STATUS     mandatory
    DESCRIPTION
      "An INTEGER value."
    ::= { intTableEntry 2 }

intValue2 OBJECT-TYPE
    SYNTAX     INTEGER
    ACCESS     read-write
    STATUS     mandatory
    DESCRIPTION
      "Another INTEGER value."
    ::= { intTableEntry 3 }
```

Converting intList to intTable required adding a definition for the intTable object, including an INDEX clause in the SEQUENCE definition, and adding a variable to the SEQUENCE declaration itself. You can see by the SEQUENCE OF intTableEntry SYNTAX in the intTable object that this table object is a list of intTableEntry objects.

Because intTable may contain zero or more intTableEntry rows, an index must be used to address each row in a table. We must declare that one or more of the MIB variables in the IntList list are to be used as the indexes into the table. In the intTable example, we declared the index using the INDEX clause in the intTableEntryobject.

Assume that the intTable object maintained by an agent contains four rows; its members and their values are shown in Table 4-7.

You can see in Table 4-7 that intTable contains four separate but identical copies of the intTableEntry list. That is, the format of each row is identical. Each member

Table 4-7. An Example of the Format of intTable

Row 1	intEntryId = 1	intValue1 = 10	intValue2 = 34
Row 2	intEntryId = 2	intValue1 = 9	intValue2 = 10
Row 3	intEntryId = 4	intValue1 = 10	intValue2 = 22
Row 4	intEntryId = 7	intValue1 = 85	intValue2 = 22

in the table is an independently instantiated columnar variable that contains its own data. Members of lists and tables are therefore no different from other MIB variables, with the exception that list and table variables are referenced within the context of a table or table entry by SNMP operations.

Each member in a table is referenced using the table index (or indexes) value as the instance identifier. I said earlier that each scalar variable may only have a single instance, and this instance is referenced by appending the instance identifier ".0" to the variable's OID. A variable in a table, however, may have zero or more instances. To address a specific variable instance, we append the index of the row to its OID.

For example, to reference intValue2 in row 3 we use the OID,

    intValue2.4

and to reference intEntryId in row 1 we use the OID:

    intEntryId.1.

The INDEX clause in the SEQUENCE object definition indicates which members in the table are the indexes. The value of each index member must be unique to all the other instances of the same member. A table with identical index values cannot be accessed properly.

In intTable the index member data type is an INTEGER and the index values are 1, 2, 4, and 7. There is no requirement that the index values be contiguous or in any sort of lexical order. The only requirements are that all index values be unique within their instance and that no columnar variable be indexed using only ".0" (or else an agent might confuse a columnar variable with a scalar). We could infer that there are rows 3, 5, and 6 that are not currently instantiated, but this is not necessarily so. If we changed the data type of the index to OCTET STRING, the values "Fred," "Wilma," "Barney," and "Betty" could just as well be used as index values to reference the table rows.

Note that a list does not require an INDEX clause. Lists contain one and only one instance of each variable. This is why the members in an ordered list are always referenced using an instance identifier of ".1".

Each index defined for a table increases the dimension of the table by one. One of the most common examples of multi-index table access is the tcpConnTable

table defined in the tcp group of MIB-II. This table is referenced using four index values, which are the addresses and ports of the local and remote ends of each TCP connection. The syntax of this reference follows:

```
tcpConnTable.<local IP addr>.<local port>.<remote IP addr>.<remote port>
```

So to reference the tcpConnState variable of a specific connection, you would need IP addresses and ports of the connection to reference the value. Here's an example of this unusual looking reference:

```
tcp.tcpConnTable.tcpConnEntry.tcpConnState.199.35.10.47.139.199.35.12.25.1029
```

Note that there are no default table indexes. You must explicitly specify all indexes defined by a table entry to reference a table variable.

At this point you may be asking, "Where is the number of rows in a table defined in the MIB?" It would seem that the intTable object definition in our previous example should contain subtyping that describes the number of rows that intTable may contain. However, the SMI does not define a construct used to declare the possible number of rows that may be instantiated in a table. According to RFC 1212, a table may contain zero or more rows, and each row may contain one or more columnar scalar objects. This effectively makes the number of rows present in any table at any given moment "implementation-dependent."

You may be wondering how to Get and Set the variable in a table if you don't know the index values of the rows, and which rows—and which members of each row—are instantiated. The magic that makes requesting data from tables possible is the GetNext operation (explained later in this chapter).

Lists and tables are quite capable of creating complex data structures and arrays of complex data structures. But what about creating a simple array?

As defined by ASN.1, SEQUENCE OF is used to create a list containing only a single data type. So to declare an array of INTEGER values we could simply declare something like the following:

```
MyArray ::= SEQUENCE OF INTEGER
MyArray myArray ::= { 1, 1, 2, 5, 7, 9  }

intArrayTable  OBJECT-TYPE
    SYNTAX     MyArray
    ACCESS     read-only
    STATUS     mandatory
    DESCRIPTION
      "An array of INTEGER values."
    ::= { myMib 1 }
```

Unfortunately, this works only under ASN.1 proper. The subset of ASN.1 defined for SNMP in the SMI only allows SEQUENCE OF to specify the SEQUENCE type.

To define an array of INTEGER, OCTET STRING, or OBJECT IDENTIFIER values, we would need to define a table that declares a SEQUENCE that contained a member used to store an INTEGER value, and a second member to store the index. If you were to remove the intValue2 member from the intTable example, you would have a table that can be used as an array of INTEGER values.

Before you start trying all sorts of clever things with lists and tables, here are a few more SMI design limitations that help keep SNMP simple:

- Enumerated textual conventions are not allowed in a SEQUENCE. For example, you are not allowed to do this:

```
Employee ::= SEQUENCE {
    id          INTEGER,
    level       INTEGER { director(1), manager(2), grunt(3) }
}
```

- When declaring the member of a SEQUENCE, subtyping is commonly applied in the OBJECT-TYPE definition of each member, and not in the member declaration itself. You can, however, use subtyped textual conventions in a SEQUENCE definition:

```
IdType ::= INTEGER(0..6)
LevelType ::= INTEGER { director(1), manager(2), grunt(3) }
Employee ::= SEQUENCE {
    id          IdType,
    level       LevelType
}
```

- You cannot nest a SEQUENCE within a SEQUENCE. In other words, you can't do this in an SNMP MIB:

```
Employee ::= SEQUENCE {
    fullName    DisplayString,
    Address ::= SEQUENCE {
        street    DisplayString,
        city      DisplayString,
        state     DisplayString,
        zipCode   DisplayString
    }
}
```

- By the same restriction, a table is not allowed to nest other tables. Under ASN.1, nested SEQUENCE and SEQUENCE OF types are allowed; to reduce the complexity of implementing SNMP, the SMI disallows this ability.

Although these "no lists in a list" and "no tables in a table" restrictions may seem intolerable to you, it is possible for a table to reference other tables using common and multiple index values.

Object Identifiers

Each variable defined within a MIB is referenced by a unique OBJECT IDENTI-FIER, or OID. An OID is the location of a managed object within the MIB namespace, and is analogous to the address of a variable in memory, or the path-name in a file system. The OID of a MIB object is also referred to as the object's *identity* or *registration*.

OIDs are arranged in a hierarchical, inverted tree structure. This is the same type of structure that is used by the MS-DOS and UNIX file systems and the Windows registry. In a typical tree-structured file system, the location of a file is specified by starting with a point of origin (usually called "the root directory") and is followed by a list of each directory or folder that occurs between the root and the file. Each directory name is delineated by a special separator character, and the very last name in the path is that of the file itself. The blueprint of the entire file system is referred to as the directory tree.

This also happens to be the same pattern used to reference OIDs. The OID tree begins with the root and expands downwards into branches. Each point in the OID tree is called a node, and each node will contain one or more branches, or will terminate with a leaf node. Only leaf nodes may contain management data. The blueprint for a collection of OIDs (both branches and leaves) is referred to as a MIB namespace, or a subtree of the complete OID tree. The entire OID tree from the root on down is referred to as the *MIB naming tree*. Figure 4-1 shows a partial diagram of the SNMP MIB tree defined by the SMI.

At the top of the MIB naming tree is the root. The root forms three branches or children, which have the OIDs of ccitt(0), iso(1), and joint-iso-ccitt(2). All OIDs begin with one of these three branches. The root itself does not have an OID, and is therefore never directly addressed, so its existence is only implied.

Each node is enumerated using a non-negative, 32-bit integer value called a sub-identifier. All OIDs are written out starting from the root as a sequence of subidentifiers in dot notation:

```
1.3.6.1.2.1.1.2
```

Each node is also assigned a human-readable name. If the node is a branch, the name is a textual convention. If the node is a leaf object, the name is an object descriptor. Referencing a node by name allows an OID to be rendered as a human-readable sequence of textual labels. Numerical and textual subidentifiers may be mixed in the same OID. The following OIDs all reference the same MIB object:

```
1.3.6.1.2.1.1.2
1.3.6.1.2.1.1.sysObjectID
iso.org.dod.internet.mgmt.mib-2.1.2
```

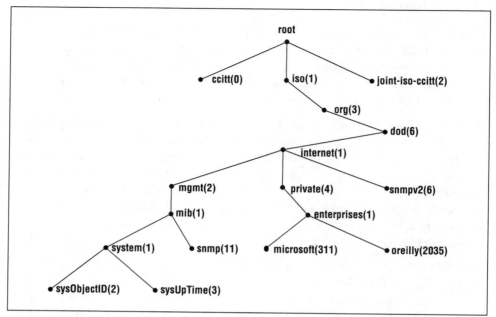

Figure 4-1. The SNMP section of the MIB naming tree

```
iso.org.dod.internet.mgmt.mib-2.system.sysObjectID
iso(1).org(3).dod(6).internet(1).mgmt(2).mib-2(1).system(1).sysObjectID(2)
```

You will also note the similarities between OIDs and the notation used by the MS-DOS and Unix file systems and the Windows registry:

```
C:\WINDOWS\SYSTEM32\Drivers\Etc\Service\Service
/usr/local/bin/rogue
HKEY_LOCAL_MACHINE\SOFTWARE\Microsoft\SNMP\CurrentVersion
```

Internet-standard network management is defined under the iso(1) branch, so it's very likely that all of the OIDs that you will be working with will begin with 1.3.6.1. From the SNMP point of view, you will always be working with OIDs in the mib (1.3.6.1.2.1) or enterprises (1.3.6.1.4.1) branches of the MIB naming tree.

Now that we've described the type of data structures and formats used to describe management information, let's delve into the messages used to exchange this information between SNMP management systems and agents.

The SNMP Message

All information that is exchanged between hosts using the SNMP protocol is in the format of SNMP messages. On a TCP/IP network, each SNMP message is encapsulated in the payload of a UDP datagram.

The entire SNMP message is always BER-encoded. If you aren't fluent in reading BER, then hex dumps of raw SNMP messages will be of little use to you. In this case, you will need the service of a protocol analyzer that is capable of decoding SNMP messages (such as the NetXRay network protocol analyzer demo on the CD-ROM), and providing you both a hex dump of the SNMP message and a human-readable listing of the information that it contains.

My advice is to both use a protocol analyzer and spend the time learning BER so you can double-check what the analyzer is telling you; after all, the analyzer is just a piece of software written by a programmer, and it can have bugs just like any other program.

The SNMP message (see Figure 4-2) consists of a very simple preamble followed by an Application Protocol Data Unit (APDU) or, as it is often referred to, an SNMP PDU. The preamble contains information used to verify the authenticity of an SNMP message (described later in this chapter). The PDU header contains information specific to the SNMP message, such as the type of operation to perform. The PDU body contains the actual data used to perform the specified SNMP operation.

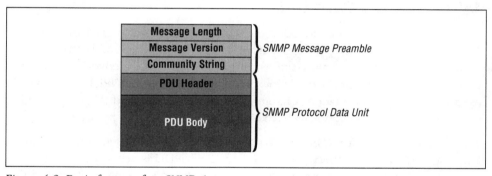

Figure 4-2. Basic format of an SNMPv1 message

SNMP Message Preamble

The SNMP message preamble contains three fields, and all SNMPv1 messages contain the same preamble:

Message Length
A 16-bit integer used to indicate the total length of the message in octets minus two (the length of the Message Length field itself is not included in this value).

Message Version

A single octet value used to indicate the version of the SNMP protocol that encoded the message. Valid values are 0 for SNMPv1, 1 for SNMPv2, and so forth.

Community String

The sequence of octet values that specifies a management community of the host that is to receive the message. This field varies in length and the name is not likely to be longer than 128 octets (and is typically much shorter).

NOTE   SNMP management systems and agents are not required to support SNMP messages larger than 484 bytes, but are encouraged to do so if system resources permit. Agents implemented on very small systems may strictly abide by this rule, but most network management systems are implemented on workstations with plenty of memory and CPU horsepower, so they should be able to handle much larger messages.

SNMP Protocol Data Unit

Chapter 2, *Network Basics*, looked at the concept of a Protocol Data Unit, or PDU. A PDU is an independent block of information that is exchanged between two or more entities using a communications protocol, such as the network services in a protocol stack. Each protocol defines one or more types of PDUs that will be used to exchange information. Chapter 2 also briefly examined the PDUs used by Ethernet, IP, and UDP. Now let's have a look at the PDUs used by SNMP.

There are five different SNMPv1 PDUs defined by RFC 1157: GetRequest, GetNextRequest, SetRequest, GetResponse, and Trap. Each PDU is actually a template that an SNMP management system or agent fills in with specific information and then sends on its way.

The popular way to represent the data structure of a PDU is by using ASN.1 notation, as you can see in RFC 1157 and most texts written on SNMP. But these ASN.1 illustrations only show the PDU fields that specifically contain management data and leave out the low-level information that is important to the protocol itself. (I'll try to fill in those blanks.) And because you may not yet be familiar with ASN.1, I'll use a block diagram to illustrate the internals and SNMP messages and PDUs (see Figure 4-3).

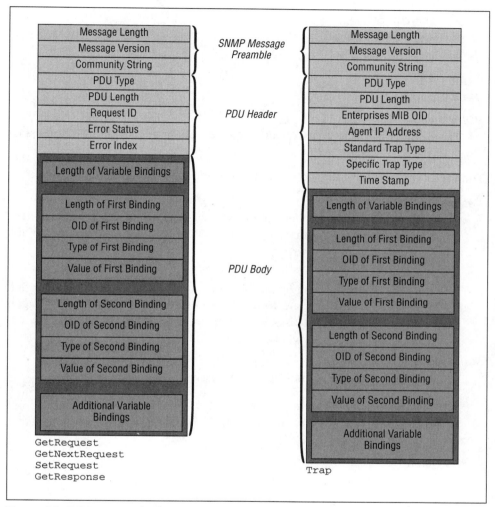

Figure 4-3. SNMPv1 PDU formats

PDU header

The header of the PDU is identical for all of the request messages and the GetResponse message. The Trap PDU header, however, is very different because of the specialized use of the trap message. The first two header fields are identical for all SNMPv1 messages:

PDU Type

Indicates the type of SNMP operation represented by this message. These are accepted values defined in RFC 1157:

0   getRequest

1   getNextRequest

2   getResponse

3   setRequest

4   trap

PDU Length

The number of octets that appear in the remaining part of the SNMP message after the PDU Length field.

The following fields are defined in the PDU header of the Trap PDU:

Enterprises MIB OID

The OID of the management enterprise that defines the trap message. This value is represented as an OBJECT IDENTIFIER value and has a variable length.

Agent IP Address

The network address of the agent that generated this trap message. This field contains an IP address in the form of an OBJECT IDENTIFIER. If the agent resides on a network that uses a network addressing scheme other than IP (such as IPX), this address will be all zeros (0.0.0.0).

Standard Trap Type

Identifies the type of trap message. The following values are defined:

0   coldStart

1   warmStart

2   linkDown

3   linkUp

4   authenticationFailure

5   egpNeighborLoss

6   enterpriseSpecific

Specific Trap Type

Indicates the specific trap as defined in an enterprise-specific MIB. If the Standard Trap Type value is 6, this field will contain a value greater than zero which indicates which TRAP-TYPE object in the MIB identified in the Enterprises MIB OID field defines this Trap PDU. If the Standard Trap Type is a value other than 6, its value is 0 and is not used.

Time Stamp

A 32-bit unsigned value indicating the number of centiseconds that have elapsed since the (re)start of the SNMP agent and the sending of this trap message. This field is initialized to the value stored in the MIB-II sysUpTime variable at the time the trap message was sent.

The following fields are defined in the PDU header of all other SNMP request and response messages:

Request ID

A handshaking value used to correlate a response message with a request message. This is most useful if a management system sends multiple request messages out at the same time and needs to correlate the response messages received with each request message sent. (The next section describes this field in detail.)

Error Status

The value indicating the success or failure of the SNMP operation. A non-zero value indicates that an error occurred. Here are the possible values for this field, as defined by RFC 1157. (For an agent to be fully compliant with SNMPv1, the readOnly error must not be used and noSuchName used in its place.)

Value	Message	Description
0	noError	Operation successful; no errors occurred
1	tooBig	The response message is too big in size to send
2	noSuchName	The specified OID is not supported by the agent, or there is no "next" OID
3	badValue	The value or data type specified for a SetRequest varbind was incorrect
4	readOnly	Attempted to write a value to a read-only MIB variable
5	genErr	A non-protocol specific error occurred while reading or writing a MIB variable

Error Index

A ones-based index value that indicates which variable binding in the message caused the specified error. A value of 1 indicates that the first variable binding was the cause, 2 indicates that the second was the cause, and so on. If Error Status is non-zero, but Error Index is zero, this may indicate that the variable binding that caused the error could not be determined, or that the error was not specifically caused by information in the variable bindings (as is often the case with the tooBig and genErr errors). If both Error Status and Error Index are zero, the operation completed successfully.

Request ID

Most high-level communications protocols define a header field containing handshaking information used to match a response message with a specific request message. This information is usually referred to as a synchronization value or a correlation tag. In the SNMP protocol, this value is stored in the Request ID field of the request and GetResponse messages.

The Request ID is missing from most descriptions of SNMP messages that you will encounter in other SNMP texts. This is because the Request ID field does not contain information related to management data. Instead, it is part of the hand-shaking mechanism used by management systems to correlate a response message with a specific request message. The agent does not use the Request ID value, but it is responsible for copying the value into the Request ID field of the response message it sent in reply to the request.

A management system uses the Request ID value to determine which response message is a reply to which request message that it sent. For example, suppose that a management system sends three GetRequest messages with Request ID values of 123, 234, and 345. The management system then starts a timer for each message that is sent to keep track of how much time has passed between the sending of the request and the arrival of the response.

When each GetRequest message is processed, the agent will copy its Request ID value into the GetResponse message that it will send back to the management system as a reply. As each response message arrives, the management system matches the request ID to the appropriate message timer, and then kills the timer. If a timer expires before the associated GetResponse message is received, the message is assumed to have been lost and another message is sent; if the number of message retries has been reached, the management application stops sending repeated request messages and reports that the agent is not responding.

The value of the Request ID also indicates which functional area of a management system sent the request, and is used to return the response to the same thread. For example, message 123 might have been sent in a request for some inventory data; message 234 in a request of alarm data; and message 345 in a request of performance data. If each message were sent by a different thread (or process), each response message could be recognized by its RequestID value and routed to the correct handling routine.

This will only be possible if the management application can select the request ID, or at least can determine what the Request ID is of each message that is sent. Many SNMP APIs automatically generate the Request ID of each request message and grant only read-only access to this value, not allowing it to be changed by management applications.

Variable bindings

The *variable bindings* (or *varbinds* for short) are the actual data payload of each SNMP request and response message. Management data that is transported back and forth inside SNMP messages is stored in the varbinds list of each message. All SNMP messages, with the exception of trap messages, contain at least one variable binding. Most SNMP messages are not of any use unless they are shuttling management data.

Variable bindings are so named because they bind an OID name (or identity) with a value. The OID is that of a single managed object defined in a MIB. The value may be any of the ASN.1 scalar data types defined by the SMI for use with SNMP, or the ASN.1 NULL value if the value field is not used. If a value is specified, its data type must match that of the object whose OID is specified in the same binding. The size of each binding and the number of bindings that may be included in any PDU is variable.

There is no field in the PDU that indicates the number of variable bindings the PDU contains. A PDU must be fully parsed and the varbinds counted to discover their quantity. Varbinds are numbered starting with one, and there is no limit to the number of varbinds that may be contained within an SNMP message (although you may quickly hit your head on the physical size limitation of the SNMP message itself, imposed by the SNMP agent and the network).

SNMP guarantees that the order of the varbinds in a GetResponse message will be the same as in the corresponding request message. The actual order of the varbinds in a message is of no significance to an agent (see the section on the SetRequest message for more information on the significance of varbinds).

SNMP Request Messages

Each SNMP operation is initiated by a management system sending an SNMP request message to an agent. The request message contains information required by the agent to perform the specific operation on the data that it maintains in its MIBs. There is one request message defined per SNMP operation. Although each message uses the same common SNMP message format I described earlier, each message has its own unique set of characteristics and problems, mostly incurred from the behavior defined for each SNMP operation itself.

GetRequest message

The GetRequest message is used by a management system to retrieve values from the managed objects maintained by an agent. Each GetRequest may be used to request the value of one or more MIB variables. The variables may be located in different private MIBs, but all of the MIBs must be supported by the agent receiving the GetRequest message.

Each GetRequest message contains one or more variable bindings. Each varbind specifies a single OID whose value a management system needs to retrieve.

Because the GetRequest is only used to retrieve the values of specific scalar, list, and table variable instances, the OID specified in each varbind must also include the instance identifier of the variable, or a noSuchName error will result. The value field in each varbind is not used in a GetRequest message, so they are initialized with ASN.1 NULL values.

Figure 4-4 shows a typical GetRequest transaction between a management system and an agent.

52	Size of Message	65
0	SNMP Version	0
public	Community Name	public
0	PDU Type	2
39	Size of PDU	52
2159	Request ID	2159
0	Error Status	0
0	Error Index	0
28	Size of Variable Binding List	41
12	Size of First Varbind	23
1.3.6.1.2.1.1.2.0	OID of First Variable	1.3.6.1.2.1.1.2.0
NULL	Type of First Variable	2
NULL	Value of First Variable	1.3.6.1.4.1.311.1.1.3.2
12	Size of Second Varbind	14
1.3.6.1.2.1.7.4.0	OID of Second Variable	1.3.6.1.2.1.7.4.0
NULL	Type of Second Variable	65
NULL	Value of Second Variable	250

Additional Variable Bindings

GetRequest ➡️   ⬅️ GetResponse

Figure 4-4. A GetRequest message and its GetResponse message

The GetResponse message returned in reply to a GetRequest contains the values requested if no protocol error occurs. The varbinds list in the GetResponse will be a duplicate of the varbinds list in the GetRequest, except that value fields in the varbinds list will contain the object values requested by the GetResponse message.

Here are some possible errors that may occur during the processing of a GetRequest message:

noSuchName

> An OID specified in the varbinds list was not found in the MIBs supported by the agent (often caused by an incorrect or omitted instance identifier). The noSuchName error is also returned if an OID is not within the MIB namespace supported by the agent.

tooBig

> The resulting GetResponse message containing the requested values is too big to be sent back to the management system by the agent. This error is determined only by a master agent. Subagents cannot detect this problem.

genErr

> For some reason a MIB variable value could not be read by the agent.

Remember the "all or nothing" rule of SNMPv1: if an operation on one of the varbinds fails, then none of the values requested are returned. In this case, the varbind list of the GetResponse is an exact duplicate of the GetRequest message.

GetNextRequest message

GetNextRequest, like GetRequest, is used to retrieve values from the managed objects maintained by an agent. The GetNextRequest message is also identical in format to the GetRequest message. Where GetNextRequest differs is in the behavior of the GetNext operation itself.

GetNextRequest is used primarily to "walk" through tables and retrieve the values of the specified entry members (variables). GetNext, unlike Get, does not require that the instance identifier of each variable be specified in its OID.

If you perform a GetNext using the OID of a scalar variable, without specifying the instance identifier, you will receive the correct value of the variable in response. For example, a GetNext performed using this varbind data,

```
OID   = 1.3.6.1.2.1.1.4
Value = NULL
```

will return this data in response (as least on my system it does):

```
OID   = 1.3.6.1.2.1.1.4.0
Value = OCTET STRING - "J. D. Murray"
```

As you can see, the "next" variable from the OID specified was the one and only instance of this scalar variable. If you specified the instance identifier as well, you would have still received the next variable value. For example:

```
OID   = 1.3.6.1.2.1.1.4.0
Value = NULL
```

returns:

```
OID   = 1.3.6.1.2.1.1.5.0
Value = OCTET STRING - "PPRO - 200"
```

Figure 4-5 illustrates the contents of a GetNextRequest message, and the resulting GetResponse, specifying these two OIDs in the variable bindings.

52	Size of Message	66
0	SNMP Version	0
public	Community Name	public
1	PDU Type	2
39	Size of PDU	53
112234	Request ID	112234
0	Error Status	0
0	Error Index	0
28	Size of All Variable Bindings	42
12	Size of First Varbind	15
1.3.6.1.2.1.1.2.0	OID of First Variable	1.3.6.1.2.1.1.3.0
NULL	Type of First Variable	67
NULL	Value of First Variable	1924065
12	Size of Second Varbind	23
1.3.6.1.2.1.7.4.0	OID of Second Variable	1.3.6.1.2.1.7.5.1.1.0.0.0.0.1025
NULL	Type of Second Variable	64
NULL	Value of Second Variable	0.0.0.0
	Additional Variable Bindings	

GetNextRequest →   ← GetResponse

Figure 4-5. A GetNextRequest message and its GetResponse message

This behavior is essential for retrieving data from tables when the instance identifiers (or row indexes) are not known. If you always know the index values of each row in a table, then a Get operation would suffice for all your SNMP data retrieval needs. But you don't, so it can't.

To start walking through a table, all you need is the name of the table, and the entry, and you'll need the entry members whose values you need to retrieve. To GetNext all of the values in each row of a table, issue one GetNextRequest message per row plus one. The variable bindings of each GetNextRequest message will specify the OIDs of each of the variable in the row. The values returned will be those of the variable in the next row.

Let's take a look at a GetNext operation performed on a table containing two columns (variables) and three rows (instances):

```
wiseTable.wiseEntry

wiseIndex    wiseGuy
1            Shadrach
2            Meshach
3            Abednego
```

This walk will begin with a GetNextRequest that contains two variable bindings, one for each entry member. The OIDs are specified without object identifiers, and this will return to us the values contained by the members in the first row of the table. It will take exactly four GetNext operations to retrieve all of the values in this table (but remember that we don't yet know how many rows, if any, are in this table).

Here are the varbinds (see Example 4-4) of the GetNextRequest and GetResponse messages resulting from the walk. For clarity, we will use textual labels to represent the OIDs. Note that the numbers used to match the responses with the requests serve the exact same function as the SNMP message Request ID values.

Example 4-4. Sample varbinds

```
GetNextRequest 1
   OID   = wiseTable.wiseEntry.wiseEntry
   Value = NULL
   OID   = wiseTable.wiseEntry.wiseGuy
   Value = NULL

GetResponse 1
   OID   = wiseTable.wiseEntry.wiseEntry.1
   Value = 1
   OID   = wiseTable.wiseEntry.wiseGuy.1
   Value = "Shadrach"

GetNextRequest 2
   OID   = wiseTable.wiseEntry.wiseEntry.1
   Value = NULL
   OID   = wiseTable.wiseEntry.wiseGuy.1
   Value = NULL

GetResponse 2
   OID   = wiseTable.wiseEntry.wiseEntry.2
   Value = 2
   OID   = wiseTable.wiseEntry.wiseGuy.2
   Value = "Meshach"
```

Example 4-4. Sample varbinds (continued)

```
GetNextRequest 3
  OID   = wiseTable.wiseEntry.wiseEntry.2
  Value = NULL
  OID   = wiseTable.wiseEntry.wiseGuy.2
  Value = NULL

GetResponse 3
  OID   = wiseTable.wiseEntry.wiseEntry.3
  Value = 3
  OID   = wiseTable.wiseEntry.wiseGuy.3
  Value = "Abednego"

GetNextRequest 4
  OID   = wiseTable.wiseEntry.wiseEntry.3
  Value = NULL
  OID   = wiseTable.wiseEntry.wiseGuy.3
  Value = NULL

GetResponse 4
  OID   = wiseTable.wiseEntry.1
  Value = 1
  OID   = theNextMibVariable.0
  Value = "1-800-998-9938"
```

In the first GetNextRequest, we initialize the varbinds list with one varbind per member in each table row. No instance identifiers are specified because we don't know the instance values of the variables in the first row (or any rows). The GetResponse message that is returned contains the names, instance identifiers, and values of the variables in the first instantiated row.

The OIDs returned in the first GetResponse are then used as the requested variable OIDs in the second GetNextRequest. The GetResponse returns the names and values of the variables in the next row instance. This pattern of using the OIDs returned in the GetResponse messages as the OIDs in the next GetNextRequest message is followed until we have retrieved the data in all of the instantiated rows in the table.

The management system knows that the end of the table has been reached when a GetResponse is returned that contains an OID of a variable that is outside the table's namespace. This is an indication that the walk has stepped past the end of the table, that all of the table data has been retrieved, and that all of the values returned by this final GetResponse should be discarded.

If the table is located at the very end of the agent's set of managed objects, and thus there are no other variables past the table to get, then a noSuchName error is returned. This indicates that we attempted to walk past the end of the agent's MIB namespace itself. This is an annoying error to receive when walking a table. MIB designers should take care that only scalar, and never columnar, variables appear last in a MIB.

What you may have noticed from this example is that the last GetResponse returned an OID and value that was also returned by the first GetResponse. This is because GetNext walks through tables by column, and from the top of each column to the bottom. Figure 4-6 illustrates a walk-through of a three-column table containing three rows. Each entry member is walked separately, and it requires ten GetNext operations to traverse the entire table.

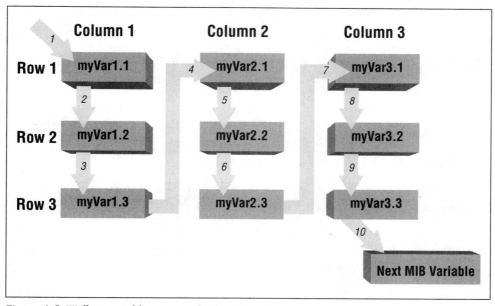

Figure 4-6. Walking a table one member at a time

The walk begins at the first member of the first column and walks down each column until an OID outside of the table is returned. When a table is walked by rows, the same pattern is followed, but some or all of the columnar variables are walked through at the same time (see Figure 4-7).

You can see that the last GetNext operation wraps around to the top of the next column, or to the next MIB variable that lexically follows the table. When this occurs, the walk through the entire table is complete.

In these examples, we used a GetNext operation to retrieve all of the data in a table, one member or one row at a time. But there is no restriction on which member values may be retrieved by a single GetNextRequest. Values stored in different rows, in different tables, and in different MIBs may all be retrieved using a single GetNextRequest message. The only requirement is that all the variables

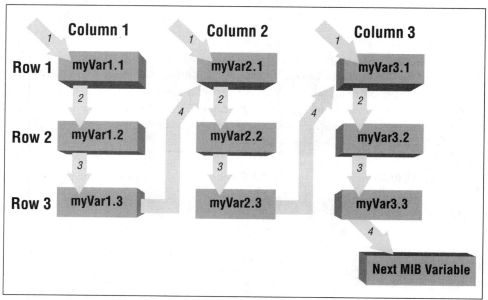

Figure 4-7. Walking a table one row at a time

whose values are requested must be supported by the agent to which the Get-NextRequest message is sent.

If you think that you now have tables nailed down, let me just briefly mention a bit of a MIB land mine you will eventually encounter when walking through MIBs. These are the dreaded sparse tables or, to put it another way, tables that are a few entry members shy of a full spread.

In a previous section, we conceptualized tables as spreadsheets, but they aren't quite the same thing. If a cell in a spreadsheet does not contain data, then the cell is merely uninitialized. If we examine the cell, we simply get no data from it. But in an SNMP table, not only may entry variables be uninitialized (as we have seen), but they may also exercise a little existential versatility and not exist at all. In other words, when walking MIB tables, you cannot assume that every variable in every row of every table is instantiated. And when a MIB table contains such "holes" in its fabric, it is referred to as a *sparse table*.

Note that the GetNext operation has absolutely no problem walking sparse tables. The problems occur, however, when a management system receiving the table data fails to recognize the holes present in the row data, and does not adjust the OIDs in the varbinds of the GetNextRequest messages it sends to the agent so that it walks the table properly.

A sparse table is essentially made of columns that are of different lengths. When walking through a table by rows, you naturally expect all of the data returned in a single GetResponse to be of the same row. If a row is missing an instance of one or more members, then the next member instance might be on the next row, or on the row after that.

Figure 4-8 shows the GetNext operation from the previous example, but with two members of the table missing. It is clear that the variables returned in a single GetResponse are not all from the same rows. And the walk across the shorter columns will jump to the next column before the walk is finished on the longer columns.

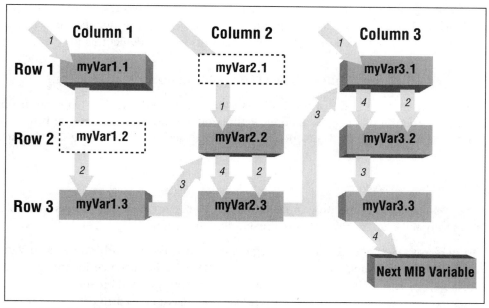

Figure 4-8. A problematic walk through a sparse table

A management system will only notice an entry member hole by comparing the instance identifiers (index) of each member variable in the same entry. If all of the members are of the same row, then they will all have the same index value(s).

If a row variable is not instantiated, then the value of the next available instance of that variable is returned, regardless of the row that instance might occupy. And the index value of the variable's OID will not match the other members of the row. If there are no more instances of the variable, then the value of the instance of the variable in the next column is returned.

Properly walking a sparse table requires recognizing that a variable instance is missing, and simply rerequesting the same variable until its index matches the indexes of the other OIDs in the request row. Until the index matches, the management system should ignore the value returned in the varbind.

The possible errors that may occur in response to the processing of a GetNextRequest message are the same as those of the GetRequest message:

noSuchName
> There are no more managed objects following an OID specified in the varbinds. In other words, a GetNext was requested using the OID of the last variable in the MIB namespace. The noSuchName error is also returned if the specified OID is not within the MIB namespace supported by the agent.

tooBig
> The resulting GetResponse message containing the requested values is too big to be sent back to the management system by the agent. This error is determined only by a master agent; subagents cannot detect this problem.

genErr
> For some reason a MIB variable value could not be read by the agent.

The "all or nothing" rule of SNMPv1 also applies to GetNext: if an operation on one of the varbinds fails, then none of the values requested are returned. In this case, the varbind list of the GetResponse is an exact duplicate of the GetNextRequest message.

SetRequest message

The Set operation is the only mechanism that a management system has available to modify the management data maintained by an agent.

To perform a Set, a SetRequest message is created with one varbind per MIB variable value to set. Each varbind contains an OID with the instance identifier of the variable to set and the new value. The management system then sends the SetRequest to an agent and waits for the GetResponse message to arrive. The agent will step through the varbinds and cache each value. If no processing errors occur, then each of the values is assigned to its respective MIB variable. If an error occurs during processing (noSuchName, badValue, readOnly, tooBig, or genErr), then none of the values specified in the varbinds will be set.

If the GetResponse message indicates noError, the ErrorStatus value is zero. If the GetResponse message indicates that an error occurred during the Set operation, the ErrorStatus and ErrorIndex values specify the error and which varbind caused the error (if it can be determined). In either case, the varbinds in the GetResponse message are identical to that of the SetRequest message.

The order in which the MIB variables appear in the variable bindings of a SetRequest message should have no effect on how they are modified by the agent. As quoted from RFC 1157:

"Each variable assignment specified by the SetRequest-PDU should be affected as if simultaneously set with respect to all other assignments specified in the same message."

What this means is that all modifications that are made to MIB variables specified in a single SetRequest message are to be regarded by an agent as occurring at the same time. If the design of a node requires that the value of a specific MIB variable is to be set before another MIB variable value may be set, you cannot perform both Set operations using the same SetRequest messages and expect to achieve the desired result.

For example, if a node requires you to set the value of the openGarageDoor variable before you can set the value of the backTheCarIntoTheDriveway variable, you must set each variable using two separate SetRequest messages. The order in which the value assignments appear in the variable binding of a single SetRequest message is of no significance.

When a GetResponse denoting a successful Set operation has been received, it might seem safe to assume that the MIB variables specified in the varbinds that now store the new values and are ready to be accessed use a Get or GetNext operation. This is, however, not a safe assumption. SNMP itself is only one link in a chain of the entire mechanism that is used to Get and Set management data. Although SNMP may have been successful in its part of setting the new values, other links in the chain could fail, unbeknownst to SNMP.

A noError GetResponse is only an indication that the SNMP agent successfully passed the value on to another process or operating system call that is now responsible for setting the value. As previously mentioned, the ErrorStatus field is an indication that an error occurred only within the operation of the SNMP protocol. It is quite possible that a failure to permanently set the value occurred after the noError GetResponse was sent, or that the actual setting of the value will not occur until several seconds (or longer) after the GetResponse was received by the management system.

Ideally, the agent should not return a GetResponse until the values set are accessible using a GetRequest. But the SNMP agent process might have to continually query the MIB variable until it returns the new value. If the agent is implemented on a single-threaded operating system, this will keep the agent from responding to any other SNMP requests either until it times out or until the value is actually set.

This problem is solved by other system and network management protocols with an "In Process" message that is an indication to a management system from an agent that it is working on the request. An InProcessResponse message would be sent by an agent if a request were to take longer than a second or two to complete. Once completed, a proper GetResponse message would then be sent by the agent.

While the concept of an InProcessResponse message sounds great, its operation would place a tremendous burden upon an SNMP agent. For example, if a SetRequest containing 30 new MIB values was received by an agent, the agent would not only need to set the new values, but it also would need to continually poll the node's operating system and its own MIB database to verify that all 30 values are actually set before it may send a GetResponse. And while engaged in setting and polling, the agent would also be sending periodic InProcessResponse messages as an indication to the management system that it is still working on its SetRequest operation. Support of the InProcessResponse message therefore violates SNMP's "minimal impact upon the managed node" rule.

Because an SNMP management system cannot use a successful GetResponse as an indication that the SetRequest data has actually been set, it should perform every Set operation using four steps:

1. The management system performs a Get on the MIB variables to determine their current value.

2. It sends the SetRequest message specifying the new values.

3. It checks the GetResponse message returned by the agent to make sure that the Set operation completed successfully.

4. It performs a GetRequest on the MIB variables again to verify that they are all indeed set to the new values. If some or all of the variables are not set, the management system waits for a specific period of time and then performs the GetRequest again. If they are still not set, the SetRequest may be performed again or the management system may continue to poll. (See Figure 4-9.)

You will also find a slight modification of this four-step Set procedure useful when using a SNMP management API that doesn't give you an indication of whether a Set operation had been completed successfully.* With your management application unable to determine when (or if) the GetResponse had been received, and the value of its ErrorStatus field, you are therefore left with only one alternative: getting the MIB value, performing the SetRequest, waiting a predetermined length of time for the Set operation to complete, and then getting the variable again to see if the Set operation was successful.

If this seems like an awful lot of work just to set the value of a variable, remember that the SNMP agent is running as a low-priority process on the network node. Rather than indulge in cycle-consuming error handling, an agent

---

* At least one very popular SNMP management API available for both UNIX and Windows does not provide this obviously necessary feature.

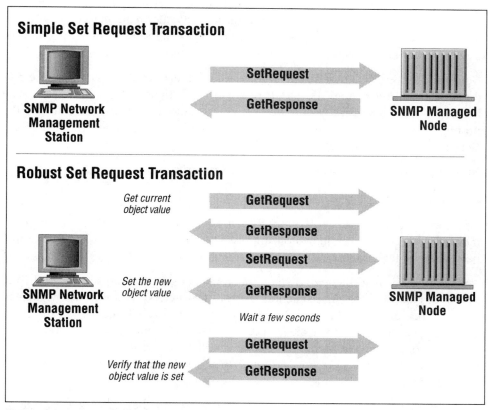

Figure 4-9. Steps in the Set operation

may be designed just to give up on a problematic operation in favor of processing other messages it has received. The philosophy here is that in such an event, a management system should be able to cope.

GetResponse Errors

When you are troubleshooting a failed SNMP operation, the ErrorStatus and Error-Index values present in the GetResponse message provide the bulk of your high-level debugging information. You must know exactly what kinds of problems may cause these errors if you are going to debug an SNMP problem in a timely manner.

RFC 1157 describes a set of rules used by agents to determine if a specific SNMP operation has been processed successfully. You will use these same rules to design the SNMP message parsing code in all of the extension agents that you write. You will also use these rules when attempting to determine what went wrong when an agent sends your management system a GetResponse message with a non-zero value in the ErrorStatus field.

The Get and GetNext operations may only result in noSuchName, tooBig, and genErr errors. The Set operation may result in badValue, readOnly, noSuchName, tooBig (very unlikely), and genErr errors. Of course, all operations return noError if no protocol errors occurred during processing of the request message.

Note that the ErrorStatus and ErrorIndex values are only used to indicate errors that have occurred within the SNMP protocol itself; they are not used to indicate alarms or faults on a managed node. Network problems must be identified by the proper interpretation of management data stored in the variable bindings of the GetResponse and Trap PDUs.

Now let's have a look at each SNMPv1 protocol error in detail.

tooBig error

The tooBig error is an indication that the size of the resulting GetResponse message exceeded some limitation imposed by the network or agent and cannot be sent (or at least cannot be sent in an unfragmented packet).

An agent may be designed to limit the total length of GetResponse and Trap PDUs to a "reasonable" size (such as 512 or 1024 octets), possibly due to limited memory resources. If the cumulative size of all the requested data causes the GetResponse message to exceed the agent's size limitation, a GetResponse message containing the identical variable bindings found in the request message is returned; the tooBig error is indicated in the ErrorStatus field. The ErrorIndex value of the GetResponse message is zero.

A message size limit is typically based on the size of the network connection's Maximum Transfer Unit (MTU). The MTU is the largest single packet that can be transported across a specific network link. This limit is determined by the data link layer interface. Larger packets are normally fragmented by the network (IP) layer into multiple smaller packets, and are reassembled when they are received. Data that must avoid being fragmented into multiple packets (usually because of the extra overhead involved in fragmentation and reassembly) must be less than the size of the MTU.

For an Ethernet network, the MTU is typically the maximum size of an Ethernet frame payload (1500 octets). You might think that each message could therefore have varbind data up to 1500 octets in length. But remember that other data (the IP, UDP, SNMP message, and PDU headers) must also fit into the payload. For both Ethernet and UDP, an MTU of 1492 is quite common. Therefore, a GetResponse message containing varbind data greater than 1400 octets in length in an SNMP message may inspire a tooBig error.

So be careful about how many MIB values you request using a single SNMP request message, and be mindful of the maximum possible size of each OCTET STRING. When in doubt, request the data using several smaller SNMP messages.

TIP   The MTU of a network connection can be found by looking at the
             1.3.6.1.2.mib.interfaces.ifTable.ifEntry.ifMtu variable. You can also
             use the *ping* command to test the MTU size by specifying the send
             buffer size and setting the "don't fragment" flag. To find the MTU
             value, try starting with a buffer size of 1500 and work downward:*

             ```
             ping -f -l 1500 <address>
             ```

noSuchName error

The noSuchName error is an indication that an OID specified in a variable
binding was not found by an agent in its supported MIB namespace. The Error-
Index value indicates the specific variable binding that contains the unfound OID.

The GetRequest and SetRequest operations require that exact OID and instance
identifiers be specified in each variable binding. If any OID is incorrect, or if the
instance identifiers are incorrect or omitted, then a noSuchName error will result.
A GetNextRequest may also result in a noSuchName error if there is not another
variable supported by the agent to get.

A noSuchName error is resolved by comparing the OID that caused the error with
the agent's MIB to discover if the OID does not, in fact, exist. If it does exist, then
the MIB database maintained by the agent must be searched using GetNext operations to determine if the variable instance specified in the OID does exist.

badValue error

The badValue error indicates that the value specified for a MIB variable in a SetRequest operation is incorrect. The value may be the wrong specified data type, or
have a length or value outside the range specified for the variable. The ErrorIndex
value in the PDU indicates which variable bindings contain the erroneous value.

Each new value specified for a MIB variable by a SetRequest must be of the same
data type as the variable. For example, a management system may ask to set the
value of an INTEGER variable, but send an OCTET STRING value in the variable
binding that contains the INTEGER value's OID. The agent will recognize the data
type mismatch and return a badValue error. Even if an INTEGER value were
stored in the variable binding, the agent would interpret the value as an OCTET
STRING because that is the data type specified in the variable binding.

---

* See "Default MTU Size for Different Network Topology," Microsoft Knowledge Base, article Q140375,
3-26-97, and "Diagnoses and Treatment of Black Hole Routers," Microsoft Knowledge Base, article
Q159211, 3-28-97.

MIB variables may also have assigned to them a specific scope to which the new value must conform. As we have seen, both INTEGER and OCTET STRING variables may be subtyped only to allow values in a specific range, or strings of specific lengths. If the new value is outside the length specified for the OCTET STRING variable, then a badValue error will result. For example, suppose that a SetRequest that specifies an OCTET STRING 32 octets in length is to be assigned to a MIB variable that is declared as only containing an OCTET STRING from 6 to 28 octets in length. This situation will generate a badValue error.

To resolve badValue errors, you need to look at the OBJECT-TYPE definition of the variable in the MIB. The SYNTAX clause gives you a specification of the data type and range of the MIB variable. The DESCRIPTION section contains information about the acceptable range of values that may be assigned to the variable.

readOnly error

The readOnly error occurs when a SetRequest message attempts to assign a new value to a variable that is defined in the agent's MIB with a read-only ACCESS mode—or so it would seem.

The definition of the SetRequest message in RFC 1157 clearly shows readOnly as a possible value to be returned in the errorStatus field of the SetRequest PDU. Unfortunately, the actual definition of how to determine when a readOnly error has occurred was accidentally omitted from the SetRequest PDU description. Therefore, to be completely compliant with the SNMPv1 standard, the readOnly error status must never be returned by an agent.[*]

So what do you do if an agent receives a SetRequest message that specifies a read-only MIB object? Looking back to RFC 1157 we see that for any object specified for a set operation that is not available, a noSuchName error should result. The phrase "not available" is interpreted to mean both "setting the value of a read-only object and not in the agent's MIB view."

To determine if a noSuchName error resulted from a MIB variable being read-only or not existing in the agent's supported set of managed objects, you must use a GetRequest performed on the variable. A management system will typically precede a Set operation with a Get operation to retrieve the value of the MIB variable before changing it to confirm that the value has indeed changed.

genErr error

The genErr error indicates that some error has occurred that does not fit into any of the other error status categories. The variable binding that caused the genErr

---

[*] SNMPv2 defines a notWritable error that is identical in meaning to readOnly in SNMPv1.

may be indicated in the ErrorIndex value if it can be determined by the agent. However, many genErr responses are simply returned with an ErrorIndex value of zero.

Probably the most frequent cause of genErr errors is when the agent encounters an error reading or writing a MIB variable on the local system. Suppose that the MIB variable data is accessed via the node's operating system or a database, and an error is returned to the agent when it reads or writes the data. The agent has no choice but to send a genErr as a response to the management system's request. Unfortunately, there isn't a field in the GetResponse message that is used to store an agent-defined error code that could be used to return a more specific indication of what caused the genErr.

Not to belabor the point, but let me mention again that a protocol analyzer does come in very handy when you are troubleshooting SMNP protocol errors. The cause of a badValue or noSuchName error is often very apparent when you look at the data in the variable bindings of both the request and response messages. Otherwise you might waste a lot of time poking through your code trying to find a logic or data error—this has never happened to me. :-)

SNMPv1 Traps

Traps are unrequested event report messages that are sent from an SNMP agent to a management system.* The generation of a trap by an agent indicates that some predefined condition or event has occurred that may be of interest to a manager. Traps are identical in concept to interrupts generated by a hardware device or signals generated by an operating system. That wonderful "A General Protection Fault has occurred" message so familiar to Windows programmers is a type of trap response as well.

The term *trap* is exactly what it sounds like—a trap waiting to be sprung. When an SNMP agent detects that a predetermined event has occurred, trap messages are generated by the agent and sent to specific network addresses, called *trap destinations*.

Residing at each trap destination is (we hope) an active network management process that will receive all trap messages generated by the agent and will report them in a trap log. If the management process, or *trap receiver*, is in the form of an interactive application, then it may also present audible and visual indications that a trap has been received.

---

* Traps may also be described as unsolicited responses, asynchronous notifications, event reports, and autonomous messages.

A management system may determine what kind of event caused the agent to generate the trap by examining the data stored in the variable bindings of each trap message. The varbinds will contain the identity and values of MIB variables that provide information on the specific event. All of the MIB variables in the Trap PDU varbinds must reside within the MIB view supported by the agent that generated the trap.

Many trap messages do not contain any variable bindings. This is because there may be no data associated with the event that inspired the generation of the trap, or the presence of the trap message itself is all that is required to convey the necessary information. How many words do you need printed on a red flag to understand what it means?

SNMPv1 traps are certainly simple, sparse of features, and considered by some to be ill-defined. Regardless of what you may think of SNMPv1 traps, their design is written in standards stone and will not change.

TRAP-TYPE Macro

The TRAP-TYPE macro described in RFC 1215 is used to define the traps associated with a specific MIB. Although a TRAP-TYPE macro appears very similar in format to the OBJECT-TYPE macro, a trap is not a MIB variable and does not have an OID. Instead, each trap is referenced by the OID of the MIB that defines the trap, and by a non-negative enumeration uniquely assigned to each trap in the same MIB.

Here is an example of a TRAP-TYPE macro used to define a mythical trap in a private MIB:

```
oraUnit OBJECT IDENTIFIER ::= { enterprises 2035 1 }

unitOnFire TRAP-TYPE
    ENTERPRISE  oraUnit
    VARIABLES   { shelfId, slotIndex, unitId, unitIsToastState }
    DESCRIPTION
      "This trap is used to indicate if a unit is now on fire,
      or a fire previously detected has been extinguished. The
      variables shelfId, slotIndex, and unitId are used to
      identify the unit and its location. The value of
      unitIsToastState indicates if a fire is present (1), or
      not (2)."
    ::= 1
```

The Trap Identifier is "unitOnFire" and is a textual label used to give a human-readable name to the trap. The OID of the management enterprise that defines this trap is specified in the ENTERPRISE clause. The VARIABLES clause specifies the MIB variables whose OIDs and values are copied into the variable bindings of the trap message. The variables are specified in the order in which they are stored. If the trap is not defined to include any MIB data, then the VARIABLES clause is omitted and the trap message will not contain a varbind list. The DESCRIPTION in this example is a fairly helpful bit of text used for deciphering the use and meaning of this trap. The number that follows the DESCRIPTION is the private MIB enumeration for this trap.

Trap PDU

The Trap PDU (see Figure 4-10) is slightly different in format from the other SNMPv1 request and response messages. The preamble and body sections are identical in format to the other PDUs, but the header contains a few extra fields required to support the trap data. The ErrorStatus and ErrorIndex fields found in the other PDUs are missing from the Trap PDU, as there are no SNMP protocol errors associated with the trap message.

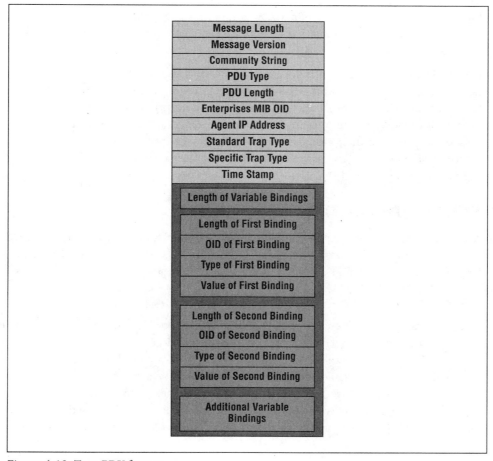

Figure 4-10. Trap PDU format

The identity of a trap message is determined by examining the values contained in the Enterprises, Standard Trap Type, and Specific Trap Type fields of the Trap PDU. If the Trap Type value is zero through five, then the trap is one of the generic SNMP traps defined by the snmp group of MIB-II. The OID stored in the Enterprise field will be iso(1).org(3).dod(6).intenet(1).mgmt(2).mib(1).snmp(11), and the value of the Specific TrapType field will be zero.

If the Trap Type value is six, then this trap is an enterprise-specific trap that is defined in a private MIB residing in the iso(1).org(3).dod(6).intenet(1).private(4). enterprises(1) namespace defined by the SMI. The OID specified in the Enterprises field indicates exactly which management enterprise defines the trap, and the Specific Trap Type value will store the enumeration value of the trap as specified in the TRAP-TYPE macros that defines the trap.

Specific instances of a trap message are identified using the Time Stamp value found in the PDU. The order in which a series of trap messages was received from an agent may be determined by comparing the time stamp values. This is very important for determining the current state of a two-state trappable event, such as "the unit is on fire," and "the fire is out; everything is OK."

RFC 1157 defines seven traps for use by SNMPv1 agents. Six of these traps are described as "generic," and are the traps that may be commonly generated by any SNMP agent. The seventh trap is described as enterprise-specific and is used to define all device-specific traps used by private organizations. It is not possible to define new generic traps; only new enterprise-specific traps may be defined, and a MIB designer is free to define as many enterprise-specific traps as desired (and believe me, they often do).

SNMPv1 Generic Traps

An SNMP agent is not required to implement generic traps that are not required. Several generic traps you will find used by most agents (e.g., coldStart and authenticationFailure), and some you may find used infrequently (e.g., egpNeighborLoss).

coldStart traps

coldStart traps indicate that a device has just powered up or has performed a complete reinitialization (hard-reset). The configuration of the device may have changed and any data collected prior to the reset may have been lost. Such data is usually stored in volatile memory and is cleared by a hard reset or when the device loses power. A restart might also be necessary before the device recognizes a change in the system parameters (such as IP address or active network port) or configuration (a non-plug-and-play piece of equipment is added or removed).

A coldStart trap is also an indication to the other members of its SNMP community that the agent is available to service SNMP requests. If problems occur during initialization that would prevent the agent from correctly responding to SNMP requests, then the coldStart trap should not be sent.

The Time Stamp value in the coldStart Trap PDU may be zero or close to zero, indicating that the SNMP process has just started. If the node has also just (re)started, then this time stamp is an accurate indication of the system start time. If only the SNMP agent process, but not the entire operating system, has restarted, then the time stamp will not be a proper reflection of the system start time.

warmStart trap

The warmStart trap is an indication that a device has reinitialized, but that neither the device configuration nor the stored data have changed. The device may be expected to continue in the same state of operation as before the reinitialization. When a device performs a warm start, it typically has time to write data to disk or non-volatile memory, including its current configuration and operational state. When the device completes its warm start, it may read persistent data from disk or non-volatile memory, and then resume normal operation.

linkDown trap

The linkDown trap is an indication that a communications link or a port on a network node has failed. The affected interface is identified in the first variable binding of the Trap PDU data as the name and value of the ifIndex instance in the MIB-II interfaces group of the link that went down. However, this information is not necessarily helpful in determining the effect that the downed link will have on the operation of the node.

Many network communications devices maintain multiple communications links, so the sending of a linkDown trap by an agent is not necessarily an indication of a critical fault. If one communication link goes down, its traffic may be transparently routed through another available channel. It is also possible that the link that went down was not in service at all.

However, if many links have gone down, or if all links are in use and none are available for the traffic to switch to, then a linkDown trap indicates a critical or catastrophic failure. If a downed link is the channel used to send SNMP messages, then you will never see a linkDown—or any other trap—at all.

linkUp trap

A linkUp trap is an indication that a communications link or a port on a node has come up and is ready for service. The affected interface is identified in the first variable binding of the trap PDU data as the name and value of the ifIndex instance in the MIB-II interfaces group. The linkUp trap is only supported on devices with multiple communication links (such as routers and workstations).

authenticationFailure trap

The authenticationFailure trap indicates that an agent has received an SNMP message that cannot be authenticated. This is typically an indication that the SNMP PDU contained an unrecognized community name, or that the message was sent from a node residing at a network address not authorized to send SNMP requests to the agent.

The authenticationFailure trap does not contain any variable bindings (or, really, any useful information); to do so would make it necessary to store this information as variables in the MIB-II snmp group. This is unfortunate, as it would be very helpful to know the community name and source network address of the SNMP message that failed authentication.

egpNeighborLoss trap

The egpNeighborLoss trap is generated by an Exterior Gateway Protocol (EGP) router agent when an EGP peer router listed in its neighbor table (egpNeigh-Table) has stopped responding. Support for this trap is mandatory by all devices that implement EGP. It will be used only in the management of networks that contain a large number of EGP nodes. EGP itself is an IP router protocol defined by RFC 904.

Using Traps

Traps sound like a really good idea. When a managed node on a network experiences a problem, it gathers a few pieces of descriptive information and sends it to a management system in the form of a trap. The management system can then act to correct the problem brought to its attention by the preemptive alert.

In theory, traps are all well and good, but in application there are a couple of hitches. Because SNMP is built upon the UDP connectionless transport protocol, message reception acknowledgment must be handled by the software that is using SNMP. When a management system sends a GetRequest, GetNextRequest, or SetRequest message it expects to receive a GetResponse message in return. If the response is not received within the specified time-out period, the management system can send the message again, or give up and log that the managed node is not responding.

SNMP traps, however, have no associated response message. In fact, a trap itself is an unsolicited response message sent by an agent. And once an agent sends a trap, it does not expect an acknowledgment message from any of the nodes that received and processed the message. In fact, the agent does not care if anyone at all received the trap.

So how is trap handshaking to be handled? Without a trap acknowledgment message, a trap can be sent by an agent, and be lost somewhere on the network; no one will know or even care. What's worse, most major network problems involve severe network congestion, poor or faulty communication links, misconfigured routing tables, and the failure of physical devices. These network problems reduce the likelihood of a trap message—and information regarding a critical or catastrophic event—from reaching its destination.

You may conclude from this description that traps under SNMP are not well thought out, and many people would agree with you. However, if we compare the concepts of acknowledged traps versus unacknowledged traps, we can recognize both the smart and the stupid sides of these models.

NOTE   This discussion of trap message acknowledgment is purely academic. Neither SNMPv1 nor SNMPv2 has a mechanism for acknowledging traps, and using one would represent a nonstandard implementation of SNMP. Nevertheless, I'm explaining the situation so you will understand completely why you should not consider designing a system of network management based on SNMP that relies in any way on traps.

On the smart side, unacknowledged traps allow an agent to send a trap and then immediately get back to monitoring the node. The agent doesn't need to waste cycles listening for the trap acknowledgment, and then resending the trap if it doesn't receive one. This also solves a problem that occurs if the agent times out before the trap ACK is received and ends up sending a second, duplicate trap.

Trap acknowledgment can be especially time consuming when a trap has been sent to multiple destinations and over a congested network. The added acknowledgment messages only add to the network congestion. And after all, if a node is sending traps then there are likely to be problems occurring on the network. You would want to keep the network as uncongested as possible for the "real" management messages to flow.

On the stupid side, traps (properly implemented) are indicators of the presence of significant conditions and events. If a trap message sent by an agent is "lost in the Ether," the network management system may be severely delayed in discovering a serious or critical network fault.

A trap acknowledgment mechanism would allow a dropped trap to be re-sent by an agent within a few seconds. In the unlikely event that a delayed trap ACK resulted in a management system receiving duplicate traps, the management system software could be designed to recognize duplicate traps and disregard them.

Perhaps the best solution would be an optional trap acknowledgment mechanism. Each trap message would include a flag indicating whether or not the agent expected a trap acknowledgment from a management system. A network administrator could therefore choose to implement or not implement trap handshaking.

Traps in themselves are not corrective actions. They are just reports used to indicate that a condition has been detected, or an event has occurred, that might be of interest to a network manager. Once a trap is received, it is up to the network manager to decide whether further action should be taken, or whether the trap should be ignored.

Trap messages are not intended by applications to contain large amounts of information (although by design they may contain volumes). If a network node generates a trap, then it is very likely that the node, or its corner of the network, is in trouble. Rather than devote a significant amount of system time and resources to the collection of information, the network node generates a trap containing minimal information on the problem (type and severity of alarm condition, location of problem, and so forth). The information in the trap message is used to tell a management process where to poll for additional management information needed to diagnose and resolve the problem.

Using a Protocol Analyzer

Now that I have covered the logical construction of messages, datagrams, packets, and frames, let's have a look at what the data really looks like as it's flying through the air, across the copper, or down the fiber. To do this, we need to use a special piece of software tool called a protocol analyzer. As I've mentioned, a protocol analyzer is an invaluable tool for observing the conversation occurring between two computers on a communications link or monitoring all of the traffic flowing across a network.

If you are attempting to debug a problem with network software, it is very helpful to see the data being sent and received by a node. Without an analyzer, all you can do is put some debugging code in the software processes running at either end of the network link and try to capture some useful information. This method is very invasive and time-consuming, and it's not possible at all unless you have access to the code at both ends of the link.

If we instead drop a protocol analyzer in between the network nodes to eavesdrop on their exchange of messages, we can see all of the data that is being exchanged without disrupting the current operational state of the network. This is very similar to the way that a doctor can listen to your heart and take your temperature without interfering with the current operational state of your body.

NOTE   All of the protocol analyzer screenshots featured in this book are taken from NetXRay by Cinco Networks Incorporated. The NetXRay Packet Viewer window makes excellent use of the Microsoft tree view control to illustrate the structure and content of network packet data. NetXRay also contains several nice features specifically used for troubleshooting SNMP. Appendix A, *References*, contains detailed information on NetXRay, including the fully functional NetXRay demo program provided on the CD-ROM that accompanies this book.

Trap Message

Figure 4-11 shows a captured SNMPv1 trap message. The Ethernet frame, IP packet, UDP datagram, and SNMP message sections are each expanded to show their data. The Ethernet frame contains the MAC addresses of the two nodes involved in the message exchange and identifies the protocol used as IP. At the very end of the message you can see the CRC value that is located inside the FCB of the Ethernet frame.

The IP header contains the information used to get the packet from one host to another. The IP addresses of the source and destination hosts are shown, along with the type of IP protocol data contained within the IP packet: UDP datagram. The UDP header shows the port numbers that were used to send and receive the trap.

The SNMP message section contains the information in which we're really interested. The message preamble shows the total size of the message (44 bytes), the SNMP version (1), and the community to which the trap response belongs ("public"). The PDU header contains the total size of the PDU (31 bytes) and the message type (4), the management enterprise that defines this trap (1.3.6.1.2.1.311.1.1.3.1.1), the IP address of the agent host that generated the trap (128.128.128.3), and the generic and specific type of trap (0 and 0). The time stamp of when the trap was generated (the sysUpTime value when the trap was generated) shows a value of zero, which is typical for coldStart traps. There is no variable binding data associated with this trap.

GetRequest Message

Figure 4-12 illustrates a GetRequest message that is requesting the sysContact MIB-II variable value. We see the preamble data field common to all SNMPv1

Figure 4-11. A coldStart trap message

messages, and the error and request-id fields not present in trap messages. The variable bindings store the OID and the instance of the variable being requested. Most remaining fields in the message are initialized to zero or ASN.1 NULL.

GetResponse Message

The GetResponse message containing the requested sysContact value is illustrated in Figure 4-13. The format of the PDU is exactly the same as the GetRequest, but several of the fields are now initialized with data. The three important things to note are that the requested data is available in the variable binding ("Contact: James D. Murray"), that the Request ID value in the GetResponse is the same as in the GetRequest, and that no errors occurred during the request (ErrorStatus and ErrorIndex are zero).

The GetNextRequest and GetResponse message pairs appear in essentially the same way. The only difference is that the approximate OIDs specified in the GetNextRequest variable bindings are replaced in the GetResponse message with the exact OIDs found by the agent.

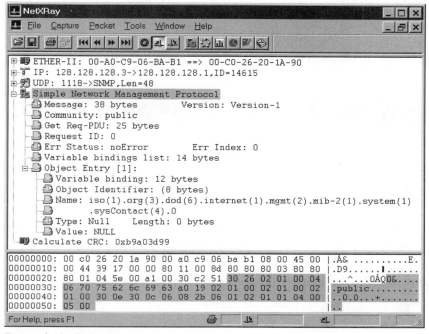

Figure 4-12. GetRequest message

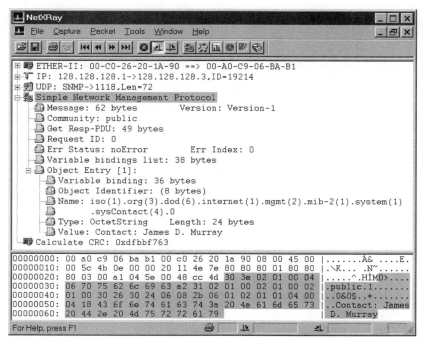

Figure 4-13. GetResponse message

SetRequest Message

Figure 4-14 shows a SetRequest message. Once again, a SetRequest message has the same format as the GetRequest, GetNextRequest, and GetResponse messages. This SetRequest is setting the value of the sysLocation MIB-II variable—the new value visible in the single variable binding.

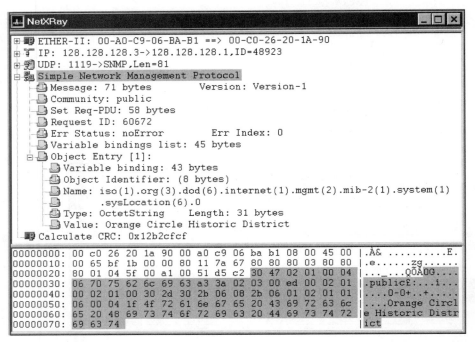

Figure 4-14. SetRequest message

Figure 4-15 shows the GetResponse message returned in response to the SetRequest message. This would be just another uneventful GetResponse message, except that we see an error has occurred. The sysLocation field in the agent's MIB has an ACCESS-LEVEL of read-only, so a readOnly error is indicated by the ErrorStatus field, and the ErrorIndex value points to the first variable binding. If you take a quick look at the MIB, you'll see that sysLocation is, in reality, a read-write variable, so the agent must have a bug in its database or code.[*]

---

[*] See "Windows 95 SNMP Agent Allows Only Read-Only Access," Microsoft Knowledge Base, article Q159567, 11-16-96.

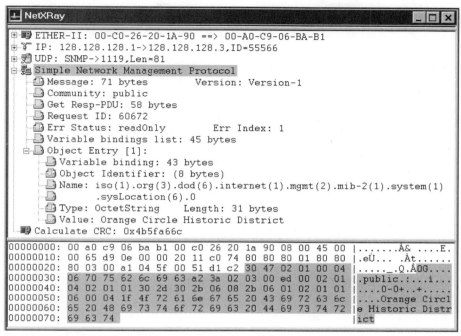

```
NetXRay                                                        _ □ ×

⊞ 🖳 ETHER-II: 00-C0-26-20-1A-90 ==> 00-A0-C9-06-BA-B1
⊞ 🔻 IP: 128.128.128.1->128.128.128.3,ID=55566
⊞ 📲 UDP: SNMP->1119,Len=81
⊟ 🍱 Simple Network Management Protocol
      📄 Message: 71 bytes          Version: Version-1
      📄 Community: public
      📄 Get Resp-PDU: 58 bytes
      📄 Request ID: 60672
      📄 Err Status: readOnly        Err Index: 1
      📄 Variable bindings list: 45 bytes
   ⊟ 📄 Object Entry [1]:
      📄 Variable binding: 43 bytes
      📄 Object Identifier: (8 bytes)
      📄 Name: iso(1).org(3).dod(6).internet(1).mgmt(2).mib-2(1).system(1)
      📄      .sysLocation(6).0
      📄 Type: OctetString    Length: 31 bytes
      📄 Value: Orange Circle Historic District
   🖳 Calculate CRC: 0x4b5fa66c

00000000: 00 a0 c9 06 ba b1 00 c0 26 20 1a 90 08 00 45 00  |.......À& ....E.
00000010: 00 65 d9 0e 00 00 20 11 c0 74 80 80 80 01 80 80  |.eÜ... .Àt......
00000020: 80 03 00 a1 04 5f 00 51 d1 c2 30 47 02 01 00 04  |....._.Q.ÀOG....
00000030: 06 70 75 62 6c 69 63 a2 3a 02 03 00 ed 00 02 01  |.public.:...í...
00000040: 04 02 01 01 30 2d 30 2b 06 08 2b 06 01 02 01 01  |....0-0+..+.....
00000050: 06 00 04 1f 4f 72 61 6e 67 65 20 43 69 72 63 6c  |....Orange Circl
00000060: 65 20 48 69 73 74 6f 72 69 63 20 44 69 73 74 72  |e Historic Distr
00000070: 69 63 74                                         |ict
```

Figure 4-15. GetResponse message

II

SNMP Details

This part of the book provides detailed information for developers on how to write NT SNMP agent and management code.

Chapter 5, *Getting Started with the SNMP Service*, describes the installation, operation, and removal of the Microsoft SNMP service and its components under Windows 95 and Windows NT. It also examines the SNMP service configuration parameters and how to modify them using both the System Policy Editor and the registry.

Chapter 6, *Using the Extension and Utility APIs*, provides an in-depth look at the Microsoft SNMP Extension and Utility APIs. It includes working code examples that demonstrate the operation of each API call, along with a walk-through of the *SNMP.H* header file.

Chapter 7, *Writing Extension Agents*, discusses how to write an extension agent. It includes many working code examples that show you how to implement each SNMP Extension API call and use it in an extension agent, as well as how to collect management data stored in both process memory and the registry. It also covers how to build, install, test, debug, and remove extension agents.

Chapter 8, *Implementing Traps*, explains how to write an extension agent DLL that is capable of sending SNMP traps. It examines methods for collecting management information and detecting trappable events, and it provides recommendations for how, when, and where to send traps.

Chapter 9, *Using the Management API*, is an in-depth look at the Microsoft SNMP Management API. This API is used to write simple SNMPv1 management applications that run under Windows NT (and, with a bit of fudging, under Windows 95 as well). It includes many working code examples that demonstrate the operation of each API call, as well as a walk-through of the *MGMTAPI.H* header file.

Chapter 10, *Writing Network Management Applications*, discusses how to design an SNMP management application that uses the SNMP Management API to send, receive, and process SNMPv1 request messages and to receive SNMPv1 traps. It also discusses the problems of performing SNMP management.

5

Getting Started with the SNMP Service

This chapter describes how to install, uninstall, configure, and test the Microsoft Windows SNMP service. We'll also have a look at how the SNMP service works with the Win32 and SNMP APIs.

The Windows SNMP Services

As we've mentioned, SNMP is implemented as a Win32 system service. Under Windows NT there are actually two SNMP services. The first is the SNMP agent service (*SNMP.EXE*). The agent processes SNMP Request messages that it receives from SNMP management systems and sends GetResponse messages in reply. The agent specifically handles the interface with the Windows Socket (WinSock) API, SNMP message parsing, and ASN.1 and BER encoding and decoding. The agent is also responsible for sending trap messages to SNMP management systems. The SNMP agent service is available under both Windows NT and Windows 95.

The second service is the SNMP trap service (*SNMPTRAP.EXE*), which listens for traps sent to the NT host and then passes the data along to the Microsoft SNMP management API. The SNMP trap service is not available under Windows 95, for reasons that I'll explain later in this chapter.

The SNMP agent service is also referred to in Microsoft literature as the "Windows NT extendible SNMP agent." An "extendible" agent allows MIB information to be dynamically added and supported as required. For the programmer this means that to enable the SNMP agent service to support a new MIB object, you need not update and recompile the agent's code. Instead, an external "subagent" will be modified and used by the agent to process all of the management requests that it receives, and to create all of the traps that it sends. These subagents are called extension agents, and are written by you. Figure 5-1 illustrates the relationship of the two SNMP services, the Service Control Manager (SCM), and the extendible agent under Windows NT.

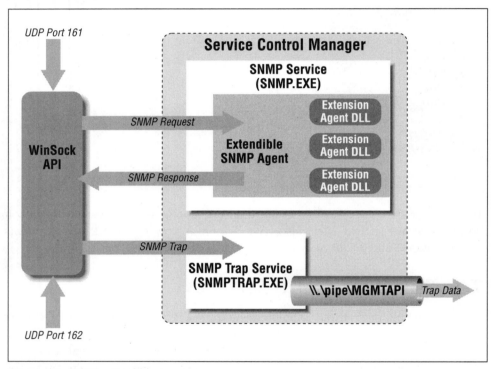

Figure 5-1. SNMP extendible agent

Both SNMP services are controlled by the SCM (I'll explain more about the SCM later in this chapter). The extendible agent resides within the SNMP service. It receives SNMP messages across the network using the WinSock API, and passes the message data to one or more of the loaded extendible agents for processing. Each extension agent is actually a DLL that is responsible for performing GetRequest, GetNextRequest, and SetRequest operations on MIB variables specified in the message. The SNMP trap service simply receives trap messages from the WinSock API and passes the data along using a named pipe server.

Figure 5-2 shows more detail of the interaction between the SNMP service, a set of extension agents, and the SNMP and WinSock APIs. SNMP messages are received from the WinSock API via the UDP/IP protocol services. The SNMP agent BER-decodes and authenticates the messages it receives and, using the SNMP API, passes the data on to the extension agent(s) responsible for processing the MIB objects specified in the message. The resulting data is then passed back to the extendible agent, formatted as a GetResponse message, and sent back to the management system. If the message specifies a MIB object that is not supported by any extension agents loaded by the SNMP service, then a noSuch-Name error will be returned.

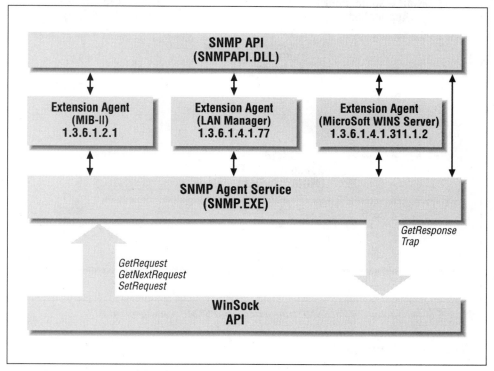

Figure 5-2. Interaction of the SNMP agent service and the SNMP API

The function of the SNMP trap service is to listen for SNMP trap messages sent by other SNMP agents and then to forward the data to the Microsoft SNMP manage-ment API, specifically to the *MGMTAPI.DLL*, via a named pipe server. The trap data is then sent to any applications that are using the management API to listen for traps. Figure 5-3 shows the interaction of the SNMP trap service with an SNMP management application and the SNMP, management, and WinSock APIs. The management application sends and receives SNMP messages using the Management API and calls the SNMP API for memory allocation and data conversion functions.

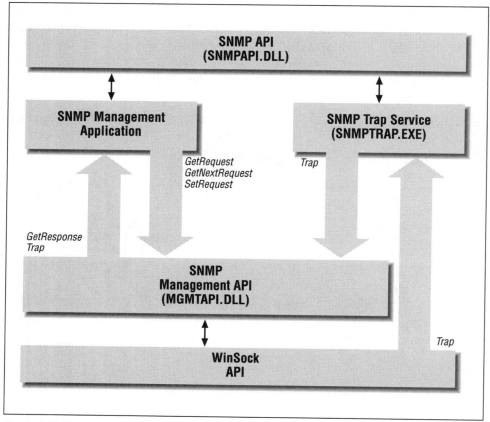

Figure 5-3. Interaction of the SNMP trap service and SNMP management API

What Is a Service?

Before we delve into the SNMP services any further, it might be helpful to look at exactly what a *service* is.

The Windows NT SNMP Service Control Manager (SCM) is made up of (among other things) a collection of services. A service is actually a special type of Win32 application that interfaces with the SCM using the Win32 API. Services are essentially background processes (or *daemons* in UNIX vernacular) used to monitor hardware devices and other system processes. You can find a master listing of all services installed on a system in the registry under the *HKEY_LOCAL_MACHINE\ SYSTEM\CurrentControlSet\Services* key.

There are actually two types of services: *system services* and *device services*. If you double-click on the Services applet in the Control Panel you will be presented with a listing of all the system services currently installed. Each system service monitors and maintains a specific process (Event Log, Computer Browser, Messenger, DHCP Server, and so forth). If you have a program that needs to continually monitor a process or port, or to support the operation of many different applications, then you have a good candidate for a system service.

Device services (also called *drivers*) are used to control specific hardware peripherals installed on the workstation (hard and floppy drives, SCSI host adapter, CD-ROM, NIC, and so forth), and to interface software applications to hardware devices. Double-clicking on the Devices applet in the Control Panel will present you with a listing of all the device services currently installed on your system.

A service is started and stopped by the SCM when a user logs in and out, or the service may be set to continually run even if no user is logged in. Service information is stored in the registry and is maintained by the SCM. See the section "Starting and Stopping the SNMP Services" later in this chapter for more information on the features of the SCM.

Services Under Windows 95

Windows 95 does not have a Service Control Manager, or even a rudimentary equivalent. All services installed under Windows 95 are started when Windows 95 starts up, and are stopped when Windows 95 shuts down.

When Windows 95 starts up, all of the service applications listed under the RunServices and RunServicesOnce registry keys are started; they are stopped when Windows 95 shuts down. When the SNMP service is installed, the *SNMP.EXE* executable file is listed under the RunServices key. Entries found in the Run and RunOnce keys are run when a user logs in and are stopped when the user logs out. The entries in the RunOnce and RunServicesOnce keys are deleted from the registry after the applications are started. All four of these keys are located in the registry under the *HKEY_LOCAL_MACHINE\Software\Microsoft \Windows\CurrentVersion* key.

Under Windows 95, most services are stopped and restarted by either logging out of Windows and back on again, or by restarting the system. This is an extremely tedious process if you are constantly changing service parameters while developing software, or debugging a problem in an application. Some services can attach themselves to the task bar and present a menu allowing them to be paused (disabled) or stopped as needed.

The SNMP service under Windows 95 may be stopped and started by either restarting the system or by using the MS-DOS Console window. The command "SNMP" will start the service, and the command "SNMP -close" will stop it. You will be frequently stopping and starting the SNMP service to reload and test any extension agent DLLs that you are developing.

If you wish to install a Windows 95 service, or prevent a service from starting, you must modify the RunServices key directly. This key has the following syntax:

```
<app name> <path><executable name> <option 1> <option 2> ...
```

For the SNMP service the default key name and value appears as follows:

```
SNMP agent    "C:\WINDOWS\SNMP.EXE"
```

If you want to set some of the SNMP agent's command-line options, you can add them in this registry key as follows:*

```
SNMP agent    "C:\WINDOWS\SNMP.EXE /LOGLEVEL:10 /LOGTYPE:2"
```

You can also start a service in the MS-DOS Console window by executing the service application directly on the command line:

```
C:\> SNMP
```

See the section "Starting and Stopping the SNMP Services" later in this chapter for more information on the SNMP service's command-line options.

SNMP Agent and Management APIs

Microsoft SNMP extension agents and SNMP management applications gain access to the SNMP services using the SNMP extension agent and SNMP Management APIs. These APIs are accessed using a standard set of header files and import libraries distributed with the Win32 SDK, and a set of two SNMP API DLLs distributed as part of the SNMP services. The SNMP agent service and SNMP trap service both make use of the SNMP APIs.

Extension agents are implemented as 32-bit, multithreaded DLLs using the Microsoft SNMP API. The agent's code must include the header file *SNMP.H* and link the import library *SNMPAPI.LIB*. All extension agents use the *SNMPAPI.DLL* library at run-time for making calls to the SNMP API.

Figure 5-4 shows the file and library components used to build an extension agent DLL. The compiled source file(s) include *SNMP.H* and other required header files. The compiled object files are linked with the *SNMPAPI.LIB* import library and the module definition (*.DEF*) file. The resulting DLL is loaded by the SNMP service and uses *SNMPAPI.DLL* to make calls to the SNMP API.

SNMP management applications are implemented as 32-bit Windows applications, or as MS-DOS Console Mode programs, using the Microsoft SNMP Management

---

* Note that these command-line options are only supported by the checked build of the Windows NT *SNMP.EXE* file.

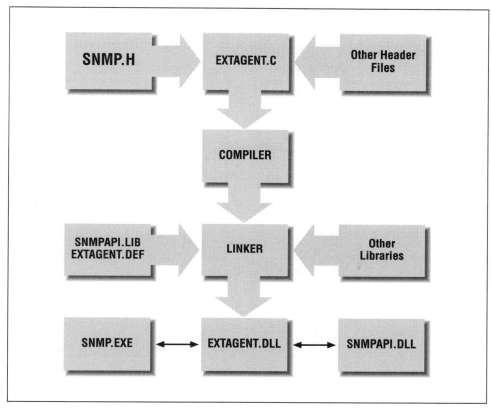

Figure 5-4. Building an SNMP extension agent

API. Access to the Management API is gained by compiling with the *MGMTAPI.H* header file and linking with the *MGMTAPI.LIB* import library. Because management applications will use function calls from the SNMP API, the *MGMTAPI.H* header file includes *SNMP.H*. Once import libraries *SNMPAPI.LIB* and *MGMTAPI.LIB* have been linked, the management application will then access both the *SNMPAPI.DLL* and *MGMTAPI.DLL* libraries at run-time.

Figure 5-5 shows the components and process used to build an SNMP management application using the Microsoft SNMP management API. The compiled source file(s) includes *MGMTAPI.H* and other required header files. The compiled object files are linked with the *SNMPAPI.LIB* and *MGMTAPI.LIB* import libraries and the application's module definition (*.DEF*) file. The resulting *.EXE* is run under Windows and uses *SNMPAPI.DLL* and *MGMTAPI.DLL* to make calls to the SNMP and Management APIs. Although the management application will not access the SNMP agent service itself, it does receive trap information from the SNMP trap service via the Management API.

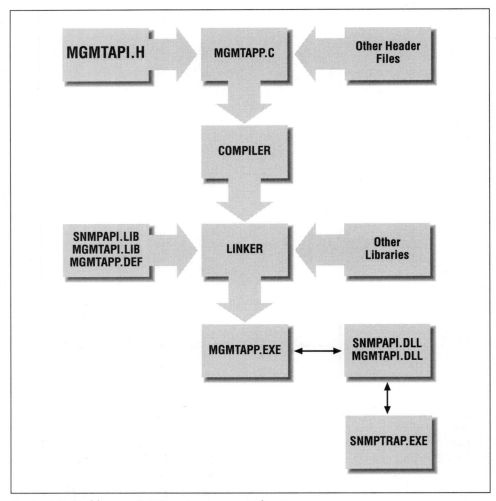

Figure 5-5. Building an SNMP management application

NOTE   Extension agents must be compiled as multithreaded DLLs. If you
                are compiling extension agent code using Microsoft C you will have
                to specify the /MD command-line flag. *MSVCRT.DLL* is the multi-
                threaded dynamic link import library for the *MSVCRT?0.DLL* dynam-
                ic link C run-time library. If an application was linked using Visual
                C++ 4.x, then the name of the dynamic link C run-time library will
                be *MSVCRT40.DLL*. Multithreaded C and C++ applications and DLLs
                compiled using Visual C++ require that the *MSVCRT.DLL* be present.

The SNMP API and Windows NT 3.51

Under Windows NT 3.51, the SNMP API was contained in the static library *SNMP.LIB*. Static libraries, however, cannot be accessed by non-compiled languages, such as Visual Basic. Microsoft has therefore discontinued support for the static *SNMP.LIB* library in favor of the dynamic link library *SNMPAPI.DLL*.

The *SNMPAPI.DLL* distributed with NT 4.0 is not directly compatible with NT 3.51. Microsoft has therefore released a version of the *SNMPAPI.DLL* library specifically for Windows NT 3.51 This file is found in the Win32 SDK version 4.0 in *\MSTOOLS\SNMPAPI* and should be installed in the *%SystemRoot%\SYSTEM32* directory of the Windows NT 3.51 system. Use the *SNMPAPI.LIB* import library distributed with the Win32 SDK 4.0 in place of the obsolete *SNMP.LIB* static library when you're building applications that call the SNMP API.[*] There are also several problems associated with extension agents developed using the SNMP API under versions of Windows NT earlier than 3.51.[†]

Most of these problems have to do with memory allocation and have been fixed by the revision of the extension agent code to only allocate memory using the SNMP API, and simply recompile using *SNMPAPI.LIB*.

No SNMP Management Service for Windows 95

Both Windows NT and Windows 95 support the SNMP agent service and API. Only Windows NT, however, supports the Microsoft SNMP trap service and Management API. Therefore, Microsoft does not provide an API for building SNMP management applications under Windows 95.

Why this oversight? And is it an oversight? Probably not. If you look at the Microsoft network management model for Windows 95[‡] you will notice that in the big picture of Windows system and network management, Windows 95 is conceptualized only as a system to be managed, and not as a tool to provide management. Microsoft's plan points to the Systems Management Server running on Windows NT as the ideal management platform. If this does not fit into your system management plan, you may instead choose one of the many third-party SNMP management tools available for Windows 95.

---

[*] See Microsoft Knowledge Base, "PRB: SNMP Applications Reference SNMPAPI.DLL on NT 3.51," article Q157599.

[†] See Microsoft Knowledge Base, "PRB: SNMP Extension Agent Gives Exception on Windows NT 3.51," article Q130562 and Microsoft Knowledge Base, "FIX: SNMP Sample Generates an Application Error," article Q124961.

[‡] See Windows 95 System Management Architecture, Backgrounders and White Papers, MSDN Library.

Why do so many vendors implement management systems only on Windows NT and not include support for operation under Windows 95? When compared to Windows NT, Windows 95 is a rather weak management platform. NT is far more robust than Windows 95. Its true preemptive multitasking makes it more stable. But the biggest advantage NT has is its security.

As we described in Chapter 1, *Introduction to SNMP*, SNMPv1 is not a very secure protocol. Perhaps the best way to secure network data is by encrypting the protocol messages themselves—a capability which SNMPv1 does not support. If the protocol itself cannot be secured, then security must come from the network elements that provide access to both the protocol and to the network itself. Windows NT, when configured and managed properly, is a very secure operating environment.

If you do need to implement SNMP management applications for use under Windows 95, take a look at the product references in Appendix A, *References*, and the product demos on the CD-ROM. There are several SNMP management libraries that will enable you to do Windows 95 implementation.

TIP   If you are thinking of moving the *SNMPTRAP.EXE* trap service and *MGMTAPI.DLL* library over to Windows 95 on the off chance that they might work, don't bother. SNMPTRAP is implemented specifically as a Windows NT service and will not be properly started by Windows 95. SNMPTRAP also uses a named pipe server to communicate trap information to the *MGMTAPI.DLL* library, and named pipe servers are not supported under Windows 95.

However, when *MGMTAPI.DLL* is moved to Windows 95, the Management API functions used to send and receive SNMP messages (but not receive traps) do work as expected. It is therefore possible to write Microsoft management applications that run under Windows 95.

Differences Between Windows NT and Windows 95 SNMP

Support of the Management API is not the only area where the SNMP service differs between Windows 95 and NT. We've noted that the lack of a Service Control Manager under Windows 95 requires the use of the MS-DOS Console window's command line to manually start and stop the SNMP service. Here is a complete list of deficiencies of the SNMP service under Windows 95:[*]

---

[*] See Microsoft Knowledge Base, "Differences Between Windows 95 and Windows NT SNMP," article Q139462.

- No support for the Management API (see the tip above)

- No support for the SNMP trap service

- The SNMP service cannot be configured using the Control Panel Network applet

- The System Policy Editor does not support all SNMP service parameters

Is the Microsoft SNMP Service and API Right for You?

The SNMP APIs discussed in this book are the creation of Microsoft specifically for the Win32 operating environment. These APIs are not portable to other operating systems (including the Macintosh), and are not compatible with other SNMP APIs, such as HP OpenView and WinSNMP.[*]

You might be tempted to say that an SNMP API exists for Java and that Java is a universal computer language; therefore, a universal API for SNMP does exist. However, this would only be true if Java were used universally by everybody and existed on every platform. But the programmers who are required to use C++, Delphi, Perl, and Visual Basic would hardly consider a Java SNMP API to be universal.

There is also the question of the robustness of the SNMP service itself. Searching through the Microsoft Knowledge Base articles using the keyword "SNMP" reveals that the SNMP service has had its share of bugs. And the single-threaded extendible agent will perform poorly when concurrently accessed by multiple—and demanding—management applications.

When you start to test your own extension agents, you will find that the majority of the time required to service an SNMP request is spent inside your extension agent and executing your code. SNMP performance problems are therefore typically the fault of some inefficient code that you have implemented, and not of any delays caused by the SNMP service itself.

So should you use the Microsoft SNMP agent or buy a third-party agent? That's really a decision you'll have to make based on your own testing and observation. The benefits of the Microsoft SNMP service and APIs include the following:

- Included standard with Windows NT Workstation and Server, and with Windows 95 OSR2

- Available as a free "CD-ROM Extra" for Windows 95

- Easy to install and configure

---

[*] Windows NT 5.0 will include WinSNMP 1.1a and full backwards compatibility with the existing Microsoft SNMP Management API.

- The agent is extendible and operates as a system service

- The agent complies with version 1 of the SNMP protocol (See Chapter 4, *Inside SNMP*, for an exception regarding the Set operation.)

- The SNMP service is actively maintained by Microsoft

While there seem to be no disadvantages to using the SNMP service as a standalone SNMP agent, there are a few things you need to consider about the Microsoft SNMP API.

One issue is complexity. Most SNMP APIs give you access to MIB databases, MIB compilers, data collection mechanisms, and other high-level features typically associated with SNMP agents and management systems. The Microsoft SNMP API only supports basic SNMP agent and management functions. If you need database access, then you must use the ODBC API; if you need low-level network access, then you must use the WinSock API; if you need to report a trap, then you must use the event logging API, and so forth. Experienced Win32 programmers might not consider this a disadvantage, but having to utilize so many different APIs (rather than a single, uniform API) does make the learning curve a bit steeper.

Another possible disadvantage is portability or, more precisely, the lack of it. If your code needs to run only under Win32 hosts, then you have no problems. But if your SNMP management or agent software needs to run under UNIX, the MacOS, or even Windows 3.1, and you want to reuse the code that you've written, the Microsoft SNMP API should *not* be your choice.

A final reason why you might choose not to use the Microsoft SNMP service is the apparent lack of human technical support—or even lack of knowledge about the service—on the part of Microsoft. If you are ever in a quandary over whether to use a native Win32 mechanism or to purchase a third-party alternative, try giving Microsoft's technical support a call and see what in-depth knowledge they have on the internals of their own products. Many people who have called looking for the SNMP service and API have received insufficient responses. This has prompted some of the people to ask for help on the Internet, or to disregard the use of the Microsoft SNMP API altogether. (Still others have been prompted to write books!)

Installing the SNMP Service

The Microsoft SNMP service is installed just as any other network service would be under Windows NT and Windows 95. The only requirement is that you first install a TCP/IP protocol stack under Windows before you install the SNMP service. The Microsoft TCP/IP-32 protocol stack is included with Windows NT and

Windows 95. And under Windows NT you must be logged into an account with Administrator privileges to install and configure the SNMP service.

If you have not already installed TCP/IP, refer to the Windows manuals, resource kit help file, or third-party TCP/IP stack documentation for information on how to install TCP/IP.* Once you are up and running with TCP/IP, you will be ready to install SNMP.

Table 5-1 lists all of the files that are installed as part of the Windows NT SNMP service.

Table 5-1. Files Installed as the SNMP Service

File	Description
INETMIB1.DLL	Extension agent implementing MIB-II (1.3.6.1.2.1)
LMMIB2.DLL	Extension agent implementing the LAN Manager MIB 2 (1.3.6.1.2.1.77.1.3)
MGMTAPI.DLL	SNMP Management API Library
MIB.BIN	Compiled MIB data used by the Management API
SNMP.EXE	SNMP agent service executable
SNMPTRAP.EXE	SNMP trap service executable

Several Microsoft networking products have MIB modules and extension agents that are distributed for each product to support an SNMP management interface. The MIBs listed in Table 5-2 are distributed with the Windows NT Resource Kit and with the Win32 Software Development Kit 4.0. All other MIB files are also included on the book's CD-ROM.

Table 5-2. Microsoft MIBs and Extension Agents

File	Description
DHCP.MIB	Extension agent implementing the DHCP server MIB (1.3.6.1.4.1.311.1.3)
DHCPMIB.DLL	Extension agent is part of the DHCP server installation
FTP.MIB	Microsoft Internet Information Server FTP server MIB (1.3.6.1.2.1.77.1.7.2.1)
GOPHERD.MIB	Microsoft Internet Information Server gopher server MIB (1.3.6.1.2.1.77.1.7.4.1)
HTTP.MIB	Microsoft Internet Information Server HTTP server MIB (1.3.6.1.2.1.77.1.7.3.1)
INETMIB1.DLL	Extension agent implementing MIB-II (1.3.6.1.2.1)
INETSRV.MIB	Microsoft Internet Information Server MIB (1.3.6.1.2.1.77.1.7.1.1)

---

* *Networking Personal Computers with TCP/IP*, by Craig Hunt (O'Reilly & Associates), contains a detailed description of the installation and configuration of TCP/IP under Windows NT 3.51.

Table 5-2. Microsoft MIBs and Extension Agents (continued)

File	Description
LANMAN.MIB	Original LAN Manager MIB. Superseded by *LMMIB2.MIB*
LMMIB2.MIB *LMMIB2.DLL*	Extension agent implementing the LAN Manager MIB 2 (1.3.6.1.2.1.77.1.3)
WINS.MIB *WINSMIB.DLL*	Extension agent implementing the WINS server MIB (1.3.6.1.4.1.311.1.2)

The extension agents DLLs for MIB-II (*INETMIB1.DLL*) and for LAN Manager (*LMMIB2.DLL*) are installed with the SNMP service. All other extension agent DLLs are installed when their respective services are installed.

Looks like MIB-I; Tastes Something like MIB-II

Note that the extension agent *INETMIB1.DLL* actually supports several, but not all, MIB-II objects as defined in RFC 1213. This extension agent DLL probably supported MIB-I (RFC 1156) prior to the March 1991 publication of MIB-II; and when *INETMIB1.DLL* was updated for MIB-II, it was not renamed appropriately. The RFC1156Agent registry key also bears this legacy.

The most important deficiency in *INETMIB1.DLL* is the lack of support for the snmp group of MIB-II (1.3.6.2.1.11). The IETF has declared support for the snmp group of MIB-II as being mandatory for all network nodes that implement SNMP. The snmp group was added when MIB-I was revised to MIB-II, but INETMIB1.DLL has yet to follow this revision.

Installing SNMP Under Windows NT 4.0

Follow these steps to add the SNMP service to a Window NT 4.0 system with TCP/IP installed:

1. Log in to the system using an account with Administrator privileges.
2. Double-click on the Network applet in the Control Panel.
3. Click on the Services tab.
4. Click on the Add button.
5. Click on the SNMP Service entry in the Network Service list box.
6. Click on the OK button.

Installing SNMP Under Windows NT 3.51

Follow these steps to add the SNMP service to a Window NT 3.51 system with TCP/IP installed:

1. Log in to the system using an account with Administrator privileges.

2. Double-click on the Network applet in the Control Panel.

3. Click on the Add Software button.

4. Click on the TCP/IP Protocol And Related Components entry in the Network Software list box.

5. Click on the Continue button.

6. Click on the SNMP service entry in the Windows NT TCP/IP Installation Options dialog box.

7. Click on the Continue button.

8. Enter the path to the Windows NT installation files.

9. Click on the Continue button.

For information on the SNMP Service Properties window that appears after the installation is finished, refer to the later section "Configuring the SNMP Service."

Once you have installed and configured the SNMP service, be sure to update the system with the Windows NT 4.0 Service Pack 2 or later, or the Windows NT 3.51 Service Pack 5 or later. The SNMP agent and libraries have been modified in these service packs to fix several known problems. If you have installed the latest service pack before adding the SNMP service, then you will need to reinstall the service pack after adding the SNMP service to update the necessary files.

Installing SNMP Under Windows 95

Installing the SNMP service under Windows 95 is a bit complex. Under the original distribution of Windows 95 (4.00.950) the SNMP service is not a standard network component. It is not included on the Windows 95 installation floppy disks, or CAB file distributions, or in the Windows 95 Resource Kit.

Instead, the SNMP service is bundled as a network management service in the Windows 95 installation CD-ROM. You will find the SNMP service stored as the self-extracting archive file *SNMPZP.EXE* in the *\ADMIN\NETTOOLS\SNMP* directory on the Windows 95 CD-ROM, and on the Microsoft FTP site in the *ftp://ftp.microsoft.com/Products/Windows/Windows95/CDRomExtras/AdministrationTools/NetworkTools/* directory. Once you obtain *SNMPZP.EXE*, move it to an empty directory or floppy disk and execute it. The archive will extract the following files:

```
INETMIB1.DLL  50,512   07-11-95   9:50a
SNMP.EXE      89,088   07-11-95   9:50a
SNMP.INF       3,008   07-11-95   9:50a
SNMP.TXT       1,110   08-17-95   1:28p
README.TXT     1,412   08-17-95   1:22p
LICENSE.TXT    3,315   08-15-95   9:13a
```

The file *SNMP.EXE* is the actual SNMP agent. When started by Windows 95 it will load the *INETMIB1.DLL* extension agent that allows the Windows 95 workstation to respond to MIB-II requests and send traps. The *SNMP.INF* file is used to install the SNMP service and contains a wealth of information on the registry keys created and used by the SNMP service.

TIP   If you have Windows 95 OEM Service Release 2 (4.00.95b), the SNMP service is included in the distribution as a standard network component. Therefore, don't bother obtaining *SNMPZP.EXE* before installing the SNMP service. The SNMP service files were not changed by Windows 95 Service Pack 1 or OSR2.

To install the SNMP service, double-click the Network applet in the Control Panel. The Configuration tab will display all of the network components presently installed. The TCP/IP network protocol must be installed before the SNMP service will operate. Click the Add button, select Service from the Select Network Component Type dialog box, and click the OK button and wait for Windows to finish building a driver information database.

Click the Have Disk button and select the *SNMP.INF* file in the directory where you expanded the *SNMPZP.EXE* archive (this "Have Disk" step isn't necessary with OSR2). Select "Microsoft SNMP Agent" and click the OK button. You should now see "Microsoft SNMP agent" displayed in the Configuration panel of the Network window.

Windows 95 may insist on copying several network files that are already in your *%SystemRoot%\SYSTEM* directory. You must either insert the Windows 95 installation floppy disks or CD-ROM and let it recopy these files, or simply enter the *%SystemRoot%\SYSTEM* directory as the source from which to copy the file. You will then be prompted to restart Windows 95. The SNMP service will not become active until the restart has completed.

At this point, the *SNMP.EXE* file is in the *%SystemRoot%* directory and the *SNMP.INF* file is in the *%SystemRoot%\INF* subdirectory. For some unknown reason, the *SNMP.INF* file does not contain instructions to copy the *INETMIB1.DLL* library to the *%SystemRoot%\SYSTEM* directory. You must perform this crucial step yourself or the SNMP agent will not respond properly to MIB-II requests.

Under Windows 95, the SNMP service does not have a menu item, a properties window, or any user interface. SNMP is configured by either installing and using the System Policy Editor, or by editing the Windows 95 Registry directly. The SNMP service is started when Windows 95 starts, and is stopped when Windows 95 is shut down. It may also be started and stopped from the MS-DOS Console window using the commands "SNMP" and "SNMP -close."

For information on configuring the Windows 95 SNMP service, refer to the later sections "Windows 95 System Policy Editor," "Using the System Policy Editor," and "SNMP and the Registry."

Configuring the SNMP Service

Most of the information used by the SNMP service that you will need to configure is available in the SNMP Service Properties window accessed via the Services tab in the Network applet. This window will also appear after the SNMP service is initially installed. The SNMP Service Properties window does differ in appearance between Windows NT 3.51 and 4.0, but the information is basically the same. To configure the SNMP service you must be logged into an account with Administrator privileges.

To open the SNMP Service Properties window, double-click the Network applet in the Control Panel, click on the Services tab, select the SNMP Service from the Network Services list, and click the "Properties . . ." button.

The Microsoft SNMP Properties window should now be visible. The three tabs contain most of the SNMP service configuration information that is stored in the Windows registry. The Agent tab (see Figure 5-6) contains the values for the sysContact, sysLocation, and sysServices MIB-II variables. The use of these variables is explained in the section "SNMP and the Registry" and in Chapter 4.

The Traps tab (see Figure 5-7) allows you to configure the IP or IPX addresses or DNS host names of the trap destinations. The case-sensitive community name that is encoded in each trap message must also be specified. Up to five trap destination addresses may be entered per community name.

To add a new trap destination community name, click in the combo box and highlight the community name that is there (if any). Enter the new community name and click the Add button. Now click the "Add..." button under the Trap Destinations list box. Enter the address or host name of a trap destination. Repeat this step as necessary.

The Security tab (see Figure 5-8) enables the sending of authentication traps and configures the communities that are considered valid by the SNMP agent. If no community names are listed, then all community names are accepted. The agent

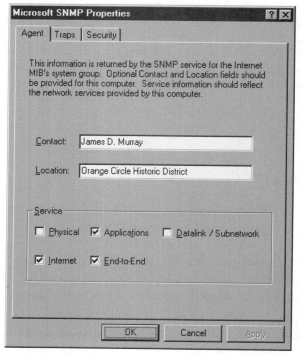

Figure 5-6. The SNMP Service Properties Agent tab

may also be configured to accept SNMP messages only from specific management hosts; to do this, you must specify the host's name or its IP or IPX address.

All security settings are global to the agent. For example, you can't associate a specific community name with only a single management host address. All permitted managers are considered by the SNMP service to be members of all the community names listed. And the concept of read-only community names is not supported.

New or updated properties information is not written to the registry until you click the Apply or OK buttons. Clicking the Cancel button or hitting the Escape key will discard any changes you have made in the Properties window.

Windows 95 System Policy Editor

The Windows 95 System Policy Editor allows you to edit the configuration of user accounts, user groups, and the network. Some, but not all, of the SNMP service's parameters may be configured using the Policy Editor. You can change those parameter values not supported by the Policy Editor by directly modifying the registry.

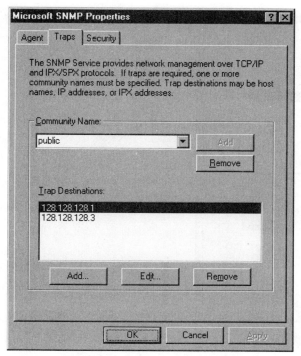

Figure 5-7. The SNMP Service Properties Traps tab

You can find the Policy Editor self-extracting archive (*POLICY.EXE*) in the *\ADMIN\APPTOOLS\POLEDIT* directory on the Windows 95 CD-ROM, on the Microsoft FTP site in the *ftp://ftp.microsoft.com/Products/Windows/Windows95/CDRomExtras/AdministrationTools/ApplicationTools/* directory, and in the Windows 95 Resource Kit. Sample policies are available in the Windows 95 Resource Kit, and on the Windows 95 CD-ROM in the *\ADMIN\RESKIT\SAMPLES \POLICIES* subdirectory.

Installing the System Policy Editor

Install the System Policy Editor by following the same installation steps used for other Windows 95 components:

1. Select Add/Remove Programs from the Control Panel.

2. Select the Windows Setup tab.

3. Click the Have Disk button.

4. Enter the path of the *POLICY.INF* file.

5. Select the components you wish to install by clicking the check boxes.

6. Click the Install button.

7. Click the OK button.

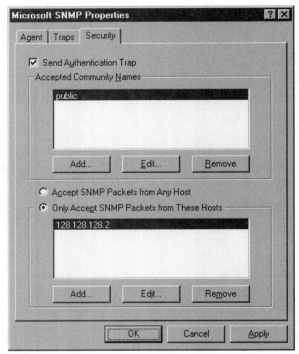

Figure 5-8. The SNMP Service Properties Security tab

The System Policy Editor will appear in the Start, Programs, Accessories, and System Tools menu.

Using the System Policy Editor

Start the System Policy Editor and select Open Registry from the File menu. The Local User and Local Computer icons will appear. Double click on Local Computer. On the Policies tab, select Local Computer, Network, and SNMP in the tree control. Four SNMP configuration options are shown (see Figure 5-9). Clicking on an SNMP option will display its configuration parameters.

You enable each option by placing a check in the check box by its name and entering the configuration information. You disable an option by removing the check. This will cause the associated information to be deleted from the registry. The Policy Editor will, however, save the information and restore it to the registry in case you enable the option again. You can change the option as described later.

All modifications made to the system policies are saved to the system registry. The registry is not actually modified until the File/Save menu item is selected. These are the options:

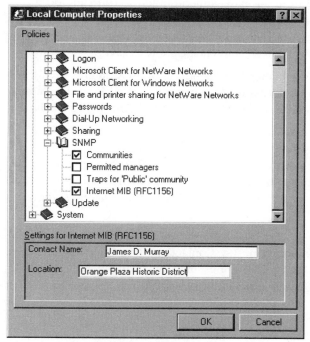

Figure 5-9. The SNMP service properties

Communities

Allows you to specify the SNMP communities to which the SNMP agent belongs. All listed communities are considered authentic by the SNMP agent, and the agent will process all requests sent to it by members of its own community. The default community is "public." If no communities are listed, or the "Communities" box is not checked, then request messages sent by any management system will be processed by the SNMP agent.

You can add a new community string by clicking "Communities" in the Policies tab, clicking the Show button, clicking the Add button on the Show Contents dialog box, entering the name of the new community, and clicking OK.

You can remove a community name by selecting the name from the Show Content dialog box and clicking the Remove button. These values are stored in the \Services\SNMP\Parameters\ValidCommunities registry key.

Permitted managers

A listing of IP or IPX addresses of network hosts that are allowed to make management requests of the SNMP agent. If no addresses are listed, or if the "Permitted managers" box is not checked, then the SNMP agent will process request messages received from all management systems. You can add a new permitted management host by clicking on "Permitted managers"; then click the Show button, click the Add button in the Show Contents dialog box, and enter a host name, IP or IPX address, and click on OK to save.

You can remove a permitted manager by using the Show Contents dialog box by clicking on the name or address of the manager and clicking the Remove button. These values are stored in the *Services\SNMP\Parameters\Permitted-Managers* registry key.

Traps for 'Public' community

Allow you to specify up to five trap destinations. Traps with the 'public' community name will be sent to each hostname, IP, or IPX network address listed. These values are stored in the *Services\SNMP\Parameters\TrapConfiguration* registry key.

Internet MIB

Allows you to set the Contact Name (sysContact) and Location (sysLocation) strings defined in RFC 1213. These strings may be changed by clicking on "Internet MIB (RFC 1156)" and entering the new strings in the edit fields. These values are stored in the *Services\SNMP\Parameters\RFC1156Agent* registry key. Note that the MIB-II system name (sysName) is not configurable using the System Policy Editor, but you may set it directly in the registry.

Starting and Stopping the SNMP Services

Under Windows NT, the SNMP service and trap service are started and stopped using the Services applet in the Control Panel. The name of the SNMP service is "SNMP" and the name of the trap service is "SNMP Trap Service." These are also the registered names used by these services to report events in the Windows NT system event log.

The Services window indicates the current status and startup type parameter of each service. Services may have a current status of Started, Paused, or Stopped. The startup type indicates how the service is to be started; here are the possible startup types:

Automatic

The service starts when the system starts.

Manual

The service must be manually started by a user or process after system startup.

Disabled

The service cannot be started.

Both the SNMP service and trap service may be Started and Stopped, but not Paused.

The default service parameter for the SNMP service is Automatic startup. The SNMP trap service, however, is set to Manual startup by default. If you will be using traps, be sure to change the trap service to Automatic startup. You do this by clicking on "SNMP Trap Service" in the Services window. Then click on the Startup button, click the Automatic radio button, and then click OK. Click on the Start button to start the SNMP trap service.

TIP   When the SNMP service is started, it reads the *snmp* port number listed in the *%SystemRoot%\SYSTEM32\DRIVERS\ETC\SERVICES* file (*%SystemRoot%\SERVICES* under Windows 95) and listens to this port for SNMP request messages. This port is *161/udp* by default, but may be changed to another port number to allow only a specific management system to send requests to the agent. The SNMP service must be stopped and restarted for the snmp port number to be read.

Starting and Stopping Under Windows NT

Starting and stopping the SNMP service is something you will be doing quite a bit if you plan on writing, testing, and debugging SNMP extension agents. You must stop and start the SNMP service each time you need to load an extension agent for testing. You will quickly find that the Services window is a very tedious way to repetitively start and stop the SNMP service.

Fortunately, under Windows NT most network services can also be controlled using the Network Redirector (*NET.EXE*) and the Service Controller (*SC.EXE*) from the MS-DOS Console window.

You can start the SNMP service from the MS-DOS command line using the following command:

```
C:\> NET START SNMP
```

When the SNMP service is started, *SNMP.EXE* is loaded by the Service Control Manager, and all of the extension agents listed under the *HKEY_LOCAL_ MACHINE\System\CurrentControlSet\Services\SNMP\Parameters\ExtensionAgents* registry key are loaded into memory and initialized. It typically requires only a few seconds to start the SNMP service, but the actual time depends on the number of extension agent DLLs that are being loaded and the time they each require to fully initialize. In any event, if any Windows NT service does not fully start within 30 seconds, the startup is aborted.[*]

---

[*] See Microsoft Knowledge Base, "Dealing With Lengthy Processing in Service Control Handler," article Q120557.

The SNMP service has two flags that can only be set using NET or SC.

The syntax of the NET command line is as follows:

```
NET START SNMP [/LOGLEVEL:level][/LOGTYPE:type]
```

The LOGTYPE and LOGLEVEL flags control the event logging messages generated by the SNMP service:

LOGLEVEL

> A numeric value in the range 1 to 20. Presumably, the greater the LOGLEVEL value, the more detailed events that will be logged. Experimentation, however, has shown that a LOGLEVEL of 10 seems to produce the most logging information.

LOGTYPE

> A bitfield value that indicates where logging information is to be written. A value of 2 specifies that SNMP events are to be written to the *%System-Root%\SYSTEM32\SNMPDBG.LOG* file. A value of 4 has log messages written to the Windows NT system event log. A value of 6 writes message to both the debug file and the event log.

These options are only supported by the checked build of *SNMP.EXE.*

Here's my personal advice:

1. Always use the checked builds of *SNMP.EXE, SNMPTRAP.EXE,* and *INETMIB1.DLL* when developing extension agents.

2. Use the log messages produced by the checked build of *INETMIB1.DLL* as an example of the type of debug log messages to include in your own extension agents.

3. Don't bother logging detailed debugging information to the event log. Typical SNMP activity can cause hundreds of debugging messages to be logged in just a few seconds. This defeats the purpose of the event log as a device to report significant system events. It is also more convenient to have SNMP debug messages logged to an editable file on disk, although debug messages written to the file do not include the sometimes useful time stamps found in the event log.

You can stop the SNMP service from the MS-DOS command line by using the following command:

```
C:\> NET STOP SNMP
```

When the service is stopped, all extension agent DLLs are unloaded from memory and Windows NT will no longer respond to SNMP requests or send traps. You must stop the SNMP service before you can load a new or revised extension agent DLL. Stopping the service will allow you to overwrite the previous extension agent DLL without causing a sharing violation. Starting the SNMP service will load and initialize the new extension agent DLL.

You can start and stop the SNMP trap service in the same manner as the SNMP service:

```
C:\> NET START SNMPTRAP
C:\> NET STOP SNMPTRAP
```

The trap service does not support any command-line options.

You can get help on the NET command by using the HELP modifier:

```
C:\> NET HELP START SNMP
```

You can find complete information on the command for the MS-DOS Network Redirector in the *%SystemRoot%\SYSTEM32\NTCMDS.HLP* help file.

You can also start and stop the SNMP service, and any other service, using the Service Controller (*SC.EXE*) included with the Win32 SDK. SC is actually an MS-DOS command-line version of the Service Control Manager and provides all the functions supported by the SCM. SC gives you more accurate control and information about system services than either NET or the Services Control Panel applet.

Issue SC commands as follows:

```
sc <server> [command] [service name] <option1> <option2>... .
```

SC uses RPC to control services on remote systems. If the service is on the local system, you can omit the <server> name. SC uses the same command syntax as NET to start and stop the SNMP service and trap service:

```
C:\> SC START SNMP /LOGLEVEL:20 /LOGTYPE:6
C:\> SC STOP SNMP
C:\> SC START SNMPTRAP
C:\> SC STOP SNMPTRAP
```

SC also lets you query the current status of a service:

```
C:\> SC QUERY SNMP
   SERVICE_NAME: snmp
       TYPE              : 10  WIN32_OWN_PROCESS
       STATE             : 4   RUNNING
                              (STOPPABLE,NOT_PAUSABLE,IGNORES_SHUTDOWN)
       WIN32_EXIT_CODE   : 0(0x0)
       SERVICE_EXIT_CODE : 0(0x0)
       CHECKPOINT        : 0x0
       WAIT_HINT         : 0x0
```

You can find the complete code for SC in the Win32 SDK and on the MSDN CD-ROM. Refer to the MSDN article "Using SC.EXE to Develop Windows NT Services" for more information.

Starting and Stopping Under Windows 95

There is no Service Control Manager under Windows 95. You must use the MS-DOS Console window to manually start and stop the SNMP service. The SNMP service is started by executing *SNMP.EXE* directly:

```
C:\> SNMP
```

The SNMP service is stopped by using the undocumented (or at least sparingly documented) "-close" flag:

```
C:\> SNMP -close
```

There is also a "-help" flag, but it isn't very helpful.

SNMP Service Event Log Messages

The free build of *SNMP.EXE* contains only a few basic event log messages, as shown in Table 5-3. The checked builds of *SNMP.EXE* and *INETMIB1.DLL*, however, contain much more detailed logging information, much of which is self-explanatory. These messages are not available under Windows 95, as there is no checked build of *SNMP.EXE* or *INETMIB1.DLL* for Windows 95.

Table 5-3. SNMP Service Event Log Messages

Message	Description
The SNMP service has started successfully.	The SNMP service has started and is running. (This message is logged regardless of the failure of any extension agent DLLs to successfully load or initialize.)
The SNMP service has stopped successfully.	The SNMP service has been stopped. SNMP requests and traps are no longer being serviced.
The SNMP service is ignoring trap destination <name or address> because it is invalid.	A trap destination host name or network address listed in the registry is badly formed or illegal.
The SNMP service registry key <key> is missing or misconfigured.	An expected key in the SNMP registry branch is missing or badly formed.
The SNMP service is ignoring extension agent key <key> because it is missing or misconfigured.	A registry key providing information about a specific extension agent is missing or badly formed.
The SNMP service is ignoring extension agent DLL <DLL file name> because it is missing or misconfigured.	An extension agent listed in the registry has failed to load or properly initialize. A failure to load may be due to the extension agent's DLL failing to properly initialize, an incorrect path to the DLL specified in the registry, or the DLL missing from the location specified in the registry.
The SNMP service has encountered a fatal error.	An unspecified error has caused the SNMP service to terminate.

Table 5-3. SNMP Service Event Log Messages (continued)

Message	Description
The SNMP service is not designed for this operating system.	The SNMP service was started under an incorrect version of Windows. The Windows 95 and Windows NT *SNMP.EXE* executables are not interchangeable and will not start under the incorrect Windows environment. It is also possible that the current SNMP services will not be compatible with future versions of Windows 95 and Windows NT.

Removing the SNMP Service

Normally there is no need to remove the SNMP service unless the initial installation has failed and you must attempt a reinstallation. You can temporarily stop or disable the service using the Services applet in the Control Panel (Windows NT), or by removing the "SNMP Agent" value from the *HKEY_LOCAL_MACHINE\ SOFT-WARE\Microsoft\Windows\CurrentVersion\RunService* registry key (Windows 95).

The steps to remove the SNMP service are nearly identical on all flavors of Windows.

Removing Under Windows NT 4.0

1. Double-click on the Network applet in the Control Panel.
2. Click on the Services tab.
3. Click on the SNMP Service entry in the Network Services list box.
4. Click on the Remove button.
5. Click on the Yes button.

You will be prompted to restart Windows. The SNMP service will not be stopped and fully uninstalled until the restart has completed. Alternately, you can stop the SNMP service using the SCM or MS-DOS Console window.

Removing Under Windows NT 3.51

1. Double-click on the Network applet in the Control Panel.
2. Click on the SNMP Service entry in the Installed Network Software list box.
3. Click on the Remove button.
4. Click on the Yes button.

You will be prompted to restart Windows. The SNMP service will not be stopped and fully uninstalled until the restart has completed.

Removing Under Windows 95

1. Double-click on the Network applet in the Control Panel.

2. Click on the Microsoft SNMP Agent entry in the Installed Network Components list box.

3. Click on the Remove button.

4. Click on the OK button.

You will be prompted to restart Windows. The SNMP service will not be stopped and fully uninstalled until the restart has completed.

The SNMP service may be removed manually by deleting its associated keys from the registry. Windows 95 reads the *%SystemRoot%\INF\SNMP.INF* file to determine which keys to delete. The following *HKEY_LOCAL_MACHINE* keys are deleted from the registry:

> *SYSTEM\CurrentControlSet\Services\SNMP*
> *SOFTWARE\Microsoft\RFC1156Agent\CurrentVersion*
> *SOFTWARE\Microsoft\Windows\CurrentVersion\RunServices\SNMP agent*

The *SNMP.EXE, SNMP.INF,* and *INETMIB1.DLL* files, however, are not removed from disk and remain in the *%SystemRoot%* subdirectories. You cannot reinstall the SNMP service using the *SNMP.INF* file that remains in the *%SystemRoot%\INF* subdirectory. You must use the original files supplied with the *SNMPZP.EXE* archive.

SNMP and the Registry

If you are interested in the modifications made to the registry when an application, service, or other Windows components is installed, then check out the installation file (*.INF*) for the application. The INF file lists all keys added or modified in the registry during the installation. The INF file itself is typically copied to the *%SystemRoot%\INF* or *%SystemRoot%\SYSTEM32* subdirectory. After installing the SNMP service you will find the *OEMNSVSN.INF* (Windows NT) or the *SNMP.INF* (Windows 95) installation file there.

NOTE   Many applications will add, modify, and delete registry keys during normal operation. To monitor changes to the registry as they happen, use the Registry Monitor (Regmon) and RegSpy95 utilities that are available on the Web at *http://www.ntinternals.com/* and are also included with the O'Reilly book, *Inside the Windows 95 Registry*, by Ron Petrusha.

Now let's have a look at the registry keys used by the SNMP service. If you need to change an SNMP parameter, it is very convenient to use the Registry Editor (RegEdit), but only if you know the name and location of the key you need to edit, and the possible values that may be assigned to the key. The Win32 API and Visual Basic provide several functions that allow you to manipulate the registry from within your applications (also described in the Petrusha book).

The SNMP registry keys are stored in the *HKEY_LOCAL_MACHINE* key and are identical on both Windows 95 and Windows NT. All of the data in *HKEY_LOCAL_MACHINE* is stored in the *SYSTEM.DAT* registry file.

Under Windows NT, the SNMP service software package is referenced in the *HKEY_LOCAL_MACHINE\SOFTWARE\Microsoft\SNMP* key:

```
HKEY_LOCAL_MACHINE\SOFTWARE\Microsoft\SNMP\CurrentVersion
   Description          "Simple Network Management Protocol service that enables
                        a Windows NT computer to be administered remotely with
                        an SNMP management tool."
   InstallDate          0x33191abe
   MajorVersion         0x00000004
   MinorVersion         0x00000000
   OperationsSupport    0c00000086
   RefCount             0x00000000
   ServiceName          "SNMP"
   SoftwareType         "service"
   Title                "SNMP Service"
HKEY_LOCAL_MACHINE\SOFTWARE\Microsoft\SNMP\NetRules
   InfName              "oemnsvsn.inf"
   InfOption            "SNMP"
```

This information is described in the *%SystemRoot%\System32\OEMSNVSN.INF* file used to install the SNMP service. Under Windows 95, the information on the SNMP service and installations can be found in the *HKEY_LOCAL_MACHINE\Enum\Network\SNMP* and *HKEY_LOCAL_MACHINE\System\CurrentControlSet\Services\Class\NetService* keys:

```
HKEY_LOCAL_MACHINE\Enum\Network\SNMP\0000
   Class             "NetService"
   CompatibleIds     "SNMP"
   ConfigFlags       10 00 00 00
   DeviceDesc        "Microsoft SNMP agent"
   Driver            "NetService\0002"
   MasterCopy        "Enum\Network\SNMP\0000"
   Mfg               "Microsoft"

HKEY_LOCAL_MACHINE\System\CurrentControlSet\Services\Class\NetService\0002
   DriverDesc        "Microsoft SNMP agent"
   InfPath           "SNMP.INF"
   \Ndi
      DeviceID       "SNMP"
      HelpText       "The SNMP agent provides administrators with
                     configuration information about this computer."
```

```
InfSection      "SNMP.ndi"
InstallInf      ""
\Compatibility
   RequireAny
\Install
   (Default)    "SNMP.Install"
\Interfaces
   DefLower     "WinSock"
   Lower        "WinSock"
   LowerRange   "WinSock"
\Remove
   (Default)    "SNMP.Remove"
```

Under no circumstances should you need to modify the information in these registry keys. This information is used to identify the SNMP service, and it can only be changed by Microsoft itself.

The keys you are most likely to need to modify are under the *HKEY_LOCAL_MACHINE\System\CurrentControlSet\Services\SNMP\Parameters* registry key (see Figure 5-10).

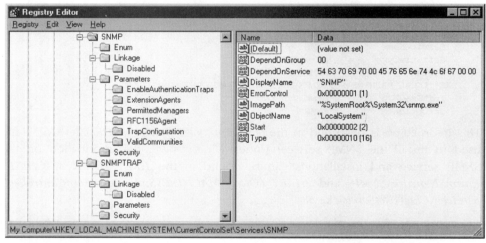

Figure 5-10. The SNMP registry keys

All of the SNMP parameters that are changed by the System Policy Editor or SNMP Service Properties window (and all of the parameters that aren't) are found under the SNMP key:

```
HKEY_LOCAL_MACHINE\System\CurrentControlSet\Services\SNMP
  \Parameters
    \EnableAuthentication
       switch       01 00 00 00
    \ExtensionAgents
       1               "SOFTWARE\Microsoft\LANManagerMIB2Agent\CurrentVersion"
       2               "SOFTWARE\Microsoft\RFC1156Agent\CurrentVersion"
```

```
    \PermittedManagers
        1              "123.123.123.123"
        2              "12345678.1234567890AB"
    \RFC1156Agent
        sysContact     "James D. Murray"
        sysLocation    "City of Orange Plaza Historic District"
        sysServices    4c 00 00 00
    \TrapConfiguration
        \public
            1          "123.123.123.123"
    \ValidCommunities
        1              "public"
        2              "private"
```

The parameters are summarized below:

EnableAuthentication

A Boolean value used to indicate whether an authentication trap is to be sent
if a PDU with an invalid community name is received by the SNMP agent. A
value of 1 (the default) enables authentication traps; a value of 0 disables the
traps. The trap is sent to all trap destination addresses listed in the *TrapConfiguration* key.

NOTE   The *TrapConfiguration* key disables the sending of the trap but
          does not disable the authentication process itself. This key was
          named Authtrap under Windows NT 3.1.

ExtensionAgents

An enumerated listing of each extension agent DLL that is loaded when the
SNMP service is started. The DLLs are loaded in the order in which the entries
appear in this key. Each entry is a pointer to a location in the registry of the
SOFTWARE key that contains the name and path of the specific extension
agent DLL. The *INETMIB1.DLL* is installed with the SNMP service. The first
value in the *ExtensionAgents* key points to the key describing the location of
the *INETMIB1.DLL* extension agent DLL:

```
HKEY_LOCAL_MACHINE\SOFTWARE\Microsoft\RFC1156Agent\CurrentVersion
Pathname                  "%SystemRoot%\System32\inetmib1.dll"
```

The *HKEY_LOCAL_MACHINE\SOFTWARE* key is used to store the parameters
of all software packages installed in the Windows workstation. The format of
the keys in this section are *SOFTWARE\MyCompany\MyApp\Settings*.

When you add custom extension agents, you will create new keys typically
based on the enterprise name to which the MIB is registered. For example,
the sample toaster MIB belongs to Epilogue, so the key describing the location of the Toaster extension agent DLL should be as follows:

```
HKEY_LOCAL_MACHINE\SOFTWARE\Epilogue\ToasterAgent\CurrentVersion
  Pathname                    "testdll.dll"
```

If you install the sample agents on the CD-ROM included with this book, their location will be described by the following registry key:

```
HKEY_LOCAL_MACHINE\SOFTWARE\O'Reilly\NtSnmpBook\Agents\CurrentVersion
  \MinAgent
    Pathname                  "minagent.dll"
  \RegAgent
    Pathname                  "regagent.dll"
  \TrapAgt1
    Pathname                  "trapagt1.dll"
```

If the path is not specified with the DLL file name, the default directory *%SystemRoot%\System32* is searched under Windows NT and *%System-Root%\System* under Windows 95. If a DLL listed is not found or fails during loading, a mention is made in the Windows NT event log.

PermittedManagers

An enumerated listing of the IP or IPX network addresses of SNMP management devices permitted to make requests of the SNMP agent. If an SNMP request is received from an address that is not in this list, the request is not processed and no response (or authentication trap) is returned. If no network addresses are listed in PermittedManagers, all received management requests are accepted.

RFC1156Agent

Contains the values of the read-write objects defined by the System group in the MIB-II Internet MIB. This information is read by *INETMIB1.DLL* when it is loaded by the SNMP service.

sysContact

The name of the user who manages the Windows workstation. The *sysName* key is the administratively assigned name of the Windows workstation. The *sysLocation* key value is the physical location of the workstation. And, the *sysServices* key contains a 7-bit binary value used to indicate the type of services the managed device may provide. This value is created by OR'ing the bits, from the table below, together.

Bit Field	Functionality	OSI Layer	Example
0x01	Physical	1	Repeater
0x02	Datalink/Subnetwork	2	Bridge
0x04	Internet	3	Multi-homed router
0x08	End-to-End	4	Host with a network address
0x10	End-to-End Interface	5	Session management protocols
0x20	Applications Interface	6	Terminal Protocols
0x40	Applications	7	SNMP Agent

Under Windows NT, these values are changed by using the SNMP Service Properties panel. Under Windows 95, they are changed either by using the System Policy Editor or by modifying the registry directly.

For Windows NT, the *sysDesc* is built out of several pieces of information in the registry. The registry keys queried to build the Windows NT *sysDesc* follow:

```
HARDWARE\DESCRIPTION\System\CentralProcessor
HARDWARE\DESCRIPTION\System\Identifier
SOFTWARE\Microsoft\Windows NT\CurrentVersion\CurrentVersion
SOFTWARE\Microsoft\Windows NT\CurrentVersion\CurrentBuildNumber
SOFTWARE\Microsoft\Windows NT\CurrentVersion\CurrentType
```

For example, the *sysDesc* for my workstation appears as follows:

```
Hardware: x86 Family 6 Model 1 Stepping 7 AT/AT COMPATIBLE
Software: Windows NT Version 4.0 (Build Number: 1381 Uniprocessor Free)
```

For Windows 95 the sysDescr is always "Microsoft Corp. Chicago Beta."*

TrapConfiguration

A listing of communities and hosts to which SNMP agents will send traps. This key contains one or more subkeys named after the trap communities. Each community name key contains an enumerated listing of IP or IPX network addresses. The community installed by default is "Public." Each network address listed under Public will be sent trap PDUs with the community name "Public." Additional keys may be added for other communities; for example:

```
\TrapConfiguration
   \Public
      1            "132.123.122.103"
   \Private
      1            "132.123.122.103"
      2            "12345678.1234567890AB"
```

Note that the SNMP agent encodes the community name in a trap PDU using the same alphabetical case as the *TrapConfiguration* subkeys. Community names are compared as strings of octet values. Therefore, the names "Public," "PUBLIC," and "public" identify three different SNMP communities. The Windows registry, however, is case-insensitive, and would regard these names as the same three key names. If you are having a problem with seemingly identical community names failing to compare, be sure to check the case of the names.

This key was named *TrapDestinations* (addresses to send trap, no default) and *TrapCommunity* (community name of traps, default "public") under Windows NT 3.1.

---

* See Microsoft Knowledge Base, "BUG: Windows 95 SNMP System Description Is Incorrect," article Q139461

ValidCommunities

An enumerated listing of the SNMP communities to which the SNMP agent belongs. Any request PDU received by the SNMP agent that does not belong to one of the listed communities will not be processed, and an authentication trap will be sent if the *EnableAuthentication* key value is 1. The default community name is "public" and additional community names may be added. If no community names are listed in *ValidCommunities*, all PDUs received are considered valid. This key was named *CommunityNames* under Windows NT 3.1.*

Once again, community names are case-sensitive. The community string in all received PDUs will be compared to the case-sensitive names stored under the *ValidCommunities* key. The first unidentical pair of octets to be found by the string comparison causes the PDU to fail authentication. If all octets are identical, then the authentication succeeds. A problem was identified in the SNMP agent under Windows NT 3.5 where the community name comparison would stop as soon as all the octets in one string had been compared. For example, the community names "public" and "publichouse" would have compared as identical.†

The *SNMPTRAP* key contains the configuration information used by the SNMP trap service (see Figure 5-11). There is very little data in the *SNMPTRAP* key and its subkeys, and you will not be making any modifications here. This key is not present in the Windows 95 registry.

Installing an Extension Agent DLL

When you finish writing and debugging your extension agent DLLs (covered in Chapter 7, *Writing Extension Agents*) you will need some way to distribute them. One way is to use any one of several Windows application installation programs available as commercial or shareware products. If you also need to install some other Windows application, such as an SNMP network management system or network monitor, this is the way to go.

The Microsoft extension agents distributed for Windows 95 and Windows NT are installed using device information (*.INF*) files. When you install the SNMP service, Windows NT reads the device information file *OEMNSVSN.INF* (Windows 95 reads the *SNMP.INF* file) to install the service application. The *INF* file is a custom setup script that instructs Windows how to install a set of files, where to copy them, and how to modify the registry and *INI* files.

---

* See Microsoft Knowledge Base, "SNMP Agent Responds to Any Community Name," article Q99880.

† See Microsoft Knowledge Base, "Windows NT 3.5 SNMP Agent Responds to Incorrect Communities," article Q130421.

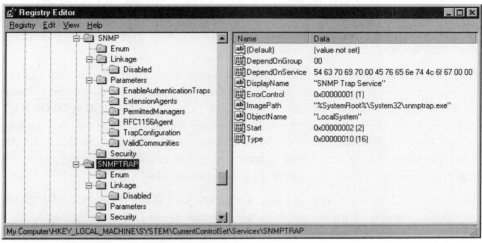

Figure 5-11. The SNMPTRAP registry keys

The Windows 95 Resource Kit describes how to create INF files and includes the Batch INF Script Editor utility (the kit and all utilities are available on the Internet as described in Appendix A). I recommend that you use the INF format supported by Windows 95 and not the older INF format supported only by earlier versions of Windows NT. This will allow you to write a single INF file that can be used under both Windows 95 and Windows NT.

While you are developing extension agents, and to make "quick fixes," you will use the Registry Editor to add, modify, and remove extension agent registrations. You can also temporarily disable the loading of a specific extension agent by changing its name or path in the registry. A warning posted to the event log by the SNMP service will verify that the extension agent was not loaded.

TIP   If you don't have RegEdit in your Start menu or as a desktop icon, then you can find it under Windows NT4 and Windows 95 as *%SystemRoot%\REGEDIT.EXE*, and under Windows NT 3.x as *%SystemRoot%\REGEDT32.EXE*.

Extension agent DLLs will typically be installed in the *%SystemRoot%\SYSTEM32* subdirectory under Windows NT, and in *%SystemRoot%\SYSTEM* under Windows 95, but they may also be located anywhere on your local file system. When the SNMP service is started, it reads from the registry the physical location of all extension agent DLLs that it is to load.

The installation of extension agents is performed using the same procedure under both Windows NT and Windows 95. The SNMP service must be installed before any extension agents may be installed. To determine whether the SNMP service is installed, you can check for the existence of the *HKEY_LOCAL_MACHINE\ SYSTEM\CurrentControlSet\Services\SNMP* registry key, which is created when the SNMP service is installed.

Each extension agent must be registered using a unique key in the registry. Because extension agent DLLs are associated with specific hardware or software vendors, the registration keys are located under the *KEY_LOCAL_MACHINE\SOFT-WARE* key, which stores registry information specific to the software configuration of the system. To install the O'Reilly extension agents included on the CD-ROM, you will make an *O'Reilly\SNMP\ExtensionAgents* branch to contain all of the registration information for the O'Reilly extension agents.

Figure 5-12 shows the *HKEY_LOCAL_MACHINE\SOFTWARE\O'Reilly\SNMP\ExtensionAgents* branch of the registry. Each extension agent DLL is registered using a separate key and a subkey, *CurrentVersion*, which stores the absolute pathname of the extension agent DLL. This is the actual information read by the SNMP service to locate the extension agent DLLs on disk.

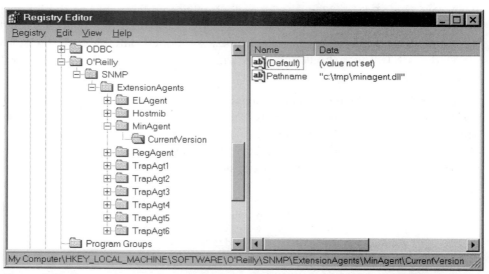

Figure 5-12. Extension agents registered under HKEY_LOCAL_MACHINE\SOFTWARE\O'Reilly

Create the *HKEY_LOCAL_MACHINE\SOFTWARE\O'Reilly\SNMP\ExtensionAgents* in the registry and one key for each extension agent you wish loaded by the SNMP service. Under each extension agent key, create a *CurrentVersion* key with the string value name "Pathname" and data value set to the absolute pathname of the extension agent DLL (e.g., *%SystemRoot%\System32\inetmib1.dll* or *D:\Agents\O'Reilly\MINAGENT.DLL*).

If the extension agent DLL stored in "Pathname" cannot be loaded or is missing, the SNMP service will mention this fact in the Windows NT event log (no warning message is given under Windows 95). Note that if you misspell the key value name "Pathname," the SNMP service will not be able to find the extension agent and will simply ignore it. No warning message will be written to the event log and you will be left scratching your head for an hour or more until you find the problem.*

Next, you need to point the SNMP service to the registration keys of the extension agents that you need to have loaded. This indication is given in the SNMP service configuration registry keys located at *HKEY_LOCAL_MACHINE\SYSTEM\ CurrentControlSet\Services\SNMP\Parameters.*

The subkey *ExtensionAgents* contains an enumerated listing of string values that contain the name of each registration key of the extension agents that are to be loaded, not including the *HKEY_LOCAL_MACHINE* top-level key name. Add to the list the registration keys of the extension agents you wish loaded. Figure 5-13 shows the *ExtensionAgents* key on my machine.

Name	Data
(Default)	(value not set)
1	"SOFTWARE\Microsoft\LANManagerMIB2Agent\CurrentVersion"
10	"SOFTWARE\O'Reilly\SNMP\ExtensionAgents\RegAgent\CurrentVersion"
11	"SOFTWARE\O'Reilly\SNMP\ExtensionAgents\ELAgent\CurrentVersion"
12	"SOFTWARE\O'Reilly\SNMP\ExtensionAgents\Hostmib\CurrentVersion"
2	"SOFTWARE\Microsoft\RFC1156Agent\CurrentVersion"
3	"SOFTWARE\O'Reilly\SNMP\ExtensionAgents\MinAgent\CurrentVersion"
4	"SOFTWARE\O'Reilly\SNMP\ExtensionAgents\TrapAgt1\CurrentVersion"
5	"SOFTWARE\O'Reilly\SNMP\ExtensionAgents\TrapAgt2\CurrentVersion"
6	"SOFTWARE\O'Reilly\SNMP\ExtensionAgents\TrapAgt3\CurrentVersion"
7	"SOFTWARE\O'Reilly\SNMP\ExtensionAgents\TrapAgt4\CurrentVersion"
8	"SOFTWARE\O'Reilly\SNMP\ExtensionAgents\TrapAgt5\CurrentVersion"
9	"SOFTWARE\O'Reilly\SNMP\ExtensionAgents\TrapAgt6\CurrentVersion"

Figure 5-13. Extension agents paths under \SNMP\Parameters\ExtensionAgents

Uninstalling an extension can be performed to temporarily disable the loading of a specific extension agent (like the one that GPFs each time it processes an OCTET STRING MIB variable and crashes the SNMP service, or even the Service Control Manager itself), or to remove an extension agent registration from the registry completely. Just delete the extension agent's registry key.

---

* Please benefit from my personal experience.

After performing any modifications to the SNMP registry keys, you need to stop and then restart the SNMP service for the extension agents to be unloaded and reloaded, and for any changed parameters to take effect.

Under Windows NT, you should always check the event log after loading any new extension agents to make sure that the DLLs were found and successfully loaded (see the earlier section "SNMP Service Event Log Messages" for SNMP service errors that may appear in the event log). Windows 95 does not provide an indication of whether an extension agent DLL was not found or failed to success-fully load, so you'll need to use an SNMP management utility, such as SNMPUTIL (described in the next section), to check whether the extension agent is responding.

SNMPUTIL: Testing the SNMP Service

Once the SNMP service has been installed and configured, and the system has been rebooted, the workstation will respond to SNMP queries. Both Windows NT and Windows 95 install the MIB-II extension agent; NT also installs the LAN Manager extension agent. So now all that's left to do is make a query to the SNMP agent and check for a response.

Microsoft provides an SNMP management utility, SNMPUTIL, that you can use to test the functionality of the SNMP service. In fact, you'll probably be using SNMPUTIL to test your own extension agents. The only unfortunate fact is that SNMPUTIL is written using the Microsoft SNMP Management API, so it won't run under Windows 95 (unless you copy *MGMTAPI.DLL* from a Windows NT system to your Windows 95 *%SystemRoot\SYSTEM* directory). To test an extension agent running on a Windows 95 system, you'll need an SNMP management application written using an API that operates under Windows 95 (such as WinSNMP), or you'll need to send management queries from a Windows NT host over a network.

SNMPUTIL is actually a Win32 SDK sample program used to demonstrate how to use the SNMP Management API. SNMPUTIL is an MS-DOS program and is typi-cally run in the MS-DOS Command window. SNMPUTIL is only available in the Win32 SDK and on the companion CD-ROM for the book *Internetworking with TCP/IP on Windows 4.0* from Microsoft Press.

TIP   If you don't have SNMPUTIL, then use the SNMPTOOL utility includ-ed on this book's CD-ROM. SNMPTOOL is an SNMP management utility that greatly improves on SNMPUTIL in several ways. Full source code is included.

The SNMPUTIL example includes an external makefile and is compiled using *NMAKE*. If you are using the Microsoft Development Studio (or other development platform) you will need to import the makefile and convert it to a project file. This procedure is described fully in the MDS Help file (under "makefiles, converting"). Here's the abbreviated run down of this procedure for Microsoft Visual C++ 4.x:

1. Select Open Workspace from the File menu.

2. Select "All Files (*.*)" in the "Files of type" combo box.

3. Select the directory where the project is stored (typically *\MSTOOLS\ SAMPLES\WIN32\WINNT\SNMP\SNMPUTIL*).

4. Select "Makefile" and click the Open button.

5. A message box will appear asking if you really want to convert the makefile to a Developer Studio workspace. Click the "Yes" button.

6. A Save As dialog box will appear, allowing you to save the new makefile to a different file name. If you want to keep the old makefile, then select a new name (*MAKEFILE1.MAK* is the default).

7. Select Rebuild All from the Build menu.

The command-line syntax of SNMPUTIL is shown below:

```
usage:  snmputil [get|getnext|walk] agent_address community oid [oid ...]
        snmputil trap
```

You can use SNMPUTIL to send a single GetRequest or GetNextRequest message. You can also have SNMPUTIL walk an entire MIB using a volley of GetNextRequest messages that listen for traps. It's usually best to open two MS-DOS Console windows and use SNMPUTIL in the first window to perform requests; start SNMPUTIL in the second window to listen for traps.

You will notice that SNMPUTIL does not include the Set operation. The current Management API does include the ability to perform Set requests, but this functionality was not included in the SNMPUTIL sample program, probably because of the extra overhead required on the command line. The SNMPTOOL utility on the CD-ROM supports the Set operation and the ability to read command-line data from a file.

Here are a few ways to use SNMPUTIL to test your SNMP service installation. Let's assume that the IP address of the agent is 189.112.208.25 and that a valid community name is "public."

1. Request the sysDesc from the agent using a GetRequest:

```
SNMPUTIL get 189.112.208.25 public 1.1.0
```

If you are querying an object in the MIB-II view, it is not necessary to supply the "1.3.6.1.2.1" OID prefix. For a get operation, you must always supply the ".0" instance identifier.

2. Request the sysDesc from the agent using a GetNextRequest:

```
SNMPUTIL getnext 189.112.208.25 public 1.1
```

A getnext does not require an instance identifier. If you were to perform a GetNextRequest on "1.1.0," you would receive a GetResponse containing the value of "1.2.0".

3. Request a non-MIB-II variable:

```
SNMPUTIL getnext 189.112.208.25 public .1.3.6.1.4.1.77.1.3
```

When you use SNMPUTIL to get or GetNext a value from a MIB other than MIB-II, you must prepend a "." to the OID. Otherwise, SNMPUTIL will infer that the entire OID you specified on the command line should first be appended to "1.3.6.1.2.1" before performing the operation.

4. Walk the MIB-II system subtree:

```
SNMPUTIL walk 189.112.208.25 public 1
```

You will receive a listing of the objects and values in the MIB-II System group.

5. Walk the entire MIB-II subtree:

```
SNMPUTIL walk 189.112.208.25 public .1.3.6.1.2.1
```

You will receive a listing of all MIB-II objects supported by the INETMIB1.DLL extension agent.

6. Configure the SNMP service to send traps to the host that is running SNMPUTIL. Now start up a second MS-DOS Console window and start SNMPUTIL listening for traps:

```
SNMPUTIL trap
```

From the first MS-DOS window, make a request but specify a community name that is not recognized by the agent. This will cause an authentication trap to be generated by the agent:

```
SNMPUTIL getnext 189.112.208.25 fred 1.1
```

In the trap window you should see the authentication trap (assuming that "fred" is not a valid community):

```
snmputil: trap generic=4 specific=0
from -> 189.112.208.25
```

When a message fails authentication, no response other than the trap is returned. SNMPUTIL will send the request a total of three times and wait six seconds between requests before giving up. One trap per response will be sent to the trap window.

NOTE   The agent must have authentication traps enabled and at least one
community name registered for this test to work.

---

7. You can also easily test traps by receiving the coldStart trap sent by the SNMP
   service when it is first started. With SNMPUTIL listening for traps in the
   second window, stop the SNMP service and then restart it. You will see the
   following indication by SNMPUTIL that it has received the coldStart trap sent
   by the extendible agent:

   ```
   snmputil: trap generic=1 specific=0 from -> 189.112.208.25
   ```

   Other methods of testing extension agents and the SNMP service are detailed
   in Chapters 7, 8, and 10.

6

Using the Extension and Utility APIs

This chapter describes the functions and data type definitions found in the Microsoft SNMP Application Programming Interface (API). You'll use this API to write extension agent DLLs capable of sending trap responses and processing SNMP requests sent to the Windows NT SNMP agent. Management API (MGMTAPI) applications also use the SNMP API for memory allocation and data conversion functions.

The SNMP API is actually a collection of four separate APIs used to construct the SNMP service, all extension agents, and SNMPv1 management applications. The APIs are as follows:

Extension API

This API is used as the standard interface to exchange data between the SNMP service and extension agent DLLs. When you're writing an extension agent, you'll implement the functions in this API to control how the extension agent processes request messages and sends traps.

Management API

SNMP management applications are implemented using the SNMP Management API. This API allows both Windows applications and MS-DOS Console programs to send GetRequest, GetNextRequest, and SetRequest messages, and to receive GetResponse and trap messages. Extension agent DLLs typically never need to call functions defined by the Management API.

Utility API

A collection of functions that enables both extension agents and SNMP management applications to easily create and manipulate data objects used by the SNMP API.

Service API

Win32 API functions that are used to implement the SNMP service (*SNMP.EXE*). This API is not called by management applications or extension agents.

NOTE   The Microsoft SNMP APIs were still undergoing development at the time this material was published. This information reflects the SNMP APIs as supplied by the initial release of Windows NT 4.0 and changes made by NT4 Service Pack 2 (December 1996).

Overview of the SNMP APIs

In Chapter 5, *Getting Started with the SNMP Service*, we discussed how to build extension agent DLLs and management applications using the *SNMPAPI.LIB* and *MGMTAPI.LIB* import libraries. Now we need to look at how the SNMP API is used in the operation of both extension agents and management applications.

An extension agent DLL must implement the SNMP Extension API to communicate with the extendible agent. The SNMP service provides the interface to the WinSock API for all network communications required by the extension agent. Both extension agents and MGMTAPI management applications also use the SNMP Utility API for performing memory allocation and data manipulation functions.

The Management API performs all SNMP management operations (Get, GetNext, and Set), and allows the management application to receive trap data from the SNMP trap service (*SNMPTRAP.EXE*). Both the trap service and the Management API interface to the WinSock API for all network communications required by the management application.

Both extension agents and management applications are, of course, free to use calls to other APIs, including the Win32 API.

Extension API

The Extension API is a set of four functions (summarized in Table 6-1) that are implemented in each extension agent DLL. The SNMP service and extension agent DLLs use this API to exchange data when servicing requests and traps.

The prototypes for these functions are found in *SNMP.H;* the code for the functions is found in each extension agent.

Table 6-1. SNMP Extension API Functions

Function	Usage
SnmpExtensionInit	Performs extension agent initialization and MIB object registration
SnmpExtensionInitEx	Provides multiple MIB object registrations
SnmpExtensionQuery	Processes Get, GetNext, and Set requests
SnmpExtensionTrap	Called to collect trap data from the extension agent

Management API

The Management API* is a set of seven functions (summarized in Table 6-2) used for implementing SNMP management applications as either Win32 applications or MS-DOS console programs. This API allows SNMP management applications to send SNMP request messages and receive SNMP response messages, including traps.

The prototypes for these functions are found in *MGMTAPI.H;* the code for the functions themselves are located in *MGMTAPI.DLL,* and are linked using *MGMTAPI.LIB.* The Management API is described in detail in Chapter 9, *Using the Management API.*

Table 6-2. SNMP Management API Functions

Function	Usage
SnmpMgrClose	Closes a network socket connection with an agent
SnmpMgrGetTrap	Retrieves buffered trap data from agent
SnmpMgrOidToStr	Converts an AsnObjectIdentifier to an OBJECT IDENTIFIER
SnmpMgrOpen	Opens a network socket connection to an agent
SnmpMgrRequest	Sends a Get, GetNext, or Set request to an agent
SnmpMgrStrToOid	Converts an OBJECT IDENTIFIER to an AsnObjectIdentifier
SnmpMgrTrapListen	Registers a management application to receive traps

Utility API

The Utility API is a collection of 14 functions (summarized in Table 6-3) used by extension agents and management applications to dynamically create and destroy memory objects that they exchange with the SNMP service and MGMTAPI. The prototypes for these functions are found in *SNMP.H;* the code for the functions themselves is located in *SNMPAPI.DLL,* and they are linked using *SNMPAPI.LIB.*

---

* Microsoft's documentation seems to be evenly divided between the names "Manager API" and "Management API." The title "Microsoft SNMP Management API" is more accurate, so that is what is used here.

Table 6-3. SNMP Utility API Functions

Function	Usage
SnmpUtilDbgPrint	Prints debug message to log file
SnmpUtilMemAlloc	Allocates memory
SnmpUtilMemFree	Frees allocated memory
SnmpUtilMemReAlloc	Reallocates memory
SnmpUtilOidAppend	Appends AsnObjectIdentifier objects
SnmpUtilOidCmp	Compares AsnObjectIdentifier objects
SnmpUtilOidCpy	Copies an AsnObjectIdentifier object
SnmpUtilOidFree	Frees an allocated AsnObjectIdentifier object
SnmpUtilOidNCmp	Compares N number of AsnObjectIdentifier OID subidentifiers
SnmpUtilPrintAsnAny	Prints an AsnObjectIdentifier value to the standard output
SnmpUtilVarBindCpy	Makes a copy of an RFC1157VarBind object
SnmpUtilVarBindFree	Frees an allocated RFC1157VarBind object
SnmpUtilVarBindListCpy	Makes a copy of an RFC1157VarBindList object
SnmpUtilVarBindListFree	Frees an allocated RFC1157VarBindList object

Service API

The Service API is used to construct the actual SNMP service (*SNMP.EXE*). This API is found in the *SNMPAPI.DLL* library as of the release of NT4 SP2. The function prototypes have not been included in the current release of *SNMP.H*, and the documentation for the SNMP Service API has not yet been released by Microsoft.[*] Table 6-4 simply lists the names of the SNMP API functions exported by *SNMPAPI.DLL*.

Table 6-4. SNMP Service API Functions

SnmpSvcAddrIsIpx	SnmpSvcGenerateTrap
SnmpSvcAddrToSocket	SnmpSvcGenerateWarmStartTrap
SnmpSvcBufRevAndCpy	SnmpSvcGetEnterpriseOID
SnmpSvcBufRevInPlace	SnmpSvcGetUptime
SnmpSvcDecodeMessage	SnmpSvcInitUptime
SnmpSvcEncodeMessage	SnmpSvcReleaseMessage
SnmpSvcGenerateAuthFailTrap	SnmpSvcReportEvent
SnmpSvcGenerateColdStartTrap	SnmpSvcSetLogLevel
SnmpSvcGenerateLinkDownTrap	SnmpSvcSetLogType
SnmpSvcGenerateLinkUpTrap	

---

[*] These functions will most likely not be formally documented until the release of the Windows NT 5 SDK.

The following sections describe the *SNMP.H* header and the
Utility APIs. Chapter 9 describes the Management API. As
mation on the Service API is not yet available from Mic
available, it will be included in a future edition of this book.

The SNMP.H Header File

All C and C++ source code modules that use the SNMP API must include the
header file *SNMP.H*. This header file is included in the Win32 SDK along with the
SNMPAPI.LIB and *SNMPAPI.DLL* libraries. *SNMP.H* contains all of the constants,
data type definitions, and function prototypes used by the SNMP API. You will
find it very useful to have a copy of *SNMP.H* in an edit buffer to use for reference
as you are writing your extension agents.

The definitions in *SNMP.H* are used by both SNMP management applications and
extension agent DLLs. The SNMP service itself also uses *SNMP.H*, and many of the
definitions found in *SNMP.H* are only used by the code for the extendible agent.
There are no differences in the SNMP header files or APIs between the Intel,
Alpha, and MIPS Windows NT platforms.

NOTE   The discussion in this chapter is based on the *SNMP.H* file, included
              with the November 1996 Win32 4.0 SDK dated 11-26-96 12:00pm,
              which is 16,987 bytes in size (no other form of version stamping is
              used with this file). Use this file in place of any earlier revisions of
              SNMPAPI.H that you may encounter.

Let's have a look at the contents of *SNMP.H*. In this discussion, excerpts from
SNMP.H are followed by their descriptions.

Constant Definitions

The first section of the *SNMP.H* file contains the constant definitions:

```
#include <windows.h>

#ifdef _cplusplus
extern "C" {
#endif
```

As with many Windows header files, the *WINDOWS.H* header is the source of
most standard Win32 constants and data type definitions. The *SNMPAPI.LIB* library
is a C language library and must be linked as such when used in C++ programs.:

```
#define SNMPAPI    INT
#define SNMP_FUNC_TYPE    WINAPI
```

Most SNMP API functions that return a value use the INT (32-bit unsigned integer) data type for the return value. Memory allocation functions return the type LPVOID, which must be cast to the appropriate data type.

WINAPI under Win32 has the _stdcall directive that explicitly declares a function to use the calling convention used by the Win32 API. Functions declared using the _stdcall directive have a specific calling convention.

- Arguments are passed in order from right to left.

- Arguments are passed by value.

- Called functions clear the stack.

- There is no case translation.

- The "mangled" (or "decorated" in Microsoft-speak) function name syntax is the following: _<function name>@<bytes in argument list>.

- The source must include a function prototype.

The /Gz Microsoft C compiler flag specifies that all functions not declared using another calling convention will use _stdcall.

```
#define SNMPAPI_NOERROR            TRUE
#define SNMPAPI_ERROR              FALSE
```

These are rather wordy definitions for TRUE and FALSE. Many of the functions in the Extension, Management, and Utility APIs return TRUE on success and FALSE on failure. Memory allocation functions return NULL on failure.

```
#define SNMP_MEM_ALLOC_ERROR          1

#define SNMP_BERAPI_INVALID_LENGTH    10
#define SNMP_BERAPI_INVALID_TAG       11
#define SNMP_BERAPI_OVERFLOW          12
#define SNMP_BERAPI_SHORT_BUFFER      13
#define SNMP_BERAPI_INVALID_OBJELEM   14

#define SNMP_PDUAPI_UNRECOGNIZED_PDU  20
#define SNMP_PDUAPI_INVALID_ES        21
#define SNMP_PDUAPI_INVALID_GT        22

#define SNMP_AUTHAPI_INVALID_VERSION  30
#define SNMP_AUTHAPI_INVALID_MSG_TYPE 31
#define SNMP_AUTHAPI_TRIV_AUTH_FAILED 32
```

These are definitions used to indicate errors in memory allocations, BER and PDU encoding, and PDU authentication. These values are returned by GetLastError when a Service API function fails.

```
#define SNMP_GENERICTRAP_COLDSTART    0
#define SNMP_GENERICTRAP_WARMSTART    1
#define SNMP_GENERICTRAP_LINKDOWN     2
```

```
#define SNMP_GENERICTRAP_LINKUP          3
#define SNMP_GENERICTRAP_AUTHFAILURE     4
#define SNMP_GENERICTRAP_EGPNEIGHLOSS    5
#define SNMP_GENERICTRAP_ENTERSPECIFIC   6
```

These are the possible values for the generic-trap field in the Trap PDU. All of these generic-trap types are defined by RFC 1157. If you are writing an extension agent for a private enterprise MIB that supports traps, then it will specify the SNMP_GENERICTRAP_ENTERSPECIFIC generic-trap type when sending a private enterprise trap. All other generic-trap type definitions are only used by the *INETMIB1.DLL* extension agent.

```
#define ASN_UNIVERSAL             0x00
#define ASN_APPLICATION           0x40
#define ASN_CONTEXTSPECIFIC       0x80
#define ASN_PRIVATE               0xC0

#define ASN_PRIMATIVE             0x00
#define ASN_CONSTRUCTOR           0x20
```

These are BER definitions. They are used only by the SNMP Service API.

```
#define ASN_INTEGER           (ASN_UNIVERSAL|ASN_PRIMATIVE|0x02)
#define ASN_OCTETSTRING       (ASN_UNIVERSAL|ASN_PRIMATIVE|0x04)
#define ASN_NULL              (ASN_UNIVERSAL|ASN_PRIMATIVE|0x05)
#define ASN_OBJECTIDENTIFIER  (ASN_UNIVERSAL|ASN_PRIMATIVE|0x06)
```

These are UNIVERSAL ASN.1 data types used by the extension agents to identify and validate MIB data.

```
#define ASN_SEQUENCE          (ASN_UNIVERSAL|ASN_CONSTRUCTOR|0x10)
#define ASN_SEQUENCEOF        ASN_SEQUENCE
```

These are table constructor definitions. MIB variables are only ASN.1 primitive types, so you probably won't be using these constructor definitions in any extension agents that you write.

```
#define ASN_RFC1155_IPADDRESS   (ASN_APPLICATION|ASN_PRIMATIVE|0x00)
#define ASN_RFC1155_COUNTER     (ASN_APPLICATION|ASN_PRIMATIVE|0x01)
#define ASN_RFC1155_GAUGE       (ASN_APPLICATION|ASN_PRIMATIVE|0x02)
#define ASN_RFC1155_TIMETICKS   (ASN_APPLICATION|ASN_PRIMATIVE|0x03)
#define ASN_RFC1155_OPAQUE      (ASN_APPLICATION|ASN_PRIMATIVE|0x04)
#define ASN_RFC1213_DISPSTRING  ASN_OCTETSTRING
```

These are APPLICATION types defined in RFC 1155—these definitions are used to more clearly document the type of MIB variables supported by an extension agent.

```
#define ASN_RFC1157_GETREQUEST     (ASN_CONTEXTSPECIFIC|ASN_CONSTRUCTOR|0x00)
#define ASN_RFC1157_GETNEXTREQUEST (ASN_CONTEXTSPECIFIC|ASN_CONSTRUCTOR|0x01)
#define ASN_RFC1157_GETRESPONSE    (ASN_CONTEXTSPECIFIC|ASN_CONSTRUCTOR|0x02)
#define ASN_RFC1157_SETREQUEST     (ASN_CONTEXTSPECIFIC|ASN_CONSTRUCTOR|0x03)
#define ASN_RFC1157_TRAP           (ASN_CONTEXTSPECIFIC|ASN_CONSTRUCTOR|0x04)
```

These are SNMP request and response type definitions. The SNMP service uses these values to indicate to the extension agent what type of request has been received. ASN_RFC1157_GETRESPONSE and ASN_RFC1157_TRAP are used only by the SNMP service.

Data Type Definitions

The next section of *SNMP.H* contains data type definitions that you will constantly use while designing and implementing extension agents and management applications. All of these data types are derived from fundamental Windows data types defined in *WINTYPES.H*. The only thing that you need to keep in mind regarding the size of these data types is that a BYTE is an 8-bit char value, and all of the other data types used are signed (INT, LONG) or unsigned (BOOL, UINT, DWORD) 32-bit integer values.

```
typedef struct {
    BYTE * stream;       // pointer to octet stream
    UINT   length;       // number of octets in stream
    BOOL   dynamic;      // true if octets must be freed
} AsnOctetString;
```

This is the definition of the ASN.1 OCTET STRING data type. An OCTET STRING is an array of 8-bit bytes, a length value indicating the number of elements in the array, and a Boolean value indicating whether the memory allocated for the BYTE array should be freed by the extendible agent when the AsnOctetString variable is destroyed. The dynamic flag should never be set to TRUE if the value of stream is statically allocated. Mismanaged AsnOctetString variables are a prime source of memory leaks within extension agents.

```
typedef struct {
    UINT   idLength;     // number of integers in oid
    UINT * ids;          // pointer to integer stream
} AsnObjectIdentifier;
```

This is the data type definition of the ASN.1 OBJECT IDENTIFIER constructor. An OBJECT IDENTIFIER is simply a variable that stores a "dotted decimal" Object Identifier (OID). It is represented by an array of UINTs and a length value indicating the number of elements in the array. There is no dynamic flag in AsnObjectIdentifier because the responsibility of freeing the memory allocated for the ids stream is left to the extension agent. Dynamically allocated AsnObjectIdentifier variables are also a common source of memory leaks in extension agents.

```
typedef LONG                    AsnInteger;
typedef DWORD                   AsnCounter;
typedef DWORD                   AsnGauge;
typedef DWORD                   AsnTimeticks;
```

These are UNIVERSAL and APPLICATION integer-based data types. AsnInteger is a signed 32-bit value used to store INTEGER types. AsnCounter, AsnGauge, and AsnTimeticks are all unsigned 32-bit values and are used to store SMIv1 Counter, Gauge, and TimeTicks values respectively.

```
typedef AsnOctetString          AsnSequence;
typedef AsnOctetString          AsnImplicitSequence;
```

These type definitions are not used by extension agents or management applications.

```
typedef AsnOctetString          AsnIPAddress;
typedef AsnOctetString          AsnDisplayString;
typedef AsnOctetString          AsnOpaque;
```

These are SMIv1 APPLICATION data types based on the AsnOctetString type. The name of each type definition indicates the format of the string data it contains based on its description in RFC 1155. For example, an AsnIPAddress variable can be expected to contain a stream of exactly four BYTE values that represent an IP address. An AsnDisplayString is an octet stream that contains only printable ASCII characters and is 0 to 255 characters in length. An AsnOpaque is used to store an arbitrary series of BER-encoded byte values.

```
typedef AsnObjectIdentifier     AsnObjectName;
typedef AsnIPAddress            AsnNetworkAddress;
```

These type definitions are used to either clarify the purpose of their base data type definition or to confuse the programmer. The name of an object is its OID value, so the AsnObjectName redefinition makes a bit of sense. Just be sure that you don't confuse OBJECT IDENTIFIER with object descriptor, which is the human-readable label given to an OBJECT-TYPE in a MIB.

Defining the type AsnNetworkAddress based on AsnIPAddress, however, is a bit of a misnomer. A NetworkAddress (as defined in RFC 1155) is a listing of different protocol family addressing formats, of which IpAddress is the type of only one choice—the Internet family (and the only choice in SMIv1). It would be more correct if AsnNetworkAddress were a union that contained an AsnIPAddress variable named "internet."

```
typedef struct {
    BYTE asnType;
    union {
        AsnInteger              number;
        AsnOctetString          string;
        AsnObjectIdentifier     object;
        AsnSequence             sequence;
        AsnIPAddress            Address;
        AsnCounter              counter;
        AsnGauge                gauge;
        AsnTimeticks            ticks;
```

```
        AsnOpaque                arbitrary;
    } asnValue;
} AsnAny;

typedef AsnAny              AsnObjectSyntax;
```

AsnAny is a structure that stores data of any of the ASN.1 types defined in *SNMP.H*. This structure is used to define variable bindings that are passed between an extension agent and the SNMP service, and is used as a formal parameter data type by several SNMP API functions.

```
typedef struct vb {
    AsnObjectName   name;      // variable's object identifier
    AsnObjectSyntax value;     // variable's value (in asn terms)
} RFC1157VarBind;
```

RFC1157VarBind is the definition for a single SNMP PDU variable binding. Each binding contains an OBJECT IDENTIFIER and its length, and the object value and its data type. Data passed between the SNMP service and extension agents is in the form of variable bindings stored in a variable binding list.

```
typedef struct {
    RFC1157VarBind * list;     // array of variable bindings
    UINT             len;      // number of bindings in array
} RFC1157VarBindList;
```

RFC1157VarBindList is the definition for a variable binding list. This structure contains a pointer to an array of RFC1157VarBind structures and a count of the number of varbinds in the list. This data type is found in the parameters list of several SNMP API functions.

```
#define SNMP_LOG_SILENT    0x0
#define SNMP_LOG_FATAL     0x1
#define SNMP_LOG_ERROR     0x2
#define SNMP_LOG_WARNING   0x3
#define SNMP_LOG_TRACE     0x4
#define SNMP_LOG_VERBOSE   0x5
```

These are values used as the first parameter of the SnmpUtilDbgPrint function. This function is not documented, so the meaning of each value can only be presumed.

```
#define SNMP_MAX_OID_LEN   0x7f00 // max number of elements in oid
```

This is the maximum number of subidentifiers in an object identifier that is supported by the SNMP service. A more practical limit to the number of subidentifiers in an OID is 128.

```
#ifndef SNMPSTRICT

#define SNMP_oidcpy              SnmpUtilOidCpy
#define SNMP_oidappend           SnmpUtilOidAppend
#define SNMP_oidncmp             SnmpUtilOidNCmp
```

```
#define SNMP_oidcmp          SnmpUtilOidCmp
#define SNMP_oidfree         SnmpUtilOidFree

#define SNMP_CopyVarBindList SnmpUtilVarBindListCpy
#define SNMP_FreeVarBindList SnmpUtilVarBindListFree
#define SNMP_CopyVarBind     SnmpUtilVarBindCpy
#define SNMP_FreeVarBind     SnmpUtilVarBindFree

#define SNMP_printany        SnmpUtilPrintAsnAny

#define SNMP_free            SnmpUtilMemFree
#define SNMP_malloc          SnmpUtilMemAlloc
#define SNMP_realloc         SnmpUtilMemReAlloc

#define SNMP_DBG_free        SnmpUtilMemFree
#define SNMP_DBG_malloc      SnmpUtilMemAlloc
#define SNMP_DBG_realloc     SnmpUtilMemReAlloc

#endif // SNMPSTRICT
```

These are definitions used to support older SNMP Utility API function names. Under Windows NT 3.x, the SNMP Utility library used the SNMP_* function names and was stored in the *SNMP.LIB* static link library. Under NT 4.0, *SNMP.LIB* was discarded and these functions were moved to the *SNMPAPI.DLL* dynamic link library. Furthermore, they were renamed using the SnmpUtil* function naming convention.*

Most Microsoft code examples that use the SNMP APIs use these older API names. You should always use the SnmpUtil* names in your extension agent code. Defining SNMPSTRICT in your code will disable support for the older SNMP_* function names.

The remaining code in *SNMP.H* is the SNMP Utility API function prototype definitions. These API functions are covered later in this chapter.

SNMP API Data Types

This section describes each of the ASN.1 data types specified by SMIv1 for use in the SNMPv1 protocol. It also looks at the equivalent C data type definitions that you will use when converting a MIB module to C code for use in your extension agents.

There are only three primitive (or UNIVERSAL) ASN.1 data types that are allowed by the SMIv1 to be used in SNMP MIB modules: INTEGER, OCTET STRING, and

---

* This was done primarily to enable languages that cannot link to a static C library—most notably Visual Basic—to use the SNMP API.

OBJECT IDENTIFIER. All of the other data types are derived from these three data types.

INTEGER

AsnInteger represents the SMIv1 INTEGER type. Neither ASN.1 nor SMIv1 assigns any definite size to the INTEGER data type. Many SNMP agent implementations, including the Microsoft SNMP service, define an INTEGER as a signed, 32-bit value in the range -2147483648 to 2147483647.

In Chapter 4, *Inside SNMP*, we described how the SIZE clause of a MIB variable may be used to restrict the range of an object type. It is very important to understand how to correctly interpret such INTEGER subtypes because the extension agents you write will be responsible for all range checking of values for objects.

Range checking is used primarily to determine whether the value in the variable bindings of a SetRequest is within the bounds given in the SYNTAX clause for the specified MIB variable. SetRequest values that are out of the range specified by the INTEGER subtype (or system default) are rejected with a badValue error. If no subtyping is present for a specific INTEGER variable, the agent must assume the system's default range for the INTEGER type.

OCTET STRING

AsnOctetString represents the SMIv1 OCTET STRING type. Under ASN.1 an OCTET STRING is an ordered stream of octets representing textual or binary data. And as we've seen, an AsnOctetString object is simply an array of BYTE values and an unsigned integer specifying the number of values in the array. A byte value of zero (NULL) stored in an AsnOctetString object does not mark the end of the string.

Neither ASN.1 nor SMIv1 assigns any definite maximum length to the OCTET STRING type. Agent implementations will limit the size to something practical for the system (such as 256, 512, or 1024 octets). Under the Microsoft SNMP service, the limit is how much memory your extension agent may allocate, or whatever you consider to be practical. Note that an OCTET STRING value must be passed in an SNMP message, which is typically restricted in length to between 484 and 1490 octets.

An extension agent is responsible for checking the length of each OCTET STRING value specified in a SetRequest. If the length of the new OCTET STRING is not within the range(s) specified for the MIB variable, the agent must return a badValue error. If the OCTET STRING in the SetRequest is within the SIZE range specified in the MIB, but the string value exceeds the system's maximum limit on the length of OCTET STRINGs or a memory allocation error occurs, then a genErr error should be returned.

AsnOctetString variables may be statically or dynamically allocated. You may statically or dynamically allocate the array of BYTE values used to store the OCTET STRING value itself. Example 6-1 shows how to create AsnOctetString objects both at compile-time and at run-time.

Example 6-1. Creating and initializing AsnOctetString objects

```
#include <snmp.h>

BYTE bString[] = "My string";

/* Compile-time static allocation and initialization */
AsnOctetString os = { bString, sizeof( bString ) - 1, FALSE };
AsnOctetString os2;
AsnOctetString *pOs;
printf("%*s\n", os.length, os.stream );

/* Compile-time static allocation and run-time dynamic initialization */
os2.length = sizeof( bString ) - 1;
os2.stream = (BYTE *) SnmpUtilMemAlloc( os2.length );
os2.dynamic = TRUE;
memcpy( os2.stream, bString, os2.length );
printf("%*s\n", os2.length, os2.stream );
SnmpUtilMemFree( os2.stream );

/* Run-time dynamic allocation and initialization */
pOs = (AsnOctetString *) SnmpUtilMemAlloc( sizeof( AsnOctetString ) );
pOs->length = sizeof( bString ) - 1;
pOs->stream = (BYTE *) SnmpUtilMemAlloc( pOs->length );
pOs->dynamic = TRUE;
memcpy( pOs->stream, bString, pOs->length );
printf("%*s\n", pOs->length, pOs->stream );
SnmpUtilMemFree( pOs->stream );
SnmpUtilMemFree( pOs );
```

OBJECT IDENTIFIER

AsnObjectIdentifier represents the SMIv1 OBJECT IDENTIFIER type. The AsnObjectIdentifier object is an array of UINT values and an unsigned integer specifying the number of elements in the array (which is also the number of subidentifiers in the OID).

Neither ASN.1 nor SMIv1 assigns any definite maximum size nor maximum number of subidentifiers that may be present in the OBJECT IDENTIFIER type. However, subidentifiers are commonly defined as 32-bit unsigned integer values (0 to 4294967295), and the practical limit on the number of subidentifiers in an

OID is typically 128. There is no subtype or SIZE clause to restrict the length of an OBJECT IDENTIFIER.

AsnObjectIdentifier objects may be statically or dynamically allocated. Example 6-2 shows how to create them both at compile time and run time.

Example 6-2. Creating and initializing AsnObjectIdentifier objects

```
#include <snmp.h>

/* Compile-time static allocation and initialization */
UINT wOid[] = { 1, 3, 6, 1, 4, 1, 9999, 1 };
AsnObjectIdentifier oid = { sizeof( wOid ) / sizeof( UINT ), wOid };
AsnObjectIdentifier oid2;
AsnObjectIdentifier *pOid;

/* Compile-time static allocation and run-time dynamic initialization */
oid2.idLength = sizeof( wOid ) / sizeof(UINT);
oid2.ids = (UINT *) SnmpUtilMemAlloc( oid2.idLength * sizeof(UINT) );
memcpy(oid2.ids, wOid, oid2.idLength * sizeof(UINT) );

SnmpUtilMemFree( oid2.ids );

/* Compile-time dynamic allocation and initialization */
pOid = (AsnObjectIdentifier *) SnmpUtilMemAlloc( sizeof(AsnObjectIdentifier) );
pOid->idLength = sizeof( wOid ) / sizeof(UINT);
pOid->ids = (UINT *) SnmpUtilMemAlloc( pOid->idLength * sizeof(UINT) );
memcpy( pOid->ids, wOid, pOid->idLength * sizeof(UINT) );

SnmpUtilMemFree( pOid->ids );
SnmpUtilMemFree( pOid );
```

APPLICATION Types

The SMIv1 defines several new data types for use specifically in the SNMPv1 protocol. Each of these types is a redefinition of the INTEGER and OCTET STRING simple types.

The INTEGER-based APPLICATION types are Counter, Gauge, and TimeTicks. *SNMP.H* defines the 32-bit unsigned data types AsnCounter, AsnGauge, and AsnTimeticks to represent these SNMv1 types. The range of each of these types is always 0 to 4294967295.

The OCTET STRING-based APPLICATION types are IpAddress, DisplayString, and Opaque, and are defined in *SNMP.H* using the AsnOctetString data type. IpAddress is always four octets in length and is assumed to store a 4-byte IPv4 address. A DisplayString variable always contains 0 to 255 printable characters. And the octets stored in an Opaque object always represent the BER serialization of ASN.1 values.

SNMP.H also defines AsnSequence and AsnImplicitSequence as AsnOctetString types, but these types are not used by extension agents or management applications.

The Extension API

The four functions found in the Extension API are implemented in extension agent DLLs and are called by the SNMP service. Three of these functions, SnmpExtensionInit, SnmpExtensionQuery, and SnmpExtensionTrap, must appear in every extension agent DLL. The fourth, SnmpExtensionInitEx, is optional and is present only if needed. Each extension agent DLL uses only the Extension API to communicate with the SNMP service. No active thread of execution is required in an extension agent DLL, but one may be created if needed.

A View to a MIB

Microsoft's SNMP documentation incorrectly uses the term *MIB view* to describe the set of managed objects supported by an extension agent. A MIB view is an administratively defined collection of managed objects that are all made locally accessible by a single SNMP agent. The objects in a MIB view are determined by the administrative policy for access control and not by the access methods of the managed objects. The collection of objects supported by an extension agent is therefore not a MIB view, and is instead simply a set of registered objects. The SNMP service has only one MIB view, which contains all of the objects accessible from all loaded extension agents.

SnmpExtensionInit

When the SNMP service starts up, it reads from the registry a list of all of the extension agent DLLs it is to load. After an extension agent DLL is successfully loaded, the SNMP service calls the SnmpExtensionInit function defined in the DLL to supply the extension agent with some startup data, and also receives service initialization information from the DLL. Figure 6-1 illustrates the data passed between the SNMP service and an extension agent using SnmpExtensionInit.

Here is the function prototype of SnmpExtensionInit:

```
BOOL WINAPI SnmpExtensionInit(
    DWORD                  dwTimeZeroReference,    /* IN */
    HANDLE                 *phPollForTrapEvent,    /* OUT */
    AsnObjectIdentifier    *pSupportedView );      /* OUT */
```

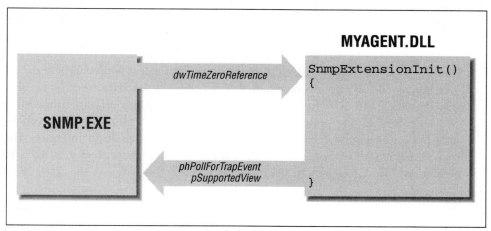

Figure 6-1. Data passed using SnmpExtensionInit

SnmpExtensionInit must return TRUE if the initialization succeeded, or FALSE if the initialization fails in some way. If FALSE is returned, the SNMP service will not register the extension agent, and the failure of the extension agent to start is noted in the system event log. The extension agent DLL will remain loaded in memory, but will never be called by the SNMP service.

The parameters are described here:

dwTimeZeroReference

This time value is the number of centiseconds that have elapsed since the SNMP service was started. This value must be stored by the extension agent and subtracted from the value returned by the GetTickCount Win32 API call, divided by 10 to determine the amount of time the system has been up. The resulting value is used as part of the data included with all trap PDUs, and in any MIB variables that keep track of the system uptime as well. This reference value will not represent the actual system startup time if the SNMP service has been restarted since the system was booted up.

NOTE   The 32-bit time value returned by GetTickCount will wrap to zero after 49.71 days (4294967295 milliseconds). If you believe that it is possible for a Windows system to not require restarting within this duration, then your code will need to check whether the current time value is less than the dwTimeZeroReference value and adjust accordingly.

---

phPollForTrapEvent

> This is the handle of the event that will be asserted by the extension agent when it needs to send a trap. This event is created by the extension agent using Creativeness, is passed to the SNMP service using phPollForTrapEvent, and the event is triggered by the extension agent using SetEvent. The extension agent signals this event when it has collected the data for a Trap PDU and it needs the SNMP service to call the SnmpExtensionTrap function to retrieve the data and send the trap message. The extension agent is responsible for closing this event handle before it is unloaded from memory. The value of this handle is set to NULL if the extension agent does not need to send traps.

pSupportedView

> The object identifier of the MIB subtree supported by the extension agent. This value is an OID that represents the branch of the MIB tree that is supported. For example, specifying a subtree OID of 1.3.6.1.4.1.9999.1 indicates to the SNMP agent that this extension agent will handle all SNMP requests that specify MIB variables that begin with this OID prefix. If multiple extension agents register the same subtree OID, varbinds specifying objects in that subtree will only be passed to the first extension agent that registered the OID. Multiple subtrees are registered with the SNMP service using the optional SnmpExtensionInitEx API call.

WARNING   Never set the pSupportedView pointer or its contents to NULL. Doing so disables the SNMP service's ability to service all loaded extension agents.

Example 6-3 shows a minimal SnmpExtensionInit that supports traps. If your extension agent doesn't have a need to generate traps, you will not need to call CreateEvent or use the hTrapEvent variable. Most extension agents will have additional initialization that must be performed after the DLL has completely loaded. Such initialization includes allocating memory, creating threads and processes, and writing to the system event log. SnmpExtensionInit is where such initialization will occur.

Example 6-3. A typical implementation of SnmpExtensionInit

```
#include <snmp.h>

DWORD dwTimeZero = 0;
HANDLE ghTrapEvent = NULL;
UINT OID_Prefix[] = { 1, 3, 6, 1, 4, 1, 2035, 1, 10 };
AsnObjectIdentifier OidMibPrefix = {
    sizeof( OidMibPrefix ) / sizeof( UINT ),
```

Example 6-3. A typical implementation of SnmpExtensionInit (continued)

```
    OidMibPrefix
};

BOOL WINAPI SnmpExtensionInit(
    DWORD    dwTimeZeroReference,
    HANDLE *phPollForTrapEvent,
    AsnObjectIdentifier *pSupportedView )
{
    BOOL fResult = TRUE;

    /* Create an event asserted by the extension agent when a trap occurs */
    *phPollForTrapEvent = CreateEvent( NULL, FALSE, FALSE, NULL );

    if ( *phPollForTrapEvent != NULL )
    {
        /* Save the trap event handle for use by the extension agent */
        ghTrapEvent = *phPollForTrapEvent;

        /* Convey the managed subtree to the extension agent */
        *pSupportedView = MIB_OidPrefix;

        /* Record the time the DLL was loaded */
        dwTimeZero = dwTimeZeroReference;

        /*
        ** Perform extension agent-specific initialization here
        */
    }
    else
        fResult = FALSE;     /* CreateEvent() failed */

    return( fResult );    /* Return initalization result */
}
```

SnmpExtensionInitEx

When an extension agent is loaded (and following the call to SnmpExtensionInit), the SNMP service performs a GetProcAddress call on the DLL in an attempt to find the address of the function SnmpExtensionInitEx. If this function is present in the extension agent DLL, then the service calls it repeatedly to obtain the OIDs of additional MIB branches or subtrees registered by the extension agent; one subtree OID is returned per call. If SnmpExtensionInitEx is not present, no additional MIB subtrees are supported by the extension agent DLL. Figure 6-2 illustrates the data passed between the SNMP service and an extension agent using SnmpExtensionInitEx.

Here is the function prototype of SnmpExtensionInitEx:

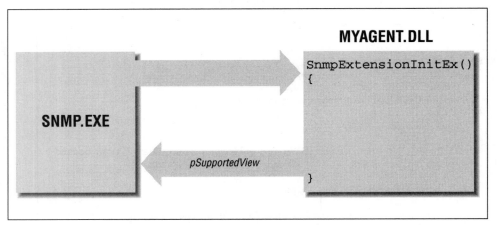

Figure 6-2. Data passed using SnmpExtensionInitEx

```
BOOL WINAPI SnmpExtensionInitEx(
    AsnObjectIdentifier *pSupportedView )              /* OUT */
```

The SNMP service obtains multiple MIB subtree OIDs by repeatedly calling SnmpExtensionInitEx until it returns the value of FALSE. There is no harm in including in an extension agent an SnmpExtensionInitEx function that only returns FALSE.

This function has only a single parameter, pSupportedView, described here:

pSupportedView

> This is the OBJECT IDENTIFIER of an additional MIB subtree supported by the extension agent. If multiple extension agents register the same subtree OID, varbinds specifying objects in that subtree will only be passed to the first extension agent that registered the OID. It is also useless for an extension agent to register the same subtree multiple times.

> WARNING   The memory for the object passed in pSupportedView is not freed by the SNMP service, so you must free it on a subsequent call to SnmpExtensionInitEx, or pass a pointer to a statically allocated AsnObjectIdentifier variable. Never set this pointer or its contents to NULL.

Example 6-4 shows an implementation of SnmpExtensionInitEx that registers three additional MIB subtree with the SNMP service. A static index is used to step through the array of AsnObjectIdentifier objects. A value of TRUE is returned while there are additional MIB subtrees to register.

Example 6-4. A typical implementation of SnmpExtensionInitEx

```
#include <snmp.h>

UINT OidMibPrefixes[][] = {
    { 1, 3, 6, 1, 4, 1, 2035, 10,  2 },
    { 1, 3, 6, 1, 4, 1, 2035, 10,  3 },
    { 1, 3, 6, 1, 4, 1, 2035, 10, 10 },
};

AsnObjectIdentifier OidMibViews[] = {
    { sizeof( OidMibPrefixes[0] ) / sizeof( UINT ), OidMibPrefixes[0] },
    { sizeof( OidMibPrefixes[1] ) / sizeof( UINT ), OidMibPrefixes[1] },
    { sizeof( OidMibPrefixes[2] ) / sizeof( UINT ), OidMibPrefixes[2] },
    { 0, 0 },
};

BOOL WINAPI SnmpExtensionInitEx(
    AsnObjectIdentifier *pSupportedView )
{
    BOOL fResult = TRUE;
    static UINT nViewCount = 0;

    /* Check if there are any managed subtrees remaining */
    if ( OidMibViews[nViewCount].idLength != 0 )
    {
        *pSupportedView = OidMibViews[nViewCount];
        nViewCount++;
    }
    else
        fResult = FALSE; /* No more MIB additional views */

    return( fResult );
}
```

SnmpExtensionQuery

The variable bindings of each authenticated GetRequest, GetNextRequest, and SetRequest message received by the SNMP service is passed on to the appropriate extension agent via a call to the SnmpExtensionQuery function. The extension agent then determines whether the request is valid (i.e., the OIDs specified in the request exist, there are no writes to a read-only variable, and so forth); it also processes the request (reads or writes MIB variables) and collects data to be returned in a response message by the SNMP service. Figure 6-3 illustrates the data passed between the SNMP service and an extension agent using SnmpExtensionQuery.

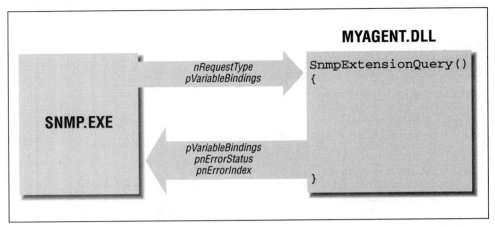

Figure 6-3. Data passed using SnmpExtensionQuery

This is the function prototype of SnmpExtensionQuery:

```
BOOL WINAPI SnmpExtensionQuery(
    BYTE                nRequestType,           /* IN */
    RFC1157VarBindList  *pVariableBindings,     /* IN OUT */
    AsnInteger          *pnErrorStatus,         /* OUT */
    AsnInteger          *pnErrorIndex )         /* OUT */
```

SnmpExtensionQuery should return TRUE if the query was successfully processed, or FALSE if the query failed. If an SNMP request resulted in a protocol validation or processing error (noSuchName, badValue, etc.), SnmpExtension-Query will return TRUE because the query itself succeeded (although it may have resulted in an SNMP error). FALSE should be returned only if SnmpExtension-Query encounters an operational or system error (e.g., memory allocation failure) and is unable to continue processing the variable bindings in a message. If FALSE is returned, the SNMP service returns the GetResponse message with an error status value of 5 (genErr), an error index of 1, and no variable bindings.

Most of the processing performed by an extension agent occurs in SnmpExten-sionQuery. Each variable binding in an SNMP request must be resolved by following the rules described in RFC 1157. Exactly how to code SnmpExtension-Query to resolve SNMP requests depends on the programmer writing the code. All processing required to service a request must occur before SnmpExtension-Query returns.

The parameters are described here:

nRequestType

> This is the type of SNMP request being passed to the extension agent by this call. This value may be one of the following values defined in *SNMP.H*:

```
ASN_RFC1157_GETREQUEST          160     GetRequest
ASN_RFC1157_GETNEXTREQUEST      161     GetNextRequest
ASN_RFC1157_SETREQUEST          163     SetRequest
```

pVariableBindings

This is the list of variable bindings contained within the request message that are within the MIB subtrees registered as supported by the extension agent. Each binding in this list must be parsed, and the specified Get, GetNext, or Set operation applied to its OID and value. The memory in this list is allocated by the SNMP service. If the extension agent changes any variable-length data pointed to by pVariableBindings (AsnOctetString or AsnObjectIdentifiers objects), it must first free and reallocate the memory in the specific RFC1157VarBind object before changing the value. The pVariableBindings object itself need not be freed and reallocated.

pdwErrorStatus

This is the errorStatus value to be included in the GetResponse message. If an error occurs during the validation or processing of the message, the extension agent will return a non-zero value in pdwErrorStatus. The following errorStatus values are defined in *SNMP.H* (for tooBig, note that an extension agent will never return a tooBig error because it has no way to determine if this situation exists):

Value	Message	Description
1	SNMP_ERRORSTATUS_TOOBIG	Response is too big to send in one message
2	SNMP_ERRORSTATUS_NOSUCHNAME	Specified OID does not exist
3	SNMP_ERRORSTATUS_BADVALUE	Value to set is wrong type or out of range
4	SNMP_ERRORSTATUS_READONLY	Attempted to set a read-only variable
5	SNMP_ERRORSTATUS_GENERR	Some other error occurred

If no errors occur, then a value of zero (SNMP_ERRORSTATUS_NOERROR) is returned in pdwErrorStatus. It is important that pdwErrorStatus be initialized by the extension agent before SnmpExtensionQuery returns. Do not assume that it contains a valid value when SnmpExtensionQuery is called.

pdwErrorIndex

This is the index of the variable binding that caused the error. This value will be zero if no specific binding caused the error or if no error occurred. This value is included in the GetResponse message. It is important that pdwError-Index be initialized by the extension agent before SnmpExtensionQuery returns. Do not assume that it contains a valid value when SnmpExtension-Query is called.

Example 6-5 shows one possible implementation of SnmpExtensionQuery that examines each variable binding in turn and passes it to a ResolveVarBind function, which then performs the specified operation on the data. Chapter 7, *Writing Extension Agents*, contains much more detail on the implementation of SnmpExtensionQuery.

Example 6-5. A typical implementation of SnmpExtensionQuery

```
#include <snmp.h>

BOOL WINAPI SnmpExtensionQuery( BYTE byRequestType,
    RFC1157VarBindList *pVariableBindings,
    AsnInteger *pErrorStatus, AsnInteger *pErrorIndex )
{
    UINT i;
    BOOL fResult = SNMPAPI_NOERROR;

    /* Resolve each variable binding in the request */
    for ( i = 0; i < pVariableBindings->len; i++ )
    {
        /* On a Get or GetNext retrieve a value from the MIB */
        *pErrorStatus = ResolveVarBind( &pVariableBindings->list[i],
            byRequestType );

        /* Check if a GetNext went beyond supported range of managed objects */
        if ( *pErrorStatus == SNMP_ERRORSTATUS_NOSUCHNAME )
        {
            if ( byRequestType == MIB_ACTION_GETNEXT )
            {
                *pErrorStatus = SNMP_ERRORSTATUS_NOERROR;

                /* Move the OID outside of the registered view */
                SnmpUtilOidFree( &pVariableBindings->list[i].name );
                if ( SnmpUtilOidCpy( &pVariableBindings->list[i].name,
                    &MIB_OidPrefix ) == FALSE )
                {
                    variableBindings->list[i].name = NULL;
                    fResult = SNMPAPI_ERROR;
                }
                else
                    pVariableBindings->list[i].name.ids[MIB_PREFIX_LEN - 1]++;
            }
        }

        /* Return any indication of error to the extendible Agent */
        if ( *pErrorStatus != SNMP_ERRORSTATUS_NOERROR )
        {
            *pErrorIndex = i + 1;
            fResult = *pErrorStatus;
        }
    }
```

Example 6-5. A typical implementation of SnmpExtensionQuery (continued)

```
    }
    return( fResult );
}
```

SnmpExtensionTrap

SnmpExtensionTrap is polled by the SNMP service to acquire information that is then used to generate a trap message. A poll occurs when the event handle created in, and passed to the SNMP service by, SnmpExtensionInit is signaled by the extension agent. One trap is generated per poll and SnmpExtensionTrap is continually polled until it returns a value of FALSE. Figure 6-4 illustrates the data passed between the SNMP service and an extension agent using SnmpExtensionTrap.

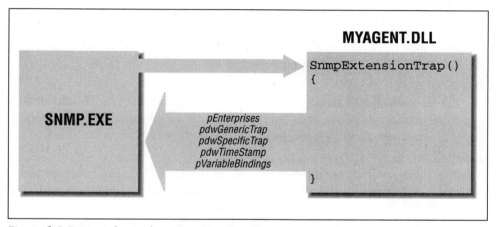

Figure 6-4. Data exchanged via SnmpExtensionTrap

This is the function prototype of SnmpExtensionTrap:

```
BOOL WINAPI SnmpExtensionTrap(
    AsnObjectIdentifier    *pEnterprise,          /* OUT */
    AsnInteger             *pdwGenericTrap,       /* OUT */
    AsnInteger             *pdwSpecificTrap,      /* OUT */
    AsnTimeticks           *pdwTimeStamp,         /* OUT */
    RFC1157VarBindList     *pVariableBindings)    /* OUT */
```

The parameters are described here:

pEnterprise

This is the OID of the management enterprise whose registration authority defines the trap. This OID is included in the enterprise OID field of the Trap PDU. The memory used by this parameter is not freed by the SNMP service, so you must either pass the OID as the address of a static AsnObjectIdentifier structure or free memory allocated for this OID the next time SnmpExtension-Trap is called.

pdwGenericTrap

This is the value of the generic-trap field in the Trap PDU. The extension agent must supply this value to indicate which of the seven generic traps defined by RFC 1157 this trap is:

Message	Value	Type of Trap
SNMP_GENERICTRAP_COLDSTART	0	coldStart Trap
SNMP_GENERICTRAP_WARMSTART	1	warmStart Trap
SNMP_GENERICTRAP_LINKDOWN	2	linkDown Trap
SNMP_GENERICTRAP_LINKUP	3	linkUp Trap
SNMP_GENERICTRAP_AUTHFAILURE	4	authenticationFailure Trap
SNMP_GENERICTRAP_EGPNEIGHLOSS	5	egpNeighborLoss Trap
SNMP_GENERICTRAP_ENTERSPECIFIC	6	enterpriseSpecific Trap

Most extension agents will only generate traps of the SNMP_GENERICTRAP_ ENTERSPECIFIC generic-trap type identifier.

pdwSpecificTrap

This is the value of the specific-trap field in the trap PDU. Each trap defined in an enterprise-specific MIB contains an enumerated value that is specified in this parameter. Generic traps must pass a specific-trap type value of zero.

pdwTimeStamp

This is the value of the time-stamp field in the Trap PDU. Each trap contains a time stamp representing the number of centiseconds that have elapsed since the SNMP agent became active. This value is calculated by subtracting the value returned by GetTickCount divided by 10 from the dwTimeZeroReference value received in SnmpExtensionInit.* It is a common mistake to return the time-stamp field data as a millisecond rather than as a centisecond value as defined by the SMIv1 TimeTicks data type.

pVariableBindings

These are variable bindings that are included in the Trap PDU. The extension agent must build and initialize the entire varbind list using the following steps:

    a. Dynamically allocate an RFC1157VarBindList object.

    b. Dynamically allocate an RFC1157VarBind object in the list.

---

* The SnmpSvcGetUptime function is also used to retrieve the agent uptime value for trap data, but this function won't become officially available until the release of the Windows NT 5 SDK.

c. Initialize the RFC1157VarBind object with the data defined for the varbind of the specific trap.

d. Repeat steps 2, 3, and 4 for each remaining varbind in the Trap PDU.

e. Pass the pointer of the RFC1157VarBindList object to the SNMP service using the pVariableBindings parameter.

After the trap is sent, the SNMP service deallocates this memory using SnmpUtilVar BindListFree. (AsnOctetString object data is only freed if the dynamic flag is set to TRUE.) Don't ever allow the extension agent to deallocate this memory or use the pointer to the RFC1157VarBindList object after SnmpExtensionTrap has returned.

The extension agent will signal the SNMP service that one or more traps are waiting to be generated by using SetEvent and the phPollForTrapEvent event handle initialized in SnmpExtensionInit:

```
/* Signal the SNMP service that we need to generate a trap */
SetEvent( ghTrapEvent );
```

SnmpExtensionTrap will then be called by the SNMP service. The PDU header and variable binding data for one trap is loaded into its function parameters. SnmpExtensionTrap then returns with a value of TRUE indicating that the parameters contain valid trap data and that SnmpExtensionTrap should be polled again. Each additional poll is used by the SNMP service to retrieve data for another trap, and by the extension agent to clean up any local memory allocated for the previous trap.

Each trap generated will require one poll of SnmpExtensionTrap. A final poll of SnmpExtensionTrap that returns FALSE is an indication that no more traps are waiting to be generated; any data residing in the function parameters is to be considered invalid.

Example 6-6 shows a very simple implementation of SnmpExtensionTrap. When SnmpExtensionTrap is called by the SNMP service, the data for trap two defined by the 1.3.6.1.4.1.2035.1.4 enterprises MIB is loaded into the function parameters. A return value of TRUE indicates that valid trap data is being passed and that the SNMP service should call SnmpExtensionTrap again. The second call returns FALSE to indicate that there are no more traps to generate.

Example 6-6. A typical implementation of SnmpExtensionTrap

```
#include <snmp.h>

UINT OidTrapMibPrefix[] = { 1, 3, 6, 1, 4, 1, 2035, 1, 4 };
AsnObjectIdentifier OidTrapMib = {
    sizeof(OidTrapMibPrefix) / sizeof(UINT), OidTrapMibPrefix };

BOOL WINAPI SnmpExtensionTrap(
```

Example 6-6. A typical implementation of SnmpExtensionTrap (continued)

```
    AsnObjectIdentifier *pEnterprise,            /* OUT */
    AsnInteger          *pdwGenericTrap,         /* OUT */
    AsnInteger          *pdwSpecificTrap,        /* OUT */
    AsnTimeticks        *pdwTimeStamp,           /* OUT */
    RFC1157VarBindList  *pVariableBindings )     /* OUT */
{
    static BOOL fResult = FALSE;

    if ( fResult == FALSE )
    {
        /* Specify the OID of the trap to send */
        *pEnterprise = OidTrapMib;

        /* Trap is enterprise-specific */
        *pdwGenericTrap = SNMP_GENERICTRAP_ENTERSPECIFIC;

        /* Specific trap type as defined in trap MIB */
        *pdwSpecificTrap = 2;

        /* Calculate the time stamp in centiseconds */
        *pdwTimeStamp = (GetTickCount() / 10) - gdwTimeZero;

        /* VarBinds associated with this trap (in this case, none) */
        pVariableBindings->list = NULL;
        pVariableBindings->len = 0;

        fResult = TRUE;
    }
    else
        fResult = FALSE;     /* No more traps to send */

    return( fResult );
}
```

A more detailed explanation of trap implementation is found in Chapter 8, *Implementing Traps.*

The Utility API

The Utility API is divided into two sets of functions: memory management and data manipulation. The majority of SNMP Utility functions are used to manipulate objects declared using the complex data types defined in *SNMP.H.*

SnmpUtilMemAlloc, SnmpUtilMemReAlloc, and SnmpUtilMemFree

The SnmpUtilMem* functions are used to allocate, reallocate, and deallocate memory objects in the SNMP and Management APIs. As previously mentioned, an extension agent should never call Win32 (LocalAlloc or GlobalAlloc) or compiler-supplied memory management functions (malloc, realloc, and free) when allocating memory that will be used by the SNMP or Management APIs.

The SNMP service is sometimes required to free memory that has been allocated by an extension agent. Extension agents and management applications are also sometimes required to free memory allocated by the SNMP service or MGMTAPI. To prevent memory leaks caused by the inability to successfully free memory allocated from different heaps, all dynamic objects are allocated and deallocated from the same heap using the SnmpUtilMem* functions.

The parameters and return values of these functions are patterned after the standard C memory management functions malloc, realloc, and free. They also return pointers rather than memory handles.

Win32 Memory Management

In Win32, there is no distinction between local heap and global heap, or near pointers and far pointers. All memory allocations come from the same 2GB virtual low-memory address space available to all user processes. Fixed pointers to memory, such as those returned by malloc and SnmpUtilMemAlloc, are not pointers to actual physical memory, but instead point to a page map of virtual addresses that correspond to physical memory locations. When Win32 performs memory management by moving pages of memory, the virtual address stored in each pointer is not affected.

Dynamic memory objects (or, as they are more conventionally known, blocks of memory) are allocated using SnmpUtilMemAlloc. The syntax and usage of SnmpUtilMemAlloc is the same as that of malloc:

```
AsnOctetString os;
char szString[] = "An Octet String";

os.Length = lstrlen( szString );
os.stream = (BYTE *)SnmpUtilMemAlloc( sizeof( BYTE ) * os.Length );
if ( os.stream )
    memcpy( os.stream, szString, os.Length );
```

SnmpUtilMemAlloc takes as its only parameter the number of 8-bit bytes to allocate. The pointer returned must be cast to the appropriate data type. If SnmpUtilMemAlloc fails, then the NULL value is returned.

You often need to call SnmpUtilMemAlloc multiple times to allocate all of the memory required for a complex data structure. To create an RFC1157VarBindList containing a single RFC1157VarBind that stores an AsnOctetString requires three calls to SnmpUtilMemAlloc, as shown in Example 6-7.

Example 6-7. Using SnmpUtilMemAlloc to create a single variable binding

```
UINT MibVar1Prefix[] = { 1, 3, 6, 1, 2, 1, 9999, 1, 0 };
AsnObjectIdentifier OidMibVar1 = {
    sizeof(MibVar1Prefix) / sizeof(UINT), MibVar1Prefix };
char szString[] = "Another Octet String";
RFC1157VarBindList VarBinds;
VarBinds.list = NULL; VarBinds.len  = 1;

/* Allocate a single variable binding object in a list */
VarBinds.list = (RFC1157VarBind *)SnmpUtilMemAlloc(
    sizeof(RFC1157VarBind) * VarBinds.len );
if ( VarBinds.list != (RFC1157VarBind *)NULL )
{
    VarBinds.list->name.idLength = OidMibVar1.idLength;
    VarBinds.list->name.ids = (UINT *)SnmpUtilMemAlloc(
      sizeof(UINT) * VarBinds.list->name.idLength );
    if ( VarBinds.list->name.ids != (UINT *)NULL )
        memcpy( VarBinds.list->name.ids, OidMibVar1.ids,
            sizeof(UINT) * VarBinds.list->name.idLength );
    VarBinds.list->value.asnType = ASN_OCTETSTRING;
    VarBinds.list->value.asnValue.string.length = strlen( szString );
    VarBinds.list->value.asnValue.string.stream = (BYTE *)SnmpUtilMemAlloc(
      sizeof(BYTE) * VarBinds.list->value.asnValue.string.length );
    if ( VarBinds.list->value.asnValue.string.stream != (BYTE *)NULL )
    {
        memcpy( VarBinds.list->value.asnValue.string.stream, szString,
          VarBinds.list->value.asnValue.string.length );
        VarBinds.list->value.asnValue.string.dynamic = TRUE;
    }
}
```

Here we have allocated memory for a single element in the VarBinds.list array, the OID of the variable binding, and the OCTET STRING data stored in the variable binding. If there were multiple variable bindings it would be necessary to access them using an index into VarBinds.list; with only a single element, this is not necessary.

We can create multiple variable bindings in an RFC1157VarBindList by initially using SnmpUtilMemAlloc—or as an afterthought by using SnmpUtilMemReAlloc, as shown in Example 6-8.

Example 6-8. Using SnmpUtilMemReAlloc to create multiple variable bindings

```
/* Allocate two more variable binding objects in a list */
UINT MibVar2Prefix[] = { 1, 3, 6, 1, 2, 1, 9999, 2, 0 };
AsnObjectIdentifier OidMibVar2 = {
    sizeof(MibVar2Prefix) / sizeof(UINT), MibVar2Prefix };
UINT MibVar3Prefix[] = { 1, 3, 6, 1, 2, 1, 9999, 3, 0 };
AsnObjectIdentifier OidMibVar3 = {
    sizeof(MibVar3Prefix) / sizeof(UINT), MibVar3Prefix };
```

Example 6-8. Using SnmpUtilMemReAlloc to create multiple variable bindings (continued)

```
RFC1157VarBind *pList;
VarBinds.len = 3;

pList = (RFC1157VarBind *)SnmpUtilMemReAlloc(
    VarBinds.list, sizeof(RFC1157VarBind) * VarBinds.len );
if ( pList != (RFC1157VarBind *)NULL )
{
    VarBinds.list = pList;

    /* Second varbind */
    VarBinds.list[1]->name.idLength = OidMibVar2.idLength;
    VarBinds.list[1]->name.ids = (UINT *)SnmpUtilMemAlloc(
      sizeof(UINT) * VarBinds.list[1]->name.idLength );
    if ( VarBinds.list[1]->name.ids != (UINT *)NULL )
        memcpy( VarBinds.list[1]->name.ids, OidMibVar2.ids,
          sizeof(UINT) * VarBinds.list[1]->name.idLength );
    VarBinds.list[1]->value.asnType = ASN_INTEGER;
    VarBinds.list[1]->value.asnValue.number = 1234;

    /* Third varbind */
    VarBinds.list[2]->name.idLength = OidMibVar3.idLength;
    VarBinds.list[2]->name.ids = (UINT *)SnmpUtilMemAlloc(
      sizeof(UINT) * VarBinds.list[2]->name.idLength );
    if ( VarBinds.list[2]->name.ids != (UINT *)NULL )
        memcpy( VarBinds.list[2]->name.ids, OidMibVar3.ids,
          sizeof(UINT) * VarBinds.list[2]->name.idLength );
    VarBinds.list[2]->value.asnType = ASN_INTEGER;
    VarBinds.list[2]->value.asnValue.number = 5678;
}
```

SnmpUtilMemReAlloc changes the size of a previously allocated memory object. This function takes as its two parameters a pointer to the existing memory object to resize, and the new size of the memory object in 8-bit bytes. New memory is allocated for an increase in size; memory is deallocated for a reduction in size.

This function returns a pointer to the new memory object on success, and returns a NULL value on failure. Store the returned value in a temporary pointer variable in case NULL is returned, or you will overwrite the pointer to the original memory object.

SnmpUtilMemFree frees any memory object allocated using SnmpUtilMemAlloc or SnmpUtilMemReAlloc. A pointer to the memory object to free is the only parameter; there is no return value:

```
AsnOctetString os;
os.Length = 10;
os.stream = (BYTE *)SnmpUtilMemAlloc( sizeof( BYTE ) * os.Length );
if ( os.stream )
{
    SnmpUtilMemFree( os.stream );
    os.stream = (BYTE *)NULL;
}
```

In a previous example, an RFC1157VarBindList is initialized using three calls to SnmpUtilMemAlloc. You might expect to deallocate this object using three calls to SnmpUtilMemFree as follows:

```
SnmpUtilMemFree( VarBinds.list->value.asnValue.string.stream );
SnmpUtilMemFree( VarBinds.list->name.ids );
SnmpUtilMemFree( VarBinds.list );
```

You could do this, but you might instead want to use the very useful SNMP Utility API functions; these functions handle the memory deallocation of complex data structures.

The Utility API includes several functions that are very useful for working with AsnObjectIdentifier, RFC1157VarBind, and RFC1157VarBindList objects. If it were not for these functions, you would eventually get around to writing your own functions to copy, append, free, and even display the contents of the SNMP API complex data types. (Actually, you will eventually discover that you will still need to write a few useful functions that are not currently included in the SNMP API.)

Each of these utility functions shares the unfortunate design misfeature of generating a protection fault if an unexpected NULL pointer is passed in any of their parameters. It would be nice if the utility functions simply and gracefully failed when this occurred, but they don't. So always first check that your pointers are pointing somewhere—preferably to the correct object in memory—before calling an SNMP or any Win32 API function.

SnmpUtilOidAppend

SnmpUtilOidAppend appends two AsnObjectIdentifier objects together in memory. Here's the function prototype of SnmpUtilOidAppend:

```
SNMPAPI SNMP_FUNC_TYPE SnmpUtilOidAppend(
    AsnObjectIdentifier *pDstObjId,      /* IN OUT */
    AsnObjectIdentifier *pSrcObjId)      /* IN */
```

The parameters are described here:

pDstObjId

This is the destination AsnObjectIdentifier object that will be modified.

pSrcObjId

This is the source AsnObjectIdentifier object that contains the OID that will be appended to the destination object.

The value stored in the source AsnObjectIdentifier object is appended to the destination object. The source is unmodified and memory is allocated for the destination object as needed. You may either statically or dynamically allocate the source object, but you must dynamically allocate the destination using SnmpUtilMemAlloc, as shown in Example 6-9.

Example 6-9. Using SnmpUtilMemAlloc for dynamic allocation

```
UINT SrcOid[] = { 5, 6, 7, 8, 9 };
AsnObjectIdentifier MibSrcOid = { sizeof( SrcOid ) /
    sizeof( UINT ), SrcOid };
AsnObjectIdentifier *pMibDstOid;

pMibDstOid = (AsnObjectIdentifier *)SnmpUtilMemAlloc(
    sizeof( AsnObjectIdentifier ) );
if ( pMibDstOid )
{
    pMibDstOid->idLength = 4;
    pMibDstOid->ids = (UINT *)SnmpUtilMemAlloc(
      sizeof(UINT) * pMibDstOid->idLength );
    pMibDstOid->ids[0] = 1;
    pMibDstOid->ids[1] = 2;
    pMibDstOid->ids[2] = 3;
    pMibDstOid->ids[3] = 4;

    /* pMibDstOid is 1.2.3.4 */
    /* MibSrcOid is 5.6.7.8.9 */
    if ( SnmpUtilOidAppend( pMibDstOid, &MibSrcOid ) == TRUE )
    {
        /* pMibDstOid is now 1.2.3.4.5.6.7.8.9 */
    }
}
SnmpUtilOidFree( pMibDstOid );
```

In this example a source OID with five subidentifiers is statically allocated at compile-time. A destination OID is dynamically allocated at run-time and initialized with an OID containing four subidentifiers. SnmpUtilOidAppend concatenates the source to the destination and allocates memory for the additional five subidentifiers present in the source OID.

If the destination object pointer is NULL, a copy of the source object is made:

```
UINT SrcOid[] = { 5, 6, 7, 8, 9 };
AsnObjectIdentifier MibSrcOid = { sizeof( SrcOid ) /
    sizeof( UINT ), SrcOid };
AsnObjectIdentifier *pMibDstOid = NULL;

if ( SnmpUtilOidAppend( pMibDstOid, &MibSrcOid ) == TRUE )
{
    /* pMibDstOid points to a copy of the *pSrcOid object */
}
SnmpUtilMemFree( pMibDstOid );
```

SnmpUtilOidAppend returns TRUE if the operation was successful and FALSE if an error occurred; examples of errors are a memory allocation failure or the passing of a static destination object.

SnmpUtilOidCmp and SnmpUtilOidNCmp

SnmpUtilOidCmp and SnmpUtilOidNCmp compare the OID values stored in two AsnObjectIdentifier objects. These functions return a value greater than zero if the first OID is greater than the second, a value less than zero if the second OID is greater than the first, and zero if both OIDs are identical.

Here are the function prototypes of SnmpUtilOidCmp and SnmpUtilOidNCmp:

```
SNMPAPI SNMP_FUNC_TYPE SnmpUtilOidCmp(
    AsnObjectIdentifier *pObjIdA,      /* IN */
    AsnObjectIdentifier *pObjIdB)      /* IN */

SNMPAPI SNMP_FUNC_TYPE SnmpUtilOidNCmp(
    AsnObjectIdentifier *pObjIdA,      /* IN */
    AsnObjectIdentifier *pObjIdB,      /* IN */
    UINT                Len)           /* IN */
```

The parameters are described here:

pObjIdA

This is the first AsnObjectIdentifier object value to compare.

pObjIdB

This is the second AsnObjectIdentifier object value to compare.

Len

This is the maximum number of subidentifiers to compare.

The objects compared may be statically or dynamically allocated. Example 6-10 compares two statically allocated AsnObjectIdentifier objects.

Example 6-10. Comparison of two statically allocated objects

```
int nResult;
UINT dwA[] = { 1, 3, 6, 1 };
UINT dwB[] = { 1, 3, 6, 1 };
AsnObjectIdentifier OidA = { sizeof( dwA ) / sizeof ( UINT ), dwA };
AsnObjectIdentifier OidB = { sizeof( dwB ) / sizeof ( UINT ), dwB };

nResult = SnmpUtilOidCmp( &OidA, &OidB ); /* nResult is 0 */
```

An OID is evaluated to be greater or lesser than another OID by comparing each subidentifier in identical positions in both of the OIDs. The nResult value in the previous example will be zero because the subidentifier values in each position of the OIDs are identical.

If the first OID is greater than the second, the return value is greater than zero; this value is equal to the difference of the first non-matching subidentifier returned. When comparing the following OIDs,

```
1.3.6.2
1.3.6.1
```

the value 1 is returned because the difference of the first nonidentical subidentifiers is 1 (2 - 1). If you reverse the position of the OIDs in the comparison,

```
1.3.6.1
1.3.6.2
```

the return value is -1 (1 - 2). The following comparison will return -10:

```
1.3.6.1
1.3.6.11
```

And this comparison also returns -10:

```
1.3.6.1
1.13.244.7634
```

SnmpUtilOidCmp begins its comparison at the first (most significant) subidentifier, stops when it finds a nonidentical set of subidentifiers, and then returns their difference. In the previous example, the values 6 and 244 and 1 and 7634 are never compared because the first mismatch was 3 and 13; their difference of -10 was returned.

Comparing two OIDs of unequal lengths will never result in an identical comparison. If one OID is a subset of the other, the value returned will be the number of additional subidentifiers in the longer OID. For example, a comparison of these OIDs returns a value of 2:

```
1.3.6.1.2.1
1.3.6.1
```

A comparison of these OIDs returns a value of -4:

```
1.3.6
1.3.6.1.2.1.1
```

If you need to compare the length of two OIDs, you may do so by examining the length values directly:

```
if ( dwA.idLength < dwB.idLength )
```

SnmpUtilOidNCmp is identical in operation to SnmpUtilOidCmp, but it allows the number of subidentifiers compared to be limited. The following code would return a value of 1 if SnmpUtilOidCmp were used; however, SnmpUtilOidNCmp compares only the first three subidentifiers, which are equal in comparison, so it returns a value of zero:

```
int nResult;
UINT dwA[] = { 1, 3, 6, 2 };
UINT dwB[] = { 1, 3, 6, 1 );
AsnObjectIdentifier OidA = { sizeof( dwA ) / sizeof ( UINT ), dwA };
```

```
AsnObjectIdentifier OidB = { sizeof( dwB ) / sizeof ( UINT ), dwB };

nResult = SnmpUtilOidNCmp( &OidA, &OidB, 3 ); /* nResult is 0 */
```

SnmpUtilOidCpy

SnmpUtilOidCpy makes a copy of an AsnObjectIdentifier object. Here is the function prototype of SnmpUtilOidCpy:

```
SNMPAPI SNMP_FUNC_TYPE SnmpUtilOidCpy(
    AsnObjectIdentifier *pDstObjId,    /* OUT */
    AsnObjectIdentifier *pSrcObjId);   /* IN */
```

The copy (destination) is a separate object in memory and is identical in value to the source. Both the source and the destination objects may be statically or dynamically allocated. In either case, the memory for the destination object must be allocated prior to the copy.

The parameters are described here:

pDstObjId

This is the AsnObjectIdentifier object to receive the copy.

pSrcObjId

This is the AsnObjectIdentifier object containing the value to copy.

In Example 6-11, two AsnObjectIdentifier objects are statically allocated. The source object is initialized and the destination object is not. After the copy, the destination object will contain a copy of the contents of the source object.

Example 6-11. Copying statically allocated objects

```
UINT SrcOidPrefix[] = { 1, 2, 1, 4, 1, 6 };
AsnObjectIdentifier MibSrcOid = {
    sizeof( SrcOidPrefix ) / sizeof( UINT ),
    SrcOidPrefix
};
AsnObjectIdentifier MibDstOid;

if ( SnmpUtilOidCpy( &MibDstOid, &MibSrcOid ) == TRUE )
{
        /* Copy succeeded */
}
```

Example 6-12 demonstrates a copy performed between two dynamically allocated AsnObjectIdentifier objects.

Example 6-12. Copying dynamically allocated objects

```
AsnObjectIdentifier *pMibSrcOid;
AsnObjectIdentifier *pMibDstOid = NULL;

/* Allocate the source */
pMibSrcOid = (AsnObjectIdentifier *)SnmpUtilMemAlloc(
    sizeof( AsnObjectIdentifier ) );
if ( pMibSrcOid )
{
        /* Initialize the source */
        pMibSrcOid->idLength = 4;
        pMibSrcOid->ids = (UINT *) SnmpUtilMemAlloc(
            sizeof( UINT ) * pMibSrcOid->idLength );
        if ( pMibSrcOid->ids )
        {
                pMibSrcOid->ids[0] = 1;
                pMibSrcOid->ids[1] = 2;
                pMibSrcOid->ids[2] = 3;
                pMibSrcOid->ids[3] = 4;
        }
}
/* Allocate the destination */
pMibDstOid = (AsnObjectIdentifier *)SnmpUtilMemAlloc(
    sizeof( AsnObjectIdentifier ) );
SnmpUtilOidCpy( pMibDstOid, pMibSrcOid );
```

SnmpUtilOidFree

SnmpUtilOidFree frees any memory allocated for an AsnObjectIdentifier object by SnmpUtilMemAlloc, SnmpUtilOidAppend, and SnmpUtilOidCpy.

Here is the function prototype of SnmpUtilOidFree:

```
VOID SNMP_FUNC_TYPE SnmpUtilOidFree(
    AsnObjectIdentifier *pObjId    /* IN OUT */
```

The function does not return a success or failure value, so be sure to test your application for memory leaks. Because SnmpUtilOidFree will generate an exception if it is passed a NULL pointer, be sure to check for that as well.

This function has only a single parameter, pObjId, described here:

pObjId
    This is a pointer to the AsnObjectIdentifier object to free.

SnmpUtilOidFree does not return a value indicating success or failure and will generate a protection fault if passed a NULL pointer, as shown in Example 6-13.

Example 6-13. Passing a NULL pointer to SnmpUtilOidFree

```
AsnObjectIdentifier *pMibDstOid;
pMibDstOid = (AsnObjectIdentifier *)SnmpUtilMemAlloc(
    sizeof( AsnObjectIdentifier ) );
if ( pMibDstOid )
{
    SnmpUtilOidFree( pMibDstOid );
    pMibDstOid = (AsnObjectIdentifier *)NULL;
}
```

SnmpUtilVarBindCpy

SnmpUtilVarBindCpy makes a duplicate in memory of a single variable binding structure and its contents. Here is the function prototype of SnmpUtilVarBindCpy:

```
SNMPAPI SNMP_FUNC_TYPE SnmpUtilVarBindCpy(
    RFC1157VarBind *pDstVarBind,    /* OUT */
    RFC1157VarBind *pSrcVarBind)    /* IN */
```

The parameters are described here:

pDstVarBind

This is a pointer to the destination RFC1157VarBind object to receive the copy.

pSrcVarBind

This is a pointer to the source RFC1157VarBind object to copy.

The memory required for the copy is automatically allocated; therefore, all your code needs to do is supply a pointer to store the memory address of the copy, as shown in Example 6-14.

Example 6-14. Supplying a pointer to SnmpUtilVarBindCpy

```
RFC1157VarBind *pSrcVarBind;
RFC1157VarBind *pDstVarBind = NULL;

pSrcVarBind = ( RFC1157VarBind * ) SnmpUtilMemAlloc(
    sizeof ( RFC1157VarBind ) );
if ( pSrcVarBind )
{
    /* Initalize the VarBind with an INTEGER value of 3000
       and an OID of 9.9.9.9 */
    pSrcVarBind->name.idLength = 4;
    pSrcVarBind->name.ids =
      ( UINT * ) SnmpUtilMemAlloc( sizeof( UINT ) *
      pSrcVarBind->name.idLength );
    if ( pSrcVarBind->name.ids )
    {
        pSrcVarBind->name.ids[0] = 9;
```

Example 6-14. Supplying a pointer to SnmpUtilVarBindCpy (continued)

```
        pSrcVarBind->name.ids[1] = 9;
        pSrcVarBind->name.ids[2] = 9;
        pSrcVarBind->name.ids[3] = 9;
        pSrcVarBind->value.asnType = ASN_INTEGER;
        pSrcVarBind->value.asnValue.number = 3000;

        if ( SnmpUtilVarBindCpy( pDstVarBind, pSrcVarBind ) == FALSE )
        {
            /* Copy was unsuccessful */
        }
        SnmpUtilVarBindFree( pSrcVarBind );
    }
    SnmpUtilVarBindFree( pDstVarBind );
}
```

The function returns a value of TRUE if the copy succeeds, and FALSE if there
was a memory allocation problem. Memory allocated using SnmpUtilVarBindCpy
should be deallocated using SnmpUtilVarBindFree.

SnmpUtilVarBindFree

SnmpUtilVarBindFree frees any memory dynamically allocated for an
RFC1157VarBind object by SnmpUtilVarBindCpy or SnmpUtilMemAlloc.

Here is the function prototype of SnmpUtilVarBindFree:

```
    VOID SNMP_FUNC_TYPE SnmpUtilVarBindFree(
        RFC1157VarBind *pVarBind)      /* IN OUT */
```

This function has only a single parameter, pVarBind, described here:

pVarBind
    This is a pointer to the RFC1157VarBind object to free.

SnmpUtilVarBindFree does not return a value indicating success or failure, and
will generate a protection fault if passed a NULL pointer, as shown in Example
6-15.

Example 6-15. Passing a NULL pointer to SnmpUtilVarBindFree

```
RFC1157VarBind *pVarBind;
pVarBind = ( RFC1157VarBind * ) SnmpUtilMemAlloc(
    sizeof ( RFC1157VarBind ) );
if ( pVarBind )
{
    SnmpUtilVarBindFree( pVarBind );
    pVarBind = (RFC1157VarBind *)NULL;
}
```

SnmpUtilVarBindListCpy

SnmpUtilVarBindListCpy makes a copy of an entire variable binding list and its contents. Here is the function prototype of SnmpUtilVarBindListCpy:

```
SNMPAPI SNMP_FUNC_TYPE SnmpUtilVarBindListCpy(
    RFC1157VarBindList *pDstVarBindList,    /* OUT */
    RFC1157VarBindList *pSrcVarBindList)    /* IN */
```

The function returns a value of TRUE if the copy succeeds, and FALSE is returned if there was a memory allocation problem. Memory allocated using SnmpUtilVar BindListCpy should be deallocated using SnmpUtilVarBindListFree.

The parameters are described here:

pDstVarBindList
> This is a pointer to the destination RFC1157VarBindList object to receive the copy.

pSrcVarBindList
> This is a pointer to the source RFC1157VarBindList object to copy.

The lists handled by this function may be statically or dynamically allocated; the memory required for the destination is automatically allocated, as shown in Example 6-16.

Example 6-16. Copying a variable binding list with SnmpUtilVarBindListCpy

```
RFC1157VarBindList SrcVarBindList;
RFC1157VarBindList *pDstVarBindList;

pDstVarBindList = (RFC1157VarBindList *)SnmpUtilMemAlloc(
    sizeof(RFC1157VarBindList) )
if ( pDstVarBindList )
    SnmpUtilVarBindListCpy(pDstVarBindList, &SrcVarBindList );
```

SnmpUtilVarBindListFree

SnmpUtilVarBindListFree frees any memory dynamically allocated for an RFC1157VarBind object by either SnmpUtilVarBindCpy or SnmpUtilMemAlloc.

Here is the function prototype of SnmpUtilVarBindListFree:

```
VOID SNMP_FUNC_TYPE SnmpUtilVarBindListFree(
    RFC1157VarBindList *pVarBindList)    /* IN OUT */
```

This function has only a single parameter, pVarBindList, described here:

pVarBindList
> This is a pointer to the RFC1157VarBindList object to free.

SnmpUtilVarBindListFree does not return a value indicating success or failure; it does generate a protection fault if it is passed a NULL pointer, as shown in Example 6-17.

Example 6-17. Passing a NULL pointer to SnmpUtilVarBindListFree

```
RFC1157VarBindList *pList;
pList = ( RFC1157VarBindList * ) SnmpUtilMemAlloc(
    sizeof ( RFC1157VarBindList ) );

if ( pList )
{
    SnmpUtilVarBindListFree( pList );
    pList = ( RFC1157VarBindList * )NULL;
}
```

SnmpUtilDbgPrint

SnmpUtilDbgPrint displays a printf-style string of text for debugging purposes. Here is the function prototype of SnmpUtilDbgPrint:

```
BOOL WINAPI SnmpUtilDbgPrint (
    INT    nLogLevel,    /* IN */
    LPSTR  szFormat,     /* IN */
    ...);                /* IN */
```

The parameters are described here:

INT nLogLevel

This is the severity level of the debug message. The following values are defined by *SNMP.H*:

```
SNMP_LOG_SILENT    0
SNMP_LOG_FATAL     1
SNMP_LOG_ERROR     2
SNMP_LOG_WARNING   3
SNMP_LOG_TRACE     4
SNMP_LOG_VERBOSE   5
```

szFormat

This is a format string identical to that used by printf. All of the parameters that follow szFormat are used as arguments to this format specifier.

A function prototype for SnmpUtilDbgPrint does appear in *SNMP.H*, but there is currently no published documentation on its use. I have discovered by experimenting that when an nLogLevel of SNMP_LOG_VERBOSE is used, SnmpUtilDbgPrint displays a string in the command window of the WinDbg debugger. The other values do not seem to have any effect on the other output displays typically used for debugging, including the event log, the *SNMPDBG.LOG* file, and the MS-DOS Console window.

Example 6-18 displays a string in the WinDbg command window.

Example 6-18. Displaying an object with SnmpUtilPrintAsnAny

```
#include <snmp.h>

BOOL fSuccess = TRUE;
SnmpUtilDbgPrint( SNMP_LOG_VERBOSE,
    "Initialization %s", fSuccess == TRUE ? "succeeded" : "failed" );
```

SnmpUtilPrintAsnAny

SnmpUtilPrintAsnAny displays the data stored in an AsnAny (AsnObjectSyntax) object on the standard output. This function is typically used when debugging management applications from within the MS-DOS Console window.

Example 6-19 displays the contents of an AsnAny object on the standard output.

Example 6-19. Displaying an object with SnmpUtilPrintAsnAny

```
AsnAny any = { ASN_INTEGER, 1234 };
SnmpUtilPrintAsnAny( &any );

/* The output is: "INTEGER - 1234" */
```

Undocumented Utility Functions

Several new SNMP Utility API functions were added to the SNMP API library with the release of Service Pack 2 for Windows NT 4.0 (December 1996). As of the October 1997 update of the Microsoft Developer Network CD-ROM and Knowledge Base (see Appendix B, *Microsoft Knowledge Base*), the documentation for these functions and a revised *SNMP.H* file has not been released by Microsoft.* These are the new functions:

```
SnmpUtilAnsiToUnicode
SnmpUtilIdsToA
SnmpUtilOidToA
SnmpUtilPrintOid
SnmpUtilStrlenW
SnmpUtilUnicodeToAnsi
```

If you attempt to use any new functions (those included in revisions of the *SNMPAPI.DLL* or *MGMTAPI.DLL* libraries after the initial release of Windows NT 4), your code must determine whether or not the DLLs installed on a Windows NT system include the new API functions.

---

* These functions will most likely not be formally documented until the release of the Windows NT 5 SDK.

If your management application or extension agent code attempts to use any function not present in either of these DLLs (or in any DLL, for that matter), a run-time link error will result when the function is called.

Your code can test at run-time for the existence of a function in a DLL using GetProcAddress. You pass a handle to a loaded DLL and the case-sensitive name of a function to GetProcAddress. If a function by that name is found in the DLL, a pointer to the function is returned; otherwise, a NULL value is returned:

```
FARPROC lpfnSnmpUtilPrintOid = NULL;
HANDLE  hLibrary;
hLibrary = LoadLibrary( "SNMPAPI.DLL" );
if ( hLibrary != (HANDLE)NULL )
{
    lpfnSnmpUtilPrintOid = GetProcAddress( hLibrary, "SnmpUtilPrintOid" );
    if ( lpfnSnmpUtilPrintOid == (FARPROC)NULL )
    {
        /* SnmpUtilPrintOid is not present is SNMPAPI.DLL */
    }
}
```

If the DLL that's loaded does not contain the functions you need, then you have two choices: either don't call the function, or call an alternate function that you must provide.

You may wish to experiment with some of these undocumented functions. The following section provides an example.

SnmpUtilPrintOid

SnmpUtilPrintOid displays the OID stored in an AsnObjectIdentifier object. The OID is displayed as a string on the MS-DOS console window. SnmpUtilPrintOid does not return a value.

Here is the function prototype of SnmpUtilPrintOid:

```
VOID SNMP_FUNC_TYPE SnmpUtilPrintOid (
    AsnObjectIdentifier *pOid);    /* IN */
```

This function has only a single parameter, pOid, described here:

pOid
> A pointer to the AsnObjectIdentifier object whose OID will be displayed. All subidentifiers are displayed using their numerical representation.

Example 6-20 shows how SnmpUtilPrintOid is used to display an AsnObjectIdentifier value. Because SnmpUtilPrintOid does not yet appear in the *SNMPAPI.LIB* import library and is not yet prototyped in *SNMP.H*, this example uses GetProcAddress to check whether the function exists in *SNMPAPI.DLL* and to get a reference to it.

Example 6-20. Usage examples of SnmpUtilPrintOid

```c
#include <snmp.h>

typedef VOID (* SNMPUTILPRINTOID)(AsnObjectIdentifier *);

int main()
{
    HANDLE hDll;
    SNMPUTILPRINTOID lpfnSnmpUtilPrintOid;
    UINT o[] = { 1, 2, 3, 4, 5, 6, 7, 8 };
    AsnObjectIdentifier oid = { 8, o };

    hDll = LoadLibrary( "SNMPAPI.DLL" );
    if ( hDll )
    {
        lpfnSnmpUtilPrintOid =
          (SNMPUTILPRINTOID) GetProcAddress( hDll, "SnmpUtilPrintOid" );
        if ( lpfnSnmpUtilPrintOid )
        {
            (*lpfnSnmpUtilPrintOid)( &oid );
            /* The string "1.2.3.4.5.6.7.8" is displayed */
        }
        else
            puts("SnmpUtilPrintOid not in SNMPAPI.DLL");
    }
    else
        puts("SNMPAPI.DLL not in search PATH");
    return( 0 );
}
```

Memory Management and the SNMP API

The SNMP extension API is used to pass between the SNMP service and an extension agent. But it is not always clear who is responsible for freeing dynamically allocated data. Here are the three basic rules for SNMP API memory management:

1. All memory allocated by the SNMP service is freed by the SNMP service.

2. If an extension agent dynamically allocates memory, it should also free the same memory.

3. All dynamic data passed between the SNMP service and all extension agents should be allocated using the SnmpUtilMem* function.

These rules seem simple enough, but rules 1 and 2 are complicated by several exceptions:

- The SNMP service will only free the string data stored in an AsnOctetString object created by an extension agent if the dynamic flag is set to TRUE. Otherwise, the string data must be freed by the extension agent. Do not set the dynamic flag to TRUE if the string data is statically allocated.

- The memory in the pVariableBindings parameter of SnmpExtensionQuery must be freed and reallocated if performing a GetNext operation, or a Get operation that retrieves an AsnOctetString or AsnObjectIdentifier value.

- The memory allocated by an extension agent and passed to the SNMP service via the pVariableBindings parameter in SnmpExtensionTrap is freed by the SNMP service. The extension agent must not attempt to free this memory on a subsequent call to SnmpExtensionTrap.

Extension agents are also responsible for freeing all resources that they allocate. For example, if the extension agent creates an event to signal the SNMP service to call SnmpExtensionTrap, the extension agent must also close this event before it is unloaded from memory.

Rolling Your Own SNMP API Functions

When you start using the SNMP APIs, you will quickly realize that there are several obvious functions missing that would be really handy to have. And just as you most likely have written several great string manipulation routines that aren't a part of *STRING.H*, you will end up writing your own SNMP API data manipulation functions. You can find, on the CD-ROM that accompanies this book, a small library of functions used to manipulate objects, and perform data conversions on the data objects defined in the SNMP API, and display their values.

If you happen to write any useful SNMP API or MGMTAPI API routines that you'd like to share with the rest of the Windows NT SNMP programming community, contact me via O'Reilly & Associates.

7

Writing Extension Agents

The Microsoft SNMP Extension API provides a base functionality for constructing an extension agent dynamic link library (DLL) capable of communicating with the SNMP service and interacting with network management applications using SNMP. However, there is still a considerable amount of support code that you must write in order to create a fully functional extension agent that can generate traps and process SNMP request messages.

This chapter examines in detail one possible design for implementing an extension agent, and several methods of storing and retrieving MIB data.

NOTE   The coding details in this chapter are implemented in the MIN-AGENT and REGAGENT extension agent examples on the CD-ROM accompanying this book. As you read this chapter, look over the source code for these examples. You will also find these examples to be an excellent base from which to build your own extension agent projects.

Why Build an Extension Agent?

Most of the extension agents that you write will be for the purpose of performing system or network management. Chapter 3, *Network Management and SNMP*, covered the similarities and differences between system and network management. As I said there, network management is concerned primarily with the health of an entire network. The state of an individual network device is of interest only in how it contributes to the operation of its corner of the network.

System management, on the other hand, is primarily concerned with the operation of individual devices and the service they provide. Many network devices use a management protocol to allow their status to be monitored and their operation to be controlled remotely over a network. The management systems that monitor and control these devices are concerned only with the operational state of the devices; they are not interested in the health of the network itself.

An extension agent is effectively both the interface and the database for the information used to monitor and control networks devices and processes using SNMP. The extension agent will collect and return information as requested by a management system. The device being managed may not even be aware that it is being monitored by an extension agent, or that it is attached to any type of a network at all. In such a case, the SNMP agent is acting as a management proxy for the device. Because this case is the most common one, the SNMP service is often referred to as the SNMP proxy service.

The next sections describe some useful applications for extension agents.

SNMP Agent Simulators

One very useful application for an extension agent is that of an SNMP agent simulator (or, as I like to call them, SNMP imposter agents). An extension agent may be designed to simulate—or even emulate—the agent and MIBs supported by another type of network device. For example, an extension agent can allow a Windows NT host to process SNMP requests as if they were some other type of managed or proxied device, such as a router, printer, mainframe computer, or UPS. If you were to change the sysObjectID of the SNMP service to that of the device being simulated, a management system would believe that it is actually managing the device being simulated by your extension agent.

But why would you use an extension agent in this imposterous way? Why spend the time writing up an extension agent that acts as a proxy to nothing? The answer is this: use it when you need to implement a management application, but you don't have access to the actual device(s) that you will be managing.

Often, a team of software engineers will set out to design an SNMP network management application based on the MIB of a device that does not yet exist. They will look over a list of the required features, design the look and feel of the system's user interface, argue over the languages and tools that should be used to build the system, and determine the operating system mechanisms that should be used for interprocess communication and database support.

Eventually the dust settles and a set of functional and design specifications are drafted and ratified. The software engineers are now ready to start coding. They have their application design, several proof-of-concept coding models, and a few "we think that it will work like this" guarantees from the hardware engineers working on the actual manageable device. But at this point, what if there is no actual device that speaks SNMP for the new management station to manage?

The firmware people responsible for implementing the embedded SNMP agent are also waiting for the new hardware. But at least they have a wire-wrapped prototype hooked up to a CPU emulator that they can use for testing their code. They will have to wait for the hardware engineers to finish yet another turn of the system that will fix many of the problems that are keeping their SNMP agent— and probably some of the system itself—from working properly. And it'll be ready in about three to five weeks. There will only be three initial devices made, and you can bet the software group won't be getting one of them!

So what's a software development team to do? Sit around for weeks working on personal projects that are of no revenue-earning interest to the company until the hardware and firmware are ready? (If you said "yes," then plan some additional time to work on your resume as well!) The correct answer is no. What the software team can do instead is design and code up one or more extension agents that support the MIBs of the new device. Their management application could then be tested by managing the extension agent as if it were the actual device.

The only real problem with this plan arises if the department manager doesn't like to spend time writing "throwaway software." Once the new hardware and the SNMP agent become stable and readily available, the management system development team doesn't have any reason to continue using the extension agent imposter—unless, of course, the imposter agent turns out to be useful for other things as well.

Management System Testing

Programmers commonly use SNMP network management applications to test SNMP agents. While working on this book, I certainly prodded the Microsoft SNMP service quite a bit using the HP OpenView for Windows Workgroup Node Manager, the SNMPTOOL utility (available on the CD-ROM), and the NetXRay Network Protocol Analyzer (a working demo of which is also on the CD-ROM). Such applications can continually hammer away at agents using programmed test plans and can record the results.

But how do you test a network management application? The concept of an imposter agent can be used to create an extension agent that provides a testing platform for an SNMP management application. The management application is driven by a script that allows it to exercise the testing agent with SNMP requests. The testing agent keeps a record of the requests made by the management application and reports on its performance. The management application itself must also be monitored to determine whether the data it is receiving, processing, and displaying is correct.

Having a testing agent available also gives you a "second opinion" about the operation of a management application. If an SNMP operation is failing, it might not be apparent whether the fault is with the management system making the request or with the agent returning the response. Using a protocol analyzer to take a look at the SNMP messages exchanged will usually reveal the problem—but not always. In such a case, it is handy to check the behavior of the management system against the same MIB implemented using different agent software and on a different hardware platform. It's the perfect situation for implementing a testing agent.

Learning About SNMP

Programmers who have experience using SNMP are typically either firmware engineers (who work to implement SNMP agents in embedded systems) or application programmers (who design and build SNMP management systems—ideally using a graphical, rather than a text-based, user interface). Because of the diverse specializations between firmware and software people, you will rarely find a programmer who has first-hand experience developing both SNMP management systems and SNMP agents.

The Microsoft SNMP APIs and SNMP service give the Win32 programmer a toolkit and test platform for experimenting first-hand with both SNMP management applications and agents. Although the ASN.1 and BER parsing details of the extendible agent are not accessible, the extension agent programmer must become fluent in reading SNMP MIBs,[*] processing SNMP data, storing and retrieving management data, and writing Win32 DLLs. The management API supplies the basic functions for sending request messages and receiving response messages, which are used to build SNMP management applications. The SNMP APIs therefore allow you to design and control both the agent and the management ends of an SNMP implementation.

Creating an SNMP Extension Agent DLL

Chapter 6, *Using the Extension and Utility APIs*, covered the interaction of the SNMP service and the extension agent dynamic link libraries that it loads into memory. This chapter looks at how an extension agent may go about processing

---

[*] Although the SNMP service under NT 3.x and 4 only support SNMPv1, MIB modules written using SMIv2 syntax can be implemented as extension agents. Full support of SNMPv2c will be included in the SNMP service in Windows NT 5.

SNMP requests that are received from SNMPv1 management systems. Chapter 8, *Implementing Traps*, looks at writing extension agents that support the generation of SNMPv1 traps.

If you plan to write extension agents for the Windows NT SNMP service, then you will be writing Win32 multithreaded DLLs. The "extendible" part of an SNMP agent is the ability to dynamically adapt and use information without recompiling the SNMP service code (which Microsoft doesn't distribute anyway). And the most fundamentally extendible part of Windows is its DLLs.

Although the extension agent DLLs use the multithreaded model, the extendible agent itself is only single-threaded. This means that only one SNMP request may be processed, or one trap message generated, at a time. The extension agents that you design must therefore be very quick and efficient in processing SNMP requests and in handling the collection and storage of MIB data.

Implementing Software Using the Win32 API

The Win32 API is a growing collection of functions used by Windows applications to access the Win32 operating system and its services. It would be wonderful if all Win32 API functions were implemented and had the same behavior on all Win32 platforms, but this is woefully not the case. And many hours of debugging will be the price you pay unless you learn a few details about the portability of the Win32 API.

It may seem strange to refer to the Win32 API as "portable." After all, Windows code runs only under Windows. But there are two Windows operating systems (Win16 and Win32), and several different Windows platforms (Windows, Windows for Workgroups, Windows 95, Windows NT, and Windows CE). And as I just mentioned, not all Windows applications run the same on every platform, or even run on every platform.

Prior to the release of Windows 95, a Win32 programmer only needed to keep in mind API features not available under earlier versions of Windows NT. Code using the Win32 API wouldn't run under Win16 systems* and no other Win32 systems yet existed. With the release of Windows 95 and Windows CE, and with the new features added by Service Pack upgrades, however, a considerable amount of code that is not portable between Win32 platforms has been introduced into the Win32 API.

---

* The Win32s subsystem enables single-threaded, Win32 applications to run under Win16, provided that they do not have high memory requirements. (Win32s is a lower-640K memory hog.)

There are actually four Win32 APIs:

- The Windows NT-specific API
- The Windows 95-specific API
- The Windows CE-specific API
- The common Win32 API shared by all Win32 platforms

Windows NT contains many APIs that will probably never be implemented under Windows 95, including event logging, security, and the Service Control Manager. It is generally assumed that any new APIs first implemented under Windows 95 will eventually migrate to Windows NT. Many Win32 functions common to Windows 95 and Windows NT are not supported by Windows CE, or are implemented with a reduced set of features.

To make this all a bit more confusing, additional APIs are added by periodic updates in the form of Service Packs. For example, the DirectX and Cryptographic APIs were introduced in the Windows 95-specific API in OEM Service Release 2 (OSR2), and the DirectX, Cryptographic, and ODBC APIs were all upgraded in the Windows NT-specific API by NT4 Service Pack 3. Any Windows system that does not have the respective Service Pack installed will not support these new APIs.*

The SNMP Extension, Utility, and Management APIs are native to Windows, but because the SNMP service is also available under Windows 95, the SNMP Extension and Utility APIs are part of the common Win32 API shared by Windows 95 and Windows NT. The SNMP Management API is only supported by Windows NT (although it does operate under Windows 95 as well), and it is possible that Windows CE will never support SNMP at all.

You have a choice: either you can design and verify that the extension agents you develop will operate correctly under Windows 95, or you can prevent the agents from loading under Windows 95 at all. If you do intend your extension agents to operate under Windows 95, then there are a few more things about the Win32 API that you should know.

Platform Differences in the Win32 API

Although most functions documented in the Win32 API are available under both Windows 95 and Windows NT, some Win32 API calls differ in their behavior when they are called, either in the parameters that they take or in the values that they return under different Win32 platforms. For example, functions that have a parameter of the SECURITY_ATTRIBUTE data type (including CreateFile,

---

* Unfortunately, there is no way to install only specific features of a Service Pack. It's all or nothing.

CreateProcess, and CreateThread) use the information passed in this parameter under Windows NT, but ignore it under Windows 95, where NT security is not implemented. The function GetClipboardData supports Unicode data formats under Windows NT, but not Windows 95. And the SystemParametersInfo function contains a multitude of features supported only under Windows 95 or Windows NT, but not both.

Win32 API calls that are not supported on a specific Win32 platform are stubbed out and, if called, will immediately return without performing any function. In such a case, the function will return an error code indicating that it "failed." Immediately calling the GetLastError function will return a value of 120 (ERROR_CALL_NOT_IMPLEMENTED) indicating that the function previously called is not supported under the current operating system.

If your code must run under all Win32 platforms, then you must avoid using Win32 platform-dependent API calls, or you must write your own calls to use in their place. Always check GetLastError after making a failed call to a platform-specific API call. You will also find it useful to use the GetVersionEx function to determine at runtime whether your code is executing under Windows 95 or Windows NT:

```
OSVERSIONINFO vi;
vi.dwOSVersionInfoSize = sizeof( OSVERSIONINFO );
GetVersionEx( &vi );
if ( vi.dwPlatformId == VER_PLATFORM_WIN32_NT )
{
    /* NT-specific code here */
}
```

Note that many of the functions belonging to the Win16 and Win32 APIs do not perform data validation, or at least do not perform it correctly. Often a General Protection Fault (GPF) will result from passing bad data, such as a NULL pointer or an out-of-range integer value to a Windows API function. It is a simple matter for any function to check if the data passed to it is within acceptable parameters. Many of the Windows API functions simply do not catch invalid data values and therefore generate unexpected results.

Always check that the value of your data is initialized and correct before and after passing it to any function—even if it's your own.

Windows NT Security

Some of the most frustrating things I have encountered in writing Win32 code are the security features supported by Windows NT. The most common source of frustration is with functions that operate as expected under Windows 95, but fail when called from the same code under Windows NT.

In most cases, calls to function such as ReadFile and WriteFile fail, after which GetLastError returns a value of 5 (ERROR_ACCESS_DENIED). This is an indication that the process or thread making the function call does not have permission to access the object whose handle it is using. It's annoying.

Another annoyance is running Win32 applications under Windows NT user accounts with different levels of permission. For example, consider an application that runs only under an account with "backup" permission. Windows NT will refuse to run this application under an account that does not currently have this permission bestowed. For the application to run, it must set the permission in the security token of the user account. Again, it's annoying!

To develop extension agents and SNMP management applications, you should always be logged into a user account with Administrator privileges. The SNMP service doesn't interact directly with users or the desktop interface, and only an administrator can set the policy of the SNMP service. This won't relieve you from the task of learning about the differences between a NULL SECURITY_DESCRIPTOR and a SECURITY_DESCRIPTOR with a NULL DACL, but the code in the extension agent examples on the CD-ROM tackles all of this.

Backward Compatibility

Microsoft recommends that extension agent development be performed using Windows NT 3.51 with Service Pack 5 installed, or using NT 4.0 with at least Service Pack 2 installed. Several problems with the SNMP service have been corrected in NT 4.0, but the fixes have not been backwardly applied to NT 3.51.

For Further Portability Information

For further information on Win32 API call portability, consult the following backgrounders and white papers available on the Microsoft Developers Network Web page and CD-ROM:

- "Differences in Win32 API Implementations Among Windows Operating Systems," Noel Nyman, October 10, 1996

- "Problems Encountered by Some Windows 95 Applications on Windows NT," MS Windows NT Workstation Technical Notes, Noel Nyman

- "Tips to Ensure Your Windows 95 Application Runs Under Windows NT 4.0"

If your extension agents must have full compatibility back to Windows NT 3.51, then it will be best for you to actually do your development and initial testing

under 3.51 and then test under 4.0. You must also become familiar with the problems currently pending with the SNMP service under the 3.x versions of NT.
(Appendix B, *Microsoft Knowledge Base*, contains a complete listing of all Knowledge Base articles published regarding the SNMP service.) There are also no
operational differences in the SNMP service and SNMP APIs under the Intel,
Alpha, and MIPS Windows NT platforms.

Building an Extension Agent DLL

Building an extension agent DLL requires the use of any language and compiler
that supports the creation of Win32 multithreaded dynamic link libraries, and
access to Win32 API. C and C++ are the most popular and obvious choices. How
you actually create and build an extension agent DLL will depend upon the type
of development platform you have chosen. If you use a platform such as
Microsoft Visual C++, you can simply specify that you wish to create a new
project that is a multithreaded Win32 DLL. If you want to perform all your builds
and development from the MS-DOS Console window, I still suggest using an integrated language development platform to create the project, set the options and
parameters, and generate the makefile that you will use.

To create an extension agent project, use the following project settings and build
options:

- Specify that the build target is a Win32 DLL and uses the multithreaded DLL
  runtime library (all extension agents must be compiled as multithreaded DLLs).

- Select the use of _stdcall as the default function calling convention; alternately, you may explicitly declare _stdcall or WINAPI in each function definition and prototype.

- Add *SNMPAPI.LIB* to the list of link libraries. Until you do, all of the calls
  made by your code to SNMPAPI functions will result in "unresolved external"
  link errors.

- Specify the DLL notification entry point if one is explicitly defined in your
  code. This is the function that is called when the DLL is attached and
  detached by a process or thread. If you don't explicitly define an entry point
  function in your code, the linker will include one by default. However, if you
  expect your entry point function to be called, you must pass its name to the
  linker or it won't be recognized. A commonly used name for the entry point
  function is DllMain.

- Most important, be sure to include the DLL's module definition (*.DEF*) file in
  the project. If you don't build the DLL using a *.DEF* file, then the SNMP service won't be able to access the SNMP Extension API functions in your DLL.

The Module Definition File

In its basic form, the *.DEF* file is used to define the public interface and link information to the DLL. Threads and processes that are attached to the DLL may only access the functions that are explicitly declared as exported in the *.DEF* file, using either build-time or runtime linking.

The basic *.DEF* file for an extension agent DLL is exceedingly simple and is shown here:

```
;;
;; MYAGENT.DEF
;;
;; Module definition file for MYAGENT.DLL
;;
LIBRARY MYAGENT

DESCRIPTION 'My Extension Agent'

EXPORTS
    SnmpExtensionInit
    SnmpExtensionInitEx
    SnmpExtensionQuery
    SnmpExtensionTrap
```

Under Win32, all that you need to define is the LIBRARY, DESCRIPTION, and EXPORTS sections of the *.DEF* file. You will, of course, add other sections and additional EXPORTS if your extension agent design requires them. Also, don't export the optional SnmpExtensionInitEx function if you do not define it in your extension agent.

TIP   If the SNMP service is failing to load your extension agent DLL and the SnmpExtensionInit function is not being called, check your *.DEF* file for omissions and misspellings. Or possibly, you forgot to include the *.DEF* file in your project in the first place.

About Import Libraries

If your Windows application contains explicit calls to functions defined in a DLL (this process is known as load-time dynamic linking), it must be linked at build-time with the DLL's import library to resolve the function calls made to the DLL. An import library is created during the link step when the DLL is built. The library usually has the same name as the DLL. Linking with an import library is not necessary, however, if the application calls DLL functions using runtime dynamic linking instead.

The *SNMPAPI.LIB* import library allows functions defined and implemented in the *SNMPAPI.DLL* to be linked at load-time and called by Win32 processes (the same is true of *MGMTAPI.LIB* and *MGMTAPI.DLL*). Including *SNMPAPI.LIB* in the listing of linked libraries is therefore a necessary step for building an extension agent DLL.

Normally, an import library is included with each new release of a DLL. And Microsoft does occasionally release updated revisions of *SNMPAPI.DLL* and *MGMTAPI.DLL* with a Service Pack. But unfortunately, new import libraries, header files, and checked (debugging) builds for these DLLs are not released by Microsoft (although new symbolic debugging information files are).

If you need to use a DLL, but do not have the DLL's import library, you can easily derive the import library from the DLL itself. This will allow you to use any new and updated functions present in the DLL. Of course, you must either have an updated header file that includes the prototypes of the new functions, or guess correctly at their calling parameters. In any case, you should always use import libraries derived from the DLLs that your application is linking, even if you are not using any new functions present in an updated DLL.

Creating an Import Library

Using the DUMPBIN and LIB MS-DOS utilities included with Visual C++, you can create import libraries using the following steps:

1. Create an EXPORTS dump listing of the DLL using DUMPBIN:

   ```
   DUMPBIN /EXPORTS filename.dll > filename.lst
   ```

   The resulting dump will contain a listing of all functions exported from the DLL. For example, if you perform an EXPORTS dump of the *MGMTAPI.DLL* library, you receive a listing of the following exported functions:

   ```
   ordinal hint  name

        1    0    SnmpMgrClose          (0000146F)
        2    1    SnmpMgrGetTrap        (00001EC3)
        3    2    SnmpMgrGetTrapEx      (00001EE6)
        4    3    SnmpMgrMIB2Disk       (00002210)
        5    4    SnmpMgrOidToStr       (0000178B)
        6    5    SnmpMgrOpen           (00001281)
        7    6    SnmpMgrRequest        (000014A6)
        8    7    SnmpMgrStrToOid       (0000177B)
        9    8    SnmpMgrTrapListen     (00001D7D)
       10    9    serverTrapThread      (0000183D)
   ```

2. You now use the name of each exported function listed in this dump to create a module definition file *MGMTAPI.DEF*:

   ```
   LIBRARY MGMTAPI
   ```

```
DESCRIPTION 'SNMP Management API fo

EXPORTS
        SnmpMgrClose        @1
        SnmpMgrGetTrap      @2
        SnmpMgrGetTrapEx    @3
        SnmpMgrMIB2Disk     @4
        SnmpMgrOidToStr     @5
        SnmpMgrOpen         @6
        SnmpMgrRequest      @7
        SnmpMgrStrToOid     @8
        SnmpMgrTrapListen   @9
        serverTrapThread    @10
```

3. Now you create the import library using the LIB librarian utility:

```
LIB /DEF:MGMTAPI.DEF
```

The import library (*MGMTAPI.LIB*) and the exports file (*MGMTAPI.EXP*) are created by the LIB librarian. The import library is then used to link applications that contain build-time function references to the *MGMTAPI.DLL* library. The exports file contains the export definitions of the DLL, which is used in lieu of a *.DEF* file when building the DLL.

For Further Import Library Information

For more information on import libraries, consult your compiler's documentation and the following Microsoft Knowledge Base article:

> Microsoft Knowledge Base, "How to Create 32-bit Import Libraries Without .OBJs or Source," article Q131313, 20-APR-1996

For more information on DLLs, refer to the section "Dynamic Link Libraries" of the Win32 SDK.

Installing, Starting, and Testing the Extension Agent

When you have successfully built an extension agent DLL, you will need to stop the SNMP service, copy the new DLL to the location indicated in the registry from which the DLL is loaded, and restart the SNMP service.

Under Windows NT, the SNMP service may be started from the MS-DOS Console window or from the Service Control Manager in the Control Panel. In either case, the service may only be started using an account with Administrator privileges. When you start the SNMP service under Windows NT, you will be informed that "the SNMP Service has started successfully," that "the SNMP Service is already started," or that "the SNMP Service has failed to start."

A failure to start is usually an indication that one of the extension agents has failed to respond to initialization, probably due to an infinite loop bug, or a GPF that left the SNMP service or the Service Control Manager in an unstable state. You can rename the problematic DLL or remove its entry from the registry; then attempt to restart the service.

NOTE   Under Windows 95, you start the SNMP service from the MS-DOS
                Console window by entering "SNMP" at the command line. If the
                SNMP service is already running, then you will see the message "the
                SNMP Service is already started." You can stop the SNMP service by
                using the command "SNMP -close."

Once the SNMP service has started successfully, look at the system event log using the Event Viewer. If something has gone wrong during the loading or initialization of any extension agents, you will see a warning entry (a yellow dot with an exclamation point) logged by the SNMP service. When you double-click on this entry you will probably see the message:

```
The SNMP Service is ignoring extension agent dll <the path and name of the
extension agent DLL> because it is missing or misconfigured.
```

This message indicates that something didn't go as expected during the loading or initialization of the extension agent DLL, but the SNMP service was still able to successfully start. In the spirit of event log messages, you are only told of the "what" and are left to figure out the "why."

Some reasons that a message will be generated include the following:

- The DLL notification entry point function returned a value of FALSE. If important initialization code present in this function failed, this function may be implemented to return FALSE as an indication to the SNMP service that the DLL should not be loaded into memory.

- The SnmpExtensionInit function in your extension agent returned a value of FALSE. If a serious initialization error occurs that would impair the function of the extension agent, then SnmpExtensionInit should return FALSE to prevent the SNMP service from calling the DLL to process SNMP requests.

- A bad OID value was passed to the SNMP service from SnmpExtensionInit. The third argument in SnmpExtensionInit must be a valid AsnObjectIdentifier, which informs the SNMP of the MIB subtree supported by the extension agent. Passing badly formed data, such as a NULL, will prevent the extension agent from being called by the SNMP service.

- You forgot to export the extension agent API functions in the DLL's module definition file (*.DEF*), or you forgot to include the *.DEF* file in the link step altogether. The SNMP service calls these functions when it loads the extension agent, and if they are not exported the load will fail. If this is your problem, then you probably forgot to create a module definition file for your extension agent DLL in the first place.

TIP   This message is an indication that the extension agent DLL only failed to initialize—not that it failed to load. In fact, unless the DLL entry point function returns FALSE when the DLL is first attached, the SNMP service will continue to load the extension agent although it will never be called. And if you try to over-write the extension agent DLL with a newer revision (one that includes the fix to the loading problem, I hope), you will receive a sharing violation error unless you first stop the SNMP service.

Testing an Extension Agent

Testing an extension agent requires that you be able to send SNMP requests to the SNMP service and determine that they have been properly resolved by your extension agent. You therefore need an SNMP management application that will allow you to construct SNMP messages with specific variable binding data, and that will accurately report the data returned in the GetResponse message. The SNMP service and SNMP management processes may reside on the same system, although testing over an actual network is preferable.

The obvious test tool is a network protocol analyzer, such as the NetXRay Protocol Analyzer and Network Monitor by Cinco Networks. NetXRay can both generate and display SNMP messages and is an excellent all-around testing tool. The only drawback you may encounter is that NetXRay can only monitor the network traffic between nodes with separate network addresses and interfaces. NetXRay cannot see SNMP messages exchanged by a management application and the SNMP service if they are both processes running on the same machine. (A functional demo of the NetXRay Protocol is on the CD-ROM.)

Network management platforms, such as HP OpenView for Windows Network Node Manager (32-bit) and Workgroup Node Manager (16-bit), are also useful tools for debugging extension agents. However, such management platforms are designed more for use by network administrators, and are not designed specifically as low-level protocol testing tools.

Building your own SNMP testing tool is also an option; this an excellent way to gain experience with the SNMP Management API. The Microsoft SNMPUTIL example program distributed in the MSDN is an SNMP management utility that may be used to send Get and GetNext request messages and receive traps. The SNMPTOOL example program included on the CD-ROM that accompanies this book is a much improved work-alike of SNMPUTIL that adds the ability to perform set operations and polling, provide a detailed listing of the data in GetResponse and trap messages received, and read command-line input from a file. (SNMPTOOL comes with full source code.)

Debugging an Extension Agent DLL

While testing your extension agent DLL, you will inevitably encounter unexpected behavior or the occurrence of a General Protection Fault that drives you to the conclusion that you need to use a debugger to find the problem. Up until now you've probably relied only upon your understanding of Windows, your compiler's error and warning messages, and good coding practices. But despite your knowledge, a schedule-slipping head-scratcher has turned up in your work.*

What's gone wrong?

There are three common indications that something is wrong with your extension agent DLL:

1. Your DLL will fail to load when the SNMP service is started. We've already discussed using the event log to detect when this happens. If your DLL is really hosed, then the SNMP service may not be able to start at all and will time-out. (Try putting a call to MessageBox in SnmpExtensionInit and see what happens.)

2. You will be happily sending requests and receiving responses when suddenly a GPF will occur. With luck, you will be able to faithfully reproduce the GPF and be able to isolate the section of code where the error occurs. For example, performing a SetRequest on a specific MIB object always produces a GPF, and this leads you to finding an uninitialized pointer or an array boundary overflow.

3. You see erroneous data returned in a GetResponse message, but the operation of the extension agent isn't affected. The problem might be a logical error such as referencing an incorrect entry in the MIB database, or a benign physical error such as an off-by-one bug or a cut-and-paste error.

---

* I am assuming that you are not one of those people who always develops applications using a debugger even though you are not currently experiencing any problems in your code. There's nothing wrong with this of course. You probably feel that all those extra gauges and switches that you've installed on your car's dashboard are necessary too. :-)

If you were debugging a typical Windows application, you could simply display some debugging messages on the user interface or debugging window to get a clue as to the problem that has occurred. But the SNMP service does not interact with the user or the desktop and it has no user interface. You will therefore be reduced to using functions like Beep and MessageBox to debug your code (I personally have solved many an executable mystery using Beep), or you can play it smart and use a debugger.

Debugging a Win32 service

A debugger normally starts the execution of the process that it is debugging. But in the case of Win32 services, which are usually started by the Service Control Manager or the Network Redirector, this is not possible. However, some debuggers, such as WinDbg and the Visual C++ debugger, support the ability to attach to a currently executing process.

Following these steps, attach WinDbg to the SNMP service for the purpose of debugging extension agent DLLs:

1. Start WinDbg.

2. Select "User DLLs" from the "Option" menu and enter the location of the *.DBG* files. The default directory *%SystemRoot%\SYMBOLS\DLL* should be present in the Symbol Search Path edit box. Additional directories may be specified and delimited using semicolons.

3. Choose Attach from the Run menu.

4. Select *SNMP.EXE* from the list box and click the Select button. If *SNMP.EXE* is not present in the list, then the SNMP service is not started (hit the Cancel button, start the SNMP service, and repeat step 3).

5. Choose Go from the Run menu (or click the toolbar button, or press F5).

WinDbg may also start process debugging from the MS-DOS Console window command line using the following syntax:

```
WINDBG -v -p <PID> -y <.DBG symbol file path>
```

PID is the process ID of the process to debug. The PID may be obtained using the PSTAT or PVIEW utilities included with Visual C++ and the Win32 SDK. (The PVIEW utility included with the Windows NT Resource Kit is an improved version of the Win32 SDK PVIEW.) If you specify the PID as a hexadecimal value, it must have a "0x" prefix.

Following these steps, attach the Visual C++ debugger to an executing process:

1. Open an MS-DOS Console window.

2. Start up the Microsoft Developer Studio in process debug mode by entering the following command:

```
MSDEV -p <PID>
```

3. The Developer Studio opens in debugging mode with the service running.

For Further Debugging Information

For more information on debugging Windows NT services, refer to the section "Debugging a Service" in the SDK documentation.

For more information on WinDbg, consult the WinDbg help file and the section "Debugging Programs" in the Win32 SDK Reference Help file (*WIN32SDK.HLP*).

Windows NT retail and checked builds

The Microsoft Developer Network CD-ROMs contain two sets of builds for each version of Windows NT. These sets are the retail build (or "free" build) and the checked build. The retail build is the retail version of Windows NT that is sold commercially and contains a minimal set of debugging information and fully optimized code. Additional debugging information not present in the retail build is shipped separately in the Window NT SDK as symbolic debugging files (*.DBG*) and is updated in the Service Packs.

The checked build is a special debugging version of Windows NT used for debugging drivers, services, and system code. It contains a considerable amount of error checking code and debugging symbols used to break into a debugger when an assert fails or an exception occurs. Needless to say, all of the extra debugging code causes the checked build to run more slowly than the retail build. (A checked build of Windows 95 is not currently distributed by Microsoft.)

It is not necessary to run the checked build of Windows NT when you are debugging an extension agent, or any user-level application for that matter. Checked builds are typically used only to debug kernel processes and device drivers when you are troubleshooting unexpected problems and you need detailed kernel-level diagnostic messages.

It is possible to develop SNMP applications using only the checked builds of the SNMP service and management files, and not be required to install the entire checked build of Windows NT itself. But Microsoft does not update the Windows NT checked build with the release of each new Service Pack. Instead, the debugging information for each updated component is distributed separately as *.DBG* files.

.DBG files

Debuggers that can use the symbolic debugging information in *.DBG* files, such as WinDbg, are very useful when used under the retail build of Windows. DBG files are stored in the *%SystemRoot%\SYMBOLS\DLL* directory on all NT systems, and your debugger should be configured to load the symbol files stored in this directory.

There are more than 200 *.DBG* files available in the Win32 SDK; the files for i386 machines are located in the *\SUPPORT\DEBUG\I386\SYMBOLS\DLL* directory. Each Service Pack that updates an executable or library file will include a new *.DBG* file for the updated file. You must also obtain the updated *.DBG* files with each new Service Pack that you install; if you don't do this, your debugger will complain of a mismatch error when it compares the checksum values of the new system file and the old *.DBG* file.

Only the *SNMPAPI.DBG* and *MGMTAPI.DBG* files are associated with SNMP application development under Win32. The *MGMTAPI.DBG* file is distributed with the Win32 SDK, but the *SNMPAPI.DBG* files currently is not. You can obtain *SNMPAPI.DBG* from the latest NT4 Service Pack that includes symbol files.

For Further .DBG File Information

For more information on *.DBG* files, including how to strip the debugging information from your own executables and DLLs and save it to *.DBG* files, consult the following Knowledge Base articles:

- "PDB And DBG Files - What They Are And How They Work," article Q121366, 19-JAN-1996

- "How to Set Up Windows NT Debug Symbols," article Q148659, 28-MAY-1996

- "How to Verify Windows NT Debug Symbols," article Q148660, 26-NOV-1996

- "How to Remove Symbols from Device Drivers," article Q128372, 18-SEP-1995

Inside the Extension Agent

Chapter 6 introduced the four functions of the SNMP Extension API that must be implemented to allow communication between the SNMP service and all extension agent DLLs. This chapter revisits three of these functions (SnmpExtensionInit,

SnmpExtensionInitEx, and SnmpExtensionQuery) to fill in some more of their implementation details. Chapter 8 covers the fourth function, SnmpExtensionTrap.

The information in this section describes only one possible design of an extension agent. You are perfectly free to make enhancements and improvements as you see fit. The only requirement of an extension agent is that it process SNMP requests and responses using the rules defined by RFC 1157. How you implement the code that follows these rules is up to you.

I do encourage you, however, to stay away from designs with a lot of extra overhead; these include any design whose name contains the words "object-oriented." The extra code inherent in such designs is more for the convenience of the human designers and implementers than for the machine.

Because a DLL may be used by a functionally diverse collection of applications, its code should be kept as light and efficient as possible. The majority of time spent processing an SNMP request is in the execution of extension agent code. Therefore, each extension agent must perform its processing quickly, since the single-threaded extendible agent can only process one SNMP request at a time. If you find the SNMP service slow in processing multiple requests, start looking for the bottleneck in your extension agents.

DllMain, SnmpExtensionInit, and SnmpExtensionInitEx

When an extension agent DLL is loaded by the SNMP service, the DLL entry point function is called first, the SnmpExtensionInit function is called next, and the SnmpExtensionInitEx function is called last. Each of these functions allows the DLL to perform the initialization required by both the DLL and the SNMP service.

The type of initialization that may need to be performed in any DLL includes the runtime assignment of variables, the allocation of memory for buffers and security descriptors, starting timers, and the creation of processes, threads, and events. Initialization operations specific to extension agent DLLs are performed in the SnmpExtensionInit function, and include the registration of the primary supported MIB subtree and trap event handle. The SnmpExtensionInitEx function is specifically used to register multiple MIB subtrees, but may be used for other types of non-critical initialization as well.

The DLL entry point function, often named DllEntryPoint or DllMain, is called when a thread or process attaches to or detaches from a DLL. If you do not explicitly implement an entry point function in your DLL code, then the linker will include a default entry point function for you.

Example 7-1 shows a typical DLL entry point function that creates an event object when the DLL is first attached (loaded into memory) by a process, and closes the handle when the DLL is detached (unloaded from memory). If the creation of the object fails, then the function returns FALSE and the DLL is not loaded into memory.

Example 7-1. A typical Win32 DLL entry point function

```
BOOL WINAPI DllMain( HANDLE hDll, DWORD dwReason, LPVOID lpReserved )
{
    BOOL bReturn = TRUE;

    switch( dwReason )
    {
        case DLL_PROCESS_ATTACH:
            ghDll = hDll;
            ghEvent = CreateEvent( NULL, FALSE, FALSE, NULL );
            if ( ghEvent == NULL )
                bReturn = FALSE;
            break;
        case DLL_THREAD_ATTACH:
            break;
        case DLL_THREAD_DETACH:
            break;
        case DLL_PROCESS_DETACH:
            CloseHandle( ghEvent );
            break;
        default:
            break;
    }
    return( bReturn );
}
```

DllMain

If DllMain is called with a dwReason value of DLL_PROCESS_ATTACH, and if any initialization critical to the operation of the DLL fails, then the loading of the DLL may be aborted in the entry point function by returning FALSE. This causes the process that is loading the DLL to receive an indication that the loading of the DLL failed, such as LoadLibrary returning a value of NULL. The DllMain return value is ignored by the system if dwReason is any value other than DLL_PROCESS_ATTACH.

When the DLL is unloaded from memory, DllMain is called with a dwReason of DLL_PROCESS_DETACH. The DLL now performs cleanup operations, such as closing handles, freeing memory, and notifying processes that the DLL is unloading. The DLL entry point function therefore acts as both the constructor and destructor for a DLL.

SnmpExtensionInit

Once the extension agent DLL is successfully loaded, the SNMP service calls the SnmpExtensionInit function to perform initialization operations required by both the SNMP extension agent API and the SNMP service. If the SnmpExtensionInit function is not found in an extension agent DLL, then the SNMP service will not be able to initialize the DLL. The SNMP service will then make an informational entry in the system event log indicating that a problem loading the DLL has occurred and will never call the DLL to resolve SNMP requests.

Example 7-2 shows a minimal SnmpExtensionInit function. When the SNMP service calls SnmpExtensionInit, the extension agent must at least specify the primary supported MIB subtree and the handle used by the extension agent to assert that it needs to send one or more trap messages. In this example, the extension agent specifies that its primary MIB subtree is 1.3.6.1.4.1.2035.1.5.1, and that it does not require trap support.

Example 7-2. A minimal implementation of SnmpExtensionInit

```
UINT OidPrefix[] = { 1, 3, 6, 1, 4, 1, 2035, 1, 5, 1 };
AsnObjectIdentifier MibOid = {
    sizeof( OidPrefix ) / sizeof( UINT ), OidPrefix };

BOOL WINAPI SnmpExtensionInit(
    DWORD                   dwTimeZeroReference,
    HANDLE                  *phPollForTrapEvent,
    AsnObjectIdentifier *pSupportedView )
{
    /* This extension agent does not need to generate traps */
    *phPollForTrapEvent = NULL;

    /* Register the primary managed MIB subtree with the extension agent */
    *pSupportedView = MibOid;

    return( TRUE );
}
```

This information is specified by the values returned to the SNMP service using the formal parameters of SnmpExtensionInit. The return value of TRUE is an indication that the initialization was successful.

Example 7-3 shows a more typical implementation of SnmpExtensionInit. In this example, an event object is created and its handle is passed back to the SNMP service. (This event object must be closed in DllMain when the extension agent is unloaded.) When the extension agent signals this event using SetEvent, the SNMP service will call SnmpExtensionTrap to collect trap information from the extension agent and then generate a trap message. SnmpExtensionInit also creates a thread that is used to monitor for the occurrence of events that require a trap to be generated.

Example 7-3. A typical implementation of SnmpExtensionInit

```
AsnInteger gMibVarOneStor;
AsnInteger gMibVarTwoStor;
HANDLE ghPollThread;
HANDLE ghTrapEvent;
DWORD gdwAgentStartTime;
DWORD gdwMonitorThreadId;

BOOL WINAPI SnmpExtensionInit(
DWORD                dwTimeZeroReference,
HANDLE               *phPollForTrapEvent,
AsnObjectIdentifier *pSupportedView )
{
    BOOL fResult = TRUE;

    /* Create an event to indicate that a trap needs to be sent */
    *phPollForTrapEvent = CreateEvent( NULL, FALSE, FALSE, NULL );
    if ( *phPollForTrapEvent != NULL )
    {
        /* Save the trap event handle for use by the extension agent */
        ghTrapEvent = *phPollForTrapEvent;

        /* Register the managed MIB subtree */
        *pSupportedView = MibOid;

        /* Save the start time of the SNMP service */
        gdwAgentStartTime = dwTimeZeroReference;

        /* Initialize the MIB variables */
        gMibVarOneStor = 0;
        gMibVarTwoStor = 42;

        /* Create a thread to monitor a process for trapable events */
        ghPollThread = CreateThread( NULL, 0,
            (LPTHREAD_START_ROUTINE)MonitorThread, 0, 0, &gdwMonitorThreadId );

        if ( ghPollThread == NULL )
            fResult = FALSE;    /* CreateThread() failed */
    }
    else
        fResult = FALSE;    /* CreateEvent() failed */

    return( fResult );    /* Return the initialization result */
}
```

If either of these critical initialization functions were to fail, the extension agent could not perform properly. In such a case, SnmpExtensionInit would return FALSE, indicating that the operation of the extension agent DLL is impaired and that the DLL should not be called by the SNMP service.

Other, non-critical initialization operations include specifying the primary MIB subtree, storing the SNMP start time (which is used in trap messages), and initializing local variables that are used to store MIB variable data. These operations cannot fail at runtime and therefore do not affect the return value.

SnmpExtensionInitEx

Assuming that both DllMain and SnmpExtensionInit return TRUE, the SNMP service then checks for the presence of the SnmpExtensionInitEx function in the extension agent DLL. If this function is present, it is repeatedly called by the SNMP service until it returns a value of FALSE.

Each call to SnmpExtensionInitEx is an attempt to register an additional MIB subtree supported by the extension agent. If the extension agent only supports the primary MIB subtree that it registered in SnmpExtensionInit, then SnmpExtensionInitEx may be omitted, or may be implemented to return only FALSE:

```
BOOL WINAPI SnmpExtensionInitEx(
    AsnObjectIdentifier *pSupportedView )
{
    /* No additional MIB subtrees to register */
    return( FALSE );
}
```

SnmpExtensionInitEx can be used to perform non-critical initialization operations. For example, SnmpExtensionInitEx is the perfect place to perform the runtime initialization of local variables:

```
BOOL WINAPI SnmpExtensionInitEx(
    AsnObjectIdentifier *pSupportedView )
{
    strncpy( gszString, "A String", sizeof( gszString ) - 1 );

    gpuTmp = (UINT *) SnmpUtilMemAlloc( 16 * sizeof ( UINT ) );
    gpuTmp[0] = 1; gpuTmp[1] = 3; gpuTmp[2] = 6; gpuTmp[3] = 1;

    GetWindowsDirectory( gszWinDir, sizeof( gszWinDir ) - 1 );

    /* No additional MIB subtrees to register */
    return( FALSE );
}
```

Initialization must be noncritical because once SnmpExtensionInitEx is called, the extension agent DLL is past the point where its loading can be aborted or its operation disabled.

Uninitialization

There is no counterpart to the SnmpExtensionInit function that can be called when the SNMP service detaches the extension agent DLL and unloads it from memory.* Any code that must be executed to perform cleanup operations when the DLL is detached must be placed in DllMain and executed when the value of the dwReason parameter is DLL_PROCESS_DETACH. Such cleanup commonly includes closing handles, deallocating memory, and signaling threads to exit. Chances are that you will be implementing DllMain to perform cleanup even if you end up with all of your initialization code in SnmpExtensionInit.

Supporting Multiple MIB Subtrees

The intended purpose of SnmpExtensionInitEx is to register additional MIB subtrees that the extension agent supports. Many SNMP agents support multiple MIB modules or, more precisely, multiple sections or branches in the MIB tree.

For example, if an extension agent were to register the MIB subtree 1.3.6.1.4.1.9999.1, this would be an indication that all managed objects registered in this branch were implemented by the DLL. This might be true if the number of objects were few, but any branch may contain thousands or even millions of registered objects; it would therefore be too big for any single extension agent to implement and maintain.

Instead, a single extension agent might only implement specific sub-branches of a MIB subtree. For example, under the enterprises.9999.1 branch, an extension agent might register 1.3.6.1.4.1.9999.1.5 as its primary MIB subtree, then register the following additional MIB subtrees:

```
1.3.6.1.4.1.9999.1.5
1.3.6.1.4.1.9999.1.6
1.3.6.1.4.1.9999.1.12
1.3.6.1.4.1.9999.9.2
1.3.6.1.4.1.9999.35.223.6
1.3.6.1.4.1.9999.35.223.18
```

Each of these OIDs specifies the starting node of a branch in the enterprises.9999.1 MIB tree. All objects registered under each of these branches would therefore be supported by an extension agent registering these MIB subtrees.

A more practical example is easily shown using the multiple MIB subtrees supported by the *INETMIB1.DLL* extension agent. If we walk through the INETMIB1 under Windows NT and use the RFC1213-MIB module as a map, we find that the groups sys(1), if(2), ip(4), icmp(5), tcp(6), udp(7), egp(10), and snmp(11) are registered as supported MIB subtrees. The MIB subtree containing the first group, sys(1), is registered in SnmpExtensionInit: the remaining groups

---

* The new extension agent framework in the Windows NT 5 SDK defines an SnmpExtensionClose function that will be used to perform all cleanup operations when an extension agent DLL is unloaded.

are registered in SnmpExtensionInitEx, using code that looks something like Example 7-4.

Example 7-4. A possible implementation of SnmpExtensionInitEx in INETMIB1.DLL

```
#define    VIEWCOUNT    7

BOOL WINAPI SnmpExtensionInitEx(
    AsnObjectIdentifier *pSupportedView )
{
    BOOL fResult = TRUE;
    static UINT nViewCount = 0;
    UINT MibViews[VIEWCOUNT][7] = {
        { 1, 3, 6, 1, 2, 1, 2 },      /* if */
        { 1, 3, 6, 1, 2, 1, 4 },      /* ip */
        { 1, 3, 6, 1, 2, 1, 5 },      /* icmp */
        { 1, 3, 6, 1, 2, 1, 6 },      /* tcp */
        { 1, 3, 6, 1, 2, 1, 7 },      /* udp */
        { 1, 3, 6, 1, 2, 1, 10 },     /* egp */
        { 1, 3, 6, 1, 2, 1, 11 } };   /* snmp */

    /* Check if there are any MIB subtrees remaining */
    if ( nViewCount < VIEWCOUNT )
    {
        pSupportedView->ids       = MibViews[nViewCount];
        pSupportedView->idLength = sizeof( MibViews[nViewCount] )
          / sizeof( UINT );
        nViewCount++;
    }
    else
        fResult = FALSE; /* No more MIB additional subtrees */

    return( fResult );
}
```

In this example, one additional MIB subtree is registered by the extension agent each time SnmpExtensionInitEx is called by the SNMP service. A static counter is used to iterate through the MibViews array each time SnmpExtensionInitEx is called. The MIB subtree is returned in pSupportedView using a pointer to an AsnObjectIdentifier object initialized using the OID of the MIB subtree and its length.

A value of TRUE is returned if there are more MIB subtrees to register and, therefore, SnmpExtensionInitEx should be called again. FALSE is returned as an indication that no additional MIB subtrees remain to be registered and that the SNMP service should ignore the object pointed to by pSupportedView.

This example is very simple because all of the MIB subtrees contain the same number of subidentifiers. If you were to modify the MibViews array by adding some OIDs of differing lengths, you would not get the expected results:

```
UINT MibViews[VIEWCOUNT][9] = {
    { 1, 3, 6, 1, 2, 1, 2 },       /* 1.3.6.1.2.1.2.0.0 */
    { 1, 3, 6, 1, 2, 2 },          /* 1.3.6.1.2.2.0.0.0 */
    { 1, 3, 6, 1, 4, 1, 1, 1, 1 }, /* 1.3.6.1.4.1.1.1.1 */
    { 1, 3, 6, 1, 4, 9, 7, 2 } };  /* 1.3.6.1.4.9.7.2.0 */
```

This implementation of MibViews contains four OIDs, each of a different length (specifically, a different number of subidentifiers). Because each element of an array implemented in C must be the same size, each OID that is shorter than the full width of the array will be right-padded with zeros. The resulting OIDs (shown in the comments) are definitely not what you were expecting. The solution to this problem is to initialize each OID separately, preferably using the AsnObjectIdentifier type, and not storing the OIDs in an array, as shown in Example 7-5.

Example 7-5. A more practical implementation of SnmpExtensionInitEx

```
BOOL WINAPI SnmpExtensionInitEx(
    AsnObjectIdentifier *pSupportedView )
{
    BOOL fResult = TRUE;         static UINT nViewCount = 0;
    UINT MibView1[] = { 1, 3, 6, 1, 2, 1, 2 };       /* 1.3.6.1.2.1.2 */
    UINT MibView2[] = { 1, 3, 6, 1, 2, 2 };          /* 1.3.6.1.2.2 */
    UINT MibView3[] = { 1, 3, 6, 1, 4, 1, 1, 1, 1 }; /* 1.3.6.1.4.1.1.1.1 */
    UINT MibView4[] = { 1, 3, 6, 1, 4, 9, 7, 2 };    /* 1.3.6.1.4.9.7.2 */
    AsnObjectIdentifier OidMibView1 = { { sizeof( MibView1 ) / sizeof( UINT ) }, MibView1 };
    AsnObjectIdentifier OidMibView2 = { { sizeof( MibView2 ) / sizeof( UINT ) }, MibView2 };
    AsnObjectIdentifier OidMibView3 = { { sizeof( MibView3 ) / sizeof( UINT ) }, MibView3 };
    AsnObjectIdentifier OidMibView4 = { { sizeof( MibView4 ) / sizeof( UINT ) }, MibView4 };

    /* Check if there are any MIB subtrees remaining */
    switch ( nViewCount )
    {
        case 0:
            *pSupportedView = OidMibView1;
            break;
        case 1:
            *pSupportedView = OidMibView2;
            break;
        case 2:
            *pSupportedView = OidMibView3;
            break;
        case 3:
            *pSupportedView = OidMibView4;
            break;
        default:
            fResult = FALSE; /* No more additional MIB subtrees */
            break;
    }
    nViewCount++;

    return( fResult );
}
```

Note that because SnmpExtensionInitEx is called repeatedly, poor coding makes it a good candidate for an infinite loop bug. Such a bug will hang an extension agent DLL and prevent the SNMP service from being started. On my P6-200 system running NT4 SP3, an extension agent implemented with an SnmpExtensionInitEx function that only returned TRUE was called 850 times before the Service Control Manager timed-out after 30 seconds of attempting to start the SNMP service. So make sure that your implementation of SnmpExtensionInitEx will eventually return FALSE. Also, don't plan on registering hundreds of MIB subtrees.

NOTE   The "Ex" Win32 function name suffix is commonly reserved for new functions that extend the capability of an existing function by adding additional features (for example, WriteFile and WriteFileEx). The SnmpExtensionInitEx function really doesn't fit this model; it does add an additional initialization feature not supported by SnmpExtensionInit, but it does not support any of the fundamental features implemented by SnmpExtensionInit. You therefore cannot use SnmpExtensionInitEx in place of SnmpExtensionInit, although your Win32 intuition may suggest otherwise.

Initialization and Threads

If you will be creating multiple threads and processes during initialization, then it is a practical idea to use the CREATE_SUSPENDED flag when you make calls to CreateThread and CreateProcess. This allows the thread or process to be created in a suspended state; it will not start executing until the ResumeThread function is called. Using this method, you can make sure that all threads and processes have been created successfully before allowing any of them to start running; you can also control the order in which the threads and process are started.

You may also gain some additional control if you use a thread to execute initialization code, especially to initialize a large MIB database. When an extension agent is loaded, it may need to initialize each of its MIB database variables to some default value. This default value may be obtained in a number of ways:

- Read from an external source (such as a hardware device, external database, or the Windows registry)

- Calculated from other data (as is the value of sysObjectId as maintained by *INETMIB1.DLL*)

- Hard-coded into the agent itself

Depending on the number of MIB variables, and how the initialization data is acquired, this process could require a rather long time to complete.

The Windows NT Service Control Manager only gives each service at most 30 seconds to start. Lengthy initialization procedures should therefore be handled by a separate thread, allowing SnmpExtensionInit to return TRUE before the SCM times-out and aborts the loading of the SNMP service.

All of the extension agent's MIB database initialization code could be placed in a thread procedure, the thread created in a suspended state in DllMain, and later started by SnmpExtensionInit or SnmpExtensionInitEx. When the MIB database initialization is completed, the thread could set a flag as an indication to SnmpExtensionQuery that it is OK to start processing SNMP requests.

The same flag would also indicate that requests should not be processed if the database failed to initialize. Because there is no mechanism for an extension agent to politely refuse a request, SnmpExtensionQuery can only return a value of FALSE. This will cause the extendible agent to return a response with no variable bindings and indicating that a genErr error has occurred.

If any of the initialization code in any extension agent fails, then a mention should be made in the system event log. The log entry should be very descriptive: it should give the user an indication of whether the problem was in the system environment (out of memory or resources), was a failure to properly initialize, or an unexpected runtime exception occurred.

WARNING   Do not use the _declspec(thread) statement to allocate thread local storage (TLS) in an extension agent DLL. The SNMP service uses LoadLibrary to dynamically load each extension agent DLL into memory. The use of this statement causes LoadLibrary to fail. See Microsoft Knowledge Base, article Q118816: "PRB: LoadLibrary() Fails with _declspec(thread)."

Roadmap for Processing an SNMP Request

The rules for processing an SNMPv1 request message are described by RFC 1157. These processing rules are used by SNMPv1 agents to determine whether or not a specific SNMPv1 request operation was processed successfully. And because these same rules are used to process all SNMPv1 messages, you may reuse the same SNMP message parsing code in all of the extension agents that you write.

Processing an SNMPv1 message is actually quite simple. Each request message will contain one or more variable bindings. The extension agent must iterate through each binding and apply the Get, GetNext, or Set operation specified by the message type to the OID and the data value present in each binding.

SnmpExtensionQuery

The code implemented in SnmpExtensionQuery is responsible for processing the variable bindings in an SNMPv1 request message,* for creating the variable bindings list that is present in the resulting GetResponse message, and for determining the error values in the SNMP PDU header. The majority of execution time spent in any extension agent DLL occurs in SnmpExtensionQuery. As a consequence, the majority of extension agent code that you write will be for the purpose of processing SNMP request messages.

The act of "processing a variable binding" is basically a three-step procedure:

1. The OID specified in the varbind must be matched to the OID of a MIB variable residing in the extension agent's MIB data.

2. The varbind must be validated by comparing its attributes to those of the MIB variable that it references. A varbind may fail validation if, for example, it contains data that does not match the data type specified by the MIB variable.

3. The MIB variable data must be actually written or read.

Each extension agent loaded by the SNMP service is only responsible for processing the variable bindings of a request message that specifies MIB objects residing within its supported MIB name space. If all of the MIB objects specified in the varbinds of a single message are maintained by the same extension agent, then the entire varbind list of the message is passed only to that extension agent.

Because the varbinds of a single SNMP request message may specify MIB objects maintained by several different extension agents, it is the job of the SNMP service (specifically the extendible agent) to break up the varbind list contained in a request message and send each varbind only to the specific extension agent that maintains the specified MIB object.

Figure 7-1 illustrates an example of a SetRequest message containing five varbinds that specify the OIDs of MIB variables maintained by three extension agents. The extendible agent must decide which extension agent supports the processing of which OID based on the extension agent's registered MIB subtrees. Each varbind is then passed only to the extension agent that maintains the MIB variable specified by the varbind's OID.

The varbinds are passed to each extension agent via SnmpExtensionQuery in the form of a list. SnmpExtensionQuery then iterates through each varbind in the list and applies the request operation to each MIB variable specified. The attributes of each MIB variable must be compared to the data in each varbind to determine the

---

* The new extension agent framework in the Windows NT 5 SDK defines an SnmpExtensionQueryEx function that will be used to process SNMPv2c request messages.

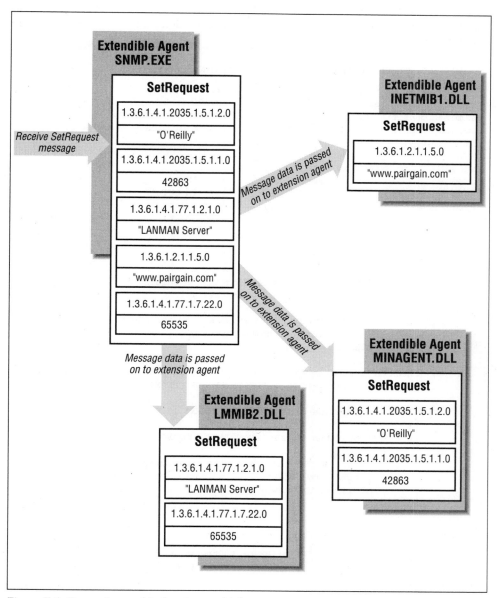

Figure 7-1. Processing varbinds using multiple extension agents

value of the ErrorStatus and ErrorIndex fields in the GetResponse message. This information is passed back to the extendible agent using the SnmpExtension-Query function parameters.

Example 7-6 shows a typical implementation of SnmpExtensionQuery. A loop iterates through the list of variable bindings and calls the ResolveVarBind function to

determine whether the OID exists in the extension agent's supported MIB
subtrees, to perform the request operation, and to determine whether the operation resulted in an error.

Example 7-6. A typical implementation of SnmpExtensionQuery

```
UINT OidPrefix[] = { 1, 3, 6, 1, 4, 1, 2035, 1, 5, 1 };
UINT OidOutOfMibView[] = { 1, 3, 6, 1, 4, 1, 2035, 1, 5, 2 };
AsnObjectIdentifier MibOid = { SIZEOFOID( OidPrefix ), OidPrefix };
AsnObjectIdentifier MibOidOutOfMibView = { SIZEOFOID( OidOutOfMibView ),
  OidOutOfMibView };

BOOL WINAPI SnmpExtensionQuery(
    BYTE                 bRequestType,        /* IN */
    RFC1157VarBindList *pVariableBindings,    /* IN OUT */
    AsnInteger           *pErrorStatus,       /* OUT */
    AsnInteger           *pErrorIndex )       /* OUT */
{
    UINT i;
    BOOL fResult = SNMPAPI_NOERROR;

    /* Iterate through each variable binding in the request */
    for ( i = 0; i < pVariableBindings->len; i++ )
    {
        /* On a Get or GetNext retrieve a value from the MIB */
        *pErrorStatus = ResolveVarBind( bRequestType,
            &pVariableBindings->list[i] );

        /* Check if a GetNext went beyond the supported range of the MIB */
        if ( *pErrorStatus == SNMP_ERRORSTATUS_NOSUCHNAME )
        {
            if ( bRequestType == MIB_ACTION_GETNEXT )
            {
                *pErrorStatus = SNMP_ERRORSTATUS_NOERROR;

                /* Return an OID outside of the registered MIB subtree */
                SnmpUtilOidCpy( &pVariableBindings->list[i].name,
                    MibOidOutOfMibView );
            }

        }

        /* Return any indication of error to the extendible agent */
        if ( *pErrorStatus != SNMP_ERRORSTATUS_NOERROR )
        {

            *pErrorIndex = i + 1; /* Point to varbind that cause the error */
            break; /* Error occurred. Stop processing the remaining varbinds */
        }
    }

    /* Flush the Set cache or cause the extendible agent to return a genErr */
    if ( bRequestType == MIB_ACTION_SET )
    {
```

Example 7-6. A typical implementation of SnmpExtensionQuery (continued)

```
        if ( *pErrorStatus == SNMP_ERRORSTATUS_NOERROR )
            fResult = FlushMibVarCache();
        else
            ClearMibVarCache();
    }
    return( fResult );
}
```

The return value of ResolveVarBind is the SNMP protocol error that resulted from performing the request operation on the data in the variable binding. It is this value that is eventually stored in the ErrorStatus field of the GetResponse PDU. A return value of 0 (noError) indicates that the varbind was processed successfully. A non-zero return value indicates that a protocol error occurred and that any remaining varbinds in the request message should not be processed. The index of the erroneous varbind is stored in the ErrorIndex field of the resulting GetResponse PDU.

There is one case when an error is not really an error. If a GetNext operation returns a noSuchName error, this is an indication that the "next" MIB variable lies outside of the range of registered MIB variables supported by this extension agent. The "next" variable is therefore the first MIB variable maintained by the extension agent that supports the next lexical MIB object.

An extension agent can indicate that a varbind should be processed by the next extension agent by changing the OID of the varbind to an OID outside of its supported MIB objects. The extendible agent will notice this discrepancy and pass the varbind to the "next" extension agent. If there is no "next" extension agent, then a noSuchName error will actually result as a response.

After the varbind list iteration is complete, we need to determine if a Set operation was being performed without error. If so, then all of the new MIB variable values that were cached during processing are now written to the MIB database by FlushMibVarCache. If an error occurred during the Set operation, the new values that were written to the cache are not written to permanent storage and must be cleared by calling ClearMibVarCache before SnmpExtensionQuery may return. This algorithm, however, does not fully conform to the processing requirement defined by SNMPv1 (see the section "A processing caveat: SetRequest").

After all of the varbind list processing is completed, we merely return TRUE if the processing was successful, or FALSE is some sort of failure occurred. If FALSE is the return value, then the extendible agent will return a GetResponse message indicating a genErr and containing no variable bindings. This is an indication to the extendible agent that a major failure has occurred within the extension agent and that the resulting variable bindings list cannot be returned. SNMPv1 does not define a case where a GetResponse message would not contain any variable bindings, so this behavior is a non-standard Microsoft extension to the functionality of SNMP.

A processing caveat: SetRequest

An extension agent must use a multi-pass approach to support SNMP's "all or nothing rule," where all of the MIB variables in a SetRequest must be successfully set, or none of the values may be set. In other words, if a protocol error results while processing one of the SetRequest varbinds, then processing stops and none of the new values specified in the SetRequest are set. This is true of GetRequest and GetNextRequest processing as well.

Unfortunately, a design flaw in the Microsoft extendible agent[*] causes this rule to be violated under one specific condition. As illustrated in the beginning of this section, a single request message may have its variable bindings broken up and processed by multiple extension agents. When a SetRequest message is processed in this way, each extension agent is responsible for internally implementing a multi-pass approach for processing these varbind values. The problem is that if a Set operation in one extension agent fails, there is no mechanism to prevent the other extension agents that are processing varbinds of the same SetRequest message from storing the new values if their processing is successful.

Looking back to Figure 7-1, the *INETMIB1.DLL* and *LMMIB2.DLL* will process their varbinds correctly, but note that the second varbind processed by *MINAGENT.DLL* will result in a badValue error (the MINAGENT MIB specifies the range of this variable to be 0 to 64). INETMIB1 and LMMIB2 will not know of the failure of the Set operation in MINAGENT and will violate the "all or nothing" rule of SNMP by storing the new MIB values of the varbinds that they processed. The GetResponse returned by the extendible agent will correctly indicate the badValue error, but the MIB variables processed by INETMIB1 and LMMIB2 will be modified to store the new values specified in the varbinds of the erroneous SetRequest message.

We could attempt to create some sort of ad hoc mechanism to synchronize all of the extension agents, but the only real solution is that the multi-pass approach for Set operations must be implemented by both the SNMP service and the extension agents. The lack of such a mechanism prevents the Microsoft extendible agent from correctly implementing the requirements of the set operation defined by SNMPv1.[†]

---

[*] To be perfectly fair, this is a common problem in most master agent/subagent designs and is not specific to Microsoft.

[†] The extendible agent under NT5 has been "fixed" by using multiphase commits to correctly handle the processing of SetRequest messages.

The MIB Database

In Chapter 1, *Introduction to SNMP*, I said that a MIB is not, in fact, a database. A MIB is merely a template or schema describing the organization of data that is used as a public interface for monitoring and manipulating network management data. However, to implement a MIB for use in an SNMP agent, the MIB must be "realized" as some sort of structure that contains the management information organized by the MIB. It is this structure that we call the MIB database.

A MIB database needs to contain one entry for each instance of a MIB variable supported by an agent. Each database record will contain information found in the OBJECT-TYPE macro that defines its corresponding leaf node. The leaf node is considered a *class* that defines the managed object, and the MIB variable is an instance of the class. As an example of a typical leaf node, let's look at the definition of the sysLocation (1.3.6.1.2.1.1.6) object as it appears in MIB-II:

```
sysLocation OBJECT-TYPE
    SYNTAX      DisplayString (SIZE (0..255))
    ACCESS      read-write
    STATUS      mandatory
    DESCRIPTION
        "The physical location of this node (e.g.,
        `telephone closet, 3rd floor')."
    ::= { system 6 }
```

Each object defined in a MIB is described by the information that is present in its corresponding OBJECT-TYPE macro definition. This information is required by an agent to process a request that specifies this particular MIB variable. If we were to map the data in sysLocation that is used by an agent into the fields of a database record, they would appear as follows:

```
Object Identifier      1.3.6.1.2.1.6
Instance Identifier    0
Data Type              OCTET STRING
Minimum Size           0
Maximum Size           255
Access Rights          readable, writeable
```

This is the basic information required to process a Get, GetNext, or Set operation performed on the MIB-II sysLocation variable. The OID of the variable in the MIB, the type and size of data that may be stored by the variable, and the access rights are all described by OBJECT-TYPE and are used by the agent.

However, several pieces of information present in the OBJECT-TYPE definition are not present in this database record. The object descriptor (sysLocation) and the data described by the STATUS and DESCRIPTION clauses are not used by the agent and are therefore not stored. The instance identifier of the object is also not stored, because sysLocation is a scalar type and therefore always has an instance identifier of ".0".

The information declared in an OBJECT-TYPE definition only forms the fundamental description of a MIB variable. Depending upon the type of database implemented, you will need additional entry fields to store implementation-specific MIB variable data to be used for searching the MIB, caching temporary data, and defining the structure of the database itself.

| *TIP* | If you need instruction and advice on how to actually write a MIB, I suggest that you pick up a copy of the excellent book *Understanding SNMP MIBs* by David Perkins and Evan McGinnis (Prentice Hall, 1997). In fact, pick up a copy of this book anyway. No one who reads or writes SNMP MIBs should be without it. |

A Simple MIB Database

An extension agent can store its MIB data in various places:

- All extension agents can store their MIB data in a central public data repository, such as in the Windows registry.

- Each extension agent can store its MIB data in a private database.

- Each extension agent can store its MIB data in local process memory.

Both the local and external storage models have their pros and cons. However, most of the time MIB data is not stored; it simply exists in the components of the device or service that is being managed. For example, the count of UDP packets received is maintained by the UDP protocol driver. When requested, the SNMP agent calls the API provided by this driver to retrieve this value. When a SetRequest is received that specifies that the value of an attribute of a managed resource is to be changed, the agent calls the API of the resource manager responsible for changing the attribute's value.

Extension agents that support only a few hundred or fewer MIB variables are the best candidates for storing MIB data in local process memory. If you avoid a design that requires dynamic insertion and deletion of objects in the MIB database, then organizing all MIB variables as a simple one-dimensional array will do nicely.

If we were to use the data types defined in *SNMP.H* to render all of the information that an agent needs to access and maintain a MIB variable into a single C structure, we might end up with the code shown in Example 7-7.

Example 7-7. A MIB database record structure

```
typedef struct _MibVars
{
    AsnObjectIdentifier Oid;   /* MIB variable OID */
    void    *pStorage;         /* Pointer to the MIB storage variable */
    void    *pTempVar;         /* Pointer to a temporary storage variable */
    BOOL    fModified;         /* True if variable value has been modified */
    BYTE    bType;             /* ASN.1 data type of variable */
    DWORD   dwMinVal;          /* Minimum end of range or length */
    DWORD   dwMaxVal;          /* Maximum end of range or length */
    UINT    uAccess;           /* Access specifier */
    UINT    (*MibFunc)(UINT, struct _MibVars *, RFC1157VarBind *);
    struct _MibVars    *MibNext;  /* Pointer to next entry in MIBVARS array */
} MIBVARS;
```

The MIBVARS data type definition defines a single element in an array used to store MIB variables. Each element in a MIBVARS array contains the following fields:

Oid

Contains the OBJECT IDENTIFIER of the MIB variable and the number of sub-identifiers that the OID contains. Refer to Chapter 4, *Inside SNMP*, for a more detailed explanation of the AsnObjectIdentifier data type.

pStorage

The address of a local variable that stores the actual MIB variable data. If the MIB variable data is stored externally to the extension agent, this pointer is not required.

pTempVar

The address of a local variable that is used to cache a new value specified by a SetRequest. If all of the variable bindings in the SetRequest were processed with no errors, the data temporarily cached in pTempVar is written to the variable referenced by pStorage; then the memory pointed to by pTempVar may be deallocated. If the temporary MIB variable data is cached externally to the extension agent, this pointer is not required.

fModified

The flag set to indicate that a SetRequest operation has changed the value of this variable. If all of the varbinds in the SetRequest message are processed without error, then each MIB variable with fModified set to TRUE will have the value in its temporary storage (pTempVar) copied to its permanent storage (pStorage) and this flag will be cleared to FALSE. If a protocol error does occur during processing, this flag will still be cleared to FALSE, but no copying will be performed.

bType

>   The ASN.1 type of the MIB variable data. This value corresponds to the ASN_*
>   types defined in *SNMP.H*:

```
ASN_INTEGER                 2
ASN_OCTETSTRING             4
ASN_RFC1213_DISPSTRING      4
ASN_NULL                    5
ASN_OBJECTIDENTIFIER        6
ASN_RFC1155_IPADDRESS      64
ASN_RFC1155_COUNTER        65
ASN_RFC1155_GAUGE          66
ASN_RFC1155_TIMETICKS      67
ASN_RFC1155_OPAQUE         68
```

>   Note that ASN_NULL is only used to indicate that a variable binding is not yet
>   initialized.

dwMinVal and dwMaxVal

>   The minimum and maximum allowed size (INTEGER and Gauge) or length
>   (OCTET STRING and OPAQUE) of the MIB variable data. These values are
>   used to perform range checking on new values specified by a SetRequest. If
>   multiple fixed or range values are specified in the OBJECT-TYPE SIZE clause,
>   the function that handles the processing of the MIB variable will need to be
>   explicitly coded to be aware of the acceptable values that may be assigned to
>   the MIB variable. No range checking is performed if dwMaxVal contains a
>   value of zero. However, this is not an acceptable value to use if the maximum
>   value that may be stored by a variable is zero (e.g., -100..0).

uAccess

>   The access mode of the MIB variable. This value indicates whether the vari-
>   able is read-only, write-only, read-write, or not-accessible. *SNMP.H* does not
>   define values for the access mode of a MIB variable, so you will be required
>   to define them in your extension agent implementation. The code examples
>   in this book use the following access mode definitions:

```
MIB_ACCESS_READ             0
MIB_ACCESS_WRITE            1
MIB_ACCESS_READWRITE        2
MIB_ACCESS_NOTACCESSIBLE    3
```

MibFunc

>   A pointer to the function that is called to perform a GetRequest, GetNextRe-
>   quest, or SetRequest operation on this MIB variable. Each MIB variable
>   therefore knows how to process itself. The arguments passed to MibFunc are
>   the type of request operation (the value of a ASN_RFC1157_* definition in
>   *SNMP.H*), a pointer to the MIBVARS element for the MIB variable, and a
>   pointer to the variable binding of the request message that specified the MIB
>   variable.

MibNext

> A pointer to the next lexical MIB object. This is the variable that would be returned if a GetNextRequest were performed on the MIB variable of this record. This address may be located anywhere in the database and need not be the next physical element in the array.

Note that you will never specify the MIB_ACCESS_NOTACCESSIBLE access mode for a MIB variable. This access mode, however, can be used when debugging to temporarily hide the existence of a variable in the MIBVARS array from searches.

Implementing a MIB Using MIBVARS

Next, let's look at how to use the MIBVARS data type for implementing a MIB database as a local array. Assume that we have an enterprises MIB residing at 1.3.6.1.4.1.2035.1.5.1, and it contains the following scalar variables:

OID	Object Descriptor	Data Type	Access Mode
1.1	oraAgentVarOneOne	INTEGER(0..64)	read-write
1.2	oraAgentVarOneTwo	OCTET STRING(SIZE(1..20))	read-write
1.3	oraAgentVarOneThree	OBJECT IDENTIFIER	read-only
2.1	oraAgentVarTwoOne	IpAddress	read-only
3.1.1	oraAgentVarThreeOneOne	Counter	read-only
3.1.2	oraAgentVarThreeOneTwo	Gauge(94..106)	read-only
3.2	oraAgentVarThreeTwo	TimeTicks	read-only

To allow an extension agent to maintain each of these MIB variables, we can code them up using local storage variables and a MIBVARS array, as shown in Example 7-8.

Example 7-8. Implementation of a MIB database

```
#define ORAAGENTVARONETWO_LEN     20
#define SIZEOFOID( Oid )     ( sizeof ( Oid ) / sizeof( UINT ) )

/* MIB enterprises OID */
UINT oraAgentPrefixOid[] = { 1, 3, 6, 1, 4, 1, 2035, 1, 5, 1 };
AsnObjectIdentifier MibOidOraAgent = {
    SIZEOFOID(oraAgentPrefixOid),
    oraAgentPrefixOid
};

/* MIB variable OID suffixes */
UINT oraAgentVarOneOneOid[]      = { 1, 1, 0 };
UINT oraAgentVarOneTwoOid[]      = { 1, 2, 0 };
UINT oraAgentVarOneThreeOid[]    = { 1, 3, 0 };
UINT oraAgentVarTwoOneOid[]      = { 2, 1, 0 };
UINT oraAgentVarThreeOneOneOid[] = { 3, 1, 1, 0 };
UINT oraAgentVarThreeOneTwoOid[] = { 3, 1, 2, 0 };
UINT oraAgentVarThreeTwoOid[]    = { 3, 2, 0 };
```

Example 7-8. Implementation of a MIB database (continued)

```
/* MIB storage variables */
AsnInteger          oraAgentVarOneOneStor = 8;
char                oraAgentVarOneTwoStor[ORAAGENTVARONETWO_LEN+1];
AsnObjectIdentifier oraAgentVarOneThreeStor;
AsnIPAddress        oraAgentVarTwoOneStor;
AsnCounter          oraAgentVarThreeOneOneStor = 0;
AsnGauge            oraAgentVarThreeOneTwoStor = 0;
AsnTimeticks        oraAgentVarThreeTwoStor = 0;

/* MIB temporary variables */
AsnInteger          oraAgentVarOneOneTemp;
char                oraAgentVarOneTwoTemp[ORAAGENTVARONETWO_LEN+1];
AsnObjectIdentifier oraAgentVarOneThreeTemp;
AsnIPAddress        oraAgentVarTwoOneTemp;
AsnCounter          oraAgentVarThreeOneOneTemp;
AsnGauge            oraAgentVarThreeOneTwoTemp;
AsnTimeticks        oraAgentVarThreeTwoTemp;

/* MIB variables array */
MIBVARS OraAgentMib[] = {
{ { SIZEOFOID( oraAgentVarOneOneOid ), oraAgentVarOneOneOid },
        &oraAgentVarOneOneStor, &oraAgentVarOneOneTemp,
        ASN_INTEGER, 0, 64, MIB_ACCESS_READWRITE,
        ProcessIntegerFunc, &OraAgentMib[1] },

{ { SIZEOFOID( oraAgentVarOneTwoOid ), oraAgentVarOneTwoOid },
    &oraAgentVarOneTwoStor, &oraAgentVarOneTwoTemp,
    ASN_OCTETSTRING, 1, 20, MIB_ACCESS_READWRITE,
    ProcessStringFunc, &OraAgentMib[2] },

{ { SIZEOFOID( oraAgentVarOneThreeOid ), oraAgentVarOneThreeOid },
    &oraAgentVarOneThreeStor, &oraAgentVarOneThreeTemp,
    ASN_OBJECTIDENTIFIER, 0, 0, MIB_ACCESS_READONLY,
    ProcessOidFunc, &OraAgentMib[3] },

{ { SIZEOFOID( oraAgentVarTwoOneOid ), oraAgentVarTwoOneOid },
    &oraAgentVarTwoOneStor, &oraAgentVarTwoOneTemp,
    ASN_RFC1155_IPADDRESS, 0, 0, MIB_ACCESS_READONLY,
    ProcessOidFunc, &OraAgentMib[4] },

{ { SIZEOFOID( oraAgentVarThreeOneOneOid ), oraAgentVarThreeOneOneOid },
    &oraAgentVarThreeOneOneStor, &oraAgentVarThreeOneOneTemp,
    ASN_RFC1155_COUNTER, 0, 0, MIB_ACCESS_READONLY,
    ProcessIntegerFunc, &OraAgentMib[5] },

{ { SIZEOFOID( oraAgentVarThreeOneTwoOid ), oraAgentVarThreeOneTwoOid },
    &oraAgentVarThreeOneTwoStor, &oraAgentVarThreeOneTwoTemp,
    ASN_RFC1155_GAUGE, 94, 106, MIB_ACCESS_READONLY,
    ProcessIntegerFunc, &OraAgentMib[6] },

{ { SIZEOFOID( oraAgentVarThreeTwoOid ), oraAgentVarThreeTwoOid },
    &oraAgentVarThreeTwoStor, &oraAgentVarThreeTwoTemp,
```

Example 7-8. Implementation of a MIB database (continued)

```
    ASN_RFC1155_TIMETICKS, 0, 0, MIB_ACCESS_READONLY,
    ProcessIntegerFunc, NULL },
};

/* Number of elements in the MIB variables array */
UINT guMibNumVars = sizeof(OraAgentMib) / sizeof(MIBVARS);
```

As you can see, this is a lot of code just to handle the processing of seven MIB variables. And the MIBVARS array will grow to a considerable size if you add dozens or hundreds more variables. We'll have a look at that problem a little later.

The definitions of the sections in the MIB database are as follows:

MIB enterprises OID

The OID of the MIB subtree that is implemented by the extension agent. This is also the OID that is passed back to the SNMP service in the SnmpExtension-Init (or SnmpExtensionInitEx) function. And this is the base OID for the variables defined in the MIB supported by this extension agent.

MIB variable OID suffixes

The unique part of each MIB variable OID, including the instance identifier. To avoid storing the entire MIB OID repeatedly in every MIBVARS element, only the OID suffix of each MIB variable is stored in the MIBVARS array. This saves a little memory, but requires that the OID of each MIB variable be reconstructed before it is used.

MIB storage variables

Used to store the current value of each MIB variable.

MIB temporary variables

A duplicate set of storage variables used to temporarily cache a new MIB variable value that is being modified by a Set operation. If the Set operation succeeds, then the extension agent should copy all temporary values to the current value storage variables.

MIB variables array

The MIBVARS array that stores and references the information for each MIB variable. A top-down search is performed on this array each time the extension agent resolves a Get, GetNext, or Set operation performed on a variable binding.

One thing you may have noticed is that the MIBVARS structure does not contain a field to store the default value of each MIB variable. Each storage variable must be initialized either at build-time or startup time with its "power-on default" value. If the MIB variable values are to persist between restarts of the SNMP service, then the values must be written by the extension agent to permanent storage and read back into memory when the extension agent is loaded.

Searching the MIBVARS Database

Before we can process a MIB variable specified in the variable binding of a message, we must first determine whether the variable exists in the extension agent's MIB. If the MIB database is a simple MIBVARS array, then we only need to compare the OID in the variable binding with the OID of each record in the MIBVARS array to find an acceptable match.

OID comparison normally occurs in a function that performs the initial processing of all variable bindings received by an extension agent. And because this function resolves a single variable binding, we name it ResolveVarBind (see Example 7-9).

Example 7-9. Function used to resolve a single variable binding

```
UINT ResolveVarBind(
    RFC1157VarBind *pVarBind,      /* IN OUT */
    UINT            nPduAction)    /* IN */
{
    UINT                i;
    MIBVARS             *pMibPtr = NULL;
    AsnObjectIdentifier TempOid;
    int                 nCompResult;
    UINT                nResult = 0;

    /* Search for a matching OID in the MIB */
    for ( i = 0; pMibPtr == NULL && i < guMibNumVars; i++ )
    {
        /* Construct the complete OID of the MIBVARS entry */
        SnmpUtilOidCpy( &TempOid, &MibOidOraAgentPrefix );
        SnmpUtilOidAppend( &TempOid, &OraAgentMib[i].Oid );

        /* Compare the varbind's OID with the OID of this MIBVARS entry */
        nCompResult = SnmpUtilOidCmp( &pVarBind->name, &TempOid );
        if ( nCompResult < 0 )     /* OID is more */
        {
            /* Passed the spot where the exact match should be */
            if ( nPduAction != MIB_ACTION_GETNEXT )
            {
                uResult = SNMP_ERRORSTATUS_NOSUCHNAME;
                SnmpUtilOidFree( &TempOid );
                break;
            }

            /* GetNext is really a Get performed on the next MIB variable */
            nPduAction = MIB_ACTION_GET;
            pMibPtr = &OraAgentMib[i];
            SnmpUtilOidCpy( &pVarBind->name, &MibOidOraAgent );
            SnmpUtilOidAppend( &pVarBind->name, &pMibPtr->Oid );
        }
        else
        if ( nCompResult > 0 )     /* OID is less */
        { /* Nothing to do */ }
```

Example 7-9. Function used to resolve a single variable binding (continued)

```
            else      /* An exact match */
                pMibPtr = &OraAgentMib[i];
    }

    /* Check if we found a match */
    if ( pMibPtr == NULL )
        uResult = SNMP_ERRORSTATUS_NOSUCHNAME;
    else           /* Process the current or next OID */
        uResult = ProcessLeafNode( nPduAction, pMibPtr, pVarBind );

    return( nResult );
}
```

ResolveVarBind simply performs an iterative, top-down search on the MIBVARS array looking for an exact match to the OID in the varbind passed to it. If an acceptable match is found, then the function ProcessLeafNode is called (more on this function later). If an exact match is not found, and the operation is GetNext, then a Get operation is performed on the next lexical variable in the MIB. Otherwise, a noSuchName error results.

Because we have chosen to save a little space by storing only the suffix of each OID in the MIBVARS array, the full OID of each MIB variable must first be constructed by concatenating the enterprises prefix stored in oraAgentPrefixOid with the OID suffix of each MIB variable. The resulting MIB variable OID is then compared to the variable binding OID using the SnmpUtilOidCmp function (explained fully in Chapter 6).

Note that we can speed up searches by storing the entire MIB variable OID in each MIBVARS entry, but this comes at the sacrifice of the MIBVARS array eating up more memory. It's your design decision, but remember that operation of the extension agent must be quick.

Example 7-10 shows three examples of searches performed using SnmpUtil-OidCmp. In each case, an OID in a variable binding is being compared to the OIDs stored in the OraAgentMib MIBVARS array. A positive value is returned if the MIB OID is less than the variable binding OID; a negative value is returned if the MIB OID is greater than the variable binding OID; and zero is returned if the two OIDs are equal.

Example 7-10. Examples of top-down searches using SnmpUtilOidCmp

```
Searching for: 1.3.6.1.4.1.2035.1.5.1.2.1.0
Comparing:     1.3.6.1.4.1.2035.1.5.1.1.1.0        1
               1.3.6.1.4.1.2035.1.5.1.1.2.0        1
               1.3.6.1.4.1.2035.1.5.1.1.3.0        1
               1.3.6.1.4.1.2035.1.5.1.2.1.0        0     <- Match for GetRequest
               1.3.6.1.4.1.2035.1.5.1.3.1.1.0     -1     <- Match for GetNextRequest
               1.3.6.1.4.1.2035.1.5.1.3.1.2.0     -1
               1.3.6.1.4.1.2035.1.5.1.3.2.0       -1
```

Example 7-10. Examples of top-down searches using SnmpUtilOidCmp (continued)

```
Searching for: 1.3.6.1.4.1.2035.1.5.1.2.1
Comparing:     1.3.6.1.4.1.2035.1.5.1.1.1.0      1
               1.3.6.1.4.1.2035.1.5.1.1.2.0      1
               1.3.6.1.4.1.2035.1.5.1.1.3.0      1
               1.3.6.1.4.1.2035.1.5.1.2.1.0     -1    <- Match for GetNextRequest
               1.3.6.1.4.1.2035.1.5.1.3.1.1.0   -1
               1.3.6.1.4.1.2035.1.5.1.3.1.2.0   -1
               1.3.6.1.4.1.2035.1.5.1.3.2.0     -1

                                              [ No match for GetRequest ]


Searching for: 1.3.6.1.4.1.2035.1.5.1.1
Comparing:     1.3.6.1.4.1.2035.1.5.1.1.1.0     -1    <- Match for GetNextRequest
               1.3.6.1.4.1.2035.1.5.1.1.2.0     -2
               1.3.6.1.4.1.2035.1.5.1.1.3.0     -3
               1.3.6.1.4.1.2035.1.5.1.2.1.0     -1
               1.3.6.1.4.1.2035.1.5.1.3.1.1.0   -2
               1.3.6.1.4.1.2035.1.5.1.3.1.2.0   -2
               1.3.6.1.4.1.2035.1.5.1.3.2.0     -2

                                              [ No match for GetRequest ]
```

As the MIB tree is traversed from lexically lesser to greater OIDs, SnmpUtil-OidCmp will return positive values. A value of zero is returned when an exact match is encountered. If the returned value is negative, then an exact match is not present in the array, and the current array OID is an approximate or "next" match.

If the MIB search is performed for a Get or Set operation, an exact match must be found or a noSuchName error will result. For a GetNext operation, either an exact or an approximate match will do. In the case of an exact match, the value of the next OID in the MIB is returned. If the match is only approximate, then a matching OID will be returned. In any case, if a MIBVARS variable is marked with the MIB_ACCESS_NOTACCESSIBLE access mode, it must be skipped over during the search.

The MIB search is stopped when an acceptable match is found, when a match is not found where it is expected, or when the end of the MIBVARS array is reached. The MIB variables must be searched in their proper lexical order; if they are not, an exact match OID may be missed, or an incorrect near-match OID may be returned.

Storing Columnar Variables

At this point we need to backtrack a little bit and discuss how the columnar variables in tables are stored in the MIBVARS array. Scalar variables are simple to store because there is only one instance of each variable in the MIB. The variables defined in the column of a table, however, may have zero or more instances in the MIBVARS array.

This would suggest to you that MIBVARS should be a linked list to allow the columns in a table, and the variables in each column, to be dynamically created and deleted as needed. You can implement this design, and you may need to if you are supporting tables that have a very large maximum number of columns or if they are of an indeterminable and indefinite size. But more than likely a table will have a definite minimum and maximum number of columns, or will be fixed in size. Two things to consider:

- A table that is fixed in size will always have all of its columns defined and accessible in the MIBVARS array, although every variable in each column need not be instantiated or initialized with a value.

- A table with a variable number of columns will also always have all of its variables defined the MIBVARS array. But, each variable may be flagged as not instantiated by having its access mode changed to MIB_ACCESS_NOTACCESSI-BLE. This is an indication that this column does not currently exist, and if access is attempted by a Get or Set operation, a noSuchName error will result. A search performed by a GetNext operation should always skip over any variables marked as MIB_ACCESS_NOTACCESSIBLE.

Of course, the original access mode of the columnar variables will need to be stored so that the variables may once again be flagged as instantiated. The temporary storage variables used to cache SetRequest data could be used to store the original mode values, or even to declare the "not accessible" state of the variables in the first place.

Also remember that variables in a table are stored lexically by columns and not by rows. When you construct entries in a MIBVARS array for a table, the order in which the variables are searched starts with the first variable in the first column, proceeds down each column until the table is traversed, and ends at the last variable in the last column.

Searching Multiple MIB Subtrees

Extension agents that support multiple MIB subtrees should implement one MIBVARS array per subtree. You can combine multiple subtrees into a single MIBVARS array, but storing hundreds or thousands of MIB variables in a single, one-dimensional array slows down searching considerably. If your extension agent does maintain thousands of MIB variables, then I encourage you to read the section "External MIB Databases," later in this chapter.

When ResolveVarBind is called, it must examine the OID stored in the variable binding passed to it and determine which MIBVARS array to search to process this

request. Example 7-11 shows ResolveVarBind modified to handle four different
MIB suntrees.

Example 7-11. ResolveVarBind modified to search four different MIB subtrees

```
UINT ResolveVarBind (
RFC1157VarBind *pVarBind,     /* IN OUT */
UINT            nPduAction)   /* IN */
{
    UINT                i;
    MIBVARS             *pMibPtr = NULL;
    MIBVARS             *pMibVar = NULL;
    AsnObjectIdentifier *pMibOid;
    AsnObjectIdentifier TempOid;
    int                 nCompResult;
    UINT                nResult = 0;
    UINT                nMibNumVars;

    /* Determine which MIB subtree is to be searched to service this request */
    if ( SnmpUtilOidNCmp( &pVarBind->name, &MibOidOraAgentOnePrefix,
      MibOidOraAgentOnePrefix.idLength ) == 0 )
    {
        pMibOid = &MibOidOraAgentOnePrefix; /* MIB branch OID */
        pMibVar = OraAgentOneMib;           /* MIBVARS array to search */
        nMibNumVars = MibOneNumVars;        /* Number of variables in array */
    }
    else
    if ( SnmpUtilOidNCmp( &pVarBind->name, &MibOidOraAgentTwoPrefix,
      MibOidOraAgentTwoPrefix.idLength ) == 0 )
    {
        pMibOid = &MibOidOraAgentTwoPrefix;
        pMibVar = OraAgentTwoMib;
        nMibNumVars = MibTwoNumVars;
    }
    else
    if ( SnmpUtilOidNCmp( &pVarBind->name, &MibOidOraAgentFourPrefix,
      MibOidOraAgentFourPrefix.idLength ) == 0 )
    {
        pMibOid = &MibOidOraAgentFourPrefix;
        pMibVar = OraAgentFourMib;
        nMibNumVars = MibFourNumVars;
    }
    else
    if ( SnmpUtilOidNCmp( &pVarBind->name, &MibOidOraAgentSevenPrefix,
      MibOidOraAgentSevenPrefix.idLength ) == 0 )
    {
        pMibOid = &MibOidOraAgentSevenPrefix;
        pMibVar = OraAgentSevenMib;
        nMibNumVars = MibSevenNumVars;
    }
    else
        return( -1 );    /* MIB subtree not supported by this extension agent */
```

Example 7-11. ResolveVarBind modified to search four different MIB subtrees (continued)

```
    /* Search for a matching OID in the MIB */
    for ( i = 0; pMibPtr == NULL && i < nMibNumVars; i++ )
    {
        /* Construct the complete OID of the MIBVARS entry */
        SnmpUtilOidCpy( &TempOid, pMibOid );
        SnmpUtilOidAppend( &TempOid, &OraAgentOneMib[i].Oid );

        /* Compare the varbind's OID with the OID of this MIBVARS entry */
        nCompResult = SnmpUtilOidCmp( &pVarBind->name, &TempOid );

        /* Additional search code here */

    }
    return( nResult );
}
```

There are four MIBVARS arrays; these are named MibOidOraAgentOnePrefix, MibOidOraAgentTwoPrefix, MibOidOraAgentFourPrefix, and MibOidOraAgentSevenPrefix. The OID of each MIB branch is compared with the OID in the variable binding passed to ResolveVarBind. SnmpUtilOidNCmp is used to compare the OIDs only up to the length of the MIB void OID prefix. If a match is found, then the addresses of the appropriate MIB OID and MIBVARS array are assigned to pointers to be used in the search. If a match is not found, then the extension agent does not support the MIB subtree of the OID and a noSuchName error will be returned.

Validating MIB Variables

Validation is actually a fairly simple process used to determine whether the operation specified by an SNMP request message is allowed to be performed. If the operation is found to be valid, then it completes successfully and returns a status of noError. If validation fails, then an SNMP protocol error is the result.

We have already covered the first step of validation by searching the MIB database for a MIB variable matching the OID specified in the varbinds. The remaining validation checks depend upon the specific operation being performed. For Get and GetNext operations it must be verified that the MIB variable is readable. For Set operations the variable must be writable. The data type of the value to set must be identical to the data type of the MIB variable, and the new value within the MIB variable must be an implicitly or explicitly specified range.

In the example in the previous section, the function ResolveVarBind calls another function, ProcessLeafNode, if an acceptable OID match is found. This function, as the name suggests, is the actual function used to finish processing a request on an individual MIB variable. ProcessLeafNode performs the MIB variable validation and, if successful, then calls the MIB variable's special processing function to perform the actual reading or writing of the variable's data.

ProcessLeafNode also has the honor of constructing the varbinds that are returned in the GetResponse message. But to do this, it must first either collect data from (Get and GetNext) or write data to (Set) the MIB database.

Reading and Writing MIB Variable Data

All the code we have discussed thus far remains nearly identical in most extension agents. At the top of the call stack is where you will find the greatest differences between extension agents.

Figure 7-2 shows the complete calling sequence required to process one variable binding. The input into this process is the type of request and the request message varbind data. And the output is the response message varbind data and the ErrorStatus value.

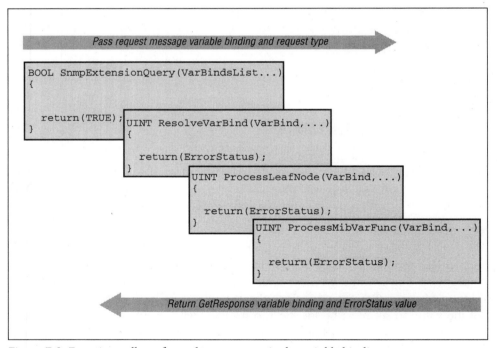

Figure 7-2. Function calls performed to process a single variable binding

The extendible agent receives an SNMP request and passes the varbinds to one or more extension agents via the SnmpExtensionQuery API call. The varbind list is iterated and each varbind is passed, one per call, to ResolveVarBind, which searches for the variable entry in the extension agent's MIBVARS array. If the extension agent supports the variable, then the varbind is passed to ProcessLeaf-Node, which performs validation of the varbind data. If it is valid, then the varbind is passed to the extension agent function defined to process this specific MIB variable (called ProcessMibVarFunc in Figure 7-2). If the entire process is successful, then the varbind is initialized with the data that it will contain in the response message, and control is returned to SnmpExtensionQuery.

ProcessMibVarFunc is the MIB processing function that is referenced in each MIBVARS entry. This is the function that performs the actual reading and writing of the data for a specific MIB variable. The implementation of these storage functions depends upon how your extension agent stores its MIB data.

You will typically implement one MIB processing function for each scalar MIB variable and one for each table. If you find that your design would then require the implementation of hundreds or thousands of MIB processing functions, then you may find it more conservative to implement only one processing function for each data type, and have the function determine where to read and write MIB data based on the OID of the variable binding passed to it.

External MIB Databases

After experiencing the sheer drudgery of coding up a MIBVARS array that contains only a few hundred MIB variables, you might decide that you should write a Perl script that converts MIB modules to MIBVARS arrays (I certainly did). While it is certainly possible to do just this, very large MIBVARS arrays are very slow to search. And while it is possible to greatly speed up OID searches by replacing the MIBVARS array with a MIBVARS btree (and I encourage you to do so), storing great amounts of MIB data locally does eat up a lot of available process memory.

Instead, you should think about ways to store the MIB database outside of your extension agents, and use an interface that makes the database easy to build and access, and quick to search. If you desire both persistence and the fastest possible access to MIB data, and are not very concerned with conserving memory, then a memory-mapped file may be your solution.

With a memory-mapped file, all MIB data is stored in a disk file using a format of your own design. When the extension agent is loaded, it maps the contents of the file into memory using the Win32 API functions CreateFileMapping and MapViewOfFile. The MIB data is then accessed as an array of BYTEs in memory. And as the MIB data is modified, the new values are written to the disk file.

Certainly a true database, such as Microsoft's JET engine, is also an alternative. Most any database will also be much faster to search than a very large MIBVARS array. And having the MIB data reside on disk, or in the memory of some other processor, reduces the overhead required by both your extension agents and the SNMP service.

An external MIB database also solves the problem of preserving MIB data in a persistent form. When the SNMP service is stopped, all of the MIB data stored in local MIB variables is lost. When the SNMP service is restarted, the extension agent is loaded and its MIB variables are initialized to their default values. Variables that lose their values during a restart are said to store *volatile data*.

If an extension agent saves its MIB data in some sort of persistent form before the service is stopped, and then reads this data when the service restarts, it can preserve its data and no MIB variable data is lost. A variable that retains its value after a restart has occurred is said to store *non-volatile data*.

If your extension agent design requires that the current value of all MIB variables be retained if the SNMP service—and Windows itself—is restarted, then you have little choice but to store the MIB data in some sort of persistent database.

A great deal of information is already published on databases and their implementation and interfaces under Win32. And tastes do vary considerably in choosing whether to use ODBC, RDO, or direct database access. Your design may also require a proprietary database format, and possibly that you use security and data encryption as well. So we won't attempt to broach the subject of Win32 databases here. But there is one very specialized database available on all Win32 systems capable of storing MIB data that is worth a quick look: the Windows registry.

Using the Windows Registry as a MIB Database

The Windows registry is normally thought of only as a replacement for the Win16 initialization (*.INI*) files, but it is capable of much more than just storing program startup information. The registry is also a very good place to store temporary data, data that needs to be isolated or hidden, and data that needs to be organized using an ordered tree structure.

Here are some of the benefits of using the Windows registry to store MIB data:

- The registry interface consists of a few, fairly simple Win32 API calls.
- The registry offers a built-in search and backup functionality.
- An identical tree structure is used by both the registry and the SNMP MIB.
- Data may be represented as a character string, integer, or binary stream.
- Data is stored as a persistent ASCII or binary file on disk.
- MIB data may be stored in a "hive" file physically separate from the central registry files.
- Registry data is easily viewed and changed using the RegEdit registry editor.

Here are some potential disadvantages of using the registry to store MIB data:

- Searches are performed in a top-down fashion and can be quite slow when traversing large amounts of data.

- Registry access may be slow due to shared use with other processes.

- Data is vulnerable to access by other system and network processes.

So once again there are trade-offs. Remember that speed is our biggest concern, so any design that accesses the registry using the fewest number of hits (reads and writes) will probably be the best.

Implementing MIBVARS in the registry

To use the registry to store MIB data, an extension agent needs to create and maintain the equivalent of a MIBVARS structure in the registry. Example 7-12 shows the format of the keys and values used by an extension agent named RegAgent to store MIB data in the registry.

Example 7-12. Registry keys and values for registry-based MIB data

```
HKEY_LOCAL_MACHINE\SNMP\O'Reilly
    \RegAgent\
        enterprises  "1.3.6.1.4.1.2035.1.5.2"
        \01.0
            AccessMode        0x00000002 (2)
            MaxValue          0x00000040 (64)
            MibFunction       "ProcessIntegerFunc"
            MinValue          0x00000000 (0)
            Modified          0x00000000 (0)
            NextOid           "02.0"
            ObjectDescriptor  "oraRegAgentInteger"
            TempVal           ""
            DataType          0x00000002 (2)
            Value             "42"
        \02.0
            AccessMode        0x00000002 (2)
            MaxValue          0x00000004 (4)
            MibFunction       "ProcessStringFunc"
            MinValue          0x00000000 (0)
            Modified          0x00000000 (0)
            NextOid           "03.0"
            ObjectDescriptor  "oraRegAgentString"
            TempVal           ""
            DataType          0x00000002 (2)
            Value             "WinNT"
        \03.0
```

The format of the MIB data in the registry is very straightforward. All of the MIB data for a specific extension agent is stored under a single key with the same name as the extension agent (in this case, "RegAgent"). This key should be located where the other registry information for extension agents is also kept. The RegAgent extension agent stores its MIB data using a registry hive file and uses the key *HKEY_LOCAL_MACHINE\SNMP\O'Reilly* as the location for its MIB data.

The RegAgent key will contain one entry per MIB subtree supported by the extension agent. RegAgent only supports one MIB subtree, so only the key *enterprises* is needed. Multiple MIB subtrees could use key names such as *MibView1*, *MibView2*, etc., or use the actual OID of the MIB subtree as the key name.

The RegAgent key contains a series of subkeys, one for each variable defined in the RegAgent MIB. Each of these OID subkeys contains all of the information needed to process the variable for an SNMP operation. The value names and data stored in each OID key will therefore be very similar to those found in the MIBVARS structure.

The name of each OID subkey is the OBJECT IDENTIFIER suffix of the MIB variable whose information it contains. It might seem more human-friendly to use the OBJECT DECRIPTOR of each MIB variable as the subkey name, but there's no guarantee that all of the variable names in a MIB will be unique. This is important as the OID subkey name is used to search for matching MIB variables.

Searches are performed using the registry API search function. The full OID of each MIB variable is assembled from the OID subkey name and the OID prefix, which is stored as the value of the enterprises field. For Get and Set operations, an exact match is required, so it is necessary to left-pad the key names with zeros or the keys will be searched in the wrong order. For a GetNext operation, the registry API is not capable of locating an acceptable approximate match. Instead, each OID subkey name must be read, and assembled into the full OID, and an SnmpUtilOidCmp comparison is made by the extension agent.

Going further

The RegAgent extension agent example on the CD-ROM is a reimplementation of the MINAGENT example that uses the registry to store MIB data (as described here). See the RegAgent example for further information on using the Windows registry to store MIB data for an extension agent.

8

Implementing Traps

The ability to send SNMPv1 traps is a feature of the SNMP Extension API that you may choose to implement in an extension agent. The use of traps is only necessary if the MIB modules used to implement an extension agent also define one or more traps. If you only need the generic SNMP traps supported by MIB-II, then simply install the SNMP service; the *INETMIB1.DLL* extension agent will handle these traps for you. But, if you are writing an extension agent using a private enterprise MIB which defines enterprise-specific traps, then you must write the support code for these traps. Just don't try it until you finish reading this chapter!

Before we dig into the trap-oriented details of extension agents and the Microsoft SNMP API, let's take both a tactical and a strategic look at the purpose and use of SNMPv1 traps themselves.

The Role of Traps

SNMP agents are typically thought of as passive, reactive processes that simply sit around waiting to be queried by network management stations. When a request is received, the management data it specifies is collected by the agent and returned to the management system as a response. The agent then sits around again, waiting for another request. This is true enough in some models, but SNMP agents do take a proactive role in network management when they send traps.

A trap is an SNMP agent's response to a predetermined event. The trap is a signal sent by an agent to one or more management systems as an indication that a predetermined event has occurred. The management system that receives a trap may do one of the following:

- Reactively poll the agent to collect more information on the occurrence of the event.

- Log the reception of the trap.

- Simply ignore the trap.

There are three different methods that can be used by a management system to monitor one or more managed nodes for the occurrence of specific events. These methods are generally referred to as the *polling-only*, *trap-only*, and *trap-directed polling* models. And as you might expect, each model has its benefits and drawbacks.

Polling-Only Method

A network management system keeps watch on a network by periodically making requests of all of the managed nodes for information describing their current state. A request for data may be spontaneous, such as a curious (or bored) manager clicking the "Send Request" button on a network management application. Or the request may be periodic, such as a system timer automatically sending a request to collect a predefined set of management data at regular intervals.

When a management system polls a managed node, it sends one or more GetRequest messages that specify the managed objects whose values are of interest to the management system. The agent collects these values from the node and sends them back to the management system in the form of a GetResponse message.

The management system will display and log the management data received and then wait a predetermined interval of time, called the *polling interval*, before performing another such poll. This model of gathering data from network nodes is referred to as *client pull* (the client pulls the data from the server). The periodic pulling of data (in this case, management information) is called *polling*. Figure 8-1 shows an example of polling.

If a fault occurs on a node, the management station will not discover the problem until the next polling cycle. The time between the occurrence of an event and its discovery is referred to as *event reaction latency*. The average latency of a specific polling operation is one-half of the polling interval; the worst-case latency is the interval of a full polling cycle.

For example, assume that a management system polls a node every ten minutes. Three minutes after a poll has completed, the node experiences a fault and is in trouble. The presence of the fault will not be detected by the management system until the next polling cycle is complete. In this case, the event reaction latency is seven minutes.

To discover as quickly as possible that important events have occurred, keep the length of the polling interval very short. The more frequently a node is polled, the sooner an event is likely to be detected after it occurs.

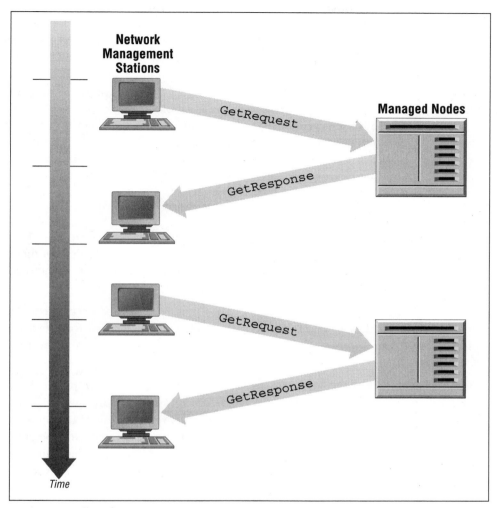

Figure 8-1. Polling for events

As the polling frequency increases, the amount of network traffic also increases, causing the available network bandwidth to decrease. Higher polling rates also limit the number of nodes that may be polled by a management system in a given period of time. Frequent polling also requires both management systems and agents to perform more work.

If the polling messages sent by a management system are intended to gather statistical data that is constantly changing (such as network load, wind speed, or signal strength), the results might be worth the amount of network bandwidth eaten up by the polling. But if the polling is constantly returning fixed data that may rarely change, then the polling is, at best, an extremely inefficient use of the network.

Event reaction latency is also affected by the number of nodes that are polled in a complete polling cycle. For example, a single network management system that is responsible for monitoring 100 managed nodes could send one poll request per second per node. It would therefore take 100 seconds to poll 100 nodes only once. Not only would this result in excessive network traffic (under typical conditions, more than 99% of all the polls would indicate that each node is normal), but on average it will take 50 seconds to detect a problem on any one node. Now 50 seconds might not seem very scary to your network managers (up the average latency to five minutes, however, and you might get a worried look), but if you are strapped with a "six seconds or less" alarm notification requirement, then you have a design problem to resolve.

Trap-Only Method

As I've said, traps are used as preemptive indications that specific events have occurred on a managed node. When the agent monitoring a node detects that a predetermined event has occurred, it will send out a trap message to all network management systems (see Figure 8-2).

Sending unsolicited data from a network node is referred to as *server push* (the server pushes the data to a client without first receiving a request for the data). And in SNMP, data is pushed from an agent to a management system in the form of a trap message.

The trap-only method seems the perfect way to detect network problems. A management system waits in idle silence to be informed by an agent that the node that it's monitoring is in trouble. When a trap is received, all of the information needed by the management system to determine the cause of the problem is included in the trap message. Minimal work is performed by both the agent and the management system while the node is normal, and no network bandwidth is required.

But a trap is of little use if it is never received. As discussed in Chapter 2, *Network Basics*, the UDP transport service used by SNMP is unreliable, and trap messages conveyed across a network could be damaged or lost at any point. It is also possible that an agent might not be provisioned to send traps to a network management system that is currently active. In such a case, the trap messages sent by an agent would not be received and processed.

Possibly the biggest problem with the trap-only method is that traps are typically implemented as reactive reports, indicating that "a problem has occurred," rather than as proactive reports, indicating that "a problem might occur." The possibility of an imminent fault can in many cases be detected by polling.

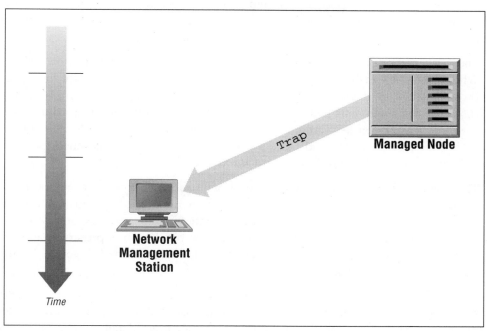

Figure 8-2. Trap event notification

For example, observing a steady rise in line signal attenuation, or the percentage of bad packets received, may indicate the slow degradation of a communications link. With trap-only event notification, a trap would likely not be sent until the link was already in an extremely poor condition, or completely out of service.

There is also a certain folly in expecting a trap message to contain all of the information necessary for a management system to determine the exact circumstances of an event's occurrence. If a trap is being generated in response to the faulty operation of a node, then it is possible that some of the node's management data is not available, or has not been properly updated. Requiring the low-priority agent process to gather many pieces of information from the faulty node's operating system may cause a considerable delay in the sending of the trap—and even risk the trap's not being sent at all.*

Trap-Directed Polling Method

If you are using the polling-only model and an event occurs between polling intervals, the management system will not become aware of the event until the next polling interval, which could be several seconds or several minutes away. And as

---

* If a genErr error results while an agent is collecting information for the variable bindings in a Trap PDU, the trap message will not be sent (or so it is hoped).

we've seen in the trap-only model, traps do give a preemptive, "heads up" on the occurrence of important events. But relying exclusively on traps risks never receiving notification about a network problem at all.

The best method, trap-directed polling, uses a combination of traps and polling. When a network management system becomes active, it will poll all of the nodes on a network to determine which ones are managed. This is referred to as a *discovery poll.* Each managed node is then polled again for more detailed management information on its current status. In this way, we establish a *baseline* of the node's management data and current operational state. (There is much more on polling in Chapter 10, *Writing Network Management Applications.*)

The management system will then periodically poll each node for an update of management information. But because traps are also used by this method to signal the occurrence of events, the polling interval can safely be much longer than it would be if traps were not used. Network bandwidth is preserved and the workload on both agents and management systems is lessened. Figure 8-3 illustrates trap-directed polling.

When the management system does receive a trap, it must determine whether a problem has actually occurred. If a problem is indicated, the management station will then poll the agent that sent the trap to gather more detailed information on the event. If the trap is purely informational in nature, the management system may simply log the reception of the trap and not take any direct action.

A trap that indicates a problem has the effect of restarting the management system's polling interval for a node. As previously discussed, a management system is configured to poll a node once every ten minutes to check on its current operational state. Seven minutes before the next poll is scheduled to start, a trap is received from the node. This trap signals that an event has been detected, which indicates that a fault has occurred. The management system will then restart its poll cycle for that node seven minutes early to obtain information on the node's current alarmed condition. The event reaction latency is reduced from seven minutes to just a few seconds.

To end this discussion I must acknowledge three facts:

1. The management of very large networks must rely heavily on traps. A network that contains many thousands of nodes cannot be managed only by polling, and therefore would be impossible to manage without the use of traps

2. The reliability of traps is directly proportional to the reliability of the network. Traps have as much chance of successfully reaching their destination as any other data conveyed using UDP (such as your email). Sending a trap over a congested network or a degraded link reduces its chance of being received in an undamaged state.

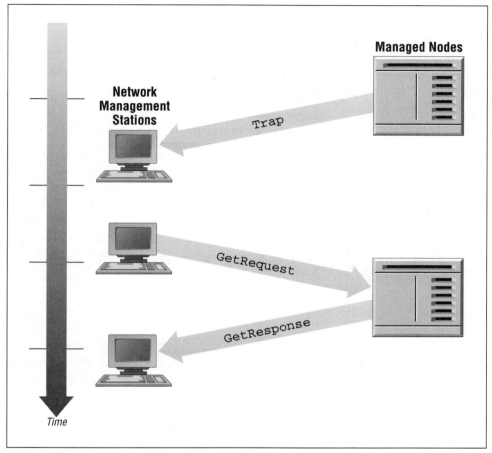

Figure 8-3. Trap-directed polling

3. The reliability of traps also depends upon how trap reporting is implemented on a network. Relying on a node to indicate when it is in trouble is not a very safe design. A node that experiences a catastrophic failure, such as sudden power failure, can't send a trap indicating that it's in trouble. You would never miss the node until it didn't respond to a poll. A better design would have a neighboring host recognize that the node was missing and raise the alarm with a trap.

SNMP Agents and Traps

An agent's job is to detect the occurrence of a trappable event, gather the data associated with the event, and send a trap message to one or more predefined network addresses.

But there's more to trap generation than obeying one or two rules. You will need to ensure that traps are usefully and successfully reported, and that trap generation itself does not affect the operation of the managed node, the network, or the agent itself.

When To (and When Not To) Generate a Trap

Only the SNMP agent can decide when to generate a trap. Specifically, the decision is made by the agent's code and the currently provisioned parameters.

An agent may generate a trap based on the occurrence of a single-state or multi-state event. *Single-state* (or *one-shot*) *events* are triggered and then are immediately reset to their normal state, such as when a momentary-contact button is clicked, a user correctly enters a password, an SNMP message fails authentication, or a database is modified. Usually there is an incrementing counter somewhere that keeps track of the number of times a specific single-state event has occurred.

A *multi-state event* toggles between two or more definite states. A typical two-state event is like a light switch, which is always either on or off. With a software switch there is also always a default or power-up state. Therefore, a two-state event has either occurred—and is still occurring—or has not occurred, and it remains in one state (called *latching*) until it's forced into the other state. Typical multi-state events that might be used to generate traps include the presence or absence of a mandatory piece of equipment, a power system switching between its primary and backup power supplies, and a communications link going in and out of service.

Multi-state events are not always determined by some definitive measure, such as the position of a switch. A variable, indefinite measure (such as the amount of free space on a hard drive or the operating temperature of a CPU) can be used to determine events. In such cases, a subjective value is chosen as a threshold for the trap generation (such as when the temperature of a CPU rises above 60°C, or when a hard drive has filled to 90% of its storage capacity). The thresholds that must be crossed to cause a trap to be generated are part of the agent's provisioning information. Human network managers determine the actual threshold values.

Edge-triggered and level-triggered events

Events may be categorized as edge-triggered or level-triggered. An event is *edge-triggered* if it occurs immediately when some sort of threshold is crossed. The *edge* is a predefined threshold boundary or state, and the trigger is the crossing of the boundary, or a transition to the predefined state. When the threshold is crossed, or the state achieved, the edge-triggered event immediately occurs.

events may be described as having a *single-edge trigger* or a ...ger. A single-edged event will occur if a threshold boundary is ... one direction. In the CPU example, the event occurs only when the temperature rises above a 60°C threshold value (see Figure 8-4). The event becomes double-edged if it also occurs when the temperature falls below the same threshold value (see Figure 8-5). It's often useful to not only know when things have heated up, but also when they have cooled off.

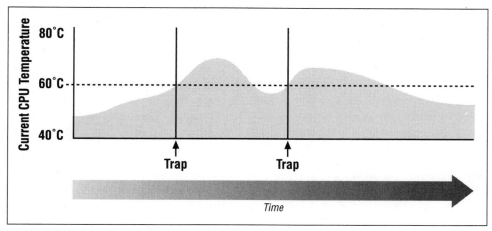

Figure 8-4. Single-edge-triggered event

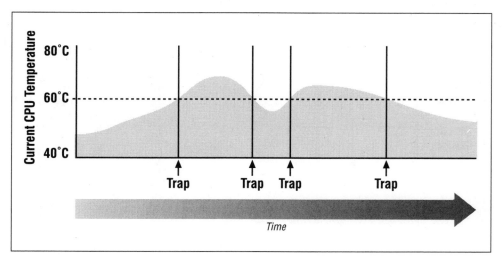

Figure 8-5. Double-edge-triggered event

A trap is usually generated immediately upon the occurrence of an edge-triggered event. The exceptions are if an agent requires that multiple events must occur—and possibly within a certain period of time (or in a certain order)—before it sends a specific trap, or if a method of restricting trap generation (throttling) is in play.

Another factor that may give rise to latency between event triggering and trap generation occurs with *level-triggered events*. Typically, a trap is sent immediately upon the agent's detection of a significant event, and only one trap message is sent. If the trap message is lost, then it might as well have never been sent at all. To reduce the risk of a trap message never being received, a trap may be sent repeatedly at periodic intervals, until the event is cleared. You can imagine a level-triggered trap as a bell that periodically rings to alert you of trouble, and continues to ring until you fix the problem.

Such events are described as periodic or level-triggered because the event occurs at regular intervals for as long as the threshold boundary remains crossed. A level-triggered event will typically be reported using a trap the moment that the agent detects that its threshold boundary has been crossed. The agent will continue to report the presence of the condition using the same trap sent at periodic intervals while the boundary remains crossed.

For example, an agent proxying an Uninterruptible Power Supply (UPS) might poll the device every 30 seconds via its serial port to determine if the unit is functioning on line power or battery power. If the UPS indicates that it is on battery power, the agent will generate a trap, and will continue to generate a trap at each 30-second polling interval, until the UPS either is back on line power or has stopped responding to the agent's polls (see Figure 8-6).

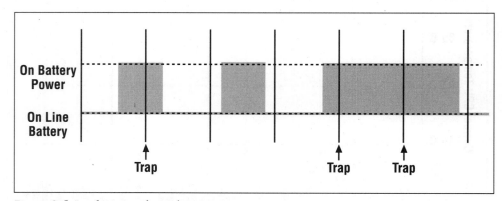

Figure 8-6. Level-triggered, single-state event

The periodic trap responses are based on the agent's 30-second polling cycle, which is never stopped. Each trap message contains the current battery level of the UPS and the estimated run-time remaining before total power failure. This information is retrieved by the agent from the UPS on every poll, is stored as management data in the agent's MIB database, and may be retrieved using a GetRequest or GetNextRequest. If the battery only maintains a five- or ten-minute reserve, then the periodic "hurry up or else!" notifications are very useful; they give the workstation operator incentive to perform a proper shutdown.

Periodic, level-triggered trap responses also help to overcome the problems of an unreliable network. If one trap message fails to reach its destination, another that might make it through will be along in a few seconds or minutes.

A level-triggered event can also occur when a measured value moves outside a predefined range. Figure 8-7 shows the plot of a value that has a normal range defined as 25% to 75%. The value is polled by the agent at fixed intervals. If the value returned by a poll is outside the predefined range, the agent generates a trap. This "out of range" trap will continue to be generated until the value moves back into its normal range.

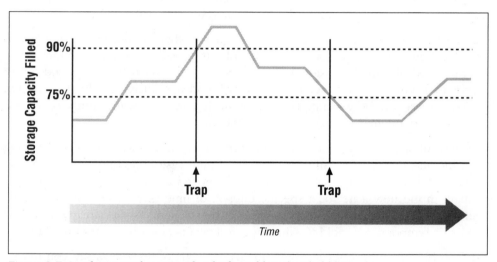

Figure 8-7. Level-triggered event with a high and low threshold boundary

There's always time . . .

Time is a variable that can be used to determine when to generate both edge-triggered and level-triggered traps. Many events may need to persist for a certain duration before they are reported. An agent must therefore first notice that a level-triggered event has occurred, and must then keep track of how long the event persists. If both the time and event thresholds are crossed, a trap is generated.

Examples of trappable events with a temporal component include a power system falling below 10% of its battery reserve for five minutes, a CPU rising above 60°C for more than 20 seconds, a hard disk with more than 90% of its storage capacity used for six or more consecutive 60-second polls, a line voltage fluctuating plus or minus ten volts for more than three seconds, and 17 or more packets with CRC errors detected on a transmission line per second.

In each of these examples there are two thresholds that must be provisioned for an agent to determine when an event has occurred and a trap is to be generated. One threshold is a physical constant (for example, line voltage and storage capacity), and the other is a measure of time. The chosen threshold values rely on a network manager's subjective definition of which events deserve notification.

Some trappable considerations

The agent must constantly poll for trappable events (checking line conditions, percentage of available resources, and so forth), and must also listen for signals that indicate that a trappable event has occurred (such as a hardware or software interrupt). As we have seen, it is also possible that two or more events need to occur, and perhaps in a specific sequence, before a trap will be generated.

A problem can occur with edge-triggered traps when a threshold boundary is crossed frequently and causes an event to be triggered many times within a very short period of time. For example, a communications link that goes in and out of service ten times in a two-second period will end up causing ten linkUp and ten linkDown traps to be generated. To report such a "flicker" with a flurry of traps is not useful to any management system or network.

To prevent spurious, knee-jerk trap reporting, you must build a form of throttling into the agent's trap generation mechanism. In the case of a communications link, the agent might require that the link transition from one state to the other and remain in the new state for a specific interval of time (say, at least two seconds) before the appropriate linkDown or linkUp trap is sent. We've already seen that adding a temporal threshold to edge-triggered events helps solve this problem.

The problem also occurs with much longer intervals of time. Let's say you have a managed host with a hard drive that's approximately 90% filled to capacity. A few files are written, and it goes up to 91%; a few files are deleted, and it goes down to 88%. Each time the 90% boundary is crossed upwards, a trap is generated indicating that "a problem is imminent"; each time the boundary is crossed on the way down, a trap is generated indicating "never mind, everything's OK."

The "wait for the trigger value to stabilize for at least two seconds before sending a trap" solution won't work here because it takes a much longer period of time for the drive's capacity to oscillate above and below the 90% threshold. We could simply provision a much longer time interval of, say, two minutes, but we may not want to eat up one of the host's few system timers for that length of time; it's certainly possible that the hard drive can be filled to 100% in less than two minutes. What we need instead are two separate threshold values: essentially, a high water mark and a low water mark (see Figure 8-8).

Assume that the hard drive is now monitored using a high threshold value of 90% and a low threshold value of 75%. A "problem is imminent" trap will be sent if the drive fills above 90% of its capacity, but the "everything's OK" trap won't be sent until the used storage capacity falls below 75%. It is very unlikely that the drive will be able to rapidly oscillate between 75% and 90% of its storage capacity, so the traps sent by the agent are restricted to a useful reporting level.

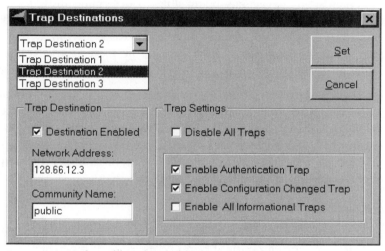

Figure 8-8. High and low threshold edge-triggered event

Trap Throttling

The ability to restrict the generation of traps under specific conditions (mentioned in the previous section) is called *throttling*. To limit the workload of the agent and to keep network traffic within reasonable levels, an agent can be throttled to send no more than "N" number of traps per second, to send traps only at periodic intervals, or to temporarily disable the sending of specific traps or all traps.

The number of network messages that a node may send within a given period of time depends upon several factors: the speed of the node's CPU, the current system work load, the amount of free system memory, the size and number of the transport stacks available for sending and receiving network messages, the number of active network interfaces available to the node, and whether the SNMP agent itself is single-threaded or multithreaded.

The speed at which network messages are exchanged and processed by a node is also clearly outside the control of the agent. Because of this, it is necessary for an agent to use throttling so as not to overtax the node by attempting to send a flood of trap messages—doing so might overflow its transport stack.

Types of trap throttling

Throttling may be fixed or variable in its implementation. With *fixed throttling*, an agent may have a fixed restriction that it may place no more than two trap messages in the transport stack per second; this restriction is always obeyed regardless of the current operational state of the node.

Variable throttling depends on the agent's being able to determine the current operational load of the node and its network stack. For example, an agent could query its node's operating system to determine the current work load in a range of 0% to 100%. The higher the work load of the system, the more restrictive the trap message throttling imposed by the agent upon itself would be.

An agent may also be designed to voluntarily throttle itself if the agent cannot keep up with its own trap generation. It is possible that events could occur on a node in an overwhelming quantity. Such a flood of events could overtax a single-threaded agent's ability to generate trap messages quickly enough to keep up with each event. A flood of trap messages is typically not useful and can threaten both the operation of the node and an already fault-ridden network.

Is it throttled or is it really choking?

The act of message throttling changes the perceived behavior of an agent. A node might be expected to generate certain traps at periodic intervals. If the agent were to become momentarily throttled, the node might stop sending these periodic traps and cause a few network managers to start scratching their heads.

What we need is some sort of indication by a node that it is currently throttled. The obvious measure is to define a MIB variable whose value is polled by a management system to determine whether or not the agent is currently in a throttled state. In addition, we could also define a trap to convey this same information to a management system when the MIB variable's value changes.

When the agent detects an event flood, it would send an enterprise-specific throttledBack trap message to all trap destinations and then cease all trap generation. The reception of this trap would indicate to a management system that, until further notice, no more traps will be sent by the node. The management system may then decide to start polling the node at an increased rate for more information, or to ignore the node's current situation altogether.

When events on the managed node have calmed to a reasonable level, the agent would send a throttledUp trap and then resume normal trap generation. Any agent indicating that it is resuming from a throttled condition should be immediately polled for new baseline management information.

Trap Destinations

SNMP agents do not broadcast traps on the network. Of all the nodes residing on a typical network, very few will host a network management system. Only a few management systems would probably be interested in the traps sent by a particular node, so there is no reason to broadcast a message in which very few, if any, network nodes would be interested.*

Rather than broadcasting traps, each SNMP agent is provisioned with the network address of one or more nodes in which to send trap messages. Each network address is referred to as a *trap destination*, and the node that resides at each destination is designated as a *trap receiver*.

An agent residing on a small system may only be able to support two or three trap destinations. Such a limitation keeps the agent from needing to consume significant amounts of processor time and transport stack space by sending traps to dozens of network addresses provisioned by over-zealous network administrators. Such a strict limit also allows agent implementers to accurately define a worst-case parameter for testing their code. (The worst case here is sending each trap generated to the maximum number of trap destinations.)

Agents residing on more robust systems may support many trap destinations. The Microsoft SNMP service documentation does not give a clue as to the total number of trap destinations that are currently supported by the SNMP service. Experimentation has shown that up to five trap destination addresses are supported per SNMP community, but the total number of trap communities supported remains a mystery.

Figure 8-9 shows a dialog box that contains several trap destination parameters that may be supported by an agent, including:

- The network address of the trap receivers

- The community name that is encoded in each trap message

- Whether the sending of traps to a certain receiver is currently enabled or disabled

Many agents also include the capability of disabling the sending of specific traps (such as authenticationFailure) or even disabling all trap generation by the agent. Trap generation is typically disabled when a node is put into "maintenance

---

* Note that this philosophy is not shared by the people who frequently email the "To_All_Associates" mailing list at your company.

mode," where changes that are made to the node's configuration and provisioning may cause an undesirable flood of traps to be generated.

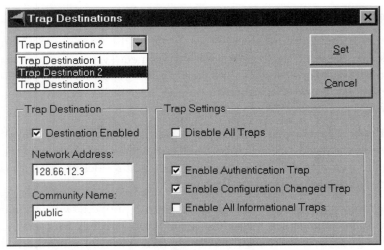

Figure 8-9. Trap Destinations provisioning dialog box

While the technicians may want a "disable all traps" capability built into an agent, system administrators tend to be a bit nervous about such features. What if someone forgets to re-enable trap generation and a problem occurs? You will never know about it unless someone using a management station notices that traps were disabled or unless the device is rebooted (assuming that "all traps enabled" is the power-on default). In the spirit of trap throttling, you might define and implement enterprise-specific trapsAreEnabled and trapsAreDisabled traps. But you would still need to hope that someone noticed these traps in the management system trap log, assuming that they made it that far.

Designing Traps

If you are adding trap support to an extension agent based on a MIB that is already written, then you don't really have too many design decisions to make. You simply code up each trap based on its TRAP-TYPE definition in the MIB, decide how the agent is to collect the Trap PDU variable binding data (if any), and have the extension agent keep an eye out for the events that inspire the traps to be generated. (If you are lucky, the events are described in the DESCRIPTION clause of each TRAP-TYPE definition.)

If you don't yet have a MIB, and therefore need to create your own TRAP-TYPE definitions, then you have two major design decisions to consider: what event(s) need to occur to cause the trap to be generated, and what management information (if any) should be included in the corresponding trap message.

In general, design your traps as lightweight messages that contain a minimal (but useful) amount of information. The information gathered for the trap should be readily available and should not take a great deal of CPU execution or wait time to collect. Also, the act of monitoring for trappable events performed by the agent should not eat up too much of a single-threaded node's CPU time or system resources.

Trap Priority Levels

Although all traps are created equal, the information they contain is not regarded equally. For example, a trap indicating that a node has just powered up is usually not regarded with the same urgency as a trap indicating that a power supply failure has just occurred.

Agents therefore often support the feature of assigning a priority (or severity) level to events that cause traps to be generated. Assigning priorities allows a management system to easily differentiate an informational trap from a trap indicating that a catastrophic failure has occurred. For example, the event indicating a power supply failure could be provisioned as a "priority one event," while a system start event might be provisioned as a lower "priority three event."

In the agent, you may assign a priority level to each event that may cause a trap to be generated. Each trappable event will have a power-on default priority level, and the priority level may be provisioned using a management system. The priority level should be stored in nonvolatile memory so it will be retained if the node is reset.

With all system events assigned a priority level, an agent may then be provisioned to send traps of different priority levels to different network addresses, to give higher priority in sending some traps when throttling is in effect, and to allow a network manager to prevent the agent from sending any "low priority" traps.

A management system may use trap priority levels to determine what course of action to take. Informational and warning traps may just be written to the trap log. Traps indicating severe or catastrophic events may cause lamps to flash, alarm bells to sound, and printed problem reports (trouble tickets) to be generated and sent to an output device, such as a printer, facsimile machine, or your pager.

Company standards

If you decide to have your agent support traps with provisionable priority levels, then you should check to see if there is already a standard in your company or industry for such levels. For example, it is common for telephone company equipment to support the assignment of priority levels to the alarm conditions that a device may report. These alarm event priority levels are typically named critical, major, minor, and informational (see Table 8-1).

Table 8-1. Sample Trap Event Reporting Levels

Event Level	Severity	Example
Critical	Catastrophic	Power supply failure
Major	Partial service-affecting	Communications link down
Minor	Minor or pending malfunction	CRC or framing errors
Informational	Event of interest has occurred	Circuit has been placed in maintenance mode
Disabled	The event is ignored by the agent and a trap is not sent	—

The priority of a trap is usually indicated in a trap log and the entry rendered using a specific color for easy recognition. For example, HP OpenView SNMP management platform uses the following colors to indicate alarm (trap) levels:

Color	Trap Priority Level
Bright red	Critical
Dark red	Major
Orange	Minor
Bright yellow	Warning
Dark yellow	Marginal
Magenta	Informational
Green	Normal
Blue	Unknown

Check the standards of your organization for the terminology and color codes used to represent event reporting levels.

Reporting the trap level

Each trap message sent by an agent may have its current event reporting level stored in a variable binding. If a management system has been specifically designed to read the priority level from the trap message, then the level of the trap may be easily reported in the management system trap log.

If storing the event reporting level in the Trap PDU variable bindings is not possible in your design, then a management system may read the currently provisioned event reporting levels for each event directly from the agent's MIB. Otherwise, the network manager must separately provision the reporting level of each event in both the agent and all of the management systems that are used to monitor the node.

Don't be surprised if you look over how one of your customers has your agent provisioned and find that most of the trap reporting levels are set to "Disabled." For each customer who finds all of the myriad of trappable events that you've defined in your MIB extremely useful, another two (or more) of your customers will find the same collection of ancillary event reports extremely annoying.

Trap Data

The reception of a trap usually indicates to a management system that a node needs to be polled to obtain additional information on the state of the node. But an enterprise-specific MIB can be huge and can contain the definitions for hundreds of managed objects; it is very helpful if a management system knows where to look in the MIB for the additional information—and specifically what to look for. This "look here for more info" help is the type of data that should be present in a trap.

When a trappable event occurs, the agent designer might be tempted to pack as much management information as possible about the event into a trap message and send it on its way. But if the agent is running as a process on the node that is in trouble, spending the CPU cycles and system resources to collect all of this trap information might hurt the system even more.[*]

The management information included in trap messages should also be useful. In a previous example, I described a trap message sent by an agent proxying a UPS that has switched to battery power. The trap message that is sent when the switch occurs should contain the current battery level of the UPS and the estimated run-time remaining before total power failure. These are good things to know when your system is in danger of losing power.

Other pieces of information available from the UPS, such as its internal temperature and the last date its battery was replaced, are not really needed in a "has switched to battery backup" situation; there is no real reason to include them in the trap message.

Table data and traps

You also have a decision to make regarding the contents of Trap PDU varbinds and table data. If a trap message is returning data that is stored in a table, should

---

[*] I've already covered the fact that network management should place as little burden as possible upon a managed node, whether the node is an 8-bit 8051 processor with 512K of available memory and running the PSOS operating system, or a 200 MHz Pentium Pro dual-processor system with 512M of memory and running Windows NT Server.

it return all of the data present in a table entry, or only return the index of the entry and let the management system specifically request data from the table entry itself?

If a table entry contains only a few data members, including all of the member values in a trap message is probably both useful and economical. But if a table entry contains many data members, it is probably impossible for the agent designer to predict the entries in which a manager will be interested.

In such a case, it would be more prudent to simply include only a single member of the entry in the Trap PDU varbinds. The instance identifier of the entry member's OID is also the index of the table entry. The management system can then use the index to request further data from the table entry. Consider the ifIndex table in the MIB-II interfaces group (1.3.6.1.2.1.2). This table contains information on all of the network interfaces currently managed by a node. Each table entry contains 22 data members, four of which are entry index values.

If an interface listed in the ifIndex table goes in or out of service, a linkUp or link-Down trap is generated by the agent. Because it is impossible for the agent to know which of the 22 values in the table entry a management system might need—or if it might require any data from this table at all—only the table entry index values of the affected interface are included in the trap message. A management system then uses these index values to request data from the table entry specified in the linkUp or linkDown trap.

In determining what data to include in a trap message, decide what information is useful to the network manager, but is also easy for the agent to obtain with minimal impact on the managed node itself. Part of this decision is based on how the trap data will be used when it is received by a management system.

Logging trap data

One of the most common places for trap data to end up is in some sort of management station trap log. This log is usually maintained by a management process called the *trap manager*, which writes an entry to the trap log for every trap message that the management system receives, including the specific information the message contains.

If you plan on having very detailed trap logs, then your design will require traps that contain a great deal of information about the event that they are reporting. It can take quite a few pieces of information to construct an informative log entry. For example, suppose that you are looking through the trap log on a management station and see the following recorded event:

```
UPS on battery power: 95% remaining; 22 minutes to failure.
```

This log entry is from the UPS example and contains three pieces of information: "on battery," "95%," and "22 minutes." Another log entry appears as follows:

```
A power short condition on line B of circuit 12 on unit Main Street has
occurred.
```

This trap was sent by an agent to report an alarm condition occurring on a communications device that is experiencing an electrical failure. The five pieces of information contained in this alarm message are "power short," "B," "12," "Main Street," and "has occurred." Now consider yet another log entry:

```
Warm start on 199.35.10.186 at 3 days, 14 hrs, 17 min, 4.45 sec
```

There is also quite a bit of information here, yet the trap that inspired this entry (warmStart defined in RFC 1215) contains no varbinds. The network address, time stamp, and trap type are standard pieces of information that are included in the header of all Trap PDUs.

You can see from these examples that even the simplest of messages can require a significant amount of management data to be collected and included in the Trap PDU varbinds before the trap can actually be sent. There is also a little useful information contained in the Trap PDU header itself.

Collecting the trap data

Trap PDUs store data using the same variable binding structure used by the other SNMP PDUs. Therefore, any data that is conveyed to a management system using a trap message must be stored as a variable in a MIB. Unlike the other SNMP PDUs, however, a Trap PDU need not include any variable bindings. Sometimes the presence of a trap message alone will be a sufficient indication of what is going on.

For example, the MIB-II coldStart trap contains no variable bindings or MIB data. The only data this trap does contain is the standard information found in the PDU header of all trap messages. Receiving only a coldStart trap indicates that the node has sustained a hard reset; no other data is required to represent this fact. It is likely, however, that most of the traps you will implement and design will contain variable bindings.

Assume the following rule about traps: A trap should be sent by an agent as soon as its associated event is detected. Therefore, poor trap design might be indicated by anything that causes latency between the time that a trappable event is detected and the time that the trap is actually sent.

What would delay the sending of the trap? Actually many things. As we have discussed, if the agent is polling for trappable events, there will be a delay between the occurrence of the event and the next poll. The trap may also include data in its varbinds that takes the agent a great deal of time (more than one or two seconds) to collect. The agent might need to obtain data from a peripheral device, which will cause the CPU (in a single-threaded operating system) to stop execution and wait until the requested data is returned. There is also the time spent dynamically constructing the Trap PDU variable bindings.

There might also be a purposeful delay (apart from trap throttling) imposed on the sending of a trap by the agent. When a management system receives a trap, it is assumed that the agent may be immediately polled to obtain the most current data. But what if there is a considerable delay between the occurrence of the trappable event and the availability of data that describes the event? In this case, the agent may be designed to delay sending the trap until all of the management data relevant to the event has been successfully updated, regardless of whether this data is actually included in the Trap PDU varbinds.

How Many Traps Are Too Many?

How many traps should you define in a trap MIB? It's not really a question of how many traps are actually defined in a MIB module, but of how often trap messages will be generated by an agent. Here's what RFC 1157 has to say:

> "Limiting the number of unsolicited messages is consistent with the goal of simplicity and minimizing the amount of traffic generated by the network management function."

Translation: go easy on the trap generation and you'll go easy on the network. How many traps you've defined in your trap MIB is not nearly as much a concern as how many traps and how often your agent will be spewing them out to the network. Network congestion, and network administrators who insist on maximal alarm and event reporting, are the main concerns.

You must realize that if you do end up defining dozens (or hundreds) of traps in your trap MIB, you will put an enormous burden on both the agent and the management system implementers who will need to code up each trap definition individually. The more complex the MIB, the more time will be required to develop the agent to service and maintain both the MIB and the specialized management application used to manage it.

Design influences the number of traps

Sometimes you can't get away with having only a few traps in a MIB. You will eventually encounter a design trade-off where you'll have to choose between implementing one trap per event versus one trap that is used to indicate the occurrence of many different events.

For example, suppose that you have a node that supports 20 different alarm events. Each alarm event has two states, "active" and "clear." Each time the state of one of these alarm events changes, a trap must be generated. How many traps do you need to implement to support all of these events? If you examine all the logical ways that these alarm events could be reported, you'll come up with the numbers 40, 20, 2, or 1:

- If you assign a single trap to each alarm and to each state, you will end up with 40 traps. Each alarm and its states would be represented by two traps—for example, alarmPowerShortActive and alarmPowerShortClear, alarmUnderVoltagedActive and alarmUnderVoltageClear, and so forth.

- If you assign one trap to each alarm, and each trap indicates the state of the alarm in its variable bindings, you will end up with 20 traps—for example, alarmPowerShort, alarmUnderVoltaged, and so forth.

- If you assign only one trap to each alarm state, only two traps will be required: alarmActive and alarmClear. Each trap will indicate in its variable bindings the name of the alarm event that has changed state.

- If both the alarm name and the alarm state are included in the Trap PDU varbinds, you will only need one trap, alarmStateHasChanged, to indicate that the state of an alarm event has changed.

So what's the best design?

Certainly, the one- or two-trap model seems the most appealing. A minimum of MIB, agent, and management application coding is required. But the collection of data necessary to construct the Trap PDU varbinds will introduce a delay (however slight) into the sending of the trap. And the event that caused the trap to be generated is not apparent until the varbind data is analyzed.

If we use the 40-trap model, we don't need any variable bindings in the Trap PDUs. When the change in the alarm event is detected, the trap is sent without needing to collect any additional data or having to construct any variable bindings. We can quickly tell exactly what event this trap is reporting by examining the specific trap ID value in the Trap PDU. But 40 traps is a lot!

In this example, you might find the best trade-off to be the 20-trap model. Each alarm event is important enough to warrant the definition of its own trap, but the state of the alarm event is easy to determine and is best stored in the variable bindings.

When you are defining a trap to report specific events, consider how many states are associated with each event, the number of traps you will need in each model, and how expensive the data is to obtain by the agent from the node. A trap is less of a burden for the agent to generate—and a management system to process—if it does not include any variable bindings. But also consider the resulting cost of needing to implement a great many individual traps.

How Not To Use Traps

While researching your agent design, you might be tempted to use traps in some creative way not intended by SNMP. Problems may arise when agents spit out traps like watermelon seeds. But this is not usually the result of a programmer really racking his brain for a way to use traps in a way that fills a hole in his operational model.

Here are some guidelines.

Don't touch RFC1213-MIB

At some point, you may decide that one or more of the generic traps supported by the snmp group of MIB-II does not contain all of the information that you need. For example, you might want to know the name of the link that went up or down or the address of the node that sent a request message that failed authentication. Your first thought might be, "I'll rewrite the MIB-II generic traps to contain the management data that I need!" Wrong!

The generic MIB-II traps defined by RFC 1157 (and RFC 1215) are written in stone. SNMPv1 guarantees that the managed objects and traps defined by MIB-II will contain the same data when generated by any managed node. Therefore, they cannot be changed by anyone for any reason. If you need more data in a trap message, your only recourse is to define a private, enterprise-specific trap used to convey the management information that you need.

Avoid implementing inProcess and operationHasCompleted traps

In Chapter 4, *Inside SNMP*, we discussed the pitfalls of an InProcessResponse message. Designing an agent to periodically send a trap that indicates that an operation requested by a management system is "in process" is likely to tax both an agent and its operating host. And using a trap to indicate that an operation "has completed" suffers from similar problems.

For example, let's say that a print job can be started by setting some of the MIB variables supported by a managed node. You would then expect to receive the GetResponse message when the print job finishes. But using this model, the management system that sent the request will time-out after a few seconds and resend the request message before the printer can get the first page in the bin.

You might decide that a successful GetResponse message indicates that the job has started, and have the agent use an enterprise-specific printJobHasCompleted trap to indicate that the print job has finished. Well, remember that traps are sent to all trap destinations provisioned in the agent. Only you will care that your print job has finished. The managers at the twelve other management systems that will receive your printJobHasCompleted trap couldn't care less.

If you design this type of trap, the agent is also placed under the extra burden of having to poll the printer to determine when the job has completed. (Yes, the printer can probably signal the agent when the job is complete, but assume in this example that it can't.) A very long print job could noticeably degrade the performance of the node for the duration of the polling. And there's no guarantee that the print job will start before the management system times-out and sends a retry message.

The best thing to do in such a case is not to use traps at all; instead, define a MIB variable whose value indicates the current status of the print operation. When the job is started, the agent will return a GetResponse within a reasonable time period to prevent the management system from timing out. The management system then polls the printJobStatus MIB variable (using a leisurely polling interval) to check when the operation has completed. The agent only polls the printer when it requests the value of the printJobStatus MIB variable. And, best of all, the other network management stations would be saved from needing to process and log unnecessary trap messages.

Station-to-station communication

Eventually, you will start to wonder how you can use SNMP to implement management station-to-management station communications. It is certainly handy to send short, human-readable messages between management stations over a network. (And implementing such a feature in a management application is most certainly a more interesting project than what your boss has you working on now!)

Under SNMPv1, there is no mechanism defined to accomplish station-to-station communications. Realizing that it isn't possible for an SNMP management station to send traps, you might get the idea to write an agent that acts as a proxy for network manager repartee.

One management station could write a message (an OCTET STRING) to a MIB variable. The agent sets this value and immediately sends a trap containing the message to another management station on the network. The receiving management station then pops up a message box displaying the message, or writes it to the trap log.

Now this is clever, and it will work too, but remember that agents may support multiple trap destinations. You probably only want your messages to go to your friend's station and not your boss' station. You must configure the agent to send traps only to the network addresses of the stations involved in the conversation. Better yet, forget about misusing traps altogether and use private email or the telephone instead!

Implementing Trap Support in an Extension Agent

The heart of trap support in an extension agent is the SnmpExtensionTrap function. Chapter 6, *Using the Extension and Utility APIs*, covered the basic operation and use of SnmpExtensionTrap. The remainder of this chapter looks at how to fully implement trap support in an extension agent.

Sending Traps

The actual sending of trap messages is handled by the SNMP service extendible agent. However, the detection of trappable events, the collection of the trap data, and the initiative to send traps originate from within extension agents.

When an extension agent detects a trappable event (more on this a bit later), it must collect any management data associated with the trap, format it as a variable binding list, and then signal the SNMP extendible agent that a trap is waiting to be sent. The extendible agent polls the SnmpExtensionTrap function implemented within the extension agent to collect the trap information, which it formats as a trap message, and then sends the message to all valid trap receivers listed in the Windows registry.

Anyone who authors a trap-generating extension agent must know how to collect and organize the trap information, and how and when to signal the SNMP agent that a trap needs to be sent.

SnmpExtensionTrap

When the SNMP service is started, all of the extension agent DLLs listed in the system registry are loaded, and the SnmpExtensionInit function in each extension agent is called by the SNMP service. At this point, the extension agent must indicate whether or not it requires trap service (as briefly explained in Chapter 6).

Example 8-1 shows sample code of the SnmpExtensionInit and SnmpExtension-Trap functions in an extension agent that does not require trap support. The value of NULL passed to the SNMP service using the phPollForTrapEvent parameter is the indication that trap support is not required. Be sure to pass a NULL value and don't set the pointer itself to NULL.

The minimal SnmpExtensionTrap function itself only returns FALSE—or would only return FALSE if it were called by the SNMP agent, but it never will be. It therefore just takes up space.

Example 8-1. Functions coded to indicate no trap support needed by the extension agent

```
BOOL WINAPI SnmpExtensionInit(
DWORD                   dwTimeZeroReference,   /* IN */
HANDLE                  *phPollForTrapEvent,   /* OUT */
AsnObjectIdentifier *pSupportedView)           /* OUT */
{
    /* Save the time that the universe began */
    gdwAgentEpoch = dwTimeZeroReference;

    /* Inform the agent of this extension agent's primary MIB view */
    *pSupportedView = MibViewOid;

    /* This extension agent never requires trap service */
    *hPollForTrapEvent = NULL;

    return( TRUE );
    }

    BOOL WINAPI SnmpExtensionTrap(
    AsnObjectIdentifier *pEnterprise,      /* OUT */
    AsnInteger          *pGenericTrap,     /* OUT */
    AsnInteger          *pSpecificTrap,    /* OUT */
    AsnTimeticks        *pTimeStamp,       /* OUT */
    RFC1157VarBindList  *pVariableBindings) /* OUT */
    {
    return( FALSE );    /* No trap data to send */
    }
```

If an extension agent may need to send traps, it must first create an event object using the CreateEvent Win32 API call, and pass the returned event handle back to the SNMP agent via the phPollForTrapEvent parameter of SnmpExtensionInit. The extension agent signals the agent using a call to SetEvent, passing to it the handle of the event object. The SNMP service then polls the SnmpExtensionTrap function in the extension agent to collect the necessary trap information.

The extendible agent formats the information it receives from calling SnmpExtensionTrap as a trap message and sends it to all of the network addresses specified in the registry to receive traps. The SNMP service will continually poll SnmpExtensionTrap to collect data for additional trap messages until a value of FALSE is returned. Multiple traps may therefore be sent each time an extension agent signals the extendible agent.

The extendible agent maintains a handle table containing the trap event object of each extension agent DLL that it has loaded. These handles are stored in an array and are supervised using the WaitForMultipleObjects API function. Because the event handle is passed directly to the extendible agent via the SnmpExtensionInit function, you don't need to specify a name for the event object when CreateEvent is called. NULL trap event handles returned by extension agents are ignored by the SNMP service.

Example 8-2 shows SnmpExtensionInit and SnmpExtensionTrap implemented for trap support. CreateEvent creates an event object to signal the SNMP service that SnmpExtensionTrap should be called. If this event object cannot be created, then SnmpExtensionInit returns FALSE, indicating that the extension agent has failed to properly initialize. In such a case, your extension agent should write an entry to the Windows NT System Event Log describing the exact problem.

Example 8-2. SnmpExtensionInit and SnmpExtensionTrap with full trap support

```
HANDLE ghTrapEvent;
DWORD gdwAgentStartTime;
DWORD gdwSpecificTrap;
UINT OidOraTrapAgentOnePrefix[] = { 1, 3, 6, 1, 4, 1, 2035, 1, 6, 1 };

AsnObjectIdentifier MibOidOraTrapAgentOne = {
sizeof( OidOraTrapAgentOnePrefix ) / sizeof( UINT ), OidOraTrapAgentOnePrefix };

BOOL WINAPI SnmpExtensionInit(
DWORD                   dwTimeZeroReference,
HANDLE                  *phPollForTrapEvent,
AsnObjectIdentifier *pSupportedView )
{
    BOOL fResult = TRUE;

    /* Create an event to indicate that a trap needs to be sent */
    *phPollForTrapEvent = CreateEvent( NULL, FALSE, FALSE, NULL );
    if ( *phPollForTrapEvent != NULL )
    {
        /* Inform the agent of this extension agent's primary MIB view */
        *pSupportedView = MibOidOraTrapAgentOne;

        /* Save the trap event handle for use by the extension agent */
        ghTrapEvent = *phPollForTrapEvent;

        /* Save the time that the universe began */
        gdwAgentStartTime = dwTimeZeroReference;
    }
    else
    {
        /*
        ** Failed to create the event object. Trap service will be
        ** unavailable to the extension agent. If this is intolerable,
        ** then return FALSE to indicate that this extension agent failed
        ** to properly initialize. Otherwise the extension agent should
        ** return TRUE and carry about its business sans traps.
        */
        fResult = FALSE;
```

Example 8-2. SnmpExtensionInit and SnmpExtensionTrap with full trap support (continued)

```
    }
    return( fResult ); /* Return initialization result */
}

BOOL WINAPI SnmpExtensionTrap(
AsnObjectIdentifier *pEnterprise,
AsnInteger          *pdwGenericTrap,
AsnInteger          *pdwSpecificTrap,
AsnTimeticks        *pdwTimeStamp,
RFC1157VarBindList  *pVariableBindings )
{
    static BOOL fCleanUp = FALSE;

    /* Send a trap */
    if ( fCleanUp == FALSE )
    {
        *pEnterprise      = MibOidOraTrapAgentOne;
        *pdwGenericTrap   = SNMP_GENERICTRAP_ENTERSPECIFIC;
        *pdwSpecificTrap  = gdwSpecificTrap;
        *pdwTimeStamp     = ( GetTickCount() / 10 ) - gdwAgentStartTime;

        pVariableBindings->list = VarBindsList.list;
        pVariableBindings->len  = VarBindsList.len;

        /* Indicate that the function parameters point to valid trap data */
        fCleanUp = TRUE;
    }
    else /* Clean up after last trap sent */
    {
        /*
        ** Clear the variable binding pointer. The memory was
        ** deallocated by the extendible agent (SNMP service).
        */
        if ( VarBindsList.list != (RFC1157VarBind *)NULL )
        {
            VarBindsList.len = 0;
            VarBindsList.list = (RFC1157VarBind *)NULL;
        }
        fCleanUp = FALSE;
    }
    return( fCleanUp );
}
```

This implementation of SnmpExtensionTrap provides data for a single trap each time the trap event is signaled by the extension agent. You pass trap data to SnmpExtensionTrap using global variables, whose values are then passed to the SNMP service using the function parameters. A static flag indicates whether a call to SnmpExtensionTrap is to provide trap data to the SNMP service or to perform cleanup operations.

When the SNMP service calls SnmpExtensionTrap, it expects to collect five items of data:

1. The registered OID of the management enterprise that defines the trap

2. The generic trap type (always 6 for enterprise-specific traps)

3. The specific trap type (the enumeration of the TRAP-TYPE macro in the MIB that defines the trap)

4. The time stamp value to be included in the Trap PDU header

5. The Trap PDU variable bindings data

The generic and specific trap types and the time stamp are 32-bit integer values. The time stamp value indicates the elapsed time since Windows was (re)started, in centiseconds (not milliseconds!). The enterprise OID is an AsnObjectIdentifier and the variable binding data is always stored in a dynamically allocated RFC1157VarBindList object.

Of the five SnmpExtensionTrap parameters, the SNMP service will free only the memory dynamically allocated for pVariableBindings. If you dynamically allocate memory for any of the other parameter values, you must be sure to free it on a subsequent call of SnmpExtensionTrap by the extendible agent. These other values are typically stored as constants, or in statically allocated variables.

Note that the SnmpExtensionTrap function must be present in every extension agent, even if trap support is not required. This is a bit odd considering the optional nature of another SNMP Extension API function SnmpExtensionInitEx. It would seem that simply omitting SnmpExtensionTrap from an extension agent DLL would not only save a little code, but may also indicate to the SNMP service that trap support is not required by the extension agent.

Binding the Variables

The managed data included in the variable bindings of a Trap PDU are specified by the VARIABLES clause in the TRAP-TYPE macro that defines the trap (described in Chapter 4). This clause specifies the managed variables whose current values are to be included in the Trap PDU and the order in which they are to appear in the variable binding list. Only managed objects supported by the agent sending the trap may be included in the variable bindings of the Trap PDU. If no VARIABLES clause is present in the TRAP-TYPE definition, then no variable bindings are present in the trap message.

The variable binding data for each Trap PDU is passed to the SNMP service as an RFC1157VarBindList object. Typically, as an extension agent collects the object values for the variable bindings, it dynamically builds the RFC1157VarBindList and initializes each RFC1157VarBind object with the collected data. A pointer to this list is returned to the SNMP service. The SNMP service also frees the memory allocated for this object.

Example 8-3 shows the skeleton of a function that is used to collect the values required by the traps supported by an extension agent. When the extension agent needs to send a trap, it calls InitiateTrap and passes to it the specific trap enumeration. InitiateTrap then collects the values for the Trap PDU variable bindings and stores them in a global RFC1157VarBindList object. If the data was collected successfully, the SNMP service is signaled to call SnmpExtensionTrap.

Example 8-3. Basic trap data collection function

```
HANDLE ghTrapEvent;
DWORD gdwSpecificTrap;
RFC1157VarBindList gVarBindsList;

BOOL CollectTrap1Data( void );

BOOL InitiateTrap( DWORD dwTrapIndex )
{
    BOOL fResult;

    switch ( dwTrapIndex )
    {
        case 1: /* Trap 1 */
            fResult = CollectTrap1Data();
            break;
        case 2: /* Trap 2 */
            fResult = CollectTrap2Data();
            break;
        case 3: /* Trap 3 */
            fResult = CollectTrap3Data();
            break;
        default:
            fResult = FALSE;
            break;
    }

    if ( fResult == TRUE )
    {
        gdwSpecificTrap = dwTrapIndex;

        /* Signal the SNMP agent to call SnmpExtensionTrap */
        SetEvent( ghTrapEvent );
    }
    return( FALSE );
}
```

Each case in InitiateTrap must gather the MIB variable data required by its specific trap, update the extension agent database using this data, and construct the RFC1157VarBindList object passed to the SNMP service by SnmpExtensionTrap.

The RFC1157VarBindList object contains the actual data stored in the variable bindings of the Trap PDU.

Example 8-4 shows the skeleton switch statement filled in with some code to collect Trap PDU variable bindings data. The trap data collection functions have been replaced with code that is used to collect the trap data and construct the RFC1157VarBindList object.

The first trap contains a single varbind with an INTEGER value. The second trap contains two varbinds, one storing an OCTET STRING value and the other an OBJECT IDENTIFIER value. The third trap contains no variable bindings.

Example 8-4. Implementation of a trap data collection function

```
HANDLE ghTrapEvent;
DWORD gdwSpecificTrap;
RFC1157VarBindList gVarBindsList;
AsnInteger gdwMibVarOneStor;
char gszMibVarTwoStor[40];
AsnObjectIdentifier gMibVarThreeStor;

BOOL InitiateTrap( DWORD dwTrapIndex )
{
    BOOL fResult = TRUE;

    switch ( dwTrapIndex )
    {
        case 1: /* Trap 1 */
            /* Collect the varbinds data */
            gdwMibVarOneStor = GetTickCount();

            gVarBindsList.len = 1;
            gVarBindsList.list = (RFC1157VarBind *)SnmpUtilMemAlloc(
              sizeof(RFC1157VarBind) * gVarBindsList.len );
            if ( gVarBindsList.list != (RFC1157VarBind *)NULL )
            {
                gVarBindsList.list[0].name.idLength = gMibVarOneOid.idLength;
                gVarBindsList.list[0].name.ids = (UINT *)
                  SnmpUtilMemAlloc( sizeof(UINT) * gMibVarOneOid.idLength );
                if ( gVarBindsList.list[0].name.ids != (UINT *)NULL )
                    memcpy( gVarBindsList.list[0].name.ids, gMibVarOneOid.ids,
                        sizeof(UINT) * gMibVarOneOid.idLength );
                gVarBindsList.list[0].value.asnType = ASN_INTEGER;
                gVarBindsList.list[0].value.asnValue.number = gdwMibVarOneStor;
            }
            break;
        case 2: /* Trap 2 */
        {
            /* Collect the varbinds data */
            DWORD dwSize = sizeof(gszMibVarTwoStor) - 1;
            GetUserName( gszMibVarTwoStor, &dwSize );
            GetSomeOid( &gMibVarThreeStor );
```

Example 8-4. Implementation of a trap data collection function (continued)

```
            gVarBindsList.len = 2;
            gVarBindsList.list = (RFC1157VarBind *)SnmpUtilMemAlloc(
              sizeof(RFC1157VarBind) * gVarBindsList.len );
            if ( gVarBindsList.list != (RFC1157VarBind *)NULL )
            {
                /* First varbind */
                gVarBindsList.list[0].name.idLength = gMibVarTwoOid.idLength;
                gVarBindsList.list[0].name.ids = (UINT *)SnmpUtilMemAlloc(
                  sizeof(UINT) * gMibVarTwoOid.idLength);
                if ( gVarBindsList.list[0].name.ids != (UINT *)NULL )
                    memcpy( gVarBindsList.list[0].name.ids, gMibVarTwoOid.ids,
                        sizeof(UINT) * gMibVarTwoOid.idLength );
                gVarBindsList.list[0].value.asnType = ASN_OCTETSTRING;
                gVarBindsList.list[0].value.asnValue.string.length =
                    lstrlen( gszMibVarTwoStor );
                gVarBindsList.list[0].value.asnValue.string.stream =
                    (BYTE *)SnmpUtilMemAlloc( sizeof(BYTE) *
                gVarBindsList.list[0].value.asnValue.string.length );
                if ( gVarBindsList.list[0].value.asnValue.string.stream !=
                  (BYTE *)NULL )
                  {
                    lstrcpy(
                      gVarBindsList.list[0].value.asnValue.string.stream,
                      gszMibVarTwoStor );
                    gVarBindsList.list[0].value.asnValue.string.dynamic = TRUE;
                  }
                /* Second varbind */
                gVarBindsList.list[1].name.idLength =
                    gMibVarThreeOid.idLength;
                gVarBindsList.list[1].name.ids = (UINT *)SnmpUtilMemAlloc(
                    sizeof(UINT) * gMibVarThreeOid.idLength);
                if ( gVarBindsList.list[1].name.ids != (UINT *)NULL )
                    memcpy( gVarBindsList.list[1].name.ids,
                        gMibVarThreeOid.ids,
                        sizeof(UINT) * gMibVarThreeOid.idLength );
                gVarBindsList.list[1].value.asnType = ASN_OBJECTIDENTIFIER;
                SnmpUtilOidCpy( &gVarBindsList.list[1].value.asnValue.object,
                    &gMibVarThreeStor );
            }
            break;
        }
        case 3: /* Trap 3 */
            break;
        default:
            fResult = FALSE;
            break;
    }

    if ( fResult == TRUE )
    {
        gdwSpecificTrap = dwTrapIndex;
```

Example 8-4. Implementation of a trap data collection function (continued)

```
        /* Signal the SNMP agent to call SnmpExtensionTrap */
        SetEvent( ghTrapEvent );
    }
    return( FALSE );
}
```

The majority of this code is simply the construction and initialization of the Trap PDU variable bindings. Note that when the data for the variable bindings is collected, its values are stored in the extension agent's MIB storage variable. Always implement rigorous error checking code to prevent passing back any ill-allocated or misinitialized variable bindings to the SNMP service.

Sending more than one trap

The design of SnmpExtensionTrap and InitiateTrap in the previous example allows only one trap to be sent each time the trap event object is signaled. This design is perfectly fine for most extension agents; however, it is possible that an extension agent may be designed so that a single event causes multiple and different trap messages to be sent to the same trap destination.

In such a case, the extension agent would need to collect the varbinds data for all of the trap messages to be sent, and store the data for each trap in a queue. When the SNMP service calls SnmpExtensionTrap, trap data would be read from the queue until empty. The Trap PDU object might appear as follows:

```
typedef struct _TrapQueue
{
    AsnObjectIdentifier *pEnterprise;
    AsnInteger          dwGenericTrap;
    AsnInteger          dwSpecificTrap;
    AsnTimeticks        dwTimeStamp;
    RFC1157VarBindList  *pVariableBindings;
    struct _TrapQueue   *pNext;
} TRAPQUEUE;
```

SnmpExtensionTrap would step through this trap queue, initialize its formal parameters using the data in a TRAPQUEUE object, and return a value of TRUE. The extendible agent then sends the trap message and SnmpExtensionTrap is then called again to gather data for the next trap. If no more TRAPQUEUE objects remain in the queue, the queue is deleted and SnmpExtensionTrap returns FALSE. The code in Example 8-5 shows an implementation of this design.

Example 8-5. SnmpExtensionTrap modified to send multiple traps from a queue

```
TRAPQUEUE *gpTrapQueue;

BOOL WINAPI SnmpExtensionTrap(
AsnObjectIdentifier *pEnterprise,
```

Example 8-5. SnmpExtensionTrap modified to send multiple traps from a queue (continued)

```
AsnInteger          *pdwGenericTrap,
AsnInteger          *pdwSpecificTrap,
AsnTimeticks        *pdwTimeStamp,
RFC1157VarBindList  *pVariableBindings )
{
    static BOOL fCleanUp = FALSE;
    static TRAPQUEUE *pQueueIndex;

    if ( fCleanUp == FALSE )
    {
        if ( gpTrapQueue )
            pQueueIndex = gpTrapQueue;  /* Get index of first queue entry */
        else
        return( fCleanUp );
    }
    else
    {
        if ( pQueueIndex->pNext == NULL ) /* No more traps to send */
        {
            /* Destroy gpTrapQueue */
            SnmpUtilMemFree( gpTrapQueue );
            gpTrapQueue = NULL;

            fCleanUp = FALSE;
            return( fCleanUp );
        }
        else
        {
            /* Free the RFC1157VarBind object */
            SnmpUtilVarBindListFree( pQueueIndex->pVariableBindings );
            /* Move to the next TRAPQUEUE entry */
            pQueueIndex += sizeof( TRAPQUEUE );
        }
    }

    /* Send Trap PDU varbind data to the SNMP service */
    pEnterprise       = pQueueIndex->pEnterprise;
    *pdwGenericTrap   = pQueueIndex->dwGenericTrap;
    *pdwSpecificTrap  = pQueueIndex->dwSpecificTrap;
    *pdwTimeStamp     = pQueueIndex->dwTimeStamp;
    pVariableBindings->list = pQueueIndex->pVariableBindings.list;
    pVariableBindings->len  = pQueueIndex->pVariableBindings.len;

    /* Indicate that the function parameters point to valid trap data */
    fCleanUp = TRUE;

    return( fCleanUp );
}
```

The InitiateTrap function would require only a slight modification. Each time
InitiateTrap is called with a specific trap number, the variables for that trap are
collected and stored as a TRAPQUEUE object, and placed in the queue.

InitiateTrap signals the SNMP service to call SnmpExtensionTrap if it is called with a pdwSpecificTrap value of zero.

An extension agent that will send many traps, and at frequent intervals, would do best to implement some sort of trap manager as a separate thread. The trap manager would allow trap messages to be queued up and sent in groups in an organized and controlled manner. Such a manager is also the ideal way to implement trap throttling in an extension agent.

When to Trigger a Trap

It is fairly straightforward to have an extension agent generate a trap once you have acquired all of the trap data to send. But it is sometimes difficult to detect the events that might require the generation of a trap in the first place.

Any condition, event, occurrence, or happenstance that is detectable by a thread or process running under Win32 is fair game to trigger a trap. The entire universe of the Win32 API, networking, databases, and Interprocess Communications (IPC) is therefore at your disposal for the detection of trappable events (and also for collecting MIB data).

The first design question, however, is not how to detect trappable events, but where to detect them.

Where to Detect a Trappable Event?

Your first answer to this question should be "inside the extension agent DLL, where else?" Using separate threads, you can certainly monitor for events and collect their associated MIB data inside an extension agent DLL. But this work can also be moved outside the DLL by using a separate process that is created by the extension agent itself.

You can use any of four distinct models for event detection and data collection:

- The extension agent performs all event detection and data collection.
- An external process performs all event detection, and the extension agent performs data collection.
- The extension agent performs all event detection, and an external process performs data collection. Data is passed to the extension agent using IPC.
- An external process performs all event detection and data collection. Data is passed to the extension agent using IPC.

Moving the event detection work to a separate process has several advantages:

- It makes the overall design more modular.

- It simplifies debugging. (The monitoring process may be stopped without affecting the SNMP service.)

- Observing the processor time being used to execute the trap event detection code is easier when implemented in a separate process.

When a trappable event has been detected by the monitoring process, it will signal the extension agent using an object created using CreateEvent. The extension agent will be listening for the signal using WaitForMultipleObjects called in a separate thread. The extension agent will then collect the management data to be included in the variable bindings.

To implement the trap monitoring code in another process, we need to create an entirely new executable program that is executed by the extension agent. This does not need to be a Windows application. In fact, if the monitor doesn't require a user interface, then a lightweight MS-DOS Console application is your best design.

The data collection too can be moved to an external process (usually the same one that is detecting the trappable events). In such a design, the monitoring process will have to move the collected data to the extension agent for storage in the MIB database and for processing by SnmpExtensionTrap. You can accomplish this move using one of the Win32 Interprocess Communication mechanisms described here.

Win32 Interprocess Communication

Win32 Interprocess Communication (IPC) allows two or more processes or threads to exchange data. Table 8-2 lists the IPC services available under Win32. The Win32 IPC mechanisms are referred to as "services" because each form of IPC is implemented as a Win32 application or driver service. Local IPC services are only capable of exchanging data locally between processes residing on the same machine and, in some cases, only between child and parent processes. Network IPC services are capable of exchanging data between processes both locally on the same system and remotely on different systems across a network.

Table 8-2. Win32 IPC Services

Local IPC services	Windows NT	Windows 95
Anonymous pipes	X	X
Clipboard	X	X
File mapping	X	X
Synchronization objects	X	X
WM_COPYDATA	X	X

Table 8-2. Win32 IPC Services (continued)

Network IPC Services	Windows NT	Windows 95
Dynamic Data Exchange (DDE)	X	X
Mailslots	X	X
Microsoft Message Queue (MSMQ)	X (NT4 only)	
Named pipe clients	X	X
Named pipe servers	X	
Network Basic Input/Output System (NetBIOS)	X	
Object Linking and Embedding (OLE)	X	X
Remote Procedure Call (RPC) 1	X	X
Remote Procedure Call (RPC) 2	X	
Windows Sockets 1.1 (WinSock)	X	X
Windows Sockets 2 (WinSock)	X	X

Not all Win32 IPC mechanisms support the same features, nor are they all appropriate for every application. Those that have many features and capabilities, such as OLE, tend to be the slowest and require the greatest amount of system overhead to operate. Simpler IPC mechanism, such as DDE, pipes, and mail slots, use fewer resources and are typically easier to implement. All MIB data is just simple INTEGER, OCTET STRING, and OBJECT IDENTIFIER data, so using a heavy-duty IPC mechanism really isn't necessary.

If you already have a preferred IPC mechanism that you like to use (and have probably already written the code for), then I encourage you to have a go at using it in your extension agent design. But there is very little reason to use a high-level networking IPC service, including NetBIOS, RPC, and OLE, with an extension agent. These IPC services are built on top of the simpler IPC services, which use far less overhead. The simpler IPC services are generally easier to implement in your code than the lower-level services, such as WinSock.

Connection-oriented IPC mechanisms, such as named pipes and DDE, require that a dedicated connection between two networked devices be established before the transport of data can occur (as with TCP). Mail slots allow the connectionless broadcasting of information to many different network processes, much like UDP. Using a network-capable IPC mechanism frees any trappable event monitoring process from needing to reside on the same system as the SNMP service. Instead, it may be located on another system connected via a network.

Several of the extension agent examples on the CD-ROM use named pipes, mail slots, file mapping, and the Windows registry to move data between external processes and extension agent DLLs.

Detecting Trappable Events

How can an extension agent actively detect trappable events? The agent typically creates a thread that polls every so often to check whether a specific condition or event has occurred. When the event is detected, the thread will gather the data required to be present in the specific trap message's variable bindings (if any), and signal the extension agent to send the trap.

An extension agent DLL may either actively poll for a trappable event, or passively sit by and wait to be notified that a trappable event has occurred. Active polling requires the use of a timer (created using SetTimer or SetWaitableTimer) that causes the extension agent to check for trappable events at specific intervals. Passive notification requires that some sort of signaling mechanism be initialized that will be triggered when the event occurs and will alert the extension agent.

The classic problem in actively polling for events is the event reporting latency that occurs between the time the event occurs and the time the extension agent "wakes up" into a polling cycle, detects the event, and generates a trap.

Polling may be quite inefficient for detecting events that do not occur very often. As with network bandwidth, we need to try to conserve the system bandwidth eaten up by the generation of dozens or even hundreds of WM_TIMER messages per minute.

Passive event notification also has its problems. Sometimes there is no way to receive an immediate notification that an event has occurred. For example, if we wanted to generate a trap each time a message was written to the system event log, we would need the Event Logging service to assert some sort of signal that would immediately notify our extension agent that such an event had occurred. If the Event Logging service didn't support a signaling mechanism used for this purpose, the extension agent would have no choice but to actively poll the Event Logging service to see if there has been any change in the number of entries in the log. (The Event Logging API does provide a NotifyChangeEventLog function.)

9

Using the Management API

This chapter describes the Microsoft SNMP Management API (introduced in Chapter 6, *Using the Extension and Utility APIs*) used to write management applications that are capable of sending requests to and receiving responses from SNMPv1 agents. Support is also included for receiving SNMPv1 trap responses.

The Management API consists of seven documented library functions. These API functions are used by management applications to interface to the WinSock and SNMP Management APIs for the purpose of sending and receiving SNMP messages. Figure 9-1 shows the three groups of management API functions and the specific data and services that they use.

The Management API itself is contained within the *MGMTAPI.DLL* library and is linked into management applications using the *MGMTAPI.LIB* import library. Both of these libraries are supplied in the Win32 SDK for Windows NT.

MGMTAPI.DLL is installed as part of the SNMP service and trap service only with Windows NT. As explained in Chapter 5, *Getting Started with the SNMP Service*, the Windows NT trap service and Microsoft SNMP Management API trap functions are not supported under Windows 95. You may, however, use the Management API under Windows 95 to send GetRequest, GetNextRequest, and SetRequest messages, and receive GetResponse messages. The Microsoft SNMP Management API for Windows NT 3.x and 4.0 is not compatible with the WinSNMP management library. MGMTAPI under NT 5.0 will use the WinSNMP API.

The Microsoft MIB Compiler

The Microsoft MIB Compiler (*MIBCC.EXE*) is an accessory tool that supports the operation of management applications. A MIB compiler converts a human-read-

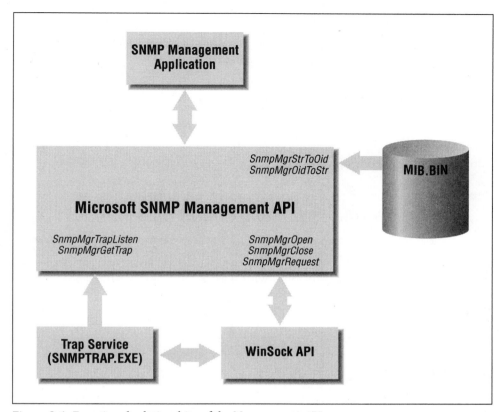

Figure 9-1. Functional relationships of the Management API

able MIB module file into a data format that can be read more easily by software. MIBCC is used to create the *MIB.BIN* file used by the Management API.

You will need to recompile *MIB.BIN* whenever you add support for new or updated MIBs to your management applications. Although the output of MIBCC may have any valid name, the file name *MIB.BIN* is the only name recognized by the Management API. This means that you must have all of your MIB files compiled into a single *MIB.BIN* file. This can be very inefficient if your collection of MIBs includes a total of many hundreds or thousands of MIB object variables.

To recreate the original *MIB.BIN* file, you will use the MIBCC compiler with the following command line:

```
MIBCC SMI.MIB MIB_II.MIB LMMIB2.MIB WINS.MIB DHCP.MIB INETSRV.MIB FTP.MIB
    GOPHERD.MIB HTTP.MIB
```

You can get a synopsis of the MIBCC command-line options as follows:

```
C:\> MIBCC /?
usage: mibcc [-?] [-e] [-l] [-n] [-o] [-t] -[w] [files...]
    MibCC compiles the specified SNMP MIB files.
        -?        usage.
        -eX       stop after X Errors. (default = 10)
        -l        do not print Logo.
        -n        print each Node as it is added.
        -ofile    output file name.  (default = mib.bin)
        -t        print the mib Tree when finished.
        -wX       set Warning level.  (1=errors, 2=warnings)
```

Note that older versions of *MIBCC.EXE* omit the "-t" options in this usage listing, although this feature is present.

For Further MIB Compilation Information

For additional information on compiling MIB files, see these Microsoft Knowledge Base articles:

- "How To Compile MIB.BIN With DHCP and WINS MIB Files Using MIBCC," article Q131776
- "How to Compile IIS MIB Files," article Q143176

MIB.BIN

MIB.BIN is a headerless, binary record format file that contains a compiled collection of the MIBs used by the SNMP management applications that reside on the local workstation. In the Management API itself, the data in *MIB.BIN* is used by only two functions: SnmpMgrStrToOid and SnmpMgrOidToStr. *MIB.BIN* is usually stored in the *%SystemRoot%\SYSTEM32* directory, but MGMTAPI searches using the PATH variable for *MIB.BIN*, so be careful that you don't have any old copies laying around that appear first in your path.

NOTE   The *MIB.BIN* file distributed with the November 1996 Win32 NT 4.0
            SDK (dated 08/09/96 01:30a and 15886 bytes in size) is a compila-
            tion of all the MIB module files included in the SDK, with the excep-
            tion of the *TOASTER.MIB* example file.*

---

* Service Pack 2 for NT 4.0 includes an updated MIB.BIN file (dated 12/14/96 01:38a and 16070 bytes in size), but the updated MIB module files were not included. A quick snoop with WinDiff reveals that only a few new MIB variables were added.

The format of the data file produced by MIBCC is not currently published by Microsoft, but it's easy enough to figure out. Looking at a formatted hex dump of a *MIB.BIN* file, you can easily see the structure of its information:

```
0000006B 00000001 00000003 00000000 00000001 iso
00000054 00000001 00000003 00000000 00000003 org
0000003D 00000001 00000003 00000000 00000006 dod
00000021 00000004 00000008 00000000 00000001 internet
00000000 00000000 00000009 00000000 00000001 directory
00000000 00000000 00000004 00000000 00000002 mgmt
00000000 00000000 0000000C 00000000 00000003 experimental
000000B1 00000001 00000007 00000000 00000004 private
00000092 00000001 0000000B 00000000 00000001 enterprises
0000007B 00000001 00000003 00000000 000000F3 ora
0000005A 00000002 0000000D 00000000 00000001 oraNtSnmpBook
```

Each record in the file contains the information for a single leaf node, stored in five 4-byte fields and a fifth, variable-length field. Here are the fields, in order:

1. Number of bytes stored in the records of the node's subnodes

2. Number of subnodes

3. Number of bytes in node name (field 6)

4. Reserved (always 0 in file)

5. Node subidentifier

6. Node name

As you can see, the output of MIBCC is not an entire compiled MIB module. Information about each node's SYNTAX, ACCESS, STATUS, and DESCRIPTION clause is not stored in the *MIB.BIN* file. The reason: the current version of the Management API does not require this information. If a future revision of the Management API introduces more sophisticated features, then it is likely the format of the MIBCC output will change to include this type of information. Or, perhaps, a new MIB compiler will be introduced to replace MIBCC.

The MGMTAPI.H Header File

The Management API uses the constants and data type definitions that are defined in the *SNMP.H* file. (This file is described in some detail in Chapter 6.) In fact, *MGMTAPI.H* includes the *SNMP.H* header file, which in turn includes *WINDOWS.H*. All applications that use the Microsoft SNMP Management API must include *MGMTAPI.H*.

Let's look at the contents of *MGMTAPI.H*:

```
#include <snmp.h>
#include <winsock.h>
#ifdef _cplusplus
extern "C" {
#endif
```

In addition to including *SNMP.H*, the *WINSOCK.H* header is also included for
support of several data types defined by the WinSock 1.1 API. The Management
API functions also use the standard C library naming conventions:

```
#define SNMP_MGMTAPI_TIMEOUT            40
#define SNMP_MGMTAPI_SELECT_FDERRORS    41
#define SNMP_MGMTAPI_TRAP_ERRORS        42
#define SNMP_MGMTAPI_TRAP_DUPINIT       43
#define SNMP_MGMTAPI_NOTRAPS            44
#define SNMP_MGMTAPI_AGAIN             45
```

These are the possible values returned by GetLastError when a Management API
function fails. They indicate the following:

SNMP_MGMTAPI_TIMEOUT
    A connection or transaction has timed-out.

SNMP_MGMTAPI_SELECT_FDERRORS
    A WinSock file descriptor error occurred.

SNMP_MGMTAPI_TRAP_ERRORS
    Errors occurred while retrieving trap data.

SNMP_MGMTAPI_TRAP_DUPINIT
    A connection for listening for traps has already been established.

SNMP_MGMTAPI_NOTRAPS
    No traps have been received.

SNMP_MGMTAPI_AGAIN
    An attempt to connect to the trap service has failed, but may be attempted
    again.

These error values are explained later in this chapter.

```
#define RECVBUFSIZE 4096
typedef SOCKET SockDesc;
```

```
typedef struct _SNMP_MGR_SESSION {
    SockDesc        fd;          // socket
    struct sockaddr destAddr;    // destination agent address
    LPSTR           community;   // community name
    INT             timeout;     // comm time-out (milliseconds)
    INT             retries;     // comm retry count
    AsnInteger      requestId;   // RFC1157 requestId
    char            recvBuf[RECVBUFSIZE];  // receive buffer
} SNMP_MGR_SESSION, *LPSNMP_MGR_SESSION;
```

The SNMP_MGR_SESSION data type stores information about an open communications link between a management application and an SNMP agent. This is mostly information maintained by the WinSock network layer. The contents and format of this structure should never be directly altered by the code in a management application.

The elements in the SNMP_MGR_SESSION have the following meanings:

fd

The socket descriptor of the network connection made to an SNMP agent. This is the value returned by the WinSock API function "socket" when a UDP socket is opened by the Management API using the destination address and port number 161.

destAddr

The address of the remote side of the network connection. All SNMP requests made in this session are sent to this address.

community

The community string used when sending SNMP messages to the agent.

timeout

The time-out value used when opening the connection or waiting for a response from the SNMP agent.

retries

The number of retry attempts to make when opening the connection or sending a request.

requestId

The current request identification value of the last message sent. (See Chapter 4, *Inside SNMP*, for more information about SNMP message request IDs.)

recvBuf

The buffer used to store received SNMP message responses.

The remaining code in *MGMTAPI.H* contains the SNMP Management API function prototype definitions; the functions are described in the following sections.

Management API Functions

The Management API is used specifically to write SNMP management applications that make requests of SNMP agents. Any SNMPv1 agent may be queried by an application built using the Management API. Chapter 10, *Writing Network Management Applications*, contains the details of designing and implementing a network management application using the SNMP Management API.

SnmpMgrOpen

SnmpMgrOpen opens a network connection with an SNMP agent. You must successfully call this function before making any requests for management information. Connections to several different agents, or multiple connections to the same agent, may be open at the same time. Trap responses may be received without the need to first call SnmpMgrOpen.

This is the syntax of SnmpMgrOpen:

```
LPSNMP_MGR_SESSION SNMP_FUNC_TYPE SnmpMgrOpen(
    LPSTR lpAgentAddress,    /* IN */
    LPSTR lpAgentCommunity,  /* IN */
    INT   nTimeOut,          /* IN */
    INT   nRetries);         /* IN */
```

If the connection to the specified agent is established, the function returns a valid pointer to an LPSNMP_MGR_SESSION structure. This pointer is used to direct SNMP requests at a specific network address, and to close the network connection. The data in the LPSNMP_MGR_SESSION structure should never be directly modified by a management application.

If the connection fails to be established, the function returns a NULL value. A call to GetLastError may return a SNMP_MEM_ALLOC_ERROR value indicating that an internal memory allocation has occurred. The majority of SnmpMgrOpen failures, however, are the result of the agent's host being unavailable or unreachable, or incorrect parameter values being passed to SnmpMgrOpen.

Note that SnmpMgrOpen does not actually establish a (virtual) connection to a managed node. UDP is a connectionless transport protocol and therefore no actual connection is made. Instead, a socket is dynamically created that is used to send SNMP messages to the address specified in the lpAgentAddress parameter.

The parameters are described here:

lpAgentAddress

> This is a NULL-terminated string containing the IP, IPX, Ethernet (MAC), address, or host name of the SNMP agent to connect. The format of the string depends upon the type of address, as follows:

IP addresses

These are specified using a four-octet, dotted-decimal notation (e.g., "128.128.10.1").

IPX addresses

These are 8.12 dotted-decimal network numbers (e.g., "12345678.12345678ABCD"). Hyphens and commas are not allowed in IPX addresses.

Ethernet hardware addresses

These are conventional, 12-octet MAC addresses (e.g., "0102030A0B0C").

Hostnames

These are also in dotted-decimal notation (e.g., "*www.microsoft.com*").

lpAgentCommunity

This is a NULL-terminated string containing the community name of the management application. This is the community string that is encoded in each Request PDU sent by the management application. It should match one of the community names supported by the SNMP agent. The community name is always case-sensitive.

nTimeOut

This is the time to wait (in milliseconds) for the socket connection to open.

nRetries

This is the number of attempts to be made when connecting to an agent. The Management API doubles the time period specified by nTimeOut for each retry attempt that is made. For example, if nTimeOut specifies 1000 and nRetries is 4, the first connect attempt fails (times-out) after 1000 milliseconds, the second attempt fails after 2000 milliseconds, the third attempt fails after 4000, and the final connect attempt fails after 8000 milliseconds.

Example 9-1 shows a typical use of SnmpMgrOpen, complete with simple error checking.

Example 9-1. A typical implementation of SnmpMgrOpen and SnmpMgrClose

```
#include <mgmtapi.h>
#include <winerror.h>

/* Open and close a connection */
DWORD dwError = NO_ERROR;
LPSNMP_MGR_SESSION lpSession;

lpSession = SnmpMgrOpen( "128.128.128.1", "public", 1400, 2 );
if ( lpSession != NULL )
  SnmpMgrClose( lpSession );
else
  dwError = GetLastError();
```

SnmpMgrClose

SnmpMgrClose closes a connection to an agent that was opened using Snmp-MgrOpen. The handle returned by SnmpMgrOpen is used by SnmpMgrClose to close the network socket that was opened for sending SNMP messages between the management application and the agent.

This is the syntax for SnmpMgrClose:

```
BOOL SNMP_FUNC_TYPE SnmpMgrClose(
    LPSNMP_MGR_SESSION lpSession);    /* IN */
```

SnmpMgrClose returns TRUE if the connection was closed, or FALSE if a failure to close the connection occurred. You can call GetLastError to determine exactly what error occurred. You can also call WSAGetLastError to check whether a WinSock error (as defined in *winsock.h*) occurred. The management application may attempt to close the connection again by calling SnmpMgrClose.

This function has only a single parameter, lpSession, described here:

lpSession
> This is the pointer to the LPSNMP_MGR_SESSION structure returned by Snmp-MgrOpen as a reference to the opened session.

See the example under "SnmpMgrOpen" for a sample of the use of SnmpMgrClose.

SnmpMgrRequest

SnmpMgrRequest sends a GetRequest, GetNextRequest, or SetRequest message to an SNMP agent. It only operates in synchronous or "blocking" mode and does not return until a response is received or until the request times out. One SNMP message is sent per call to SnmpMgrRequest.

This is the syntax for SnmpMgrRequest:

```
SNMPAPI SNMP_FUNC_TYPE SnmpMgrRequest(
    LPSNMP_MGR_SESSION  lpSession,          /* IN */
    BYTE                byRequestType,      /* IN */
    RFC1157VarBindList *pVariableBindings,  /* IN OUT */
    AsnInteger         *plErrorStatus,      /* OUT */
    AsnInteger         *plErrorIndex);      /* OUT */
```

SnmpMgrRequest returns TRUE if the request was successfully sent and a response was received; it returns FALSE if an error occurred.

GetLastError will return SNMP_MGMTAPI_TIMEOUT if the agent didn't respond within the time-out period specified in the call to SnmpMgrOpen, or SNMP_MGMTAPI_SELECT_FDERRORS if a WinSock file descriptor error occurred.

The parameters are described here:

lpSession

 This is a pointer to an LPSNMP_MGR_SESSION structure returned by a successful call to SnmpMgrOpen. This pointer indicates which network socket to use for sending the request.

byRequestType

 The type of SNMP request to send. Here are the acceptable values defined in SNMP.H:

```
ASN_RFC1157_GETREQUEST      0xA0
ASN_RFC1157_GETNEXTREQUEST  0xA1
ASN_RFC1157_SETREQUEST      0xA3
```

pVariableBindings

 These are the variable bindings of both the request message sent by the management application and of the response message received from the agent. The list pointer in this object must be dynamically allocated before the call is made to SnmpMgrRequest, even if the Request or Response PDU has no variable bindings. This object must also be freed by the management application. You should never assume that the pVariableBindings pointer you pass to SnmpMgrRequest will be the same one that is returned. SnmpMgrRequest will reallocate this object to accommodate the returned data and the pointer address may be changed.

plErrorStatus

 This is the error status in the GetResponse message returned by the agent. The possible values of this field are defined in RFC 1157 and in *SNMP.H*. Note that in a conforming SNMP agent, the readOnly error is never returned. Instead, noSuchName is returned when a Set operation is performed on a read-only object.

Value	Message	Description
0	SNMP_ERRORSTATUS_NOERROR	No error occurred
1	SNMP_ERRORSTATUS_TOOBIG	The response was too large for the agent to handle
2	SNMP_ERRORSTATUS_NOSUCHNAME	The requested OID does not exist in the supported MIB view, or is not accessible
3	SNMP_ERRORSTATUS_BADVALUE	Bad MIB variable data type specified in the variable binding
4	SNMP_ERRORSTATUS_READONLY	Attempted a write operation on a read-only MIB variable
5	SNMP_ERRORSTATUS_GENERR	Non-specific error occurred

plErrorIndex

This is the index of the variable binding in the Response PDU that created the error. The first variable binding is always 1. If the error was not caused by a specific variable binding, or there was no error, then this value will be 0.

Example 9-2 shows a function that opens a connection to an agent, sends a GetRequest for the MIB object system (sysObjectID.0 instance value), receives a GetResponse message, prints the returned sysObjectID.0 value, and closes the connection. If this request is sent to the Microsoft SNMP service agent, the printed value should be "OBJECT IDENTIFIER - .1.3.6.1.4.1.311.1.1.3.2."

Example 9-2. Function with SnmpMgrOpen, SnmpMgrRequest, and SnmpMgrClose

```
#include <mgmtapi.h>
LPSTR szAgentAddress = "128.128.128.1";
LPSTR szAgentCommunity = "public";
INT nTimeOut = 2000;
INT nRetries = 3;

DWORD MakeRequest( char *, AsnInteger *, AsnInteger * );

int main()
{
    AsnInteger nErrorStatus, nErrorIndex;

    MakeRequest( "system.sysObjectID.0", &nErrorStatus, &nErrorIndex );

    return( 0 );
}

/*
** Open a connection to 128.128.128.1, get the sysObjectID, and close the
** connection. Return the last error that occurred, or NO_ERROR.
*/
DWORD MakeRequest( char *sOid, AsnInteger *nErrorStatus, AsnInteger *nErrorIndex
)
{
    LPSNMP_MGR_SESSION lpSession;

    lpSession = SnmpMgrOpen( szAgentAddress, szAgentCommunity, nTimeOut,
        nRetries );
    if ( lpSession != NULL )
    {
        RFC1157VarBindList VBList;

        VBList.len = 1;
        VBList.list = (RFC1157VarBind *)SnmpUtilMemAlloc(
            sizeof( RFC1157VarBind ) * VBList.len );
        if ( VBList.list != (RFC1157VarBind *)NULL )
        {
                AsnObjectIdentifier oid;
```

*Example 9-2. Function with SnmpMgrOpen, SnmpMgrRequest,
and SnmpMgrClose (continued)*

```
                SnmpMgrStrToOid( sOid, &oid );
                VBList.list->name.idLength = oid.idLength;
                VBList.list->name.ids = (UINT *)SnmpUtilMemAlloc(sizeof(UINT) *
                VBList.list->name.idLength );
                if ( VBList.list->name.ids != (UINT *)NULL )
                {
                    memcpy( VBList.list->name.ids, oid.ids, sizeof(UINT) *
                        VBList.list->name.idLength );
                    VBList.list->value.asnType = ASN_NULL;

                    if ( SnmpMgrRequest( lpSession, ASN_RFC1157_GETREQUEST,
                        &VBList, nErrorStatus, nErrorIndex ) == TRUE )
                    {
                        SnmpUtilPrintAsnAny( &VBList.list->value );
                    }
                    SnmpUtilVarBindListFree( &VBList );
                    SnmpMgrClose( lpSession );
                }
        }
    }
    return( GetLastError() );
}
```

SnmpMgrStrToOid

This function converts an object identifier string to an equivalent AsnObjectIdentifier object using the data stored in the *MIB.BIN* file. The use of this function allows MIB variables to be hard-coded in management applications as text strings, rather than as AsnObjectIdentifier objects.

This is the syntax for SnmpMgrStrToOid:

```
BOOL SNMP_FUNC_TYPE SnmpMgrStrToOid(
    LPSTR                 pString,  /* IN */
    AsnObjectIdentifier *pOid);     /* OUT */
```

SnmpMgrStrToOid performs its conversion by reading data from the *MIB.BIN* file. This file is searched for by SnmpMgrStrToOid using the PATH variable, so the first *MIB.BIN* file found will be the one that is read. (This is often a source of the "but I modified and recompiled the MIB. Why isn't the data different?" bug.) If your management application includes support for non-Microsoft MIBs, then you will need to recompile *MIB.BIN* to include the MIBs that your management application uses.

SnmpMgrStrToOid assumes that all object identifiers without a leading period reside under the management subtree (1.3.6.1.2 or iso.org.dod.internet.mgmt). If you specify a source OID of 1.3.6.1.4.1.2035.10.1, SnmpMgrStrToOid will interpret it as 1.3.6.1.2.1.3.6.1.4.1.2035.10.1, which is probably not what you intended.

To instruct SnmpMgrStrToOid not to assume the management subtree, prepend a period (.) to the OID. For example, to specify an OID in the O'Reilly branch of the enterprises MIB, you would use the OID string ".1.3.6.1.4.1.2035.10.1". The same applies when using MIB node and object descriptors (e.g., ".iso.org.dod.internet.private.enterprises.oreilly.software.name").

If SnmpMgrStrToOid succeeds, it stores the object identifier data in the specified AsnObjectIdentifier object and returns a value of TRUE.

If the object identifier cannot be resolved using the data in *MIB.BIN*, or if the *MIB.BIN* file cannot be found, then SnmpMgrStrToOid returns FALSE.

The parameters are described here:

pString
> This is a NULL-terminated string containing the object identifier to convert. The identifier may have text, numerical subidentifiers, or a combination of both. For example, an identifier might be "system.sysDescr," ".1.3.6.1.2.1.1.1," or ".1.3.6.1.2.1.system.sysDescr."

pOid
> This is a pointer to an AsnObjectIdentifier object that will receive the OID value. The memory required for this object will be dynamically allocated by SnmpMgrStrToOid and should be freed by the management application after its data is no longer required.

Example 9-3 shows some examples of how SnmpMgrStrToOid may be used, and the AsnObjectIdentifier object data that results. Be sure to free the data in the AsnObjectIdentifier object after it is no longer required. You don't need to free the object before each call to SnmpMgrStrToOid.

Example 9-3. Usage examples of SnmpMgrStrToOid

```
#include <mgmtapi.h>

AsnObjectIdentifier oid;

SnmpMgrStrToOid( "1.1", &oid );
/* oid.idLength = 8 */
/* oid.ids = 1 3 6 1 2 1 1 1 */

SnmpMgrStrToOid( "1.1.0", &oid );
/* oid.idLength = 9 */
/* oid.ids = 1 3 6 1 2 1 1 1 0 */

SnmpMgrStrToOid( "system.sysName.0", &oid );
/* oid.idLength = 9 */
```

Example 9-3. Usage examples of SnmpMgrStrToOid (continued)

```
/* oid.ids = 1 3 6 1 2 1 1 5 0 */

SnmpMgrStrToOid( ".1.3.6.1.2.1.1.1", &sOid );
/* oid.idLength = 8 */
/* oid.ids = 1 3 6 1 2 1 1 1 */

SnmpMgrStrToOid( ".iso.org.dod.internet.mgmt.mib.system.sysServices", &sOid );
/* oid.idLength = 8 */
/* oid.ids = 1 3 6 1 2 1 1 7 */

SnmpUtilOidFree( &oid );
```

SnmpMgrOidToStr

SnmpMgrOidToStr converts an AsnObjectIdentifier object into a string representation of an object identifier. The OID string always contains textual subidentifiers.

This is the syntax for SnmpMgrOidToStr:

```
BOOL SNMP_FUNC_TYPE SnmpMgrOidToStr(
    AsnObjectIdentifier *pOid,      /* IN */
    LPSTR               *pString);  /* OUT */
```

SnmpMgrOidToStr performs its conversion by reading data from the *MIB.BIN* file. The function searches for this file using the PATH variable, so the first *MIB.BIN* file found will be the one that is read. If your management application includes support for non-Microsoft MIBs, you will need to recompile *MIB.BIN* to include the MIBs that your management application uses.

If the OID being converted is part of the management subtree (1.3.6.1.2.1), then SnmpMgrOidToStr will not bother including the ".iso.org.dod.internet.mib" identifier prefix in the OID string. All other OIDs outside of the management subtree are rendered as complete OIDs with textual subidentifiers and include the "." prefix.

The parameters are described here:

pOid

This is a pointer to an AsnObjectIdentifier object that contains the OID value to convert.

pString

This is a buffer to receive the NULL-terminated object identifier string.

Example 9-4 shows several examples of the use of SnmpMgrOidToStr and the input and output data.

Example 9-4. Usage examples of SnmpMgrOidToStr

```
#include <mgmtapi.h>

AsnObjectIdentifier oid;
char *pBuf = SnmpUtilMemAlloc( 80 );

SnmpMgrOidToStr( &oid, pBuf );
/* oid.idLength = 8 */
/* oid.ids = 1 3 6 1 2 1 1 1 */
/* pBuf = "system.sysDescr" */

SnmpMgrOidToStr( &oid, pBuf );
/* oid.idLength = 11 */
/* oid.ids = 1 3 6 1 4 1 77 1 1 1 0 */
/* pBuf = ".iso.org.dod.internet.private.enterprises.lanmanager.lanmgr-
2.common.comVersionMaj.0" */
```

SnmpMgrGetTrap

SnmpMgrGetTrap retrieves trap data that has been received by the SNMP trap service. The data stored in one Trap PDU is returned per call to SnmpMgrGetTrap.

This is the syntax for SnmpMgrGetTrap:

```
BOOL SNMP_FUNC_TYPE SnmpMgrGetTrap(
    AsnObjectIdentifier *pEnterprise,        /* OUT */
    AsnNetworkAddress   *pIPAddress,         /* OUT */
    AsnInteger          *plGenericTrap,      /* OUT */
    AsnInteger          *plSpecificTrap,     /* OUT */
    AsnTimeticks        *pdwTimeStamp,       /* OUT */
    RFC1157VarBindList  *pVariableBindings); /* OUT */
```

SnmpMgrGetTrap returns TRUE if a trap message was received and the data is available. SnmpMgrGetTrap returns FALSE if no trap data is present or if an error occurred. If no trap data is present, GetLastError will return SNMP_MGMTAPI_NOTRAPS. GetLastError will return SNMP_MGMTAPI_TRAP_ERRORS if an error occurred that makes any buffered trap data inaccessible; this is often caused by calling SnmpMgrGetTrap before first calling SnmpMgrTrapListen.* SNMP_MEM_ALLOC_ERROR is returned if a memory allocation error occurred.

SnmpMgrGetTrap is the only way to retrieve trap data using the Management API. It may be called periodically to poll for traps received and buffered by the trap service (as shown in Example 9-5), or perhaps only called when the event handle returned by SnmpMgrTrapListen is signaled (as shown in Example 9-6).

---

* See the Microsoft Knowledge Base, "PRB: SnmpMgrGetTrap() Fails," article Q130564.

WARNING A common source of memory leaks in applications that call MGM-TAPI is caused by the failure of the application to free the memory allocated by SnmpMgrGetTrap for the data it stores in the pEnterprise, pIPAddress, and pVariableBindings parameters.

The parameters are described here:

pEnterprise

This is the Private Enterprise Number (PEN) of the management enterprise that defines the trap. Identifying the associated MIB allows the correct interpretation of any variable bindings present in the Trap PDU. The memory for the data stored in this object is allocated by MGMTAPI and must be freed by the management application using SnmpUtilOidFree.

pIPAddress

This is the IP address of the agent that generated that trap. This value is encoded in the received Trap PDU. If a network addressing protocol other than IP was used to route the message (e.g., IPX), then this address will be "0.0.0.0". The memory for this data is allocated by MGMTAPI and must be freed by the management application using SnmpUtilMemFree.

plGenericTrap

This is the generic trap type as defined by RFC 1157. The value returned in this parameter is defined in *SNMP.H*:

Message	Value	Description
SNMP_GENERICTRAP_COLDSTART	0	The SNMP agent has just started
SNMP_GENERICTRAP_WARMSTART	1	The SNMP agent has just reinitialized
SNMP_GENERICTRAP_LINKDOWN	2	A communications link went down
SNMP_GENERICTRAP_LINKUP	3	A communications link came up
SNMP_GENERICTRAP_AUTHFAILURE	4	An SNMP message received by the agent failed authentication
SNMP_GENERICTRAP_EGPNEIGHLOSS	5	A connection was lost with a peer EGP node
SNMP_GENERICTRAP_ENTERSPECIFIC	6	This trap is defined by an enterprises MIB

plSpecificTrap

This is the specific trap type of an enterprise-specific trap. If the value of plGenericTrap is 6 (SNMP_GENERICTRAP_ENTERSPECIFIC), this value will be a zero-based index of the enterprise-specific trap, as defined by the management enterprise indicated by the OID in pEnterprise. For other generic trap types this value will be 0.

pdwTimeStamp

This is the time stamp value encoded in the received Trap PDU. This value is the number of centiseconds that the responding SNMP agent has been active.

pVariableBindings

These are the variable bindings encoded in the received Trap PDU. Only link-Down, linkUp, and egpNeighborLoss traps have variable bindings. An enterpriseSpecific trap may have variable bindings declared in its trap definition; an agent may also include varbinds in addition to those in the trap definition. If the received trap does not have variable bindings, then the list will be zero-length. The list pointer in the RFC1157VarBindList object itself must first be initialized using SnmpUtilMemAlloc before it is passed to SnmpMgrGetTrap, and the memory for the entire list is freed using SnmpUtilVarBindListFree.

WARNING   Because SnmpMgrGetTrap does not return the value of the community string of the trap message, or the network transport address of the trap message's source, you cannot determine which managed host sent the trap.

Example 9-5 shows SnmpMgrTrapListen and SnmpMgrGetTrap used to collect trap data by polling the Management API.

Example 9-5. Example of using SnmpMgrGetTrap to poll for traps

```
#include <mgmtapi.h>

#define POLLING_INTERVAL      6000
#define NUMBER_OF_POLLS         10

int                 i;
HANDLE              hTrapEvent;
AsnObjectIdentifier TrapEnterprise;
AsnNetworkAddress   TrapIpAddress;
RFC1157VarBindList  TrapVarBinds;

/* Start listening for trap events */
if ( SnmpMgrTrapListen( &hTrapEvent ) == FALSE )
{
    if ( GetLastError() = SNMP_MGMTAPI_TRAP_DUPINIT )
    {
        /* Already listening for traps! */
    }
}
```

Example 9-5. Example of using SnmpMgrGetTrap to poll for traps (continued)

```
/* Initialize the variable bindings list */
TrapVarBinds.list = (RFC1157VarBind *) SnmpUtilMemAlloc(
    sizeof( RFC1157VarBind ) );

/* Poll for traps */
for ( i = 1; i <= NUMBER_OF_POLLS; i++ )
{
    BOOL      bReceivedTrap;
    AsnInteger    TrapGeneric;
    AsnInteger    TrapSpecific;
    AsnTimeticks TrapTimeStamp;

    do
    {
        /* Check if any traps were received */
        bReceivedTrap = SnmpMgrGetTrap( &TrapEnterprise, &TrapIpAddress,
            &TrapGeneric, &TrapSpecific, &TrapTimeStamp, &TrapVarBinds );
        if ( bReceivedTrap == TRUE )
        {
            /* Received a trap */
        }

        /* Check if SnmpMgrGetTrap returned an error */
        if ( GetLastError() != SNMP_MGMTAPI_NOTRAPS )
        {
            /* An error occurred */
        }
    } while ( bReceivedTrap == TRUE );

    /* Sleep until time for next poll */
    if ( i < NUMBER_OF_POLLS )
        Sleep( POLLING_INTERVAL );
}

SnmpUtilOidFree( &TrapEnterprise );
SnmpUtilOidFree( &TrapIpAddress );
SnmpUtilVarBindListFree( &TrapVarBinds );
```

SnmpMgrTrapListen

SnmpMgrTrapListen enables a management application to receive trap messages by establishing a named pipe connection between the trap service (*SNMPTRAP.EXE*) and the *MGMTAPI.DLL* library. The SNMP trap service will be started by a call to SnmpMgrTrapListen if it is not currently active.

This is the syntax of SnmpMgrTrapListen:

```
BOOL SNMP_FUNC_TYPE SnmpMgrTrapListen(
    HANDLE *phTrapAvailable);     /* OUT */
```

SnmpMgrTrapListen returns TRUE if the Management API was able to connect to the trap service and open the named pipe server (\\.*pipe**MGMTAPI*) maintained by the trap service. All traps received by the trap service are conveyed to the Management API as BER-encoded Trap PDUs using this named pipe. All trap data received is sent to any listening applications and is buffered in a special thread created in each application by SnmpMgrTrapListen.

The function returns FALSE if an error occurred. GetLastError will return the following:

SNMP_MEM_ALLOC_ERROR
    A memory allocation error occurred.

SNMP_MGMTAPI_TRAP_DUPINIT
    The application has already called SnmpMgrTrapListen.

SNMP_MGMTAPI_AGAIN
    The Management API failed to connect to the trap service, but another attempt to connect using SnmpMgrTrapListen may be made (this is most often caused by a failure of SnmpMgrTrapListen to successfully start the trap service).

This function has only a single parameter, phTrapAvailable, described here:

phTrapAvailable
    This is a pointer to an event handle that is signaled by the trap service when trap data has been received. After being signaled, SnmpMgrGetTrap must be called to actually retrieve the data for one trap message stored in the received trap buffer. The data for additional traps is retrieved using additional calls to SnmpMgrGetTrap. The phTrapAvailable handle must be reset using ResetEvent before it can be signaled again.

Example 9-6 shows SnmpMgrTrapListen and SnmpMgrGetTrap used in an event driven design to collect trap data by waiting for a signal from the Management API.

Example 9-6. Example of using SnmpMgrGetTrap to wait for traps

```
#include <mgmtapi.h>

HANDLE      hTrapEvent;
AsnObjectIdentifier TrapEnterprise;
AsnIPAddress      TrapIpAddress;
RFC1157VarBindList      TrapVarBinds;

/* Start listening for trap events */
if ( SnmpMgrTrapListen( &hTrapEvent ) == FALSE )
{
    DWORD dwError = GetLastError();
```

Example 9-6. Example of using SnmpMgrGetTrap to wait for traps (continued)

```
    if ( dwError != SNMP_MGMTAPI_TRAP_DUPINIT )
    {
      /* Error */
    }
}
else    /* Wait for a trap(s) */
{
    DWORD dwResult;

    /* Initialize the variable bindings list */
    TrapVarBinds.list = (RFC1157VarBind *) SnmpUtilMemAlloc(
      sizeof( RFC1157VarBind ) );

    /* Receiving a trap will set an event signal */
    dwResult = WaitForSingleObject( hTrapEvent, INFINITE );
    if ( dwResult != WAIT_FAILED )
    {
      if ( dwResult != WAIT_TIMEOUT )
      {
        AsnInteger    TrapGeneric;
        AsnInteger    TrapSpecific;
        AsnTimeticks TrapTimeStamp;

        /* Loop until all traps are read from the buffer */
        while ( SnmpMgrGetTrap( &TrapEnterprise, &TrapIpAddress,
          &TrapGeneric, &TrapSpecific, &TrapTimeStamp, &TrapVarBinds ) == TRUE )
        {
          /* Do something with the trap data */
        }

        /* Check if SnmpMgrGetTrap() returned an error */
        if ( GetLastError() != SNMP_MGMTAPI_NOTRAPS )
        {
          /* Error handling */
        }
      }
    }
    ResetEvent( hTrapEvent );

    SnmpUtilOidFree( &TrapEnterprise );
    SnmpUtilVarBindListFree( &TrapVarBinds );
}
```

Memory Management and MGMTAPI

SNMP management application should always use the memory management functions of the SNMP Utility API (SnmpUtilMemAlloc, SnmpUtilMemReAlloc, and SnmpUtilMemFree) when passing data to—and freeing received data from—MGMTAPI. Chapter 6 noted (in the description of the SNMP Utility API memory management functions) that it is necessary for all dynamic memory objects passed between extension agents and the SNMP service to be allocated and freed from the same heap to prevent memory leaks. This is also true of SNMP management applications and MGMTAPI.

MGMTAPI is rather simple in its rules for memory management:

- Any data dynamically allocated by a management application and passed to an MGMTAPI function must also be freed by the application. MGMTAPI does not free your memory for you.

- The data returned by SnmpMgrGetTrap in its pEnterprise, pIPAddress, and pVariableBindings parameters is allocated by MGMTAPI and must be freed by the management application.

- Never assume that the pVariableBindings pointer you pass to SnmpMgrRequest will contain the same memory address after the function returns. The memory for this object is reallocated by MGMTAPI to store the variable binding of an SNMP request message, and the pointer may end up storing a different memory address.

10

Writing Network Management Applications

If you ask a group of software engineers about the SNMP projects that they have worked on, you will probably find that each engineer specializes in the design and implementation of either management applications or agents, but not both.* This is very common since the knowledge and experience required to write software applications and firmware programs has diverged greatly over the past ten years. And it's not often that you will find a programmer who enjoys working in both types of environments and who produces efficient code as well.

The Microsoft SNMP APIs give you the opportunity to play around with both the agent side and the management side of SNMP implementation. Although both management systems and agents share the common ground of the SNMP protocol, MIBs, and the SMI, they do have some remarkable differences in their views of the network, managed data, and their roles in the SNMP management model.

This chapter covers some of the basic planning necessary for designing and implementing SNMP network management applications. I'll also explore the types of management applications that you can design and a few of the problems you may encounter. In addition, I'll elaborate a little further on the Microsoft SNMP Management API.

---

* If they specialize in writing embedded agents, they probably refer to themselves as "firmware engineers."

Types of Management Applications

SNMP agents are conceptually "black boxes" that all operate in basically an identical manner—processing requests and sending traps based on the rules of SNMP. SNMP agents on a network differ only in the version(s) of the SNMP protocol they support, the managed objects they maintain, and how they maintain them.

From the agent's point of view, SNMP management systems are black boxes as well. From out of the darkness of the network an SNMP request message appears to the agent. The agent processes it and sends it back to the source. The agent knows little of the message sender and never directly interacts with the management application. An SNMP management application views each SNMP agent as simply a collection of managed objects associated with a port number, network address, and the management community (or communities) to which the agent belongs. If both a D4 channel bank and a General Electric refrigerator use the same MIB views, they will both most likely be managed in the same way, although they are in reality very different types of devices.

From the human manager's point of view, however, SNMP management applications are not black boxes at all. They have a well-defined user interface and vary greatly in their appearance, implementation, and use. To a manager, SNMP agents are abstract collections of information that can only be accessed using a management application, just as web pages can only be properly viewed using a web browser.

An SNMP management application may be designed for the management of network, system, or process resources. Its design may allow the management of any generic management objects, or the management of only the objects supported by a specific type of networked or proxied hardware.

Many management applications are implemented to operate in a workstation environment and under an operating system such as Windows, UNIX, MacOS, or MS-DOS; still others are written as embedded applications and live inside test equipment or a dedicated management device.

Most management applications have some sort of character or graphical user interface used to display data in a format the human manager can interpret more easily. The interface may be a simple ASCII menu, a command-line driven interactive session, or an event-driven bitmapped graphical user interface. Some management applications may implement neither, and instead generate output that must be interpreted by another device (e.g., HPGL sent to a printer, G3 compressed data sent to a facsimile machine, etc.), or by a network application (e.g., HTML sent to a web browser).

The type of management application that you write will depend primarily on how it is to be used and for what purpose. Let's look at few of the most common types of SNMP management applications.

Simple Management Tools

The simplest management applications are command-line tools designed to send single request messages and receive response messages and traps. These tools are used to gather small bits of management information, test which managed objects are implemented by an agent, debug an agent's operation on specific managed objects, and send a quick request to check if a node is alive and reachable and under SNMP management.

Simple *management tools* usually require the user to have intimate knowledge of the SNMP protocol. For the tool to be used properly, the manager must understand the concept of a management community, the structure of variable bindings, the format of ASN.1 data types, and the SNMP protocol errors.

The Microsoft SNMPUTIL example program is a very simple MS-DOS Console program that is a basic SNMP management tool. It is capable of sending Get and GetNext messages, walking an agent's MIB, and receiving traps. It is distributed as a Win32 SDK sample program with full source code as an example of how to implement an SNMP management program using the Microsoft SNMP Management API.

The SNMPTOOL program included on the CD-ROM is also a command-line SNMP management program, but it includes several features not found in SNMPUTIL, including the ability to send SetRequest messages, poll MIB variables, log all received information to a file, and read command-line information from a script file. SNMPTOOL also uses the Microsoft SNMP Management API. Full source code is included on the CD-ROM as well.

Simple management tools may also be implemented under Windows. The SimplNMS application on the CD-ROM is an example of a very simple SNMP tool implemented as a Win32 application in standard C and using the Microsoft Win32 and SNMP APIs.

Network Management Application

After spending some serious debugging time using a simple GUI or command-line management tool, you will quickly realize that there are many features that can be added to make the tool more useful and less tedious to use. DOS-based tools can quickly become very complicated to use since each new feature requires more command-line flags and arguments; moving to a menu-based design is often a great improvement. If the tool is implemented for a GUI environment, then you have an enormous collection of point-and-click, drag-and-drop, colorful, graphical, and browsable potential with which to design.

A *network management application* is typically made as generic as possible so that any MIB may be compiled and browsed, any trap message may be received and logged, any type of network device may be located and identified, and any SNMP-managed node may be queried and polled. At this point, the simple management program or application passes beyond being used as an occasional tool and graduates to the description of a management application, which may be used on a continuous basis to monitor a network and its devices.

Network Management Platform

A big drawback with generic management stations is that they are often *too* generic. To support any and every MIB, alarm message, and network device, the user interface must be as non-specific as possible. What this means is that the manager using the application must perform many repetitive, tedious, low-level procedures to carry out even the simplest of management operations. What is needed is some sort of extendible management application that can be customized for the particular network and devices that it is managing.

A *management platform* is an extendible management application. A platform typically offers the same generic features of a network management application and also supplies tools that allows the implementation of custom, specialized management applications that are written using APIs provided by the platform.

If the generic features supplied by the platform are too generic for convenient use, you can write a specialized management application to perform the same operations in only a few keystrokes and mouse clicks. The specialized application would use the basic services provided by the management platform to send complex and customized requests with few keystrokes and a single click of a button. It would also use the services of the operating system and GUI to graphically display the retrieved data, and perhaps send it to a printer or store it in a file.

Several extendible network management platforms exist for Windows (see Appendix A, *References*). The most notable of these is Hewlett-Packard's HP OpenView for Windows, also known as Workgroup Node Manager (16-bit) and Network Node Manager (32-bit). OpenView is a generic SNMP network management platform that supports many basic features, such as automatic network discovery, network topology map generation, MIB compiler and browser, trap log, and polling manager. OpenView also supplies an API (OVSNMP) that allows its services to be used to create specialized management applications, referred to as OpenView integrated applications, that perform network and system-specific management tasks. The custom management applications are typically written in C, C++, and Visual Basic.

System Management Application

Back in Chapter 3, *Network Management and SNMP*, we noted that network management is primarily concerned with maintaining the overall health of an entire network by monitoring the devices that make up the network. System management is only interested in networked devices as stand-alone entities; it is not concerned with the operation of the network itself.

Although network management stations can be used to perform system management functions (many of which are identical to network management functions), they are also too generic for convenient use by the system managers. A custom *system management application* would allow a networked device, or set of devices, to be much more easily monitored and controlled, and would not support any features required to manage the network itself.

System management applications are therefore only used for the provisioning and configuration of networked devices as separate components, or as members of a larger collection of interrelated devices. The network itself is used only as a medium for remotely controlling the devices, and the system management application has no direct control over how the network is managed.

A specialized system management application gives the manager a custom-tailored interface designed to show at a glance the condition of the nodes being monitored (see Figure 10-1). A graphical representation of the device's front panel may even be used to indicate its operational status. Just as with the custom network management applications, many routine system management tasks that may take several steps to perform using a generic management application may be performed using fewer clicks and keystrokes.

It is also a goal of most customized management applications to completely insulate the user from the protocol. To use such an application, a manager would need to know nothing of MIBs, OIDs, SNMP operations, or protocol errors. In fact, a very good design should make it impossible for a manager to determine what protocol is being used to convey the management information.

One advantage generic management stations have over customizable management applications is the ability to adapt to changes in a MIB. Once the generic application has been updated for the revised MIB module in its database, the new or revised objects become available. For a customized management application, handling changes in MIBs is not this easy. The application's user interface is usually tied quite closely to the objects defined in a MIB and the values that they may contain. Add, change, or remove objects from a MIB and it is likely that the code of the custom management application will need to be revised and recompiled, and a new release of the software product distributed. There is also a

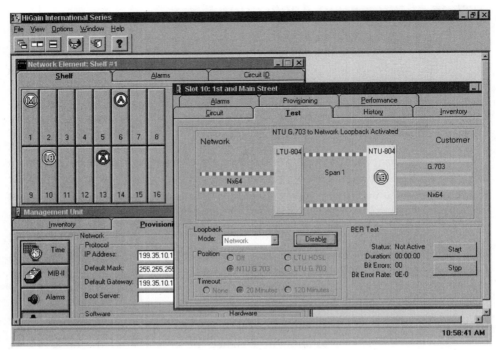

Figure 10-1. A custom system management application

significant amount of bookkeeping that a management application must do when managing nodes containing several different revisions of the same MIB. Specifically, you must know which nodes support what managed objects.

Once the development of a hardware device has leveled off (read: marketing stops pumping it up with new features), the device's MIB stabilizes as well. There may be a few corrective changes that may not affect the custom management application at all, but no significant changes occur—unless a new feature is added to the device, or the MIB is changed to support a new product family.

Another advantage generic management applications have: they are only one application, and they may manage any SNMP-managed node using only a single user interface. A custom management application only manages devices that support a specific set of MIB objects. But there is a downside. Suppose that you have a local area network containing ten types of devices, each with its own set of managed objects, and that each is managed using its own vendor-specific management application; the real estate on your 21-inch monitor can get eaten up by windows very quickly, as will most of your workstation's available memory.

Intermediate Management Systems

Not all management applications are directly used by managers and have a user interface. Occasionally, the configuration of a network may require multiple layers of management processes to efficiently oversee the entire network. Only the upper-most layer of management applications is actually used by the human managers. The mid-level management processes, often called intermediate management systems, act as network probes that collect, organize, and format management data that is then retrieved by the upper-level management applications.

Networks that contain a very large number of managed nodes are very difficult for a single management application to monitor within a reasonable period of time. The job is harder still if a great many different MIBs are supported by the network nodes. The network administrator could set up more management stations and hire more managers to examine all of the nodes, but it would be more economically feasible if the management information for all of the managed nodes could be automatically collected and made available from only a few sources.

An *intermediate* (or *mid-level*) *management system* can be used to collect management information from a specific group of managed nodes (usually ones that all support the same MIB view), or from all of the managed nodes on a specific subnetwork (see Figure 10-2). The management information collected would then be made available by the intermediate management system using a special set of managed objects that support a conglomerate of managed objects. Other management applications would then send requests to the intermediate management system rather than directly to each managed node.

A network that is composed of many remote subnetworks could have an intermediate manager on each subnetwork collecting management data and making the data available to all upper-level management applications located anywhere on the network. If the remote subnetwork is accessed via a very slow or costly link, then the intermediate manager can consolidate the management information into a more compact format (and possibly using data compression or a different management protocol) for transport across the link.

Intermediate managers are often implemented as a hybrid SNMP management application and SNMP agent. Intermediate managers that communicate entirely using SNMP must be able to both receive SNMP request messages and send SNMP response messages. They will also have the ability to receive and forward traps.

An intermediate management system can also be used as a gateway to translate one management protocol to another. The intermediate manager in Figure 10-3

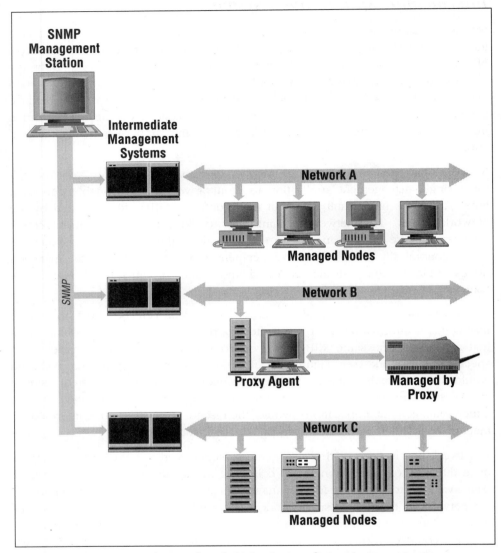

Figure 10-2. Monitoring subnetwork nodes using intermediate management systems

allows an SNMP management system to communicate with a managed node that supports a management protocol other than SNMP. The intermediate manager is only an intermediary, translating messages from one protocol to another, and does not actively collect or store management data.

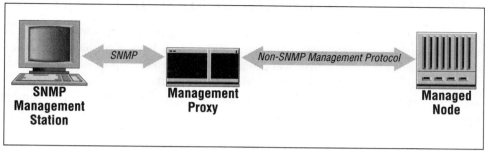

Figure 10-3. Intermediate management gateway

But Which Windows?

Before you start comparing management platforms and APIs, you must decide which Windows operating system(s) you will use to run your management application. Sometimes you don't really have a choice of platform. Your customer base will dictate the operating system you use. If your customer base mostly uses Windows NT, then Windows NT is your target system.

The operating system plays a major factor in the robustness of the management application (and agent) itself. You cannot make the assertion that your program is robust and has no bugs if the operating itself is buggy or flaky. Do not consider single-tasking and nonpreemptive multitasking operating system environments if your marketing requirements contain the phrases "mission-critical" and "fault-tolerant." I guarantee that no one other than a fellow software engineer will have sympathy for the cry "but it's Windows, not my code!"

You should also limit the number of operating systems that you attempt to support using a single body of code. A great many problems are incurred by "code once, compile many" solutions that promise that their libraries will allow you to write a single piece of code that will run under many diverse operating systems. You will find that many of your favorite problem-resolving tactics are implementation-specific and would break the multi-platform library's operational model if you implemented them.

Most multi-platform application frameworks only supply generic features that can be implemented on all supported operating systems. This means that you will end up using your own compiler switches, system-specific code libraries, and operating system API calls that will probably render at least half the application's code as platform-dependent. You will also find plenty of bugs with the framework vendor's platform-independent libraries—the libraries whose source code is not supplied unless licensed at great cost.

You may ponder if it might not have been better to write separate code for each platform in the first place. (Just a friendly warning!)

Provisioning a Management Application

Despite the diverse nature and use of SNMP management applications, they all share a few similar operational parameters. When you have a problem communicating with an agent, the cause will often be a misprovisioning of one or more of these operational parameters. Always double-check the following parameters if you experience unexpected problems while attempting to perform management operations on a node.

Network Address

A management application must know the *network address* of any node with which it needs to communicate. The network address is typically an IP or IPX address or a resolvable DNS host name. Be mindful of typos if you are entering network addresses manually. Some management applications require that you first select the node to manage from a device listing or a network topology map.

Remote Destination Port

The *remote destination port* is the network port number on the destination node that is used to receive SNMP request messages. This number is commonly the "well-known" UDP port 161. But this port number may be different if the management application is communicating with a proxy agent that does not listen to the standard SNMP port. In such a case, the destination port number will commonly be greater than 1024.

Trap Reception Port

The *trap reception port* is the network port number on the local management host that is used to receive SNMP trap messages. This number is commonly the "well-known" UDP port 162. But this port number may be different if the management application is required to listen for traps sent by an agent to a different port.

Community Name

Each SNMP agent will only accept request messages that contain as their *community string* the name of a community to which the agent belongs.[*] A management application must therefore associate a specific *community name* with each agent network address and use only that name when constructing requests that will be sent to that agent. The de facto default SNMP community name is "public."

---

[*] A management application belongs to whatever management communities it sends request messages to.

Many agents support two community names that are used by the agent to authenticate read-only and read-write access to the node. These "get community" and "set community" names must be known to the management application and be used for performing their associated operations. The community strings "public" and "private" are the de facto read-only and read-write community names.

If an SNMP agent has not been provisioned with a community name, the agent will typically respond to all request messages it receives regardless of the community string that they contain.

Response Time-Out and Request Retry Count

The *response time-out* is the interval of time that the management application will wait for a response message to be received from the agent. This interval is typically measured in deciseconds or milliseconds; if it is zero, no timeout is imposed.

The *request retry count* is the number of times the request message will be sent if a response timeout occurs. If this value is zero, no retry attempts are to be made.

Each time a request message is sent, a deadman timer (if the timer expires then the "man" has died) is started using the response timeout interval. If the response message is received, the timer is stopped. If the timer expires, then a response message was not received within the specified request timeout interval. The management application then checks the request retry count value. If it is greater than zero, it is decremented by one, the request message is resent, and the deadman timer is reset.

If the timer expires again, the retry count is decremented and the request message is sent again. This cycle continues until either a response is received or until the retry count decrements to zero (in which case the management application indicates that "no response was received from the agent").

The values of the time-out interval and number of retry attempts are judgment calls made by the network manager based on experimentation. You might start out with a two-second time-out and two retry attempts. Longer time-out values may be specified for slower managed nodes and on networks with longer end-to-end response times. Too short a time-out risks sending a second, retry request message before the response to the first request message has been received.

More than a few retry attempts usually aren't necessary. If a response isn't received after the second or third retry, the node is typically down, is too busy to respond, or there is a routing problem on the network. In each of these cases, even the most insistent manager will not receive a response.

A large number of retry attempts can be useful if you are in the act of correcting a network problem, and you are using the retry request messages to indicate when the problem has been cleared, or when an agent has come up.

Polling Interval

Management applications are commonly used to periodically retrieve the values of specific managed objects from a managed node. This retrieval of data at regular intervals is called *polling*. The most common type of polling is used to monitor data that may change—or is not supposed to change—simply to make sure that the node is still alive. The type of data often polled checks how well a node is functioning and performing its intended job.

The *polling interval* is used to determine how often each polling cycle is to begin. Depending on the size and number of messages sent each polling cycle, how long it takes the managed node to respond, and how the information is used, a polling cycle interval might be only 10 or 15 seconds in length, or a few minutes, or several hours.

Network Management Application Features

When you are designing a network management application, you might wish to consider some features that will greatly help the manager to monitor, explore, and troubleshoot a network. If you already have experience using a sophisticated SNMP management platform, such as Solstice (formerly SunNet Manager), Novell ManageWise, or HP OpenView, you are likely to be familiar already with the features I'll discuss here.

Network Discovery

Before a management system can collect detailed management information from a network, it must determine what kind of devices make up the network, how they are connected, and what their addresses are. The configuration of a network by the interconnection of its devices is called the *network topology*, and the process of determining the topology of a network by a management system is called the *network discovery*.

"A single ping, Comrade. Just one, for range"

Network discovery is most simply performed by sending an ICMP (Internet Control Message Protocol) message* to all possible host addresses on a specific subnetwork. For example, if a discovery were performed on network 200.20.2.0, a

---

* Also called a "ping," which is often described as the acronym for Packet InterNet Groper. It is more likely that this description is only a bit of net-folklore, and that "ping" is actually an onomatopoeia for the pinging sound made by a SONAR (SOund NAvigation Ranging) Doppler echo when detecting remote, underwater objects.

single ICMP message would be sent to each possible address (200.20.2.1 through 200.20.2.254) to determine which nodes are reachable and responsive.

For each ICMP response that was received, that node would be logged by the management application as currently active or "up." If a response from an address is not received, then a second ICMP would be sent just in case the first message might have been lost on the network, or possibly dropped by the node.

Using ICMP messages in this way is rather a brute force method of node detection that floods a network with packets. If many subnetworks are involved in the discovery, then thousands of ICMP messages could be sent. These messages, along with their responses, will momentarily degrade the performance of the network.

A more sophisticated and network-friendly discovery strategy is to read the ARP (Address Resolution Protocol) caches and interface tables of the local subnetwork router and management host to discover which devices are present on the network. ICMP messages can then be used to verify that the ARPable devices support IP.

Identifying SNMP-managed nodes

After completing the ICMP and ARP discovery, the management application would then send a GetRequest message to each active node to retrieve the sysObjectID (1.3.6.1.2.1.1.2.0) value of the node. If a GetResponse message is received, the management application will log the node as supporting SNMP management.

Once an SNMP-managed node is identified, the management application usually requests additional management data from the managed node. This information is used to unambiguously identify the managed node to the manager. Here's the basic management data commonly requested:

1.3.6.1.2.1.1.sysDescr.0
  The description of the system

1.3.6.1.2.1.1.sysName.0
  The human-readable name of the system

1.3.6.1.2.1.3.1.1.atPhysAddress(2), or 1.3.6.1.2.1.4.22.1.2.ipNetToMediaPhysAddress
  The physical (MAC) address of the node

1.3.6.1.2.1.3.1.1.atNetAddress(3), or 1.3.6.1.2.1.4.22.1.3.ipNetToMediaNetAddress
  The network (IP) address

Here's some explanation for the preceding information:

IP and MAC addresses
  Used to verify the network and data link identity of the node, respectively.

sysDescr value

Identifies the node by the name of its manufacturer, and possibly by its serial number and software version as well.

sysName string

Identifies the node by its human-readable name (the value of atNetAddress is used instead if sysName is blank).

Additional Identification Information

Other data from the "ip," "interfaces," and "system" groups of MIB-II is usually collected as well.

Network discovery database

All of the network configuration information gathered using network discovery is stored in a *discovery database*. This database is referenced by the management application each time the manager performs a management operation on a host. For a very simple management application that needs to keep track of only a few managed nodes, a text file or the Windows registry can be used as the database. For larger-scale management applications, use an actual database engine, such as Microsoft Access.

Network topology map

The information in the discovery database is typically displayed as a listing of active nodes, sorted first by subnetwork and then by IP address, or sorted by the sysName or sysDescr of each SNMP-managed node. This type of listing can be difficult to search and navigate if it contains thousands of entries, especially since most of them look alike. It also doesn't give a very clear depiction of which node belongs to which subnetwork on which LAN on which WAN, and so forth.* It therefore makes sense to use the network configuration information in the discovery database to create a graphical drawing that depicts the logical configuration of the network. This depiction is called a *network topology map*.

Topology maps help the manager graphically navigate a network starting at the top with each router and proceeding downward (or outward) along each subnetwork, through the servers, and finally to the end-hosts themselves. The map will be displayed using multiple windows, and each node on the map will be depicted using a specific icon denoting the type of device and the manufacturer. If the management application is actively polling the node, the icon's color will indicate the node's present status. Not only are graphical topology maps very useful, but they will impress the heck out of any boss that loves to adorn his or her office desktop with stacks of glossy marketing literature.

---

* It is not possible to discover a network's physical topology using only SNMP.

Figure 10-4 shows a view of a simple topology map window under HP OpenView for Windows. You can see a subnetwork of three end-host nodes that are user workstations. There is also an icon used to move back to the previous map.

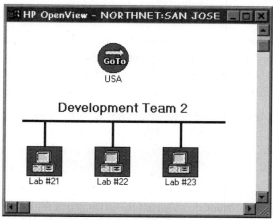

Figure 10-4. HP OpenView topology map

Polling Manager

A *polling manager* is a feature that is used to perform polling operations on multiple nodes. I previously noted that polling is used to periodically gather the values of specific managed objects, or simply to check if one or more nodes is reachable and still alive. A polling manager coordinates the information used to poll one or more nodes.

The polling manager is initialized by selecting specific node addresses from the network discovery database and storing them in a polling list. Each polling list entry contains several associated parameters used to provision how each node is polled. These parameters include the request retry and response time-out values, and the polling interval, which is typically described in seconds or minutes.

Each polling entry will also include a polling request definition that specifies the type of message to use for polling the node. If the polling is performed only to check whether the node is still alive, then a simple ICMP message sent every five or 10 minutes will do. If the polling is used to periodically collect management data using SNMP, you must specify the objects in the variable bindings of the GetRequest or GetNextRequest message.

Polling is typically performed on managed objects whose value may change over time, such as numberOfCrcErrors, pmSignalToNoiseRatio, fridgeDoorIsOpen, protectionSwitchIsEngaged, desktopMousePosition, and mostSevereAlarm.* Such objects may be polled every few hours, minutes, or seconds, depending upon how vital it is for the network manager to see their most current values.

MIB Compiler and Database

After a network discovery has been performed, the management application may now select the node to which to send management requests. To be able to reference the specific managed objects supported by each node, the management application must have access to the MIB modules used by each managed node.

MIB modules are written in ASN.1 syntax and stored as ASCII text. Just as C source code is useless to a system until compiled, MIB modules are useless to both management systems and agents until they are translated to a usable format. This is precisely the purpose of a MIB compiler.

The *MIB database* is a collection of compiled MIB modules. A management application uses the MIB database to resolve object descriptors to OIDs, convert object descriptors to numerical subidentifiers, and determine the type of data stored by a MIB object and the access it allows.

Very simple management applications may not use a MIB database. Instead, they may require that the manager build each request by manually entering the OID, data type, and data value of each variable binding. This is fine for small request messages, but is very tedious for messages with many varbinds. It also requires that the manager read and interpret the necessary MIB modules, and possibly memorize frequently used OIDs.

More sophisticated management applications read a simple listing of MIB objects created using an external SNMP *MIB compiler,* such as MIBCC. When the manager builds a request, each MIB object is specified by its object descriptor; and the object's OID and access information is read from the MIB database (see the sidebar, "Resolving MIB Database Objects").

Reading information from the MIB database is much easier than entering all of the data by hand, but the MIB compiler is usually a separate program from the management application and must be operated manually. The compiler's output is usually a simple text file that can be slow to read by the management application, especially if the MIB modules define thousands of managed objects.

Very sophisticated management applications will contain their own, built-in MIB compiler, which compiles and stores MIBs using a standard or proprietary database format. Management requests are typically built using a graphical, drag-and-drop, or point-and-click interface. Such management applications also have the

---

* Don't waste your time looking through the RFCs for these. I made them up.

Resolving MIB Database Objects

When a MIB database is compiled, the complete, unambiguous OID of each MIB object is stored. However, a management application need not use the entire OID to search the database for a specific MIB object's information. The database engine can locate a match given only a few textual or numerical subidentifiers in the OID. This is perfectly fine, but you must be aware of one pitfall.

Object descriptors must be unique within a MIB module, but there is no requirement that descriptors be unique among all MIB modules. For example, it is completely legal (although unwise) for you to create a MIB object with the descriptor "sysName," although an object with this descriptor already exists in another MIB.

If you search for an object in a MIB database only by its object descriptor, then you may end up finding the wrong object if two or more objects in the MIB database have the same descriptor. To prevent this problem from occurring, it is best to search for MIB objects based on several of their right-most or most-significant OID subidentifiers.

For example, you might search a MIB database for your sysName object as "myDevice.controlUnit.inventory.sysName," while the sysName object in MIB-II would be located by specifying "mgmt.mib-2.system.sysName." Using this strategy to increase the resolution of your MIB searches ensures that your management application will always reference the correct MIB object—assuming that it exists in the database in the first place.

capability of saving management requests in the MIB database that can be recalled and reused by the manager.

Figure 10-5 shows the HP OpenView for the Windows MIB compiler interface. The list on the left shows the MIB modules that are available to be compiled. The list on the right shows the MIBs that have been compiled and stored in the database. If an error occurs during compilation, the manager is informed and none of the new modules are added to the database. Updated MIB modules may be recompiled into the database, and the entire database may be cleared.

This approach taken by HP's MIB compiler means that only one version of any MIB module can be compiled in the MIB database. Other SNMP management platforms allow multiple versions of the same MIB module to be compiled into a single MIB database.

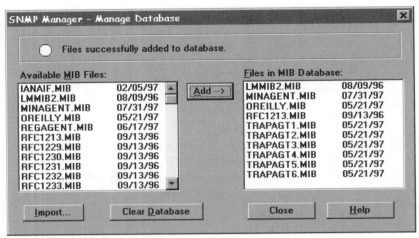

Figure 10-5. HP OpenView MIB compiler

MIB Browser

A *MIB browser* is used to locate and examine managed objects stored in a MIB database. Because "the MIB" is an inverted tree structure, the browser will use an interface similar to Microsoft Windows Explorer or File Manager. The objects in the database are browsed as if you were stepping through a directory tree, opening folders, and examining files.

MIB browsers are also used to build requests that are sent to managed nodes, usually in the form of SNMP GetNextRequest messages. The variable bindings of the request message are literally built by selecting specific MIB objects using the browser interface.

Figure 10-6 shows the HP OpenView for the Windows MIB browser interface. This is a simple point-and-click interface that is used to build management requests by stepping through each node in the MIB database, and selecting the MIB objects whose values are to be requested.

The MIB browser is also capable of sending SNMP requests and displaying the GetResponse message variable bindings data (or the error) that was returned. Figure 10-7 shows the results of the query performed by the browser in the previous figure. The name of each specified MIB object and its retrieved value is shown in the table.

MIB Walker

A *MIB walker* is a less sophisticated type of a MIB browser that is used to perform what you might call a *MIB discovery* on a managed node.

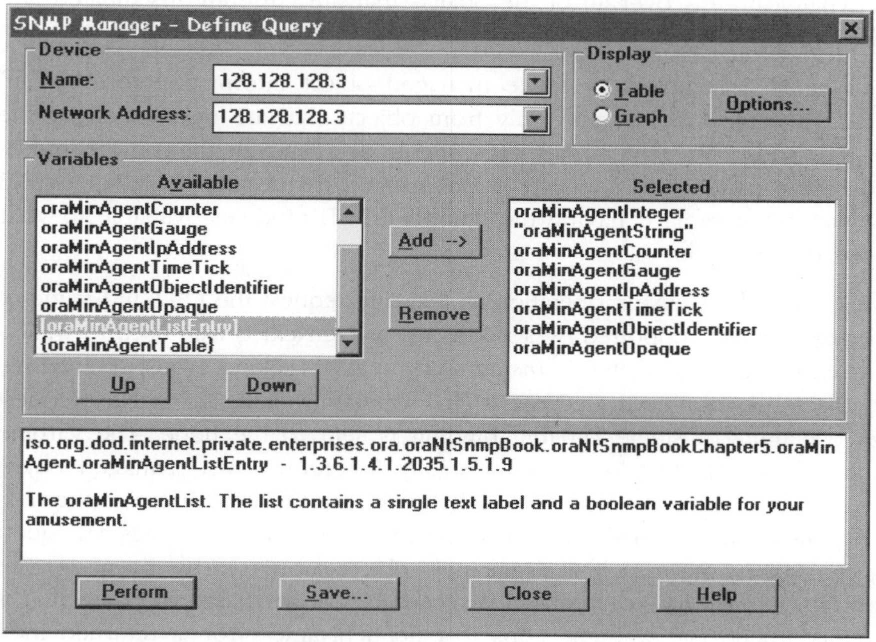

Figure 10-6. HP OpenView MIB browser

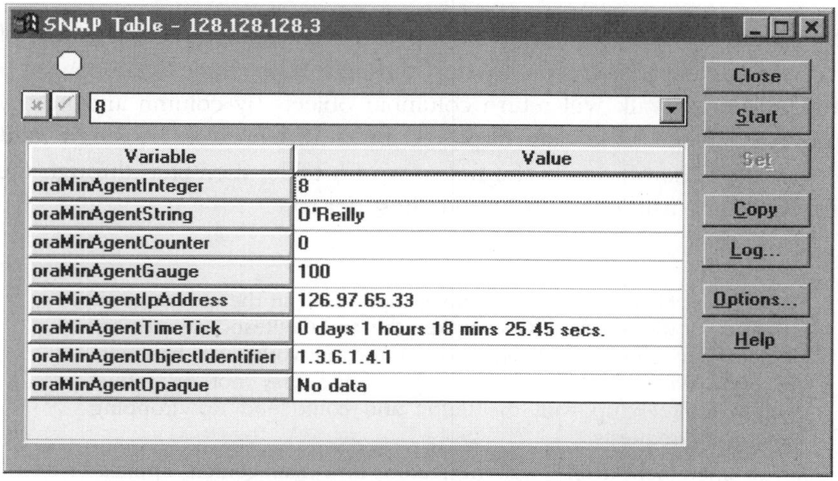

Figure 10-7. HP OpenView MIB query

Under SNMP there is no standard way to request that a managed node divulge the names, revisions, and contents of the MIB modules and objects that it supports. If you don't know what MIBs to compile for your management application to reference, then you won't be able to manage the node. MIB walking is a way to dynamically discover all of the objects that are currently instantiated and made accessible by a node at the time of the walk.

MIB walking is only able to retrieve managed object information that can be stored in a variable binding, and only from objects that are instantiated by the agent at the time of the walk. Other MIB module data, such as the ACCESS mode, DESCRIPTION, and object descriptor cannot be requested. Therefore, MIB walking will never replace having the compiled MIB modules available to your management application.

The "walk" uses the GetNext operation to lexically request the OID and value of each managed object supported by a node, just as GetNext is also used to walk a table (as explained in Chapter 4, *Inside SNMP*). MIB walking is also commonly referred to as "performing a GetNext walk." To start walking, a GetNextRequest message containing a single variable binding is sent to the node. The varbind must specify an OID that is located lexically before the first managed object supported by the node. The node will then return the OID and value of the next lexical managed object. This OID will be used to send another GetNextRequest message to request the next lexical managed object supported by the node. The OID and type of each object returned is recorded in a database, and the value is typically discarded. The walking stops if a noSuchName error is returned indicating that the end of the MIB view has been reached. Some MIB walkers may be configured to stop walking after a specific OID has been reached.

This simple walk is also called a *dumb walk* because it doesn't take advantage of the ability of the GetNext operation to step through entire tables one row at a time. In fact, the dumb walk will return columnar objects by column and not by row, as you typically see table data displayed by a MIB browser. A *smart walk* would discover all of the objects in the first row of a table, then step through the table one row at a time using one GetNextRequest per row.

WARNING   Walking the MIB of a managed node may result in the exchange of hundreds or thousands of GetNextRequest and GetResponse messages. This degrades the performance of the network, and hammers the node with request messages. The node may not be robust enough to keep up with the traffic and could end up dropping some of the requests.

If you implement a MIB walking feature in a management application, throttle the rate at which request messages are sent, and allow the throttling rate to be adjusted by the manager. Also allow the manager the capability of selecting an OID at which the walking should stop. Finally, never walk the MIB of a critical operational node.

Walking a MIB module

MIB modules themselves may also be walked.* Most MIB compilers support an option that allows a formatted, human-readable listing of the objects defined in a set of MIB modules to be generated. This is identical in concept to a map file that is generated by a linker. The OID and name of each managed object is typically depicted in their hierarchical order, as shown here:

```
1.3                     org
1.3.6                   dod
1.3.6.1                 internet
1.3.6.1.1               directory
1.3.6.1.2               mgmt
1.3.6.1.2.1             mib-2
1.3.6.1.2.1.1           system
1.3.6.1.2.1.1.1         sysDescr
1.3.6.1.2.1.1.2         sysObjectID
1.3.6.1.2.1.1.3         sysUpTime
1.3.6.1.2.1.1.4         sysContact
1.3.6.1.2.1.1.5         sysName
1.3.6.1.2.1.1.6         sysLocation
1.3.6.1.2.1.1.7         sysServices
1.3.6.1.2.1.2           interfaces
1.3.6.1.2.1.2.1         ifNumber
1.3.6.1.2.1.2.2         ifTable
1.3.6.1.2.1.2.2.1       ifEntry
1.3.6.1.2.1.2.2.1.1     ifIndex
1.3.6.1.2.1.2.2.1.2     ifDescr
```

Trap Logging

When a trap is received by a management application, its reception may be reported in several ways. The information in the trap may cause icons in a topology map to appear, change color, or disappear; a message box might be displayed; or some sort of audible or visible indication might be created by the management application to grab the attention of the manager playing FreeCell in another window. (Lucky for the network that Quake doesn't run under NT.)

One of the most common places for trap data to end up is in a database referred to as the *trap log*. When a trap is received by a management application, the information it contains is stored in the trap log, along with the time and date that the

---

* MIB browsers are used to walk MIB databases.

trap was received by the local host, and the network address of the node that sent the trap.

The manager will typically view the trap log data using a scrolling text window or table. Log entries may be selected, sorted, viewed, and deleted. The log is the first place a manager looks when diagnosing faults on the network.

Each entry in the alarm log is created when a trap message is received. The traps may be generic (MIB-II) or enterprise-specific, and any variable bindings data may be displayed if the MIB defining the trap has been compiled in the management application's MIB database.

Under OpenView, trap entries are cleared from the alarm log by performing *trap acknowledgement,* which is simply a term for marking an alarm entry as "it's been taken care of" or "it's not of any interest," and then removing the trap entry from the log. Despite the way it sounds, no acknowledgment message is actually sent to the node that generated the trap; SNMP traps are never acknowledged.

Windows traps

Under Windows NT, the event log is effectively the trap logging utility. If an application needs to report a specific condition or event, it writes a message in the event log using the Win32 Event Logging API. The administrator of the workstation periodically reads through the logged events using the Event Viewer (see Figure 10-8) to determine if any problems have occurred.

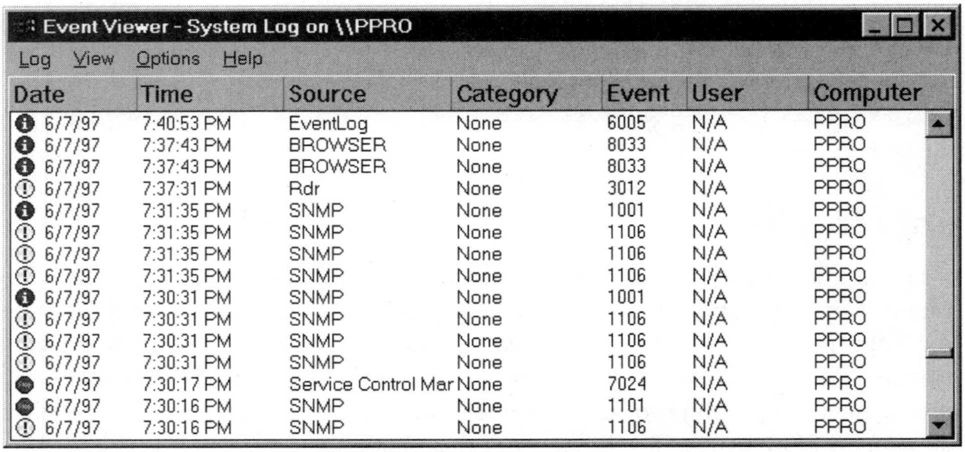

Date	Time	Source	Category	Event	User	Computer
6/7/97	7:40:53 PM	EventLog	None	6005	N/A	PPRO
6/7/97	7:37:43 PM	BROWSER	None	8033	N/A	PPRO
6/7/97	7:37:43 PM	BROWSER	None	8033	N/A	PPRO
6/7/97	7:37:31 PM	Rdr	None	3012	N/A	PPRO
6/7/97	7:31:35 PM	SNMP	None	1001	N/A	PPRO
6/7/97	7:31:35 PM	SNMP	None	1106	N/A	PPRO
6/7/97	7:31:35 PM	SNMP	None	1106	N/A	PPRO
6/7/97	7:31:35 PM	SNMP	None	1106	N/A	PPRO
6/7/97	7:30:31 PM	SNMP	None	1001	N/A	PPRO
6/7/97	7:30:31 PM	SNMP	None	1106	N/A	PPRO
6/7/97	7:30:31 PM	SNMP	None	1106	N/A	PPRO
6/7/97	7:30:31 PM	SNMP	None	1106	N/A	PPRO
6/7/97	7:30:17 PM	Service Control Mar	None	7024	N/A	PPRO
6/7/97	7:30:16 PM	SNMP	None	1101	N/A	PPRO
6/7/97	7:30:16 PM	SNMP	None	1106	N/A	PPRO

Figure 10-8. Windows NT Event Viewer

Under Windows, very serious traps that require the immediate attention of the user are displayed using message boxes. The prime example is your favorite trap and mine, the General Protection Fault.* If you are not familiar with GPFs, I'll just note that they most often occur when you are demo-ing your latest software for your company's newest customers and the CEO.

Functional Considerations and Etiquette

You may not think of management systems and agents having an "etiquette," but any device or process that communicates using a protocol always follows an implied etiquette—one that is not explicitly defined within the rules of the protocol itself. The RFCs that define SNMP occasionally recommend specific protocol etiquette practices, such as limiting the size and number of messages sent by SNMP management systems and agents. But there is no explicit advice given in the RFCs about how these aspects of proper management system etiquette are to be achieved, as they are all "implementation-specific details."

The two major areas of etiquette involve the behavior of SNMP management software as a Windows or MS-DOS application and as a network process. When interacting with other applications, all Windows applications follow a particular etiquette that is strictly enforced by the Win32 operating system. When interacting with other network processes, network processes follow a similar set of implied rules, but they are not necessarily forced to do so.

As a Win32 applications programmer, you should already be familiar with (read: live by) the rules for designing and implementing a "well-behaved" Win32 application. If you are not, then the preemptive, multitasking environment of Windows NT is a safe place for you to learn. Because of the strict isolation and control Windows NT has over each process, you will find it much harder to accidentally shoot the system in the foot than you did under the original 16-bit Windows 3.1.

Network applications must not only be well-behaved host processes, but must also be courteous to other hosts on the network and to the network itself. With the differences between a local system host and the network itself continually blurring, we find that system and network application etiquette both revolve around the same basic principles:

- Realize that you are not the only one using the system or network.

- Don't hog all of the system or network resources.

- Always limit your use of the system or network bandwidth.

- Don't attempt to unnecessarily communicate with anyone on the system or network.

---

* Under Windows NT, user-level GPFs are indicated by a message box. Kernel-level GPFs result in the stomach-sinking STOP message and the eye-popping blue screen.

All of these rules may seem like common sense, but have they ever stopped you from using the company T1 Internet connection and PointCast to continually monitor Sportsticker and CNN, or from using your web browser's news reader to download every posting from your favorite *alt.binaries.pictures.** newsgroups to your workstation? The isolation of your office or cubicle may make you feel as if you are the only one using the network, but this is by no means the case.

All of these principles of etiquette apply equally well for both SNMP management applications and SNMP agents. We can use these principles to derive a more concrete set of rules for the interaction of management systems and agents:

- Don't send request messages that contain many varbinds; send several short messages instead.

- Don't send messages in concurrent bursts; send them in a serial sequence instead.

- Don't hammer an agent with frequent and unnecessary polling.

- Don't provision an agent to send traps to more destinations than necessary.

- Realize that more than one management system may be sending requests to a single agent at the same time.

These rules are very conservative and, when used, lighten the load on both the network and the managed nodes. A very reliable network composed of nodes with robust hardware, multithreaded software, and ample available resources would modify these rules to be more liberal and to allow for greater efficiency:

- Send request messages with as many varbinds as the network MTU will allow.*

- Send messages in concurrent bursts if your management software can handle the bookkeeping.

- Use liberal discretion with polling rates.

- Consider traps to be very reliable.

Although we have already discussed these rules to some extent in other chapters of this book, they are worth reviewing from the management application point of view.

Limit the Size of the Request Messages

In Chapter 2, *Network Basics*, we discussed the types of Protocol Data Units (PDUs) that are used to send SNMP messages across a network. We also

---

* Be mindful that a successful Get or GetNext operation may return a GetResponse message that is larger than the original request message.

discussed the size limits applied to all network packets. If an SNMP message generated by a management application or an agent is so large in physical size that it must be fragmented into multiple packets, it will not be sent.

The only real control a management application has over the size of a message is the number of variable bindings it includes. The physical size of the message grows with each varbind that is added. Even with only a few varbinds, the response to a GetRequest or GetNextRequest message may contain a considerable amount of data—possibly so much that a tooBig error will be returned by the agent.

But this is a physical size problem. There is also a logical size problem that occurs when a management application sends a request message with a very large number of variable bindings. Although the physical size of the message may be small, processing a large number of varbinds puts a greater load on the agent and increases the amount of time it will take the agent to send a response. Your management application might end up sending a retry message even before the agent can return a response.

The easiest way to determine the size of a message is by using a protocol analyzer to eavesdrop on the management sessions occurring between a management application and an agent. (If you don't have a protocol analyzer, look at this book's CD-ROM; you do now.) To be safe, you might set guidelines for your management application, such as no more than 16 varbinds per message and a maximum total request message size of 1000 bytes. If you believe that the network is really robust, then try packing in as many varbinds as the network connection's MTU allows (in many cases this is actually the most efficient thing to do). Depending on what type of management you are performing, these guidelines may range from "more than generous" to "very unreasonable."

If your management application design seems to require something large, such as a SetRequest message with 72 varbinds, you need to rethink your design. Remember that the "all or nothing" philosophy of SNMPv1 dictates that if a problem occurs when performing an operation on one variable binding, the operation won't be performed on any of the variable bindings in the message. So if you use a single message to set the values of 72 MIB variables, but there is a problem with setting the value of just one of the variables, then none will be set. So please, split that monster up into several (say, about ten), bite-sized messages.

Spare the Agent (It's Probably Just a Little Guy)

Perhaps the most important rule to remember when designing a management system and agent model is that you should always have the management application perform as much of the SNMP management work as possible. Always assume that the management system is operating on a much more powerful host than the agent (visualize an Arnold Schwarzenegger and Woody Allen comparison if it helps). This, of course, is not always the case.

The most conservative advice is to design an agent to collect and store data using the least taxing implementation possible for the node. The agent should not be expected to perform complex calculations and data formatting operations just to simplify the life of a management-application-implementing software engineer. The agent should store its MIB data "in the raw" and the management application should process and format the data as required.

One request, one response

To lighten the load on an agent, consider designing your management application to have no more than one request message "on the wire" at any time. Send only a single request message and wait until you receive a response (or don't receive a response) before sending the next request (see Figure 10-9).

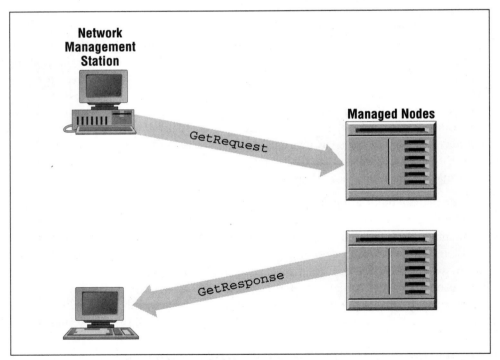

Figure 10-9. Sending and receiving sequential messages

You may find it convenient to have your event-driven design send multiple requests messages concurrently; then wait for all responses to roll in from the agent (see Figure 10-10). This design may also be a little faster than the serial "send a request, wait for a response; send a request, wait for a response" method that I am recommending, but it does place more work on the agent.

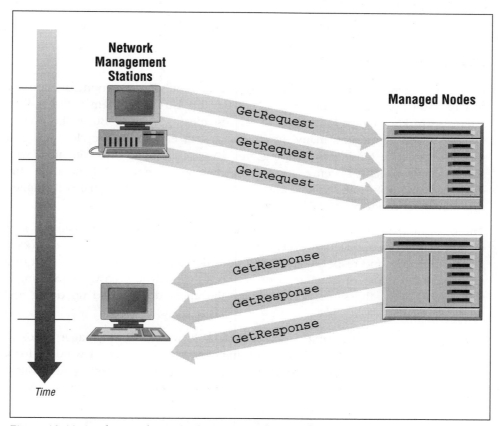

Figure 10-10. Sending and receiving concurrent messages

Each agent has a buffer where received SNMP messages are queued before they are processed. Sending multiple request messages causes this finite-sized buffer to fill up more quickly. (You might not think that this is much of a problem, but remember that other management applications might be sending messages to the same agent at that moment.) If the buffer fills to its capacity, incoming messages are dropped until the agent reads more messages from the buffer and frees up space.

Multithreaded agents are able to process messages more quickly than a single-threaded agent, which can operate on only one message at a time. While processing a request message, a single-threaded agent needs to wait for an I/O operation to complete, the agent will cease all activity-including trap event detection-until the I/O operation complete. The multithreaded agent is able to create one thread for each message pulled from the receive buffer. If one thread needs to wait for an I/O operation to complete, the other threads will continue to process their messages. Separate threads are also used for trap event detection and trap message generation.

The Microsoft extendible SNMP agent is single-threaded, so go easy on it.

Go Easy on the Polling

Polling an agent for specific management data is a very common function for management applications to perform. Usually this isn't a problem if the polling intervals are kept rather long and the request messages small. But if the polling interval is very short, and many messages are sent each polling cycle, the agent might experience problems keeping up. Now compound this situation with several management systems all polling the one agent simultaneously (the dreaded "gang poll"), and you've got an agent-breaking situation that will frighten even the most confident firmware engineers.

The most fundamental type of polling is simply a ping. An ICMP message is sent by a management application every so often to see if a node, or group of nodes, is still reachable, and responding. A ping does not actually retrieve data or require any real information processing to occur, so it is much less costly than using a Get operation for the same purpose, plus the agent doesn't end up doing any work.

The polling interval of a ping is determined by how soon the manager needs to know if a particular node is down. Five minutes might be a good window for a node of only average importance, and 30 minutes for a redundant system. But if the node is an important device, then maybe pinging every 20 seconds would be more advisable.

Polling operations that involve using Get and GetNext are typically used to monitor node performance and to detect the occurrence of faults on the node. The management application performing the polling will use a polling interval value to determine the amount of time to wait between performing each polling cycle.

You might even come up with an agent design that requires the use of the Set operation while polling. It would be highly unusual to require that a MIB variable be set with new data at periodic intervals. You also would need to consider what would happen if a SetRequest message were lost during a polling cycle.

Problems with polling

Each polling cycle is performed by the management application sending one or more request messages, usually in a serial sequence. The polling cycle is started by a heartbeat timer (a timer that fires at regular intervals and never stops) that uses the polling interval value as its trigger interval. Each time the polling timer fires, a fixed series of polling data request messages is sent to an agent and their responses are received.

Specifying the appropriate length of time for a polling interval is a judgment call on the part of the network manager. If the polling interval is too long, performance data might not be collected from the node at a useful resolution, or a fault may be present on the node for an unacceptable period of time before it is detected. If the polling interval is too short, the network will be burdened by needless, inefficient traffic. Any polling interval that can be handled by the node and does not significantly degrade the network can be considered reasonable.

Another problem of short polling intervals is *polling overlap,* where the next poll is begun before the previous poll is finished. Not only is this wasteful of network bandwidth, but it may also break the management application code responsible for handling, storing, and distributing management data.

Assume that a polling operation using three request messages is performed every 60 seconds. Under normal circumstances, all three requests are sent, and their corresponding responses are received within 10 seconds. This leaves 50 seconds of "silence" before the next poll. A manager then decides to tighten the polling interval to 20 seconds to decrease "event detection latency." This increases the response time of the management application to report a problem if a fault is detected, but it also increases the amount of network traffic (once again, this is a judgment call on the part of the network managers).

When an event does occur, and the node is really in trouble, it might be slow to respond to request messages, or it may start dropping messages that it receives altogether. Such events cause the management application to resend each lost request message, and thereby increase the length of time it takes to complete the poll. Request messages will also occasionally be lost due to network problems, although the condition of the node itself is completely normal. The poll that took 10 seconds to complete under "normal" conditions might now take 30 seconds to complete under "abnormal" conditions. But after 20 seconds, the next poll will start, and in this case, before the previous poll finishes. This is polling overlap.

You cannot rely on the polling cycle to always require a fixed amount of time to complete. Your best case might be two seconds per request message sent; your worst case would be the request time-out interval, multiplied by the number of retries, multiplied by the number of request messages sent in each polling cycle.

The simple solution to this problem is to not restart the polling interval timer until all of the data requested by a polling cycle has been received. This allows the polling to take as long as necessary to complete—or to fail—and prevents any polling overlap.

Trap reception during polling

A management system may be designed to start a polling cycle when a specific trap has been received. For example, a trap usually indicates that a fault has occurred on a node. The data in the Trap PDU will typically indicate the type of fault, the level of the fault (minor, major, or critical), and approximately where the fault physically or logically occurred. The management system receiving this trap may then poll the node for additional information on the status of the entire node.

If such a trap is received by a management system while in the middle of a polling cycle, it would be terribly inconvenient (from a software point of view) to stop and restart the cycle, or to start a second, concurrent polling cycle that polls for different information.

The trap could instead be ignored by the management system on the assumption that the management data gathered during the current polling cycle will contain information on the event. But it is possible that some of the polled data was gathered before the fault information became available to the SNMP agent. In this case, the fault would not be detected by the management application until the next polling cycle, despite the reception of the trap.

In a better design, the reception of a trap during a polling cycle is used as an indication that the management system should immediately poll the same node again after the current polling interval has completed. Using this logic, if the management data gathered by the polling cycle does not reflect the presence of the event, the data gathered by the preemptive poll will reflect the presence of the event.

Polling is not for the continuous collection of data

Management systems are only intermittent processes on a network. They are not intended to provide a reliable, node monitoring capability 24 hours a day and 7 days a week. The job of continuous monitoring and information gathering belongs to the tireless SNMP agent.

When a management system sends a request to an agent, the agent must obtain the managed object data specified in the variable bindings of the request. This data is usually maintained by the node's operating system. The agent simply retrieves the data by reading a variable or making an API call, and then copying the data to the varbinds in the GetResponse message.

In many cases, however, the data associated with some managed object might be maintained by the agent itself. The agent might be designed to spy on the node and collect statistical data that the node does not keep track of itself. This data is also made available to management systems as managed objects in the MIB.

Sometimes people misunderstand the data collection role of the management system and the agent. A design may be constructed to use a management system as a continuous, remote monitoring process used to collect data as if it were an agent. For example, every two seconds a management system might be required to poll an agent to collect important data that the management system then stored on its local disk. This sounds feasible, but there can be some significant problems:

- The SNMP request message sent by the management system may never reach the agent.

- The agent may have problems processing the request and return an error.

- The response sent by the agent may never reach the management system.

If data must be collected at precise intervals, then the delay caused by the need of the management system to send a retry message could result in the loss of important data. Neither the network nor the agent can guarantee that the management system will have its requested information every two seconds. The latency of both the network and the agent depend on their current workload. Under optimal conditions a two-second polling cycle may operate very successfully, but under less optimal conditions severe loss of data could occur. So any data requested by a management system should be considered expendable. The time interval in which the data is gathered should also not be critical; the time it takes to retrieve the data from any managed object cannot be guaranteed to be exact. (You must have a reasonable range of tolerance.)

Don't Send That Trap if No One Wants It

Previous chapters discussed the ability of agents to send traps to specific network nodes, where they are gladly received and processed. But all too often, an agent is provisioned with unnecessary trap destinations, or it retains once-valid destination addressees that now identify nodes that are not interested in processing SNMP traps. A common occurrence is an agent that sends traps to a management host that is only up at infrequent intervals, or a manager who forgets to delete a trap destination that was only used temporarily to test a specific system or network problem. In both of these cases, an agent is spewing traps to a network node that will never be processed, and is unnecessarily using network bandwidth.

Implementing Management Applications Using the Management API

Chapter 9, *Using the Management API,* covered the few functions found in the SNMP Management API. The remainder of this chapter elaborates on some of the finer points of implementing SNMP management applications using the Management API. Refer also to the SnmpTool and SimplNMS management applications on the CD-ROM as working example programs that use the Management API.

Before we jump into the "hows" and the "whys," let's have a look at a few of the "do you mind if I don'ts."

Deciding When Not to Use the Management API

The Microsoft SNMP Management API contains the bare minimum functionality necessary for constructing an SNMP management application. While the Management API does receive support from the Utility API for allocating memory and manipulating data structures, there are many advanced and useful features of SNMP session control found in other SNMP Management APIs that are currently lacking in the Microsoft SNMP Management API. I'll describe these in this section.

I'm not recommending that you never use the Management API. Unless you are building a very complex management application, the Microsoft SNMP Management API should fit your requirements. But be aware of its limitations when making comparisons with other SNMP Management packages. See Appendix A for a listing of third-party SNMP and TCP/IP toolkits.

Transportability

The Microsoft SNMP Management API will only operate under the Win32 operating systems. If you have a requirement to write a single piece of SNMP management code that must compile and run under other operating platforms, such as the X Window System and UNIX, Win16, MacOS, and the original MS-DOS, then you cannot use the Microsoft SNMP Management API.

Trap support under Windows 95

The reception of traps is not supported by the Management API under Windows 95. The SNMP trap service is required to listen for arriving traps and to transport the trap message data to the Management API via a named pipe. Because named pipe servers are not supported under Windows 95, the SNMP trap service will not operate. This is a very serious drawback if your trap-aware management application must also run under Windows 95.

Non-blocking mode support

All SNMP request and response messages are sent and received using a single call to the SnmpMgrRequest function. Although you can specify the response time-out interval and the number of request retries, SnmpMgrRequest will not return until a response message is received, or until all of the retry attempts have timed-out. This type of behavior is often referred to as *synchronous operation* or *blocking mode*.

What the Management API does not currently support is a way to control SNMP management sessions *asynchronously* using *non-blocking mode*. Such a capability would enable SnmpMgrRequest to return immediately upon sending a request message, and would allow the response message to be received using a callback function. Other non-blocking support functions would include the ability to manually resend a request message and get the status of or cancel a request in progress.

Non-blocking mode features are very useful in complex management application design. If you don't have access to such capabilities, you might have difficulty achieving the desired level of functionality in your management applications.

Usability with languages

All Microsoft SNMP APIs are not designed to be easily called using languages other than C or C++. The primary problem is the use of pointers as function arguments and the complex data types defined in *SNMP.H* and *MGMTAPI.H*. Many of the functions in the SNMP API have an argument that is a pointer to an object of the AsnAny data type (see Chapter 6, *Using the Extension and Utility APIs*). AsnAny is a struct that contains a large union. Functions that use this data type may be very difficult—if not impossible—to call from languages such as Java and Visual Basic. And making calls directly to the SNMP APIs will certainly introduce a new layer of bugs if the data is not passed correctly.

The solution is not to call the SNMP APIs directly in your application. Instead, implement the SNMP functionality that you need in a DLL, OCX, or ActiveX control written in C or C++. To perform requests and receive responses, your application will need to call only methods defined in the control and pass only integers, strings, and arrays as argument variables. Another solution is to use an SNMP API that is friendly to non-C-based languages and is specifically designed for the application development platform you will be using.

Opening and Closing a Management Session

SnmpMgrOpen and SnmpMgrClose are used by a management application to establish and terminate an SNMP management session with a managed node.

Each time SnmpMgrOpen is called, a UDP datagram socket is created and initialized using the agent's network address and the well-known port number 161.*
The session handle returned by SnmpMgrOpen is used to access the socket.
Because UDP is a connectionless protocol, no real or virtual connection is actually established to the destination node when SnmpMgrOpen is successfully
called. Opening a connection merely dynamically allocates a socket and assigns
the address and port number that it uses to send and receive SNMP messages.

Each time SnmpMgrOpen is called, a different network port on the local host is
opened; the number assigned to this port will always be greater than 1023. You
may make multiple calls to SnmpMgrOpen from the same thread, or from
different threads owned by the same process. Multiple sessions may also be
opened using the same network address.

The WinSock connection is closed and the management session is terminated
when SnmpMgrClose is called. When the session is no longer needed, be sure to
close each session opened using SnmpMgrOpen.

Sending Request Messages

As I said before, when SnmpMgrRequest is called, it does not return until either a
matching GetResponse message is received, or until all retry attempts have been
performed. During this wait, the management application will appear to freeze
because of the blocking mode operation of SnmpMgrRequest.

If your application is only performing one request at a time, you might not
consider this a problem and you might simply display the hourglass cursor or a
"Waiting for response..." message for the duration of the wait. But if your application needs to be doing multiple things (perhaps sending simultaneous requests to
other agents), then make each call to SnmpMgrRequest using a separate thread,
which is suspended or terminated when the call to SnmpMgrRequest returns.

Example 10-1 shows a thread function that is started using CreateThread, calls
SnmpMgrRequest, and then terminates. An event handle is passed to the thread
used to indicate that SnmpMgrRequest has returned and that the GetResponse
message data is available in the global variables.

Example 10-1. Example of a thread that sends a request and receives a response

```
#include <mgmtapi.h>

#define NUMEVENTMONHANDLES     8

HANDLE               ghRequestCompleted[NUMEVENTMONHANDLES];
```

---

* This port number is read from the *%SystemRoot%\SYSTEM32\DRIVERS\ETC\SERVICES* file.

Example 10-1. Example of a thread that sends a request and receives a response (continued)

```
SNMPAPI              guResult;
RFC1157VarBindList   *gpVarBinds;
LPSNMP_MGR_SESSION   ghSession;
AsnInteger           guErrorStatus;
AsnInteger           guErrorIndex;

/* Initialize GetRequest data and create thread to make the request */
{
    HANDLE ghRequestThread;
    DWORD  gdwRequestThreadId;

    /* Initialize gpVarBinds here */

    ghRequestCompleted[0] = CreateEvent( NULL, TRUE, FALSE, NULL );
    ghRequestThread = CreateThread( NULL, 0,
      (LPTHREAD_START_ROUTINE)RequestThread,
      (LPVOID)ghRequestCompleted[0], 0,
      &gdwRequestThreadId );
}

long WINAPI RequestThread( LPARAM lParam )
{
    HANDLE hCompleted = (HANDLE) lParam;

    guResult = SnmpMgrRequest( ghSession, ASN_RFC1157_GETREQUEST,
      gpVarBinds, &guErrorStatus, &guErrorIndex );

    /* Send the signal that the GetResponse data is now available
       in the global variables */
    SetEvent( hCompleted );

    return( NO_ERROR );
}

/* Wait for the request to complete */
{
    while ( 1 )
    {
        DWORD dwEventIndex = WaitForMultipleObjects( NUMEVENTMONHANDLES,
          ghRequestCompleted, FALSE, INFINITE );
        if ( dwEventIndex >= WAIT_OBJECT_0 )
        {
            if ( dwEventIndex <= WAIT_OBJECT_0 + NUMEVENTMONHANDLES )
            {
                /* SnmpMgrRequest returned and thread terminated.
                   Do something with the GetResponse data in the
                   global variables. */

                /* Reset the event */
                dwEventIndex = dwEventIndex - WAIT_OBJECT_0;
                ResetEvent( ghRequestCompleted[ dwEventIndex ] );
            }
```

Example 10-1. Example of a thread that sends a request and receives a response (continued)

```
        }
    }
}
```

A management application may create a RequestThread each time it needs to send an SNMP request message. All such threads would be called from a Request-ManagerThread that would be responsible for initializing the request data, starting the thread, and collecting the data returned by each request.

You may get the clever idea to send concurrent request messages to the same agent using multiple threads. Each thread could call SnmpMgrRequest using either a single session handle or a unique session handle opened by each thread calling SnmpMgrOpen. While this approach is certainly possible, remember that SNMP etiquette greatly discourages sending a volley of request messages to any single SNMP agent. And any agent may be serving requests from multiple management applications at the same time.

Request ID

Remember the description of the Request ID field in the SNMP Request PDU in Chapter 4? The Request ID value is used by a management application to match each response message that it receives with a specific request message that it has sent.

The Request ID is used primarily to identify a specific response message that has been received. Each time a request message is sent, a timer is started and is associated with the message's Request ID. When a GetResponse is received, the timer associated with the message's Request ID is killed. If a GetResponse is not received, its timer expires and the request message is sent again in a retry attempt; if all retry attempts have been exhausted, a "no response from host" error is returned.

The Request ID is also useful for routing the GetResponse data to the appropriate code in the management application that requested it. For example, a performance polling thread sends a GetRequest message with a Request ID of 263. The ID is noted by the management application as a record of a GetResponse message that is expected to be received, and then sends the GetRequest the specified agent.

When a GetResponse message is received, the management application compares the message's Request ID to the IDs of all pending requests to determine where to pass the data, or which thread to notify that the data has been received. In this example, the data from a GetResponse message with a Request ID of 263 is passed to the performance polling handler thread.

The Request ID itself is just a 32-bit integer. Its value is chosen by the management process and has no real significance other than that it must be unique to each request message sent during a management session. Duplicating recently used request ID values may cause the management process to mismatch responses and requests.

An SNMP agent itself does not use the value in the Request ID field. However, it is the agent's responsibility to copy the Request ID from each request message that it receives to the corresponding GetResponse message that is sent back to the management application.

The SNMP Management API automatically determines the Request ID value of each request message that it sends. When a process attaches to the *MGMTAPI.DLL*, the Request ID value is initialized to zero. Each request message that is sent using SnmpMgrRequest will increment the Request ID value by one and store the value used in the "requestId" element of the open session (SNMP_ MGR_SESSION) handle.

The requestId value is read-only and the management process cannot select what the Request ID of any SNMP request message will be. The same incrementing Request ID value is used by all calls to SnmpMgrRequest made by all threads in the process that attached to *MGMTAPI.DLL*. Opening and closing multiple session handles using SnmpMgrOpen has no effect on altering the Request ID value. The Request ID may only be reset back to zero by the process detaching and then reattaching to *MGMTAPI.DLL*.

Receiving Traps

Sending traps is part of the SNMP Extension API and is covered in Chapter 8, *Implementing Traps*. For Windows NT to receive traps, however, requires use of the SNMP trap service and the SNMP Management API. Because the trap service is not implemented under Windows 95, only Windows NT can support applications that call the SNMP Management API to receive traps.

The Microsoft SNMP trap service (*SNMPTRAP.EXE*) is stored in the *%System- Root%\SYSTEM32* subdirectory when the SNMP service is installed. By default, the trap service is set for manual start, so it won't be running when you start NT. You must start the trap service by either running the *SNMPTRAP.EXE* executable, or by using the Service Control Manager (SCM) from the Control Panel. You can also use the SCM to reconfigure the trap service to automatically start when NT starts; *MGMTAPI.DLL* will also manually start the trap service when it is needed.

The trap service monitors the protocol port designated as the SNMP trap receiver in the *%SystemRoot%\SYSTEM32\DRIVERS\ETC\SERVICE\SERVICE* file. This is typically the well-known port 162, but may be configured to a different port so as not to conflict with other SNMP services on the same system. When a socket is allocated for a port, only that process can access the port (WinSock 1.1). For this reason, a third-party SNMP management system installed under NT will usually disable the trap service to gain exclusive access to the SNMP trap port.

Each trap message received from the trap port is passed from the WinSock API to the trap service. The message is then made available to the SNMP Management API (*MGMTAPI.DLL*) using a named pipe server (\\.*pipe**MGMTAPI*) created by the trap service.

Only two MGMTAPI functions are required for an application to receive traps using the Management API. SnmpMgrTrapListen enables an application to receive traps by opening a connection to the named pipe server maintained by *SNMPTRAP.EXE*. When a trap is received by SNMPTRAP, the *MGMTAPI.DLL* library reads the Trap PDU, decodes the BER data, and makes its information available to the application via the SnmpMgrGetTrap.

An application may receive traps using either a polling model or an event-driven model (both are described in Chapter 8). In Chapter 9, code examples implementing both models are included in the sections that discuss the SnmpMgrTrapListen and SnmpMgrGetTrap functions. Previous chapters also contain example code that reads the data stored in AsnObjectIdentifier and RFC1157VarBindList objects. For additional working examples, consult the SNMP-TOOL example management program on the CD-ROM.

Bypassing the SNMP Management API to receive traps

It is possible to bypass the Management API and read incoming traps directly from the *SNMPTRAP.EXE* named pipe server. Any process needing to directly monitor traps that are received by the NT system may connect to the trap service's named pipe (\\.*pipe**MGMTAPI*) and receive trap messages.

Each message read from \\.*pipe**MGMTAPI* contains a 20-byte header followed by a BER-encoded Trap PDU. The header contains information such as the trap sender's UDP port number and IP address.* The Trap PDU data in the message body is only useful to a BER parser or as a hex dump (assuming that you read BER). And remember that Windows 95 does not support named pipe servers, so don't bother trying to get *SNMPTRAP.EXE* to run under Windows 95.

Example 10-2 illustrates a function that may be used to receive trap messages received by the trap service. Note that this example is written in the form of a

---

* Microsoft has not yet published the format of the trap messages produced by *SNMPTRAP.EXE*, so there is no guarantee that future changes to this format will be backward-compatible with the present format.

thread procedure. An MS-DOS Console program that polls for traps using the SNMP trap service is shown in the TRAPPIPE example on the CD-ROM.

Example 10-2. Example of a thread that monitors the Microsoft SNMP trap service

```
long WINAPI TrapPollingThread( LPARAM lParam )
{
    /* Open the SNMPTRAP.EXE named pipe */
    hPipe = CreateFile( TEXT("\\\\.\\pipe\\MGMTAPI"),
      GENERIC_READ|GENERIC_WRITE, FILE_SHARE_READ,
      NULL, OPEN_EXISTING, 0, NULL );

    if ( hPipe != INVALID_HANDLE_VALUE )
    {
        DWORD dwPipeState = PIPE_READMODE_MESSAGE | PIPE_WAIT;

        if ( SetNamedPipeHandleState( hPipe, &dwPipeState, NULL, NULL ) != 0 )
        {
            /* Wait for trap messages */
            while ( 1 )
            {
                DWORD dwRead;
                int nBuffer = 1024;
                BYTE szBuffer[1024];

                /* ReadFile will not return until a trap has been read */
                if ( ReadFile( hPipe, &szBuffer, nBuffer, &dwRead, NULL ) == TRUE
)
                {
                    if ( dwRead != 0 )
                    {
                        /* We have a BER-encoded trap message. The
                           data is stored in szBuffer and the number of bytes
                           is indicated by dwRead. */
                    }
                }
                else
                    break;
            }
        }
    }
    CloseHandle( hPipe );

    return ( 0 );
}
```

Using the WinSock API, you can even bypass the SNMP trap service itself and read trap messages directly from the well-known SNMP trap port. Example 10-3 illustrates a function that polls for datagrams sent to UDP port 162 on the local machine. (WinSock also supports asynchronous notification of received messages, which is the preferred method to use.) An MS-DOS Console program that polls for traps using the Winsock API is shown in the TRAPSOCK example on the CD-ROM.

Example 10-3. Example of a program that polls for traps

```c
#include <windows.h>

#define LOCALHOSTADDRESS    "128.128.128.3"

int main( void )
{
    SOCKET      s;
    WSADATA     Wsadata;
    SOCKADDR_IN sin;
    DWORD       dwRead;
    char        bBuf[512];

    WSAStartup( 0x0101, &Wsadata );

    s = socket( PF_INET, SOCK_DGRAM, 17 );     /* UDP */

    memset( &sin, 0, sizeof( sin ) );
    sin.sin_family = AF_INET;
    sin.sin_port = htons( (u_short)atoi( "162" ) );
    sin.sin_addr.s_addr = inet_addr( LOCALHOSTADDRESS );

    bind( s, (LPSOCKADDR)&sin, sizeof( sin ) );

    /* Loop here waiting for traps */
    while ( 1 )
    {
        if ( ( dwRead = recv( s, bBuf, sizeof( bBuf ), 0 ) ) != SOCKET_ERROR )
        {
            /* We have a BER-encoded trap message. The
               data is stored in bBuf and the number of bytes
               is indicated by dwRead. */
        }
    }
    WSACleanup();

    return( 0 );
}
```

III

Appendixes and Glossary

This part of the book provides references to other sources of information on SNMP and definitions of terms.

Appendix A, *References*, contains many book and Internet references for SNMP, TCP/IP, WinSock, and network management information and software.

Appendix B, *Microsoft Knowledge Base*, lists all Microsoft Knowledge Base articles through October 1997 that refer to the SNMP service and APIs.

Appendix C, *RFCs*, lists all of the RFCs (Requests for Comments) referenced in this book.

Appendix D, *What's on the CD-ROM?*, describes the book's accompanying CD-ROM. The *README.HTM* and *README.TXT* files in the CD's root directory contain detailed information about the example programs, documents, and demo and trial software packages it contains.

The *Glossary* defines the terms used in this book and in the world of NT SNMP.

References

There are many resources and references for SNMP, Win32 programming, and network management available in print and on the Internet. The information in this appendix is a small subset of these resources, but it describes those I've personally found useful.

NOTE	All of the URLs listed in this appendix were valid at the time of publication. If you discover that a URL is "not found," check for an update of this appendix (in HTML format) at the O'Reilly web site.
	Email any URL additions, updates, or corrections to me care of O'Reilly. (See the ads in this book for up-to-date information on O'Reilly's URLs and email addresses.)
	There is also an HTML version of this appendix on the CD-ROM for your browsing pleasure.

Publications

Many of the publications listed in the following sections were used in the preparation of this book. Although many of these books are excellent subject references, this is by no means an exhaustive list of all material published on the subjects of SNMP and network management.

Books

If the interest in a subject can be gauged by the number of books published in a single year, then SNMP is a topic of great interest. I estimate that there will be at least six new books published on SNMP in 1997-1998, and probably more. Now this number may not compare with the number of books on HTML published in 1996, nor the number of new and revised Java books released in 1997, but SNMP isn't nearly on the same scale of interest as topics that enable you to create web pages with waving text and bouncing logos. For SNMP, six is very substantial.

SNMP and network management

Black, Uyless, *Network Management Standards: Snmp, Cmip, Tmn, Mibs, and Object Libraries*, Second Edition, McGraw-Hill Computer Communications, 1995, ISBN 0-07005-570-X.

Carleton, Russell, *LNT Powered - SNMP Network Management*, Interlink Network Group, 1996.

Feit, Sidnie, *SNMP: A Guide to Network Management*, McGraw-Hill, 1994, ISBN 0-0-7020-359-8.

Harnedy, Sean J., *Total SNMP: Exploring the Simple Network Management Protocol*, Second Edition, CBM Books, 1997, ISBN 0-13646-994-9.

Hein, Mathis, and David Griffiths, *SNMP Version 1 & 2: Simple Network Management Protocol: Theory and Practice,* International Thomson Computer Press, 1995, ISBN 1-850-32139-6.

Leinwand, Allan, and Karen Fang-Conroy, *Network Management: A Practical Perspective*, Second Edition, Addison-Wesley, 1995, ISBN 0-201-60999-1.

Miller, Mark A., *Managing Internetworks With Snmp (Network Troubleshooting Library)*, Second Edition, M&T Books, 1993, ISBN 1-55851-561-5.

Perkins, David, and Evan McGinnis, *Understanding SNMP MIBs*, Prentice Hall, 1997, ISBN 0-13-437708-7.

Rose, Marshall T., *The Simple Book: An Introduction to Network Management*, Revised Second Edition, Prentice Hall Series in Innovative Technology, 1996, ISBN 0-13-451659-1.

Rose, Marshall T., and Keith McCloghrie, *How to Manage Your Network Using SNMP: The Network Management Practicum*, Prentice Hall, 1995, ISBN 0-13-141517-4.

Stallings, William, *SNMP, SNMPv2, and RMON: Practical Network Management*, Second Edition, Addison-Wesley, 1996, ISBN 0-201-63479-1.

TCP/IP, WinSock, and data communications

Black, Uyless D., *TCP/IP and Related Protocols*, Second Edition, McGraw-Hill Series on Computer Communications, 1992, ISBN 0-07-005560-2.

Bonner, Patrick, *Networking Programming With Windows Sockets*, Prentice Hall Computer Books, 1995, ISBN 0-13-230152-0.

Comer, Douglas E., *Internetworking with TCP/IP - Volume I: Principles, Protocols, and Architecture*, Third Edition, Prentice Hall, 1995, ISBN 0-13-216987-8.

Comer, Douglas E., and David L. Stevens, *Internetworking with TCP/IP - Volume II: Design, Implementation, and Internals*, Second Edition, Prentice Hall, 1994, ISBN 0-13-125527-4.

Comer, Douglas E., and David L. Stevens, *Internetworking with TCP/IP - Volume III: Client-Server Programming and Applications, Windows Sockets Version*, Prentice Hall, 1997, ISBN 0-13-848714-6.

Feit, Sidnie, *TCP/IP: Architecture, Protocols, and Implementation with IPv6 and IP Security*, Second Edition, McGraw-Hill, 1996, 0-07-021389-5.

Hunt, Craig, *Networking Personal Computers with TCP/IP*, O'Reilly & Associates, 1995, ISBN 1-56592-123-2.

Hunt, Craig, *TCP/IP Network Administration*, O'Reilly & Associates, 1992, ISBN 0-937175-82-X.

Quinn, Bob, and Dave Shute, *Windows Sockets Network Programming*, Addison-Wesley, 1996, ISBN 0-201-63372-8.

Stallings, William, *Data and Computer Communications*, Fourth Edition, Prentice Hall, 1994, ISBN 0-02-415441-5.

ASN.1 and BER

Steedman, Douglas, *Abstract Syntax Notation One (ASN.1): The Tutorial and Reference*, Technology Appraisals, Isleworth, Middlesex, United Kingdom, 1993, ISBN 1-871802-06-7.

Win32 programming

Appleman, Daniel, *Visual Basic Programmer's Guide to the Win32 API*, Ziff-Davis Press, 1996, ISBN 1-56276-287-7.

Brain, Marshall, *Win32 System Services: The Heart of Windows 95 and Windows NT*, Second Edition, Prentice Hall, 1996, ISBN 0-13-324732-5.

Hamilton, Dave, and Mickey Williams, *Programming Windows NT 4 Unleashed*, Sams Publishing, Indianapolis, IN, 1996, ISBN 0-672-30905.

Petrusha, Ron, *Inside the Windows 95 Registry*, O'Reilly & Associates, 1996, ISBN 1-56592-170-4.

Simon, Richard J., Michael Gouker, and Brian Barnes, *Windows 95 WIN32 Programming API Bible*, The Waite Group, 1996, ISBN 1-57169-009-3.

Windows NT administration

Pearce, Eric, *Windows NT in a Nutshell*, O'Reilly & Associates, 1997, ISBN 1-56592-251-4.

Threads

Beveridge, Jim, and Robert Wiener, *Multithreading Applications in Win32: The Complete Guide to Threads*, Addison-Wesley, 1996, ISBN 0-201-44234-5.

Lewis, Bil, and Daniel J. Berg, *Threads Primer*, Prentice Hall, 1995, ISBN 0-13-443698-9.

Phan, Thuan Q., and Pankaj K. Garg, *Multithreaded Programming with Windows NT*, Prentice Hall, 1996, ISBN 0-13-120643-8.

Shah, Devang, Steve Kleiman, and Bart Smaalders, *Programming with Threads*, Prentice Hall, 1996, ISBN 0-13-172389-8.

Periodicals

There is no shortage of periodical publications about Windows programming and management. Check out these web sites for how to subscribe:

http://www.entmag.com/
   Maintech: The Independent Newspaper for Windows NT Enterprise Computing

http://www.ntsystems.com
   Windows NT System Magazine

http://www.winntmag.com
   Windows NT Magazine

http://www.backoffice.com
   BackOffice Magazine

Also, have a look at the Open System Resources web page at:

   http://www.osr.com/

OSR publishes *The NT Insider*, a bimonthly newsletter that thoroughly and intelligently discusses the internals of Windows NT. You can subscribe to this free publication via email at *Ntinsider@osr.com*.

Internet Resources

Since SNMP is the standard network management protocol for the Internet, you might presume that there would be quite a bit of SNMP information and resources on the net. You would be correct.

Windows Development

There is a great deal of information about Win32 programming on the Internet, and the primary source of information is Microsoft itself. The Microsoft Knowledge Base, Developers Network Library, Platform Software Development Kits, Service Packs, and many sample applications are all available on Microsoft's Web and FTP sites:

> *http://www.microsoft.com/support/*
> *ftp://ftp.microsoft.com/*

Microsoft Knowledge Base

The Microsoft Knowledge Base is a collection of technical support articles describing known problems, fixes, misunderstandings, and workarounds involving all Microsoft products. You might save yourself hours or days of wasted debugging efforts by spending a few minutes searching through the Knowledge Base looking for articles that describe the Windows problems you are experiencing.

The Knowledge Base is published on the Microsoft Developers Network and Microsoft TechNet CD-ROMs (both are explained in the following sections). You can also access articles in the Knowledge Base directly on the Web at:

> *http://www.microsoft.com/support/*

See Appendix B for more information about the Microsoft Knowledge Base.

Microsoft Developers Network

The Microsoft Developers Network (MSDN) is the prime source of information for Windows developers. The MSDN contains a wealth of technical information on Microsoft products and on writing applications and drivers for all Microsoft Windows platforms.

There are several levels of MSDN subscriptions:

Library Subscription
> Contains the MSDN Library CD-ROM, with technical information, documentation, code examples, and the Microsoft Developer Knowledge Base.

Professional Subscription

   Adds all client operating systems (Windows 95 and Windows NT) and the Platform Software Development Kits (SDK) and Device Driver Kits (DDK).

Universal Subscription

   Also includes Microsoft Office 97 Developer Edition, BackOffice Test Platform, Microsoft Visual Studio 97, and the latest Microsoft Enterprise Edition development tools (Visual C++, Visual Basic, Visual J++, Visual FoxPro, Visual InterDev, and Visual Source Safe).

All three subscriptions include MSDN phone support and a 20% discount on Microsoft Press books.

You can subscribe to the MSDN as a quarterly CD-ROM-based subscription or as a free Online Membership. You can find more information about the Microsoft Developer Network at:

   http://www.microsoft.com/msdn/

Also have a look at the Microsoft Win32 Web page and newsgroups:

   http://www.microsoft.com/win32dev/
   http://www.microsoft.com/support/news/win32.htm

Microsoft TechNet CD-ROM

Microsoft TechNet is a library of service information for Microsoft products, including Service Packs, Resource Kits, updated drivers, software tools and utilities, technical notes, and the Microsoft Knowledge Base. TechNet is distributed monthly on a set of CD-ROMs, and includes an information browser and search engine.

TechNet is oriented towards support engineers and information service people rather than towards developers. TechNet does not include information on programming or using the Windows APIs.

You can find out more about Microsoft TechNet at:

   http://www.microsoft.com/technet/

Microsoft Platform Software Development Kits

The Platform Software Development Kits are collections of tools and information necessary to build Windows applications. The SDKs include link libraries, preprocessor headers, testing and debugging tools, and sample code necessary for developing applications for Windows NT, Windows 95, Windows CE, Microsoft BackOffice, and Internet Explorer.

The SDKs do not include a compiler, linker, librarian (*LIB.EXE*), or make (*NMAKE.EXE*) utility. You may use any 32-bit Windows compiler, such as Microsoft Visual C++ 4.2b or 5.0 (an abbreviated version of the Win32 SDK is included with Visual C++). All Platform SDKs are available in the Professional and Universal MSDN subscriptions.

The Platform SDKs for Windows NT, Windows 95, and Windows CE can be downloaded from:

> *http://www.microsoft.com/msdownload/*

You can find documentation and updates to the Platform SDKs at:

> *http://www.microsoft.com/msdn/sdk/*

The Microsoft Platform SDK documentation is available to all MSDN Online members.

Windows Resource Kits

Resource Kits are collections of information, tools, and utilities used to aid in the deployment and administration of Windows 95, Windows NT, and other Microsoft products. Where the Platform SDKs are strictly for Windows developers, the Resource Kits are for support engineers, system administrators, and information service people.

The Resource Kits are distributed as three different sets of books and CD-ROMs from Microsoft Press:

- *Microsoft Windows NT Workstation Resource Kit*, Microsoft Press, 1996, ISBN 1-57231-343-9.

- *Microsoft Windows NT Server Resource Kit*, Microsoft Press, 1996, ISBN 1-57231-344-7.

- *Microsoft Windows 95 Resource Kit*, Microsoft Press, 1995, ISBN 1-55615-678-2.

All Resource Kits are also distributed with the TechNet CD-ROM subscription.

Updates to the Resource Kits for all versions of Windows NT may be found at:

> *ftp://ftp.microsoft.com/bussys/winnt/winnt-public/reskit/*

Updates to the Windows 95 Resource Kits are distributed as the self-extracting archives *RKTOOLS.EXE* and *RKHELP.EXE*. These files may be found on the Microsoft FTP site in the following directory:

> *ftp://ftp.microsoft.com/Products/mspress/library/*

All of the extra programs only distributed in the Windows 95 CD-ROM, including the networking tools and SNMP service, are available at the following location:

> *ftp://ftp.microsoft.com/Products/Windows/Windows95/CDRomExtras/
> AdministrationTools/NetworkTools/*

and from the Web page:

> *http://www.micro soft.com/windows95/*

Service Packs

Service Packs are released by Microsoft as fixes and upgrades to Microsoft products. As of the publication date of this book, here are the latest Service Packs for the Win32 operating systems:

- Service Pack 1 for Windows 95 (see note about OSR2 in the next section)
- Service Pack 5 for Windows NT 3.51
- Service Pack 3 for Windows NT 4.0

Each Service Pack that is released contains all of the material in the previous Service Packs, so it is only necessary to download and apply the latest Service Pack. You can also manually install Service Pack components if you need to upgrade specific Windows components, but do not wish to apply the entire Service Pack to your Windows installation.

You can find the Windows NT Service Packs at:

> *http://www.microsoft.com/ntserversupport/content/servicepacks/
> ftp://ftp.microsoft.com/bussys/winnt/winnt-public/fixes/
> ftp://ftp.microsoft.com/Softlib/Mslfiles/
> ftp://198.105.232.37/fixes/*

You can find the Windows 95 Service Packs at:

> *http://www.microsoft.com/windowssupport/
> http://www.microsoft.com/windows95/*

The Service Packs are also distributed with the Microsoft Developer Network and TechNet CD-ROMs.

Windows software

Microsoft provides a very nice collection of links to shareware and freeware Win32 applications and utilities on its web page at:

> *http://www.microsoft.com/ntserver/tools/
> http://www.microsoft.com/windows/software/shareware/*

About OSR2

Windows 95 OEM Service Release 2 (OSR2) is technically Service Pack 2 for Windows 95, but it is only available as a full installation of Windows 95 and not as a separate Service Pack. OSR2 will only install on a system that does not have Windows presently installed. You can "fool" the OSR2 installation program by renaming the *WIN.COM* file of the existing Windows installation, installing OSR2 into an empty folder, and then renaming *WIN.COM* back again. In any case, you should never install OSR2 over an earlier version of Windows 95, because many of the components are not backward compatible.

The Downloads section of the Microsoft Win32 web page also contains many useful Win32 tools:

> *http://www.microsoft.com/win32dev/*

The SNMP service files for Windows 95 may be found at:

> *ftp://ftp.microsoft.com/Softlib/Mslfiles/SNMPZP.EXE*

NOTE   The SNMP service files are included with Windows 95 OSR2.

Emailing Microsoft

To ask general questions about Microsoft systems and network management products, send email to *manageit@microsoft.com*.

Non-Microsoft Internet Resources

There are quite a few web pages dedicated to Microsoft Windows programming and development. Here are a few you should check out:

http://www.iftech.com/oltc/nt/nt0.stm
   Marshall Brain's Excellent Win32 Programming Page

http://www.program.com/rng/index.html
   Program.com for Win32

http://www.ntinternals.com/
   NTInternals

http://www.program.com/source/index.html
   Win32 Programming

http://www.planet-source-code.com/
   Planet Source Code

http://www.kudonet.com/~ixfwin/winprog_faqs/wpw_w32_index.html
   Win32 Programming

http://www.psy.uwa.edu.au/dylan/index.html
   Dylan Greene's Windows 95 Starting Page

http://www.dc.ee/Files/Programm.Windows/
   Programming.Source.Windows

http://www.apexsc.com/vb/
   Carl & Gary's Visual Basic Home Page

Requests for Comments (RFCs)

The central site for RFCs on the Internet is the InterNIC Directory and Database Services at *ds.internic.net*. You can access RFC, STD, and FYI documents on the Web at *http://www.internic.net*, and via FTP at *ftp://ftp.internic.net*. You can locate the indexes using the following URLs:

   http://www.internic.net/rfc/rfc-index.txt
   http://www.internic.net/std/std-index.txt
   http://www.internic.net/fyi/fyi-index.txt

RFCs are archived at many other places on the Internet as well. The Ohio State server has a nice HTML archive of RFCs at:

   http://www.cis.ohio-state.edu/hypertext/information/rfc.html

At this site you can access RFCs directly using their name, such as:

   http://www.cis.ohio-state.edu/htbin/rfc/rfc1157.html

You can also request RFCs via email from *mail-server@nisc.sri.com*. Do not include a subject, and in the message body specify the RFC using the format "send rfcnnnn.txt" (e.g., "send rfc1157.txt").

SNMPv1 is defined by the following RFCs and STDs:

RFC	STD	Title
RFC 1157	STD 15	Simple Network Management Protocol (SNMP)
RFC 1155	STD 16	Structure and Identification of Management Information for TCP/IP-based Internets
RFC 1212	STD 16	Concise MIB Definitions
RFC 1213	STD 17	Management Information Base for Network Management of TCP/IP-based internets: MIB-II
RFC 1215	—	A Convention for Defining Traps for use with the SNMP

SNMPv2 is currently defined by RFCs 1902 through 1909. For a historical look at SNMP-related RFCs, see Chapter 1. All of the SNMP-related RFCs are included on the CD-ROM. See Appendix C for a summary.

Newsgroups

Usenet newsgroups are the public discussion groups of the Internet. You'll find all manner of questions and answers on SNMP, TCP/IP, and network management there. Here are several newsgroups that will probably be of interest to you:

comp.protocols.snmp
> The primary newsgroup for the discussion of the SNMP protocol. Only post to this group if you have a question relating to the SNMP protocol.

info.snmp
tnn.protocols.snmp
> Other SNMP newsgroups.

comp.dcom.net-management
> The primary newsgroup for the discussion of all network management topics.

vmsnet.networks.management.misc
> Other network management newsgroups.

comp.protocols.tcp-ip
> The primary newsgroup for the discussion of the TCP/IP protocol suite.

microsoft.public.management.*
> Microsoft management newsgroups.

comp.protocols.tcp-ip.ibmpc
comp.os.ms-windows.networking.tcp-ip
microsoft.public.windowsnt.protocol.misc
microsoft.public.windowsnt.protocol.tcpip
> Microsoft-specific newsgroups where you can post questions about using TCP/IP under Windows.

comp.dcom.lans.ethernet
> The primary newsgroup for the discussion of Ethernet LAN technology.

comp.os.ms-windows.programmer.win32
> Win32 programming newsgroups.

Frequently Asked Questions (FAQs)

FAQs were originally the *README.TXT* files for Usenet newsgroups. They were specifically intended to answer the most commonly asked questions posted to a specific newsgroup. In theory, FAQs eliminate for the experienced patrons some of the novice-inspired literary tedium. Many special-interest FAQs describing specific technologies and even commercial products have appeared over the years.

You can obtain the latest SNMP FAQ from the following FTP sites:

> *ftp://rtfm.mit.edu/pub/usenet/comp.protocols.snmp/*
> *ftp://rtfm.mit.edu/pub/usenet/news.answers/snmp-faq/*

from the following web pages:

> *http://www.pantherdig.com/snmpfaq/*
> *http://netman.cit/buffalo.edu/FAQs/*

and from the *news.answers* Usenet newsgroup.

You can request the SNMP FAQ via email by sending a message to *mail-server@rtfm.mit.edu* with the following in the body of the message:

> send usenet/news.answers/snmp-faq/part1/
> send usenet/news.answers/snmp-faq/part2/

Here are some other FAQs of interest:

ftp://rtfm.mit.edu/pub/usenet/comp.protocols.tcp-ip/
> TCP/IP

ftp://steph.admin.umass.edu/pub/faqs/ethernet.faq
> Ethernet FAQ

ftp://rtfm.mit.edu/pub/usenet/comp.os.ms-windows.programmer.win32/
> *comp.os.ms-windows.programmer.win32/FAQ*
http://www.web-span.com/pjohnson/win32_faq.txt
> Win32 programming

SNMP Mailing Lists

There are many mailing lists devoted to network management, SNMP, and the development and implementation of specific MIBs (DS1/DS3, ISDN, bridges, interfaces, etc.). Many of these mailing lists are used by Working Groups of the IETF; the archives of these lists contain a great deal of useful information. Check the IETF home page for information on the mailing lists available.

Here are the primary mailing lists for SNMPv1 and SNMPv2:

snmp@psi.com
> Discussions of SNMPv1. To subscribe, send an email message to *snmp-request@psi.com* with the body "subscribe snmp *youremailaddress*."

snmpv2@tis.com

> Discussions of SNMPv2. To subscribe, send an email message to *snmpv2-request@tis.com* with the body "subscribe snmp2 *youremailaddress*."

Archives of the messages posted to both of these mailing lists may be located by sending an email message with "HELP" in the body to the respective list servers.

The Simple Times

The bimonthly newsletter Simple Times is currently the only regularly published SNMP periodical. You can find the Simple Times on the Web at:

> *http://www.simple-times.org/pub/simple-times/issues/*
> *http://www.fv.com/pub/simple-times/*

The Simple Times is available in HTML, RTF, and PostScript formats.

You can get information about subscribing via email by sending a message to the following address with "HELP" on the subject line:

> *st-subscriptions@simple-times.org*

You can also FTP back issues from:

> *ftp://ftp.fv.com/pub/simple-times/issues/index.html*

Web Pages

If you haven't discovered the Web by now, then you have truly missed out on visiting a wondrous place (yes, even with all the advertising and the 9600bps links). Listed below are many URLs for what is likely to interest you.

SNMP

Just a few SNMP-oriented web pages:

http://www.concentric.net/~tkvallil/snmp.html
> CMIP and SNMP: An Introduction to Network Management

http://tampico.cso.uiuc.edu/~gressley/netmgmt/snmp/
> Network Management Resources for SNMP

http://cio.cisco.com/warp/public/535/3.html
> Cisco's Tutorial on SNMP

http://www.cisco.com/univercd/data/doc/cintrnet/ito/55029.htm
> Another Cisco Tutorial on SNMP

http://www.snmpinfo.com/
> David Perkin's SNMPinfo

http://snmp.net.cmu.edu/bin/snmpv2/
> SNMPv2 Working Group Problem Reports

http://www.tis.com/docs/research/network/ps/snmp/
> SNMP Security

http://www.ibr.cs.tu-bs.de/cgi-bin/sbrowser.cgi
> On-line MIB Browser

http://www.phoaks.com/phoaks/comp/protocols/snmp/resources0.html
> PHOAKS *comp.protocols.snmp* page

SNMP under development

SNMP is by no means standing still. It has many legs, but not all of them are necessarily running in the same direction. Here are the web pages where you will find news of the latest SNMP activity.

http://www.int.snmp.com/v2status.html
> Current Status of SNMPv2c, SNMPv2*, SNMPv2u, and SNMPv3

http://www.int.snmp.com/v2star.html
> SNMPv2* Web Site

http://www.fv.com/simple-times/usec/
> The USEC Resource Page

http://www.ietf.org/html.charters/snmpv3-charter.html
> SNMPv3 Working Group of the IETF

There is also a general discussion mailing list of SNMPv3. To subscribe, send an email message to *snmpv3-request@tis.com* with the body "subscribe snmpv3 *youremailaddress.*" The SNMPv3 mailing list archive is located at *ftp://ftp.tis.com/ pub/ietf/snmpv3/*.

AgentX

The goal of the SNMP Agent Extensibility (AgentX) Working Group is to define standards-track technology for SNMP agent extensibility. The resulting technology specification will allow independently developed subagents to communicate with a master-agent running on an Internet device.

You can see the latest on AgentX at:

> *http://www.ietf.org/html.charters/agentx-charter.html*
> *http://www.scguild.com/agentx/*

To subscribe to the AgentX mailing list, send an email message to *agentx-request@fv.com* with "subscribe" in the subject line. The mailing list archive is located at *ftp://ftp.fv.com/pub/agentx/*.

ASN.1 and BER

ASN.1 and BER are described in the following CCITT standards documents:

> Recommendation X.208 Specification of Abstract Syntax Notation One (ASN.1)
> Recommendation X.209 Specification of Basic Encoding Rules for Abstract Syntax Notation One (ASN.1)

ASN.1 and BER are also described in the ISO standards ISO 8824 and ISO 8825, respectively.

Officially, the X.208 and X.209 documents are only available from the ITU (at cost) at:

> *http://www.itu.int/itudoc/itu-t/rec/x/x200-499/x208_22887.html*
> *http://www.itu.int/itudoc/itu-t/rec/x/x200-499/x209_24177.html*

However, there are several collections of vintage 1988 and 1992 CCITT documents archived on the Internet and in CD-ROM collections that you may find. These documents are usually in PostScript format and formatted for A4 (European) sized paper.

ASN.1 web pages are scarce, but here are a couple:

http://www.inria.fr/rodeo/personnel/hoschka/asn1.html
> Philipp Hoschka's ASN.1 Resources

http://www.csc.vill.edu/~cassel/netbook/asn1only/node4.html
> ASN.1 Tutorial

Standards organizations

There are books and documents written on every standardization process that exists. To start, you should have a look at the following online resources:

http://www.cis.ohio-state.edu/htbin/rfc/rfc1871.html
> RFC 1871 Internet Standards Process.

http://www.cis.ohio-state.edu/htbin/rfc/rfc2200.html
> RFC 2200 Internet Official Protocol Standards.

ftp://ftp.informatik.uni-erlangen.de/pub/doc/ISO/std-faq
> Markus Kuhn's Standards FAQ.

comp.std.misc
> The *comp.std.** newsgroups contain discussions on many different computer and networking standards.

Here are the major standards bodies that define, develop, and maintain the standards for network management, TCP/IP, networking, and SNMP:

http://www.ietf.cnri.reston.va.us/
  Internet Engineering Task Force (IETF)

http://www.iab.org/iab/
  Internet Architecture Board (IAB)

http://info.isoc.org/index.html
  Internet Society (SOC)

http://www.iana.org/iana/
  Internet Assigned Numbers Authority (IANA)

http://www.irtf.org/irtf/
  Internet Research Task Force (IRTF)

http://www.iso.ch/
  International Standards Organization (ISO)

http://standards.ieee.org/
  Institute of Electrical and Electronics Engineers (IEEE)

Enterprise numbers assignment

You may apply for an SNMP network management private enterprise number from the Internet Assigned Numbers Authority (IANA) on the web at:

  http://www.isi.edu/div7/iana/forms.html

Requests for SNMP network management private enterprise number assignments may be emailed to IANA at *iana-mib@iana.org*.

Current listings of all IANA number assignments may be found at:

  ftp://ftp.isi.edu/in-notes/iana/assignments/

SNMP private enterprise number assignments are found in the list:

  ftp://ftp.isi.edu/in-notes/iana/assignments/enterprise-numbers

Network management

Not satisfied only with SNMP? It's only one small corner in the universe of network management. Here's more:

http://netman.cit.buffalo.edu/
  Network Management, University of New York, Buffalo

http://snmp.cs.utwente.nl/
  The SimpleWeb

http://www.eforc.com/cwk/net-manage.cgi
  Network Management Resource Database

http://www.cit.ac.nz/smac/nm210/
   Networks and Network Management

http://www.ldv.e-technik.tu-muenchen.de/forsch/netmanage/netmanage_e.html
   Network and System Management, Technical University of Munich, Germany

http://www.microsoft.com/products/backoffice/management/
   Microsoft System and Network Management Page

http://www.mindspring.com/~jlindsay/webbased.html
   The Web Based Management Page

http://www.microsoft.com/management/
   Microsoft Product Management

http://wwwsnmp.cs.utwente.nl/~schoenw/ietf-nm/
   IETF Network Management RFCs

http://www.elec.uow.edu.au/anmf/index.html
   Australian Network Management Forum

http://www.javasoft.com/products/JavaManagement/document.html
   Java Management Documents

http://www.aetc.af.mil/AETC-NetMgmt/nms-menu.html
   Network Management System evaluations

http://www.phoaks.com/phoaks/comp/dcom/net-management/resources3.html
   PHOAKS *comp.dcom.net-management* Page

WinSNMP

An alternative to the Microsoft SNMP Management API? Look no further than WinSNMP. Most Windows TCP/IP and SNMP management packages support WinSNMP. You can find all you need to get started in the following archives:

http://www.winsnmp.com/
   WinSNMP Tutorials, Freeware, and Information

http://www.acec.com/snmp.htm
   ACE*COMM WinSNMP

http://www.mg-soft.si/
   MG-WinSNMP SDK, MG-WinMIB SDK, WinSNMP source code examples

http://www.ftp.com/pr/wsnmp.htm
   WinSNMP Software Development Kit

ftp://sunsite.unc.edu/pub/micro/pc-stuff/ms-windows/winsnmp/
http://www.fastin.com/cdrom2/winsnmp/
   Sunsite.UNC.EDU WinSNMP archive

http://rosegarden.external.hp.com/snmp++/
   SNMP++ home page

Discussions about WinSNMP may be found on the *comp.protocols.tcp-ip.ibmpc* newsgroup and in the *winsnmp@mailbag.intel.com* WinSNMP mailing list. The membership is completely ad hoc and there is no cost to join. To join, send email to *listserv@mailbag.intel.com* with no subject and the body "subscribe winsnmp *yournamehere*."

WinSock

Here are just a few web pages and FTP archives that contain WinSock information:

http://www.winsock.com/
> Stardust WinSock Labs

http://www.sockets.com/
> Bob Quinn's WinSock Development Information Page

http://www.goodnet.com/~esnible/winsock.html
> Windows Sockets Programming

ftp://download.intel.com/IAL/winsock2/
http://www.intel.com/IAL/winsock2/index.htm
> Intel WinSock 2

http://www.data.com/Tutorials/Winsock_2.html
> WinSock 2 tutorial

http://webcom.com/~llarrow/winsock.html
> WinSock Archives, FAQs, and Related URLs

ftp://sunsite.unc.edu/pub/micro/pc-stuff/ms-windows/winsock/
> Sun's WinSock archive

ftp://ftp.microsoft.com/bussys/winsock/
> Microsoft's WinSock archive

http://www.simtel.net/simtel.net/win95/winsock-pre-bydate.html
> The Simtel.Net Windows 95 Collection

http://ftp.sunet.se/ftp/pub/pc/windows/winsock-indstate/Windows95/Develop/
> Swedish University Network Archive

http://ftp.urz.uni-heidelberg.de/ftp/pub/net/winsock/winsock-l/Windows95/Develop/
> University of Heidelberg Archive

http://www.cyfronet.krakow.pl/ftp/simw95/simtel_winsock.html
> Krakow Archive

http://www.phoaks.com/phoaks/alt/winsock/
> PHOAKS *alt.winsock.** pages

To join the Intel Windows Sockets mailing list, send email to *listserv@mailbag.intel.com* with no subject and the body "subscribe winsock *yournamehere*."

You can also find discussions on Winsock posted to the following newsgroups:

> *alt.winsock*
> *alt.winsock.programming*
> *alt.winsock.trumpet*
> *comp.os.ms-windows.app.winsock.misc*
> *comp.os.ms-windows.programmer.tools.winsock*

Also have a look at the *alt.winsock* FAQ at:

> *http://www.well.com/user/nac/alt-winsock-faq.html*
> *ftp://rtfm.mit.edu/pub/usenet/news.answers/windows/winsock-faq*

Ethernet

If you are interested in SNMP then you probably have a need for LAN technology information as well. The best place to start in this regard is with Ethernet:

http://wwwhost.ots.utexas.edu/ethernet/
> Charles Spurgeon's Ethernet Page

http://www.lantronix.com/htmfiles/mrktg/catalog/et.htm
> Ethernet Tutorial

http://netlab1.usu.edu/novell.faq/nvfaq-l.htm
> Ethernet Frame Types: Don Provan's Definitive Answer

http://pclt.cis.yale.edu/pclt/comm/ether.htm
> Overview of Ethernet networks

http://www.cavebear.com/CaveBear/Ethernet/
> Ethernet Codes Master Page

http://www.phoaks.com/phoaks/comp/dcom/lans/ethernet/resources0.html
> PHOAKS *comp.dcom.lans.ethernet* page

*http://www.yahoo.com/Computers_and_Internet/Communications_and_*
> *Networking/LANs/Ethernet/*
> Yahoo!'s Ethernet page

You can also find discussions about Ethernet posted to the *comp.dcom.lans.ethernet* newsgroup. Have a look at the *comp.dcom.lans.ethernet* FAQ at:

> *http://www.faqs.org/faqs/LANs/ethernet-faq/index.html*
> *ftp://steph.admin.umass.edu/pub/faqs/ethernet.faq*
> *ftp://rtfm.mit.edu/pub/usenet-by-hierarchy/news/answers/LANs/ethernet-faq*

Commercial SNMP Software

You are by no means stuck with using Microsoft's SNMP and TCP/IP products. There are many third-party packages that provide TCP/IP networking service, and SNMP management and agent support for Windows NT, Windows 95, and Windows 3.1. Here are just a few of the packages available:

http://www.acecomm.com/

> ACE*COMM NetPlus WinSNMP User and Developer Kit: WinSNMP/AgentX custom extensible agents (suppliers of the WinSNMP engine to Microsoft, Intel, Novell, Oracle, 3Com, Cisco, US Robotics, Microcom, DEC, and HP)

http://www.snmpinfo.com/sismic.htm

> SMICng (SNMP MIB Information Compiler Next Generation)

http://www.mg-soft.si/
http://www.abit.co.jp/varidocs/download.html

> MG-SOFT Corporation: MG-WinSNMP SDK, MG-WinMIB SDK, MIB Compiler, SNMP EasyAgent SDK, Net Inspector, various WinSNMP utilities, WinSNMP source code examples, MONET SNMP Analyzer Protocol Decoder

ftp://ftp.cinco.com/users/cinco/demo/

> Cinco Networks NetXRay Network Protocol Analyzer Demo

http://www.pantherdig.com/~snmpshop/

> The SNMP Workshop: SNMP consulting, contract software design and development

http://www.snmp.com/
http://www.int.snmp.com/

> SNMP Research International

http://www.redpt.com/

> RedPoint Software SnmpQL: SNMP tool with an ODBC interface

http://www.empiretech.com/

> Empire Technologies: Provides systems management agents for UNIX and Windows NT.

http://www.netinst.com/html/snmp.html

> SNMP Collector: An SNMP collection and analysis tool for Windows, Windows 95, and Windows NT

http://www.netinst.com/html/observer.html

> Observer: A Network Monitor and Protocol Analyzer

http://www.epilogue.com/

> Epilogue Technology Corporation

http://duras.epilogue.com/doc/snmpover.html
> Epilogue Envoy SNMP

http://www.scruz.net/~dperkins/
> SNMP test suite software

http://www.castlerock.com/
> Castle Rock Computing

http://world.std.com/~pfa/
> Paul Freeman Associates, Inc.

http://www.adventnet.com/
> Advent Network Management: Web-based SNMP Management Utilities

http://www.smplsft.com/sagent.html
> SimpleAgent and SimpleAgentPro: SNMP Agent Simulator

http://www.smplsft.com/stest.html
> SimpleTester: An Automated SNMP Agent Tester

http://www.marben.be/prodMarben/mibh.html
> MibH MIB Compiler

http://www.gordian.com/products_technologies/snmp.html
> Gordian's SNMP Agent

http://www.hp.com/go/openview/
> Hewlett-Packard OpenView for Windows

http://www.tivoli.com/
> IBM NetView

http://www.novell.com/products/managewise/
> Novell ManageWise

http://www.cpro.com/
> Computer Professionals

Noncommercial SNMP Packages

There are many SNMP agents and management tools that are available as shareware or in the public domain. Here are a few that operate under Win32:

http://www.idiom.com/free-compilers/TOOL/ASN1-1.html
> SNACC ASN.1 Compiler

ftp://ftp.fc.ul.pt/pub/net/snmp/snmpman.zip
> University of Lisbon snmpman SNMP Management Utility for Windows 3.1

http://world.std.com/~pfa/

ftp://ftp.std.com/vendors/snmp/snmp95/

> Portable, Extensible, Bilingual Open SNMP Agent by Paul Freeman Associates

http://web1.digital.net/cpro/html/cpro_snmx.html

> SNMX Simple Network Management Executive

ftp://ftp.wellfleet.com/netman/snmp/cmu/

> CMU SNMP for Windows NT

http://www.switch.ch/misc/leinen/snmp/perl/

> SNMP for Perl 5

ftp://ftp.wellfleet.com/netman/snmp/perl5/

> SNMP for Perl 5

ftp://ftp.cs.utwente.nl/pub/src/snmp/UT-SNMP/

> University of Twente

http://ftp.sunet.se/ftp/pub/pc/windows/winsock-indstate/Windows95/SNMP/

> SUNET—Swedish University Network

TCP/IP

Here are a few web sites with TCP/IP information and software, many of which offer alternatives to Microsoft's TCP/IP-32 stack:

http://www.ftp.com/

> FTP Software

http://www.dart.com/

> Power TCP Internet Toolkit

http://www.distinct.com/home.htm

> Distinct TCP/IP

http://www.kaon.co.nz/netmanage/cham.html

> Chameleon and Chameleon NFS

http://www.netinst.com/html/wscomp.html

> WinSock Companion TCP/IP Suite

http://www.dolphinsys.com/

> WinSock OCXs and VBXs for Internet and TCP/IP Software Development

http://www.lantimes.com/lantimes/buyers/index/c123.html

> TCP/IP Buyer's Guide

http://www.phoaks.com/phoaks/comp/protocols/tcp-ip/resources0.html

> PHOAKS *comp.protocols.tcp-ip* Page

http://www.microsoft.com/win32dev/netwrk/tcpiphom.htm
   Microsoft TCP/IP and Windows 95 Networking

http://pclt.cis.yale.edu/pclt/comm/tcpip.htm
   Introduction to TCP/IP

http://www.yahoo.com/Computers_and_Internet/Information_and_Documentation/
   Protocols/TCP_IP/
   Yahoo!'s TCP/IP page

MIB Module Archives and Repositories

Many manufacturers of SNMP-manageable devices have made their MIBs available on the Internet. Many universities and private organizations also archive MIBs. Here are a few FTP and web sites that currently archive MIB modules:

ftp://venera.isi.edu/mib/
   A Collection of Many Vendor MIBs

http://smurfland.cit.buffalo.edu/ftp/pub/mibs/
   Another Collection of Many Vendor MIBs

ftp://ftp.3com.com/pub/mibs/
   3Com

ftp://ftp.banyan.com/pub/mibs/
   Banyan

ftp://ftp.wellfleet.com/netman/mibs/
   Bay Networks

http://www.cabletron.com/support/mibs/
ftp://ctron.com/pub/snmp/mibs/
   Cabletron

ftp://ftp.cisco.com/pub/mibs/
http://cio.cisco.com/public/mibs/
http://www.ij.com/public/mibs/
   Cisco Systems

ftp://gatekeeper.dec.com/pub/DEC/mib/
   Digital Equipment Corporation

ftp://ftp.fore.com/pub/snmp/mibs/
   FORE Systems

http://http-mib.onramp.net/
   HTTP MIB

http://www.tylink.com/forms/mib-form
   Tylink

ftp://ftp.wellfleet.com/perm/mibs/
   Wellfleet

http://www.xyplex.com/mibs/xypmibs.html
   XYPLEX

There is also an Internet facility to convert your SMIv2 MIB modules to SMIv1 via email. Simply email an SMIv2 MIB module to *mibv2tov1@dbc.mtview.ca.us* and you will receive the SMIv1 equivalent as a reply.

B

Microsoft Knowledge Base

This appendix provides a listing of all Microsoft Knowledge Base articles published through October 1997 that contain information on the Win32 SNMP service and the SNMP APIs. If you plan to use the SNMP service or the SNMP APIs, you should become familiar with the reported problems, bugs, fixes, and workarounds currently published.

All of these Knowledge Base articles are available on the Microsoft Web Site at *http://www.microsoft.com/support*. You may use the Knowledge Base search engine on this page to find articles by searching with the keywords "SNMP" or "NtwkSnmp."

You can also reference each article directly using its Product Support Services (PSS) database number to construct the specific URL. For example, to reference PSS article Q139462 you would use the URL *http://support.microsoft.com/support/ kb/articles/Q139/4/62.asp*. Many (but not all) Win32 Knowledge Base articles are also available via FTP at *ftp://ftp.microsoft.com/bussys/winnt/kb/*.

Knowledge Base articles can also be found on the Microsoft Developers Network (MSDN) CD-ROMs and the Microsoft TechNet CD-ROMs. You can find out more information about these service products at:

> *http://www.microsoft.com/msdn/* and *http://www.microsoft.com/technet/*

The following Knowledge Base articles are organized by their product category and PSS article number. Each article is dated with its last modified date.

Win32 SDK

"PRB: WINS.MIB & DHCP.MIB Files Missing from Win32 SDK 3.5," Q121625, 02-15-1996

"FIX: SNMP Sample Generates an Application Error," Q124961, 09-29-1995

"SNMP Agent Breaks Up Variable Bindings List," Q127870, 10-18-1996

"Where to Get the Microsoft SNMP Headers and Libraries," Q127902, 09-29-1995

"How to Add an SNMP Extension Agent to the NT Registry," Q128729, 09-29-1995

"FIX: SVCGUID.H Has Wrong UDP Port for SNMP Traps," Q129061, 09-29-1995

"PRB: SnmpMgrStrToOid Assumes OID Is in Mgmt Subtree," Q129063, 09-29-1995

"PRB: Building SDK SNMP Samples Results in Unresolved Externals," Q129240, 09-29-1995

"PRB: SNMP Extension Agent Gives Exception on Windows NT 3.51," Q130562, 09-29-1995

"FIX: High CPU Usage When SNMP Retrieves Performance Counters," Q130563, 09-29-1995

"PRB: SnmpMgrGetTrap() Fails," Q130564, 09-29-1995

"BUG: SNMP Service Produces Bad 'Error on getproc(InitEx) 127'," Q130699, 09-29-1995

"BUG: Windows 95 SNMP System Description Is Incorrect," Q139461, 11-16-1995

"Differences Between Windows 95 and Windows NT SNMP," Q139462, 08-05-1996

"PRB: SNMP Applications Reference SNMPAPI.DLL on NT 3.51," Q157599, 10-25-1996

"PRB: DLLEntry in SNMP testdll Sample Does Not Get Called," Q160621, 12-09-1996

Windows 95

"SNMP Agent Does Not Respond After Returning from Suspend Mode," Q159565, 11-15-1996

"Windows 95 SNMP Agent Allows Only Read-Only Access," Q159567, 11-16-1996

Windows NT

"SNMP Agent Responds to Any Community Name," Q99880, 05-06-1997

"TCP, IP, ICMP, UDP Counters with PERFMON.EXE," Q102629, 03-25-1997

"REG: SNMP Service Entries," Q102970, 05-08-1997

"Performance Monitor Adds Event 4005 to Application Log," Q105002, 05-09-1997

"SNMP Always Returns an Error Index of One," Q112871, 05-14-1997

"Access Violation in SNMP When Processing Short OIDs," Q112872, 05-05-1997

"SNMPTRAP Quits When Sending Information," Q112873, 05-14-1997

"SNMP Fails With More Than Four Trap Sources," Q114737, 05-15-1997

"AT&T Star Sentry System Manager Requires Patch," Q119997, 08-29-1996

"SNMP Traps Sent to Wrong Port," Q124431, 08-15-1996

"Removing SNMP leaves SNMP Counters in Performance Monitor," Q128746, 03-21-1997

"Missing Network Software Components in Control Panel," Q128898, 04-13-1995

"Windows NT SNMP Agent Allows Only Read Access," Q129129, 03-21-1997

"IPX Addressing Format For Microsoft SNMP Agents," Q130013, 09-04-1996

"Windows NT 3.5 SNMP Agent Responds to Incorrect Communities," Q130421, 09-04-1996

"PRB: SNMP Extension Agent Gives Exception on Windows NT 3.51," Q130562, 09-29-1995

"Winlogon Memory Leak Caused by SNMP Components," Q131131, 08-28-1996

"How To Compile MIB.BIN With DHCP and WINS MIB Files Using MIBCC," Q131776, 09-05-1996

"Event ID 1999 Appears When Using Compaq Insight Manager," Q135528, 04-30-1996

"No Prompt to Restart When Adding SNMP Community Names," Q135597, 03-21-1997

"How to Setup Windows NT SNMP Performance Counter Agent Extension," Q139488, 04-04-1997

"SNMP Returns Corrupt MAC Address," Q139841, 03-21-1997

"SNMP Queries of Very Long OIDs May Cause SNMP Service to Hang," Q139929, 03-21-1997

"SNMP Agent Hangs on Very Long Queries," Q140463, 03-21-1997

"SNMP Trap Frames Appear to be Dropped," Q140603, 03-21-1997

"Errors Removing TCP/IP Registry Keys Using Insight Manager," Q140987, 04-24-1997

"SNMP Debug Messages Are Written to Eventlog," Q141019, 03-15-1996

"How to Automate SNMP Installation," Q142159, 01-21-1996

"DHCP.MIB and WINS.MIB Not Included in Resource Kit," Q142259, 09-06-1996

"BUG: German Windows NT 3.51 Uses Wrong SNMP-Trap Port," Q142824, 01-21-1996

"ARP -A Performs Badly When ARP Cache Contains Many Addresses," Q145587, 03-20-1997

"Err Msg in SNMPUTIL: 'error on SnmpMgrRequest 40'," Q149080, 03-26-1997

"Using Detailed Logging to Debug SNMP Issues," Q149421, 03-26-1997

"Memory Leak Using Compaq Insight Agents with SCSI Tape Drives," Q150317, 06-26-1996

"Removing TCP/IP from the Windows NT Registry," Q151237, 05-07-1997

"SNMP Trap Contains Invalid Agent ID Field," Q152079, 06-16-1997

"Agent Does Not Respond After Suspend Power Is Invoked," Q152569, 04-30-1997

"Err Msg: Event 4010: Unable to Get the Local Computer Name," Q153462, 09-07-1996

"Windows NT Operating System SNMP OID Incorrect," Q154784, 03-19-1997

"IP Received Header Error Count May Be High," Q155758, 03-27-1997

"ARP -A Causes Access Violation When Pinging Heavily," Q156284, 03-20-1997

"PRB: SNMP Applications Reference SNMPAPI.DLL on NT 3.51," Q157599, 10-25-1996

"SNMP Service Will Not Start with Event ID: 7024," Q158770, 03-19-1997

"Memory Leak in SNMP Subagents," Q160035, 03-28-1997

"SNMP Entry Point not Found," Q163595, 08-29-1997

"SNMP Query to Windows NT Returns Same Value for NTS and NTW," Q163837, 05-22-1997

"Cached IP Address Never Expires for SNMP Trap Destination," Q168451, 08-06-1997

Systems Management Server

"SMS 1.2 Allows SNMP Setup of SMS 1.1 Child Sites," Q154153, 04-24-1997

"SMS: SNMP Site Property Changes Are Not Saved," Q156629, 04-15-1997

"SMS Trace and the SNMP Trap Receiver Log File," Q158646, 04-15-1997

"SMS: How the SNMP Trap ID Relates to a Windows NT Event," Q160969, 04-15-1997

"SMS: SNMP Event Log Extension Registers Beta Version," Q161651, 05-21-1997

"SMS: Eventcmi.exe Requires Incorrect Syntax in .CNF File," Q164764, 05-21-1997

"SMS: Snmpelea 3006 Events Rapidly Fill the Application Log," Q165267, 03-24-1997

"SMS: The SNMP Agent...Is Either Not Installed or Not Running," Q165574, 03-24-1997

"SMS: SMNP Traps Are Not Sent If Trap Throttle Is Too Strict," Q165591, 03-24-1997

"SMS: SNMP Trap Translator Fails After Applying WinNT 4.0 SP 2," Q167887, 06-05-1997

"SMS: Troubleshooting SMS Windows NT Client Services Installation," Q168518, 08-12-1997

"SMS 1.2 on WinNT 3.51 Discards SNMP Traps from WinNT 4.0 Clients," Q169124, 08-18-1997

LAN Manager

"Installing the SNMP Agents on a 3Com Server," Q87663, 09-30-1994

"Installing SNMP Agents on a 3Com 3Server," Q94238, 09-30-1994

"LANMAN.MIB Does Not Compile," Q98624, 09-30-1994

Internet Information Server

"How to Compile IIS MIB Files," Q143176, 04-22-1997

Commercial Internet System

"Proper Load Order of MCIS MIBS for Use with SNMP," Q156973, 04-14-1997

C

RFCs

The following Request for Comment (RFC) documents have been referenced (or at least alluded to) in earlier parts of this book. For each, the RFC number, author, title, and date are shown. They are listed in reverse chronological order. All of these RFCs are included on the accompanying CD-ROM.

2200 J. Postel, "INTERNET OFFICIAL PROTOCOL STANDARDS," 06/97.

2089 B. Wijnen, D. Levi, "V2ToV1 Mapping SNMPv2 onto SNMPv1 within a Bilingual SNMP Agent," 1/97.

1910 G. Waters, "User-based Security Model for SNMPv2," 02/1996.

1909 K. McCloghrie, "An Administrative Infrastructure for SNMPv2," 02/28/1996.

1908 J. Case, K. McCloghrie, M. Rose, S. Waldbusser, "Coexistence between Version 1 and Version 2 of the Internet-standard Network Management Framework," 01/22/1996.

1907 J. Case, K. McCloghrie, M. Rose, S. Waldbusser, "Management Information Base for Version 2 of the Simple Network Management Protocol (SNMPv2)," 01/22/1996.

1906 J. Case, K. McCloghrie, M. Rose, S. Waldbusser, "Transport Mappings for Version 2 of the Simple Network Management Protocol (SNMPv2)," 01/22/1996.

1905 J. Case, K. McCloghrie, M. Rose, S. Waldbusser, "Protocol Operations for Version 2 of the Simple Network Management Protocol (SNMPv2)," 01/22/1996.

1904 J. Case, K. McCloghrie, M. Rose, S. Waldbusser, "Conformance Statements for Version 2 of the Simple Network Management Protocol (SNMPv2)," 01/22/1996.

1903 J. Case, K. McCloghrie, M. Rose, S. Waldbusser, "Textual Conventions for Version 2 of the Simple Network Management Protocol (SNMPv2)," 01/22/1996.

1902 J. Case, K. McCloghrie, M. Rose, S. Waldbusser, "Structure of Management Information for Version 2 of the Simple Network Management Protocol (SNMPv2)," 01/22/1996.

1901 J. Case, K. McCloghrie, M. Rose, S. Waldbusser, "Introduction to Community-based SNMPv2," 01/22/1996.

1742 S. Waldbusser, K. Frisa, "AppleTalk Management Information Base II," 01/05/1995.

1700 J. Reynolds, J. Postel, "ASSIGNED NUMBERS," 10/20/1994.

1525 E. Decker, K. McCloghrie, P. Langille, A. Rijsinghani, "Definitions of Managed Objects for Source Routing Bridges," 09/30/1993.

1493 E. Decker, P. Langille, A. Rijsinghani, K. McCloghrie, "Definitions of Managed Objects for Bridges," 07/28/1993.

1455 D. Eastlake III, "Physical Link Security Type of Service," 05/26/1993.

1452 J. Case, K. McCloghrie, M. Rose, S. Waldbusser, "Coexistence between Version 1 and Version 2 of the Internet-standard Network Management Framework," 04/1993.

1451 J. Case, K. McCloghrie, M. Rose, S. Waldbusser, "Manager to Manager Management Information Base," 05/03/1993.

1450 J. Case, K. McCloghrie, M. Rose, S. Waldbusser, "Management Information Base for Version 2 of the Simple Network Management Protocol (SNMPv2)," 05/03/1993.

1449 J. Case, K. McCloghrie, M. Rose, S. Waldbusser, "Transport Mappings for Version 2 of the Simple Network Management Protocol (SNMPv2)," 05/03/1993.

1448 J. Case, K. McCloghrie, M. Rose, S. Waldbusser, "Protocol Operations for Version 2 of the Simple Network Management Protocol (SNMPv2)," 05/03/1993.

1447 K. McCloghrie, J. Galvin, "Party MIB for Version 2 of the Simple Network Management Protocol (SNMPv2)," 05/03/1993.

1446 J. Galvin, K. McCloghrie, "Security Protocols for Version 2 of the Simple Network Management Protocol (SNMPv2)," 05/03/1993.

1445 J. Davin, K. McCloghie, "Administrative Model for Version 2 of the Simple Network Management Protocol (SNMPv2)," 05/03/1993.

1444 J. Case, K. McCloghrie, M. Rose, S. Waldbusser, "Conformance Statements for Version 2 of the Simple Network Management Protocol (SNMPv2)," 05/03/1993.

1443 J. Case, K. McCloghrie, M. Rose, S. Waldbusser, "Textual Conventions for Version 2 of the Simple Network Management Protocol (SNMPv2)," 05/03/1993.

1442 J. Case, K. McCloghrie, M. Rose, S. Waldbusser, "Structure of Management Information for Version 2 of the Simple Network Management Protocol (SNMPv2)," 05/03/1993.

1441 J. Case, K. McCloghrie, M. Rose, S. Waldbusser, "Introduction to Version 2 of the Internet-standard Network Management Framework," 05/03/1993.

1393 G. Malkin, "Traceroute Using an IP Option," 01/11/1993.

1358 L. Chapin, "Charter of the Internet Architecture Board (IAB)," 08/07/1992.

1353 K. McCloghrie, J. Davin, J. Galvin, "Definitions of Managed Objects for Administration of SNMP Parties," 07/06/1992.

1352 J. Davin, J. Galvin, K. McCloghrie, "SNMP Security Protocols," 07/06/1992.

1351 J. Davin, J. Galvin, K. McCloghrie, "SNMP Administrative Model," 07/06/1992.

1349 P. Almquist, "Type of Service in the Internet Protocol Suite," 07/06/1992.

1215 M. Rose, "A Convention for Defining Traps for use with the SNMP," 03/27/1991.

1213 K. McCloghrie, M. Rose, "Management Information Base for Network Management of TCP/IP-based internets: MIB-II," 03/26/1991.

1212 K. McCloghrie, M. Rose, "Concise MIB Definitions," 03/26/1991.

1191 J. Mogul, S. Deering, "Path MTU Discovery," 11/16/1990.

1189 L. Besaw, B. Handspicker, L. LaBarre, U. Warrier, "The Common Management Information Services and Protocols for the Internet," 10/26/1990.

1158 M. Rose, "Management Information Base for Network Management of TCP/IP-based internets: MIB-II," 05/23/1990.

1157 M. Schoffstall, M. Fedor, J. Davin, J. Case, "A Simple Network Management Protocol (SNMP)," 05/10/1990.

1156 K. McCloghrie, M. Rose, "Management Information Base for Network Management of TCP/IP-based internets," 05/10/1990.

1155 K. McCloghrie, M. Rose, "Structure and Identification of Management Information for TCP/IP-based Internets," 05/10/1990.

1108 S. Kent, "U.S. Department of Defense Security Options for the Internet Protocol," 11/27/1991.

1098 J.D. Case, M. Fedor, M.L. Schoffstall, C. Davin, "Simple Network Management Protocol (SNMP)," 04/01/1989.

1095 U. Warrier, L. Besaw, "Common Management Information Services and Protocol over TCP/IP CMOT," 04/01/1989.

1067 J. Case, M. Fedor, M. Schoffstall, J. Davin, "Simple Network Management Protocol," 08/01/1988.

1066 K. McCloghrie, M. Rose, "Management Information Base for Network Management of TCP/IP-based internets," 08/01/1988.

1065 K. McCloghrie, M. Rose, "Structure and Identification of Management Information for TCP/IP-based Internets," 08/01/1988.

1042 J. Postal, J. Reynolds, "Standard for the Transmission of IP Datagrams over IEEE 802 Networks," 02/01/1988.

1028 J. Case, J. Davin, M. Fedor, M. Schoffstall, "Simple Gateway Monitoring Protocol," 11/01/1987.

1024 C. Partridge, G. Trewitt, "HEMS Variable Definitions," 10/01/1987.

1023 G. Trewitt, C. Partridge, "HEMS Monitoring and Control Language," 10/01/1987.

1022 C. Partridge, G. Trewitt, "High-level Entity Management Protocol HEMP," 10/01/1987.

1021 C. Partridge, G. Trewitt, "High-level Entity Management System HEMS," 10/01/1987.

0904 International Telegraph and Telephone Co, D. Mills, "Exterior Gateway Protocol Formal Specification," 04/01/1984.

0854 J. Postel, J. Reynolds, "Telnet Protocol specification," 05/01/1983.

0793 J. Postel, "Transmission Control Protocol," 09/01/1981.

0792 J. Postel, "Internet Control Message Protocol," 09/01/1981.

0791 J. Postel, "Internet Protocol," 09/01/1981.

0768 J. Postel, "User Datagram Protocol," 08/28/1980.

D

What's on
the CD-ROM?

This appendix describes the contents and organization of the CD-ROM that accompanies this book. The contents of the CD-ROM are divided into three sections: example programs from the chapters, documentation, and third-party software packages.

Installing the CD-ROM

An installation program is not included with the CD-ROM itself. Many of the third-party packages contain their own installation programs. We also do not provide any programs to decompress ZIP archive files; we assume that you already have access to *PKUNZIP.EXE* for MS-DOS, or *WINZIP32.EXE* for Windows.

The *README.HTM* and *README.TXT* files in the root directory of the CD-ROM contain the description of all third-party software packages, and any last minute information that may not have made it into this appendix. *README.HTM* also contains links to all of the third-party packages available on the Internet. The \BIN directory contains the image and HTML files used by *README.HTM*. Many of the third-party README files themselves are also written in HTML, so have your Web browser handy.

When any of the program examples on this CD-ROM are updated, they will be made available from O'Reilly & Associates via FTP and HTTP. If you encounter any problems with these programs, please do not hesitate to report them to me. (See the ads in back describing O'Reilly's online services for the most up-to-date addresses.)

If you encounter any problems installing or operating the third-party software (i.e., the files in the \3RDPARTY directory), please contact the vendor of the software directly. Do not contact O'Reilly Customer Service.

Versions

The examples in this book were developed and implemented using Windows NT Workstation 4.0, Build 1381, and Service Pack 3. These examples will also run correctly on Windows NT Server 4.0. Some examples have also been tested on Windows 95 Service Pack 1 (SP1) and OEM Service Release 2 (OSR2). A few of the examples, however, use features of the Win32 API that are not present under Windows 95—most notably the SNMP trap service and the event logging API.

Many of the bug fixes made by Microsoft to the SNMP service under Windows NT 4.0 have not been retrogressively applied to Windows NT 3.51 or NT 3.1. If you are using NT 3.x, then you should check the Microsoft Knowledge Base for any uncorrected problems remaining in the SNMP services and APIs (refer to Appendix B for a listing of Knowledge Base articles related to SNMP). For NT 4.0, I recommend that you always have the SNMP service files from at least Service Pack 2 installed on your system. Under Windows 95, the SNMP service files were not changed by Service Pack 1 or OEM Service Release 2.

Book Material

Most of the code examples presented in this book are small (less than one page) and are mostly derived from the working example programs included on the CD-ROM. There is no formal documentation for the examples stored in the *BOOK* directory. However, a detailed explanation of the operation of each example program is found within the appropriate source code listings on the CD-ROM.

There is also no setup program included on the CD-ROM that will install the example extension agent DLLs, so you will need to install them by hand using the Registry Editor (RegEdit). The instructions for installing an extension agent DLL can be found in Chapter 5, *Getting Started with the SNMP Service*, in the section "Installing an Extension Agent DLL."

One last thing to consider: the example programs contained in the *BOOK* directory are simply that—examples. These programs are only intended to provide accurate, working code that you may use in your own applications. They have not been thoroughly quality tested, nor do they necessarily contain features that you may require in your own products. If you do have any interesting suggestions for extension agent features, send me some email and I'll see what I can do.

The *CHAP06 Subdirectory*

Chapter 6, *Using the Extension and Utility APIs*, details the function calls and data types of the Microsoft SNMP API. You will eventually find the need to write your own SNMP data manipulation functions, so I've included a few in the

BOOK\CHAP06 subdirectory that may be of use to you. *SNMPCONV.C* contains several routines used to convert data used by the SNMP API; the functions in *SNMPLIST.C* manipulate SNMP API list objects; and the *SNMPPRIN.C* functions are used to print the data contained in many SNMP objects to the MS-DOS Console window.

The \CHAP07 Subdirectory

Chapter 7, *Writing Extension Agents*, discusses functional concepts used to construct extension agent DLLs. The code examples used in this chapter (and in Chapter 6) are primarily drawn from the MINAGENT example extension agent DLL in the *BOOK\CHAP07* subdirectory. Briefly discussed are the changes necessary for an extension agent to use the registry for storing and retrieving data; this concept is put into practice in the REGAGENT example extension agent DLL.

MINAGENT

The Minimal Agent (MINAGENT) is an example of a Microsoft SNMP service extension agent DLL. MinAgent implements one of each type of scalar MIB variable (INTEGER, OCTET STRING, OBJECT IDENTIFIER, Counter, Gauge, TimeTicks, IpAddress, and Opaque), and one of each columnar MIB variable (list and table). All MIB variable data is stored as local variables allocated by the *MINAGENT.DLL*. MINAGENT operates under both Windows NT and Windows 95.

REGAGENT

The Registry Agent (REGAGENT) is also an example of an extension agent DLL. REGAGENT implements the same MIB variables as MINAGENT, but uses the Windows registry to store its MIB variable data. REGAGENT operates under both Windows NT and Windows 95.

The \CHAP08 Subdirectory

Chapter 8, *Implementing Traps*, details how to construct an extension agent DLL that is capable of sending SNMPv1 traps. The *BOOK\CHAP08* subdirectory contains seven example extension agents that implement traps. These projects range from the most simple trap implementation possible to complex examples that create external event monitoring processes and use Interprocess Communication (IPC). These examples illustrate the more complex details of implementing DLLs, creating processes and threads, and accessing several Win32 IPC mechanisms.

Here's a brief explanation of the function of each extension agent:

ELAGENT

The Event Log Agent (ELAGENT) monitors the event logging service of the local machine and sends a trap each time any of the three event logs (System, Security, and Application) are changed (i.e., an entry is added or the log is cleared). The MIB variables supported by ELAGENT (and defined in *ELAGENT.MIB*) allow an SNMP management system to query the number of entries in each log, clear each log individually, specify a filename to use for backing up a log before it is cleared, and see the event log entry string of the last trap that was sent. ELAGENT operates only under Windows NT.

TRAPAGT1

The Trap Agent One (TRAPAGT1) implements the three traps defined in the *TRAPAGT1.MIB* module. A trap is generated when the *TRAPAGT1.DLL* is attached by a thread, when a local timer fires every 60 seconds, and when any SNMP request message specifies the MIB variables managed by TRAPAGT1.

TRAPAGT2

The Trap Agent Two (TRAPAGT2) implements the three traps defined in the *TRAPAGT2.MIB* module. A trap is generated when a SetRequest message is received, when a local timer fires (using a slightly different timer implementation from the one used by TRAPAGT1), and when *TRAPAGT2.DLL* is unloaded by the SNMP service.

TRAPAGT3

The Trap Agent Three (TRAPAGT3) implements the three traps defined in the *TRAPAGT3.MIB* module. A trap is generated each time an external process started by *TRAPAGT3.DLL* (*TAGT3MON.EXE*) sends a periodic signal. Another trap is generated when the *HKEY_LOCAL_MACHINE\SYSTEM\CurrentControlSet\ Services\SNMP\Parameters\RFC1156Agent\sysContact* registry key is modified. A third trap is generated when the SnmpExtensionInitEx function is called when the *TRAPAGT3.DLL* is loaded by the SNMP service.

TRAPAGT4

The Trap Agent Four (TRAPAGT4) implements the two traps defined in the *TRAPAGT4.MIB* module. Traps are generated for the same events as Trap Agent Three, but file mapping is used to pass data from the monitoring process (*TAGT4MON.EXE*) to the *TRAPAGT4.DLL*. The ability to send multiple traps using a simple trap message variable binding queue is also implemented.

TRAPAGT5

The Trap Agent Five (TRAPAGT5) implements the three traps defined in the *TRAPAGT5.MIB* module. Traps are sent in response to data received from an external process, *TRAPTRG5.EXE*, which is implemented as a Windows application in Visual Basic and as an MS-DOS console program in ANSI C. The trap information is conveyed to *TRAPAGT5.DLL* using a named pipe.

TRAPAGT6

The Trap Agent Six (TRAPAGT6) implements the three traps defined in the *TRAPAGT6.MIB* module. Traps are sent in response to the signals it receives marking the occurrence of trappable events from the external process *TRAPTRG6.EXE*. Trap data is conveyed from this process to *TRAPAGT6.DLL* using mail slots.

The \CHAP10 Subdirectory

Chapter 9, *Using the Management API*, and Chapter 10, *Writing Network Management Applications*, explain how to use the Microsoft SNMP Management API to construct simple SNMPv1 network management applications. The two management utilities in the *\BOOK\CHAP10* on the CD-ROM show how the Microsoft Management API is used to send requests, receive responses, and receive traps. Two additional trap reception and diagnostic utilities are also provided.

SIMPLNMS

The Simple Network Management System (SIMPLNMS) is a sample application that uses the Win32 SDK and the Microsoft SNMP Management API to implement a very simple SNMP network management system for Win32. SIMPLNMS is capable of performing Get, GetNext, and Set operations and of receiving traps. SIMPLNMS operates under both Windows 95 and Windows NT (trap reception is not supported under Windows 95).

SNMPTOOL

The Simple Network Management Protocol Tool (SNMPTOOL) is a work-alike replacement for the Microsoft SNMPUTIL example program distributed with the Win32 SDK. SNMPTOOL is capable of performing Get and GetNext operations, receiving traps, and walking an agent's MIB (the same as SNMPUTIL).

SNMPTOOL also supports performing Set operations, polling using the Get operation, polling or event-driven trap detection, walking a complete MIB or only a specific branch, and reading command-line arguments from a file. SNMPTOOL is an MS-DOS Console program that operates under both Windows 95 and Windows

NT (trap reception is not supported under Windows 95), and its source code is an example of how to implement a SNMP management program using the Microsoft SNMP management API.

TRAPPIPE

The Trap Pipe (TRAPPIPE) is a small MS-DOS Console program used to read trap messages from the named pipe server created by the Windows NT SNMP trap service (*SNMPTRAP.EXE*). Trap Pipe displays a hex dump of each trap message received and will not interfere with any other processes that may be connected to the same pipe. This program only operates under Windows NT.

TRAPSOCK

The Trap Socket (TRAPSOCK) is functionally identical to Trap Pipe, but uses the WinSock API to read trap messages directly from UDP port 162, bypassing the Windows NT SNMP trap service completely. This MS-DOS Console program will operate under both Windows NT and Windows 95, but only if UDP port 162 is not already opened by another process.

The \APPD-A Subdirectory

Appendix A, *References*, contains many URLs to SNMP information and software available on the Internet. This appendix has also been made available on the CD-ROM in HTML format for your browsing convenience.

Documentation

The \DOCS directory contains an assortment of MIB modules, RFC standards, and SNMP documents mentioned in the book that you might find useful. Listed below are the subdirectories under \DOCS.

MIBS Subdirectories

You'll find MIB documentation in several subdirectories:

\MICROSFT
  Contains MIB modules distributed by Microsoft for their networking products, including WINS and DHCP servers and LAN Manager 2.

\MICROSFT\PERF2MIB
  Contains MIB modules generated using the Microsoft *PERF2MON* utility.

\OREILLY
  Contains the MIB modules used by all of the extension agent projects in the \BOOK\CHAP06 and \BOOK\CHAP08 subdirectories.

OTHER

Contains many private MIB modules used for managing networking equipment from vendors such as Cisco Systems, Hewlett-Packard, and Bay Networks.

The RFC Subdirectory

The subdirectory *RFC\TEXT* contains all RFC related to SNMP, MIBs, and managed objects. Other RFCs referenced in this book, such as those defining CMOT and HEMS, are included as well. See Appendix C, *RFCs*, for a summary.

The SNMP-FAQ Subdirectory

This subdirectory contains Tom Cikoski's SNMP FAQ (November 1997).

The WINSNMP Subdirectory

The subdirectory *WINSNMP* contains the WinSNMP 1.1a specification and the latest addendums for WinSNMP 2.0. You can find more references about WinSNMP on the Internet in Appendix A.

Third-Party Software

The *3RDPARTY* directory contains many trial and evaluation software packages that you may find useful in developing and testing SNMP and TCP/IP applications.

Glossary

Abstract Syntax Notation One (ASN.1)
A data definition language used for describing the structure of management data that is defined by the SMI. ASN.1 is also the ISO presentation layer standard protocol used for describing the Protocol Data Units of most OSI protocols. ASN.1 is defined in CCITT Recommendation X.208. See *MIB module, Protocol Data Unit.*

access policy
The attributes describing how, when, and by whom a collection of data or a functional processes may be accessed. See *object attributes.*

agent
A software process that provides management information about a specific device or process. An SNMP agent provides management information using the SNMP protocol. See *management information.*

alarm
A signal used to indicate the occurrence of a problem associated with a specific device or process. SNMP traps are often referred to as "alarms," "alarm events," or "alarm messages." See *fault, problem, trap.*

API *see Application Programming Interface*

AppleTalk
A network protocol suite designed by Apple Computer for use with the Macintosh computer. SNMP has been adapted for use over AppleTalk networks (RFC 1419).

application
Another name for an executable program. Typically used to differentiate a "Windows application" from an "MS-DOS Console program."

application layer
The seventh layer in the OSI reference model. The application layer is used to provide access for user applications to the services of the protocol stack. See *OSI reference model.*

Application Programming Interface (API)
A collection of functions and data defined to provide a common, standardized point of access to a specific process, hardware device, or operating system service. For example, the Win32 API is a collection of functions defined by Microsoft for accessing the services and functions of the Windows NT, Windows 95, and Windows CE operating systems. Most device drivers and application services define an API.

ARPA
Advanced Research Projects Agency. The agency of the U.S. Department of Defense responsible for the development of the APRANET. Formerly known as the Defense Advanced Research Projects Agency (DARPA). See *ARPANET.*

ARPANET
Advanced Research Projects Agency NETwork. A large-scale, packet-switched, prototype network sponsored by the Advanced Research Projects Agency of the U.S. Department of

Defense. ARPANET, whose construction was started in 1969, was the forerunner of the Internet. See *ARPA*.

ASN.1 *see Abstract Syntax Notation One*

Assigned Numbers
The title of the RFC that specifies assigned protocol port numbers used by the Internet Protocol suite. Assigned Numbers is infrequently updated and is currently RFC 2200. See *protocol port number, Request For Comments, well-known ports*.

authentication
The process of determining whether information that has been received is from a recognized and allowed source. See *validation*.

Basic Encoding Rules (BER)
The algorithm used for serializing SNMP messages into a binary format suitable for transmission across a network. All SNMP messages are encoded using a subset BER. BER is defined by CCITT Recommendation X.209. Other formally defined encoding rules for SNMP messages (DER, PER, XDR) are also available. See *serialize*.

BER *see Basic Encoding Rules*

bilingual *see multilingual*

bottleneck
A very slow channel of communication in a network. Depending on how it is used, a 1.544Mbps T1 link on a 100Mbps network could be considered a bottleneck.

branch *see MIB branch*

bridge
A device used to route packets from one network to another based on the hardware addresses of the network nodes. Bridges are used to connect two networks so they appear as a single LAN. See *Media Access Control address*.

byte
A discrete grouping of bits used to represent the character set used by a specific operating system. Eight-bit bytes are the most common; a true ASCII byte only contains seven bits, and a Unicode byte contains 16 bits (called a wide byte in MicrosoftSpeak). See *octet*.

Carrier Sense Multiple Access Collision Detection (CSMA/CD)
The control technique used by network interface controllers for accessing an Ethernet network. See *Ethernet*.

centisecond
One-hundredth of a second.

checked build
A build of Microsoft Windows NT that contains system debugging information. The checked build of NT is only distributed as part of the Microsoft Developers Network. See *retail build*.

checksum
The sum of a group of bit or byte values. Used for error checking. Checksum is a much simpler, and much less reliable, form of error detection than CRC. See *CRC*.

client
Any network process that requests information from a server. See *client-server, end-host*.

client-server
A network model used to describe nodes that "serve" information to other nodes that request information and then "consume" it. The interaction of SNMP management systems and agents is often described using the client-server model.

CMIP
Common Management Information Protocol. The network management protocol standard used by OSI networks. See *CMOT*.

CMOT
CMIP Over TCP. An implementation of CMIP used for managing TCP/IP networks. CMOT initially competed with SNMP for the status of being the recommended management protocol for TCP/IP networks. CMOT is now defunct and only exists as RFC 1189.

collection domain
The set of network elements that are being monitored by a management system.

columnar
MIB objects defined as a column-like structure. Columnar objects are the elements used to form lists and tables. See *scalar*.

community name
The administratively assigned name of a logical management domain on a network. The community name is used as a selector by the agent to specify the access to local or remote

management information and the context of the management information. The strings "public" and "private" are common default community names. See *community string.*

community profile

Information that specifies which managed objects are available to what management domain. The community profile of an SNMP managed node is the community names that it considers authentic, and therefore the management domain to which it belongs. Also called an "access profile." See *community name.*

community string

A community name physically encoded into an SNMP message header. See *SNMP message.*

configuration

The mapping of how hardware devices and software processes are interconnected. See *inventory, provisioning.*

connectionless

A term used to describe a protocol that does not first open a dedicated (or virtual) connection between a sender and receiver before exchanging information, and does not guarantee that data will be properly sent or received. UDP and IPX are examples of connectionless transport protocols. See *connection-oriented.*

connection-oriented

A term describing a protocol that opens a connection between two devices and verifies that all data exchanged has been properly sent and received. TCP and SPX are examples of connection-oriented transport protocols. See *connectionless.*

Counter

An ASN.1 APPLICATION data type defined by the SMI. A Counter is typically a 32-bit integer that stores a value allowed only to increment within the range of 0 to 4294967295.

CPU

Central Processing Unit. The microprocessor brain of a computer or embedded system. Often referred to by manufacturer or family name, model number, and operating speed, such as Intel 8051, Motorola 68030, DEC Alpha AXP 21164, PowerPC 620, 486DX4-100, MIPSR4000, HP PA-RISC 7100LC, Sun SPARC, Pentium Pro 200, and Pentium II.

CRC

Cyclical Redundancy Check. An algorithm used to detect errors that have occurred in both stored and transmitted data. CRC is commonly used to determine if network packets have been damaged and if disk files are corrupt. A single 16- or 32-bit value is generated by CRC. See *checksum.*

CRC-32

Cyclical Redundancy Check, 32-bit. See *CRC.*

CUI

Character User Interface. An application or operating system interface that is constructed entirely from graphical characters. A CUI may be as simple as a DOS or UNIX command line or menu (e.g., gopher), or it may contain complex graphics, pop-up windows, and sound effects (e.g., Procomm or Brief). See *GUI.*

DARPA

Defense Advanced Research Projects Agency. See *ARPA.*

datagram

The name given to a packet transmitted across a network using a connectionless transport protocol, such as IPX or UDP. See *packet.*

data link layer

The second layer in the OSI reference model. The data link layer is primarily responsible for establishing and maintaining a reliable low-level flow of data. See *OSI reference model.*

DCA

Defense Communications Agency. See *DISA.*

DDN

Data Defense Network. The network used by the U.S. government and military agencies. See *MILNET.*

decapsulate

To strip off outer layers of informational wrapping that encapsulate a message to obtain the data contained within. For example, you must first open an envelope and remove the letter before you can read the message that it contains. See *encapsulate, envelope.*

decisecond

One-tenth of a second.

demultiplex   *see decapsulate*

deprecated   *see MIB object status*

DISA

Defense Information Systems Agency. Formerly known as the Defense Communications Agency (DCA). It was the DCA that adopted TCP/IP as the standard network protocol for the U.S. military.

discovery domain

A partition or segment of a network that is searched for active network elements. See *network element.*

DLL   *see dynamic link library*

DMI

Desktop Management Interface. A management protocol and API defined by the Desktop Management Task Force (*http://www.dmtf.org*) that allows the standardized management of the hardware and software components of a desktop computer. The DMI agent resides in the ROM of the desktop system, and the API is used by the DMI client manager to access the management data. While SNMP can be used to perform the same type of system management operations, DMI is specifically designed for management on desktop computers and is independent of the type of network used. DMI is supported by both Microsoft and Intel.

DoD

The United States Department of Defense. See *ARPA.*

dynamic link library (DLL)

An object library containing code (and possibly data) that may be loaded and unloaded at run-time by a process running under Microsoft Windows.

edge-triggered

An event that occurs when a discrete, well-defined threshold has been crossed, such as a voltage level falling below 3.24 volts. See *level-triggered.*

element   *see network element*

emulation

To exactly duplicate the appearance and apparent function of a process or device. A management system should not be able to distinguish between an actual SNMP-managed node and an SNMP agent emulating the management operation of the node.

encapsulate

To surround a message with an outer layer of information required to successfully transport or process the message. For example, a letter must first be encapsulated inside an envelope before it can be mailed by the post office. For network packets the actual encapsulation is a series of one or more headers. See *decapsulate, envelope.*

end-host

A host that is at an end-point in a network topology map, such as a workstation or printer. An end-host (also called an "end-node") only sends and receives information and cannot provide routing functions. Used to distinguish a device from "intermediate-hosts," such as file servers and routers. Most clients in the client/server model are end-hosts. Called an "end system" in OSI terminology. See *host.*

end-to-end

The entire transmission path of information between two points. Typically used to describe the entire communication path between two hosts on a network. The time required for information to travel from one end of a path to the other and back again is described as "round trip time," and is usually measured using an ICMP messages. See *ICMP, network latency.*

enterprise identifier   *see Private Enterprise Number*

enterprise MIB

A MIB module that defines managed objects that reside within the enterprises branch (1.3.6.1.4.1) of the internet MIB subtree. Also called "vendor MIBs," "private MIBs," and "product-specific MIBs." See *Private Enterprise Number.*

enterprises

The subtree of the internet MIB (1.3.6.1.4.1) where vendor-defined managed objects are located. All objects in the enterprises subtree are registered with the IANA. See *IANA, Private Enterprise Number.*

enterprise-specific traps

SNMP trap messages defined in MIBs residing in the enterprises subtree (1.3.6.1.4.1) of the MIB. Also called "private traps" and "device-specific traps." See *trap, generic traps.*

entity

An abstract, addressable process or node on a network. In OSI terminology an entity is an active network element. See *element, host, node.*

envelope

The identification and addressing information associated with a packet. A series of headers that are filled with the necessary network addressing information and then used to encapsulate data sent to a network host. See *encapsulate, packet.*

error index

The field in an SNMP GetResponse message that indicates which variable binding caused an SNMP protocol error to be returned. See *GetResponse.*

error status

The field in an SNMP GetResponse message that indicates the protocol error that resulted by the processing of an SNMP message. See *GetResponse.*

Ethernet

A type of Local Area Network (LAN) technology that uses a passive coaxial (or twisted pair) cable, active interface hardware, CSMA/CD, and a 10- megabit-per-second data transfer rate. Ethernet was first standardized in 1973 and was later adopted in 1983 by the IEEE (802.3). The term "ether" was borrowed from 19th century Western science's attempt to define a medium used by heat and light to travel through the vacuum of space. See *CSMA/CD, LAN.*

Ethernet address

The physical address of an Ethernet Network Interface Controller. See *Media Access Control address, NIC.*

event   *see trap*

event notification   *see trap*

event reaction latency

The interval of time that elapses between an occurrence of a specific event and the moment the occurrence is detected or reported.

extendible

Having the capability of being extended. Used to describe a program that can utilize new code and data without first being modified and recompiled. A term often used in Microsoft-Speak. Compare *monolithic.*

extendible agent

The SNMP agent supported by the Microsoft SNMP service. This agent is responsible for receiving and decoding SNMP requests, passing the request information on to the appropriate subagents, retrieving the processed data, encoding it, and sending an SNMP response back to the requesting management system. The agent is deemed "extendible" because it may support any MIB objects by the run-time loading of a special DLL called an "extension agent." See *extension agent.*

extensible   *same as extendible*

extension agent

A DLL used by the Microsoft SNMP service to process SNMP requests made to specific registered managed objects. An extension agent (also called a sub- agent) receives SNMP request data (variable bindings) from the extendible agent, processes the request, and returns the resulting data (or error) back to the extendible agent. The SNMP service interfaces to all extension agent DLLs using the Microsoft SNMP API. See *extendible agent.*

FAQ

Frequently Asked Questions. A listing of answers to questions commonly asked of a specific subject. FAQ lists are found in the *news.answers* Usenet newsgroup.

fault

A problematic event or condition. Often the cause of an alarm and the reason for sending a trap. See *alarm, problem report.*

firmware

Code and data that persistently resides in non-volatile memory and does not disappear from memory when the power is removed. See *NVRAM, ROM, software.*

frame

A patterned sequence of bits on a transmission line. Network packets are frames of data found in the network and data link layers of switching networks. See *packet.*

free build   *see retail build*

gateway

A network node used to provide access to a network or to a specific group of other network nodes. Gateways often provide one or more message translation (SMTP to X.400, SNMPv2 to SNMPv1, etc.), data translation (ASCII to EBCDIC, etc.), or media translation (SLIP to Ethernet, etc.) services. The term "IP gateway" refers to a node that routes IP packets, and has been largely replaced by the term "IP router." See *router.*

Gauge

An ASN.1 APPLICATION data type defined by SNMP. A Gauge is typically a 32-bit integer that stores a value allowed to increment and decrement within the range of 0 to 4294967295.

General Protection Fault (GPF)

An indication from Windows that a process attempted to improperly access memory, usually by reading from or writing to a memory location to which it does not have legal access. Unhandled exceptions may also cause a GPF. GPFs are most commonly the result of software coding errors that result in incorrect logic or bad data passed to a function. Bad pointer values are a major source of GPFs. See *trap*.

generic traps

The SNMP standard traps defined in the mib-2 branch (1.3.6.1.2.1) of the MIB tree. These six traps are named coldStart, warmStart, linkUp, linkDown, egpNeighborLoss, and authenticationFailure. See *enterprise-specific traps, trap*.

Get

The SNMP operation used to read or "get" data from MIB variables maintained by an SNMP agent. The GetRequest message is used by a management system to perform the Get operation. The data requested by the Get operation is returned by an agent using the GetResponse message. See *GetNext, GetResponse, Set*.

GetNext

The SNMP operation used to "get data from the next" MIB variable maintained by an SNMP agent. The GetNextRequest message is used by a management system to perform the GetNext operation. The "next" variable is the next lexical variable that exists after the variable(s) specified in the GetNextRequest message. The data requested by the GetNext operation is returned by an agent using the GetResponse message. See *Get, GetResponse, Set*.

GetNextRequest

The SNMP message sent by a management application to an agent to perform a GetNext operation. See *Get, GetNext*.

GetRequest

The SNMP message sent by a management application to an agent to perform a Get operation. See *Get, GetNext*.

GetResponse

The SNMP message returned by an SNMP agent in response to receiving an SNMP request message. GetResponse is used to return the results of processing a GetRequest, GetNextRequest, or SetRequest message. See *Get, GetNext, Set*.

GPF   see *General Protection Fault*

GUI

Graphical User Interface. An application or operating system interface that uses bitmap and/or vector graphics to display data and provide operational control to the user. Rather than displaying the interface using a graphical character set (character user interface), the interface and all data are instead displayed as images and mathematical renderings. Microsoft Windows is an example of an operating system that uses a GUI. See *CUI*.

handshaking

An initial exchange of information between two devices for the purpose of establishing a proper transmission of data. Handshaking is used to identify such things as the protocol version, encoding method, and data transfer rate that will be used to transmit the data.

hardware

The physical equipment that makes up a device or system. All parts of a system that are neither software nor firmware.

HEMS

High-level Entity Management System. An early competitor in the search for a recommended management protocol for TCP/IP networks. HEMS is defined in RFCs 1021 through 1024.

heterogeneous network

A network made of devices from many different vendors; the network uses several different protocol suites. Compare *homogeneous network*.

homogeneous network

A network that contains mostly devices from the same vendor; the network uses the same networking protocols and/or provides the same type of service. Compare *heterogeneous network*.

host

On a TCP/IP network, any node that does not forward packets to another network (e.g., not a router, hub, or bridge). Hosts typically support a full TCP/IP stack through the application layer. Routers only support a stack up to the network layer. Also called "end-host." See *end-host, node.*

hub

A device that allows multiple hosts to be connected to a single physical point on a network. Also called a *switching node.*

IAB

Internet Activities Board. The standards organization that oversees the development of Internet protocols. See *IETF.*

IANA

Internet Assigned Numbers Authority. The agency that assigns Private Enterprise Numbers (PENs) and protocol numbers. See *Assigned Numbers, Private Enterprise Numbers, well-known port.*

ICMP

Internet Control Message Protocol. A TCP/IP network support protocol used to convey control, error, and informational messages (datagrams) between TCP/IP hosts. Both routers and hosts use ICMP to report problems to a packet's originating host. ICMP is also used to determine network latency and the MTU of a network connection. ICMP is defined in RFC 1122. See *Maximum Transmission Unit, network latency, ping.*

IETF

Internet Engineering Task Force. The governing body that oversees the development and standardization of all Internet protocols, including SNMP. See *IAB.*

in-band management

Management commands and messages conveyed using a device's primary data channels.

instance

A single, addressable, instantiated variable or object that contains discrete data. See *instantiate.*

instance identifier

A subidentifier used to identify a specific instance of a MIB object. Scalar objects may only have one instance and therefore always have ".0" for an instance identifier. Columnar objects use as an instance identifier the current values of the MIB objects specified in the INDEX clause of the table in which they reside. In any case, a columnar object may have any INTEGER, OCTET STRING, or OBJECT IDENTI-FIER value(s) as an instance identifier, except ".0". See *instance, MIB variable, object instance.*

instantiate

To create or bring into existence. When a variable or object is allocated it is said to be "instantiated." See *instance.*

INTEGER

An ASN.1 UNIVERSAL data type used by SNMP. An INTEGER is typically a signed 32-bit integer that stores a value in the range -2147483648 to 2147483647. An INTEGER value may also store an enumeration in the range 1 to 2147483647.

intermediate management system

A management system that collects management information from network elements and then makes the data available to other management systems. A network management proxy that provides a central point for the collection and distribution of system and network management information. Sometimes called a "management server" or "mid-level management system." See *proxy station.*

internet

A TCP/IP network. See *Internet.*

Internet

The interconnection of all TCP/IP networks (internets) to form a single, virtual, global network. This is probably how the Borg got their start. See *internet.*

internet address   *see IP address*

Internet Packet eXchange protocol (IPX)

A connectionless, user datagram service, NetWare protocol based on the Xerox Network System (XNS) Internet Datagram Protocol (IDP) and used on Novell networks. SNMP has been adapted for use over IPX networks (RFC 1420).

Internet Protocol (IP)

The network addressing protocol used by TCP/IP networks. See *IP address.*

Internet Protocol suite   *see TCP/IP protocol suite*

InterProcess Communication (IPC)

The exchange of data between two or more processes running on the same system. See *Remote Procedure Call.*

inventory

The hardware, firmware, and software components contained within a system and their identifying information (e.g., model number, serial number, revision level, manufacture date, etc.). See *configuration, provisioning.*

IP *see Internet Protocol*

IP address

A 32-bit address used by IP to unambiguously identify each node and the network to which it belongs. Each node on an IP network must have a unique IP address. IP addresses are expressed using a dotted decimal format (x.y.z.t), such as "207.25.98.2." See *Internet Protocol, TCP/IP.*

IPv4

Internet Protocol, version 4. The current network addressing scheme used by the Internet.

IPv6

Internet Protocol, version 6. The next version of IP that is to replace IPv4 and its rapidly dwindling address space. Also called Internet Protocol Next Generation (IPNG).

IPX *see Internet Packet eXchange protocol*

IPX/SPX

Internet Packet eXchange/Sequenced Packet eXchange. The Novell NetWare functional equivalent of TCP/IP. IPX is the addressing scheme used to unambiguously identify a node on a Novell NetWare network. An IPX address has an 8.12 dotted decimal format (xxxxxxxx.yyyyyyyyyyyy).

ISO

International Standards Organization.

LAN

Local Area Network. A generic term for any physical network technology designed to span only a short geographical distance and support lower data rates. A typical LAN has a maximum size of a few thousand meters and a 10 to 100 megabit-per-second data transfer rate. See *Ethernet.*

language

A standard system of encoding thoughts, feelings, ideas, and intellectual expressions in a tangible and decodable format. Compare *protocol.*

latching

A property used to describe an object whose value will not exceed the object's defined limits. An example is a thermometer with a functional range of 0˚C to 100˚C. Exposed to

lower temperatures, the thermometer will "latch" at 0˚C; exposed to higher temperatures, it will "latch" at 100˚C. The thermometer will "unlatch" when the temperature moves back into the thermometer's supported range. An SNMP Gauge object will always latch at its highest and lowest defined values.

leaf node

The end-points of a branch in the MIB tree. The name is taken from the binary tree data structure, where a leaf is a node without children. Each leaf node is a class that defines a MIB object. Also called a "leaf object." See *MIB tree.*

level-triggered

An event that occurs when a discrete, well-defined region has been entered, such as a voltage level measured in the range 3 to -3 volts. A level-triggered event is typically generated periodically for the duration that the measurement remains in the region. See *edge-triggered.*

local management

The act of monitoring and controlling a processor device by using an instrument panel or display terminal that is physically connected to the unit. See *remote management.*

managed node

A network node that supports one or more network management protocols.

managed object

An abstract term for any addressable quantity of management information. See *MIB variable.*

management application

A generic term for any software application or process that is used to manage local or remote processes and devices.

management community

A set of managed nodes all referenced as a single, logical group. See *community name.*

management domain

A discrete, logical set of network elements under active management. See *management community.*

management information

Data used to indicate the identity, state, status, and history of a managed node or network process.

Management Information Base (MIB)

A schema, blueprint, or roadmap of managed objects. The MIB acts as an API, allowing a management system to retrieve and modify management data maintained by an agent. A MIB itself is only an abstraction of data and is not actually a physical database, just as source code is only an abstraction of a program and is not a physically executable object. See *MIB database, MIB variable.*

management station

A computer or workstation used to operate management programs. See *NMS.*

management system

A generic term for anything from a simple management application to a sophisticated, proprietary, multihost network management facility. See *NMS.*

manager

A human that performs system and network management operations, typically using a computer and management software. Also a generic term for a system administrator (SysAdmin) or a network administrator (NetAdmin). The term "manager" is also commonly used when referring to management software, but this usage is incorrect, unless you prefer to refer to your computer as "the user."

mandatory *see MIB object status*

master agent *see extendible agent*

Maximum Transmission Unit (MTU)

The largest message size that may be contained within a single frame in a specific network medium. Measured in octets, the MTU for a PPP connection is typically 576 and for an Ethernet connection it is 1500. Also called "the maximum packet size."

Media Access Control (MAC) address

The hardware address of a Network Interface Controller (NIC). The MAC address is used to identify network devices and for routing network traffic. Also called a "physical address." See *OUI.*

MIB *see Management Information Base*

MIB-I

The first Internet Standard MIB. Defined by RFC 1156 and now superseded by RFC 1213 (MIB-II). See *MIB-II.*

MIB-II

The current Internet Standard MIB. MIB-II defines the standard management information that should be implemented by a network host that supports SNMP management. MIB-II is defined by RFC 1213.

MIB branch

A collection of leaf objects. A branch typically contains only leaf nodes and no other branches. See *subtree.*

MIB browser

A program used to graphically depict the structure and relationship of objects defined in the MIB. Most MIB browsers read MIB data that has been compiled from MIB modules and into a database. The MIB objects are then displayed in a hierarchical inverted tree structure and their information used to make requests of SNMP agents. This is identical in concept to browsing the contents of files and folders in a file system using File Manager or Explorer. See *MIB compiler.* Compare *MIB walker.*

MIBCC

The Microsoft MIB compiler distributed in the Win32 SDK. The output from MIBCC is used by the Microsoft SNMP Management API.

MIB compiler

A program that translates MIB modules written using ASN.1 into another data format, such as C code or a relational database. Most management systems and agents cannot read ASN.1 MIB modules directly and must first compile them into a more readable data format.

MIB database

A physical database used to store and reference data defined in one or more MIB modules. Both management systems and agents will use some sort of database to store information about MIB objects and changes made to MIB variables.

MIB module

The human-readable, ASN.1 description of SNMP MIB objects, data definitions, conventions, subtypes, and events. Because MIB modules are usually compiled into another format before they are used, they may be thought of as the source code of the MIB. See *ASN.1, MIB compiler, subtype, trap.*

MIB namespace

A set of registered MIB objects, each with a unique identity. Another term for "MIB tree."

MIB object

An abstract term for any addressable data object defined in the MIB namespace. See *MIB variable, MIB namespace.*

MIB object status

The implementation status of a MIB object. Each MIB object will have a status of mandatory (the object must be implemented by the agent), optional (the object need not be implemented by the agent), deprecated (a mandatory or optimal object that may be removed in a future revision of the MIB), or obsolete (the object is no longer supported).

MIB tree

The hierarchical collection of all MIB objects. All MIB objects are identified by their location in an inverted tree structure referred to as "the MIB tree," or simply "the MIB." The MIB tree begins at "the root" and extends into "subtrees," "branches," and terminates at the "leaf nodes."

MIB variable

The pairing of the identity of a leaf object and the value stored in an instance of the object. In other words, an instance of a MIB object, its identify, its access policy, and the value that it contains. See *columnar, leaf node, scalar.*

MIB view

An administratively defined collection of managed objects that are all locally accessible by a single SNMP agent. The managed objects specified in a MIB view may be from one or more MIB subtrees.

MIB walker

An SNMP management program used to lexically step through the instantiated and accessible MIB variables maintained by an agent. MIB walking is used to create a map of an agent's currently accessible management objects. The act of MIB walking is sometimes called "MIB discovery." Compare *MIB browser.*

Microsoft

A billion-dollar software company that was founded by a nerd and is currently owned by one of the richest men in the world. Oh—and the creator of Microsoft Windows.

MicrosoftSpeak

Marketing and technical jargon commonly found in Microsoft technical documentation and product literature.

millisecond

One-thousandth of a second.

MILNET

MILitary NETwork. The unclassified branch of the Data Defense Network (DDN). It was MILNET and ARPANET that were combined to form the Internet. See *ARPANET, DDN.*

monolithic

A single, unified, unmodifiable object used in reference to hardware or software whose function cannot be easily modified. Compare *extendible.*

MTU   *see **Maximum Transmission Unit***

multilingual

Understanding more than one language or protocol. An SNMP agent that interprets more than one version of the SNMP protocol is said to be multilingual.

multiplex   *see **encapsulate***

multistate

A physical or logical device that has two or more active states. The on-off switch on the front of your PC is a two-state device. The reset button is a single-state device. See *single-state.*

multithreaded

Having multiple threads or supporting multiple threads of execution. See *thread.*

munged

Damaged or corrupted. Used to describe bad data.

network address   *see **IP address***

network discovery

The process of detecting all of the active routers and hosts that exist on a specific network.

network element

A network node or host that supports remote management via a network and using a management agent. Any node that supports SNMP management would be considered a network element.

Network Interface Controller (NIC)

A hardware device used to connect a host system to a network. Commonly called a "network card." An Ethernet NIC is referred to as an "Ethernet card." See *Ethernet.*

network latency

The amount of delay accumulated when sending a packet from one host to another (end-to-end latency) and back to the original host (round-trip latency). Network latency is affected by the type of transmission media, the speed of the data transfer, the size of the packet, and the time spent routing the packet across the network and processing the packet by each host. An ICMP message is typically used to test network latency. See *end-to-end, ICMP.*

network layer

The third layer in the OSI reference model. The network layer is used by the transport layer to control the routing of packets from their source to their destination. TCP/IP uses IP (Internet Protocol) as its network layer protocol.

network management

The policies, processes, and activities used to monitor, control, and maintain the proper function of one or more computer networks. Network management views the network as a single system made of up discrete devices which act as a whole to provide services and conduct information. System management is more concerned with the operation of network devices as a set of discrete, independent units. Compare *system management.*

network management agent   *see agent*

network management protocol

A network protocol used by managed nodes and management systems to exchange network management information. See *management information.*

network process

A process running on a node that is accessible by other nodes. Network processes are used by a node (server) to provide data and services to other nodes (clients). An SNMP agent is a network process.

NMS

Network Management Station or Network Management System. NMS is a generic term referring to either a single software application used to provide network management capability, a collection of network management applications, or a physical workstation used to perform network management operations.

node

The connection or termination point of one or more network communication links. Any addressable device on a network. See *host.*

NT

Windows NT (New Technology). Microsoft's first 32-bit Windows operating system. NT was created after Microsoft ended its collaboration with IBM to develop OS/2.

NT4

Windows NT version 4.0.

NT5

Windows NT version 5.0.

NTS

Windows NT Server.

NTW

Windows NT Workstation.

NVRAM

Non-Volatile Random Access Memory. Random Access Memory that does not lose its data when the power is removed. NVRAM is often where firmware lives. See *Random Access Memory, ROM.*

object attributes

The properties defining the access policy and behavior of instantiated MIB objects. Such properties include the data type (INTEGER, OCTET STRING, etc.), access mode (read-only, read-write, etc.), and OID. Each object has its own set of attributes that are specified using the OBJECT-TYPE construct in the MIB module that defines the object. See *OBJECT-TYPE, Object IDentifier.*

Object IDentifier (OID)

The identification value of an object defined in the MIB. An OID is expressed as a sequence of subidentifiers in dotted-decimal notation (e.g., 1.3.6.1.4.1.2035). OIDs are analogous to path names used to identify files residing in a file system, or addresses used to identify the location of data in memory.

OBJECT IDENTIFIER

An ASN.1 UNIVERSAL data type used in SNMP to store a unique MIB object identifier. See *Object IDentifier.*

object instance

The living, allocated incarnation of a MIB object. Same thing as an "SNMP variable," or

"MIB variable." See *instance, instance identifier, leaf node.*

OBJECT-TYPE

An SNMP construct used to define scalar and columnar MIB objects. OBJECT-TYPE is used to define the data type and range, and access policy of a MIB object. See *access policy, columnar, scalar.* Compare *TRAP-TYPE.*

obsolete *see MIB object status*

octet

A discrete grouping of eight bits. Also called an eight-bit byte. See *byte.*

OCTET STRING

An ASN.1 UNIVERSAL data type used in SNMP to store a series of one or more octets. See *byte, octet.*

OID *see Object IDentifier*

Opaque

An ASN.1 APPLICATION data type defined by SNMP. Opaque is derived from the ASN.1 OCTET STRING UNIVERSAL data type and is defined by the SMI to store only BER-encoded objects.

optional *see MIB object status*

OSI

Open Systems Interconnection. A suite of communications protocols used to interconnect dissimilar devices on a network. OSI has not found wide implementation, mostly due to the availability of the lower-cost and more-efficient TCP/IP protocol suite.

OSI reference model

The standard model of computer network architecture as used by the OSI. The OSI model is used to reference and describe the layers of processing and communications protocols necessary for systems to communicate across a network. Also called the *OSI seven-layer model.*

OUI

Organizationally Unique Identifier. The three most-significant bytes of a MAC address. The OUI value unambiguously identifies the manufacturer of a Network Interface Controller. See *Media Access Control address, NIC.*

out-of-band management

Management commands and messages sent outside of a device's primary data channels.

packet

A block of data that carries the information necessary for its delivery across a switching network. This term, had it not been coined in Great Britain, might have instead been "package" or "parcel." And one might wonder why it wasn't called a "bundle." See *envelope.*

payload

The actual chunk of data that is carried across a network in a packet. SNMP messages are always found as the payload of UDP datagrams. See *datagram, packet.*

PDU *see Protocol Data Unit*

PEN *see Private Enterprise Number*

performance monitoring (PM)

Monitoring one or more network elements by polling for management data related to the operational status and performance level of the element.

physical address *see Media Access Control address*

physical layer

The first layer in the OSI reference model. The physical layer is the actual network hardware and its electrical and timing characteristics. See *OSI reference model.*

ping

A term describing an Internet Control Message Protocol (ICMP) message used to determine if a network node is reachable and responding. Ping is used as a noun ("send a ping to the host"), as a verb ("ping the host"), as an adverb ("the host is pinging"), and as an adjective ("it's a ping ping ping ping host"). (OK, I made that last one up.) The term "ping" itself is an onomatopoeia originally used in SONAR technology. See *ICMP*

polling

The act of querying a node or device at regular, periodic intervals for the purpose of collecting management data. Polling is a very basic function performed by network management systems and a fundamental operation in most models of network management. See *trap-directed polling.*

polling cycle

The complete cycle of sending one or more request (query) messages, receiving the response (reply) messages, processing the response data, and waiting until the beginning of the next polling cycle. See *polling, polling duration, polling frequency.*

polling duration

The number of polling cycles to perform. Polling duration is usually in the range 1 to infinite. See *polling, polling cycle, polling frequency.*

polling frequency

The rate at which a polling cycle is periodically started. Polling frequency is usually measured in minutes and seconds (poll host X every 120 seconds). Also called the "polling interval." See *polling, polling cycle, polling duration.*

polling interval   *see polling frequency*

port number   *see protocol port number*

presentation layer

The sixth layer in the OSI reference model. The presentation layer is used to provide encoding and encryption that allows application data to be properly interpreted and utilized by different types of host systems. See *OSI reference model.*

Private Enterprise Number (PEN)

A subidentifier used to identify a branch in the enterprises subtree (1.3.6.1.4.1) that is registered to a specific individual or vendor. For example, Microsoft's PEN is 311, so all MIB objects registered under the 1.3.6.1.4.1.311 subtree are owned and maintained by Microsoft. All PENs are assigned by IANA. Also called "enterprise identifiers." See *enterprise MIB, IANA.*

private MIB   *see enterprise MIB*

problem

A discrepancy between what is desired and what is perceived. For me, wearing a beard is not a problem because I do not perceive a discrepancy between facial hair and happiness. See *fault, problem report.*

problem report

A printed or displayed form that describes a specific problem, when it occurred, and how, when, where, and by whom it was fixed. Also called a *trouble ticket.*

proof-of-concept

The physical realization of cubicle isolation, caffeine-induced cogitation, conference room bickering, and white-board elbow. A hardware and/or software prototype that proves that your ideas work in real life.

protocol

Rules used to negotiate the exchange of a specific type of information. A management protocol is a set of rules used to unambiguously describe and convey management data. Compare *language.*

Protocol Data Unit (PDU)

A generic term for a message used by a communications protocol or a specific layer of the OSI model. A PDU contains information used to identify and authenticate the data that it encapsulates. See *SNMP message.*

protocol errors

Predefined errors that occur during the negotiation of a protocol. See *SNMP protocol errors.*

protocol port number

A number used to identify a specific network application protocol supported by a host. For example, the port number for UDP is 17, and the port number for SNMP traps is 162. See *Assigned Numbers, well-known ports.*

protocol stack

A reference to the conceptual arrangement of the layers defined in the OSI reference model. Each of the protocol layers is stacked on top of another, much as shelves are in a bookcase. One might even refer to the data being processed by a protocol stack, or the books in a bookcase, as "stackage." See *OSI reference model.*

protocol suite

A related collection of communications protocols. Also called a *protocol family.*

provisioning

The operational parameters that define how a software process or hardware device is to function. The IP address of a host, the power-on state of the NumLock key, the time and date of your workstation, and the double-click rate of a mouse are all "provisionable items." See *configuration, inventory.*

proxy

A process or device that acts on behalf of another process or device. In networking, a proxy allows a non-networked device to access (or be accessed by) the network. See *proxy agent.*

proxy agent

An agent that provides management services for a non-SNMP management agent, or for a device that does not support any management agents.

proxy station

A management system that acts as a gateway between a network and one or more management applications. See *gateway, intermediate management system.*

Random Access Memory (RAM)

Memory that is readable, writable, directly addressable, and need not be searched (e.g., hard and floppy disks) or read sequentially (e.g., magnetic tape). RAM is also volatile in nature and "forgets" its state when the power is removed. The primary memory of a computer. Software must first be loaded into RAM before it is executed. See *NVRAM, ROM.*

registry

A database supported by Win32 for storing operating system, application, and driver information. The registry is accessible via the Windows Registry Editor (RegEdit) application and the Win32 API.

remote management

The ability to monitor and control a process or device without being physically present at the system's location. Remote management usually occurs over a network or a modem link. See *local management.*

Remote Procedure Call (RPC)

A form of Interprocess Communication that is used to start and access processes on remote hosts by using local function calls. Although the function call is (possibly) made over a network, its behavior is the same as a call made to the local operating system. The apparent operation of RPC is therefore procedure-oriented rather than transmission-oriented.

Request For Comments (RFC)

The official specifications for Internet standards. All RFCs are created, reviewed, and updated by the IAB and IETF. All RFCs are freely available on the Internet. See *IAB, IETF.*

retail build

A build of Microsoft Windows NT that does not contain system debugging information. The retail build is distributed to consumers via the retail market. Also called "free build." See *checked build.*

RFC   *see Request For Comments*

RFC 1155

Structure and Identification of Management Information for TCP/IP-based internets. This standard describes the rules for defining management information and events. One of the four foundation documents that describe SNMPv1. See *SNMPv1.*

RFC 1157

A Simple Network Management Protocol (SNMP). This standard describes the format and meaning of the SNMPv1 messages exchanged between network nodes. One of the four foundation documents that describe SNMPv1. See *SNMPv1.*

RFC 1212

Concise MIB Definitions. This standard describes the format used for constructing MIB modules. One of the four foundation documents that describe SNMPv1. See *SNMPv1.*

RFC 1213

Management Information Base for Network Management of TCP/IP-based internets (MIB-II). This standard defines a common set of management information that must be supported by all SNMP-managed nodes. One of the four foundation documents that describe SNMPv1. See *SNMPv1.*

RFC 1215

A Convention for Defining Traps for use with the SNMP. This informational document describes the generic traps used by SNMPv1. RFC 1215 was never officially placed on the standards track with the other SNMPv1 documents, so it is not typically referred to as a SNMPv1 foundation document. See *SNMPv1.*

ROM

Read-only memory. Directly addressable memory that can only be read and never written. Write-once (programmable) and erasable ROM also exist. Firmware is often stored in ROM. See *NVRAM, RAM.*

route

The physical and logical path a packet follows as it travels across a network. See *end-to-end.*

router

A network device that forwards packets from one network to another. Every device on a network is either a router or a host (or sometimes both). See *gateway, end-host.*

RPC *see Remote Procedure Call*

scalar

The most primitive, fundamental, and atomic data objects. Scalar objects contain a single value and are independent of all other instantiated objects. All objects in a MIB are either columnar or scalar. A scalar MIB object may have only one instance. See *columnar.*

SCM *see Service Control Manager*

Sequenced Packet eXchange protocol (SPX)

A connection-based, reliable, sequenced transport, NetWare protocol based on the Xerox Network System (XNS) Sequenced Packet Protocol (SPP) and used on Novell networks. SPX runs on top of IPX. See *Internet Packet eXchange protocol.*

serialize

To convert data into a serial stream of octets, as in the serialization of an asynchronous (parallel) transmission into a synchronous (serial) transmission. To encode data into a binary format.

server

A network host that supplies other hosts with access to specific services. Such services may include access to printers and modems, sending and receiving news and electronic mail, archiving files and executable programs, and acting as a firewall and proxy gateway. A host that supports a SNMP agent is sometimes called a "SNMP management server." See *client, client-server, proxy agent.*

service

A special type of Win32 application used to provide a specific service or to extend the capability of the Windows operating system. The SNMP service allows a Win32 system with a TCP/IP stack to process SNMP management requests and send SNMP traps. Services typically do not interact with the Windows desktop and instead operate invisibly as background processes. See *Service Control Manager.*

Service Control Manager (SCM)

A process under Windows NT that controls all application services, such as the SNMP service. The SCM contains a database of how each service is configured; it is also an RPC server that is capable of controlling services remotely on networked NT systems. See *service.*

session

The conversation occurring between two hosts across a network. A session is usually connection-oriented (a virtual circuit), where the session itself is explicitly initiated and terminated. Hosts communicating using a connectionless (datagram) protocol may be conceptually described as "engaged in a session."

session layer

The fifth layer in the OSI reference model. The session layer manages the logical, high-level connection between two hosts. See *OSI reference model.*

Set

The SNMP operation used to write or "set" data to MIB variables maintained by an SNMP agent. The SetRequest SNMP message is used by a management system to perform the Set operation and send the new variable data to an agent. The agent uses the GetResponse message to return the results of the Set operation. See *Get, GetNext.*

SetRequest

The SNMP message sent by a management application to an agent to perform a Set operation. See *GetResponse, Set.*

SGMP

Simple Gateway Monitoring Protocol. The ancestor protocol of SNMP. SGMP is documented in RFC 1028.

simulation

A nonworking model that demonstrates the appearance and apparent operation of a device or process. The equivalent, nonscientific term is a "demo." See *emulation.*

single-edge

An event that is triggered by a threshold boundary being crossed in only one direction. See *threshold.*

single-state

A physical or logical device that has only one momentary, active state. The reset button on the front of your PC is a single-state device. The on-off switch is a two-state device. Compare *multistate.*

single-threaded

Applications that contain only a single thread of execution. Operating systems that do not support multiple threads are also described as "single-threaded." Compare *multithreaded*.

SMI

Structure of Management Information. See *RFC 1155*.

SMIv1

Structure of Management Information, version 1. The SMI used by SNMPv1. See *RFC 1155*.

SMIv2

Structure of Management Information, version 2. The SMI used by SNMPv2. SMIv2 is described in RFC 1902.

SNMP

Simple Network Management Protocol. A communications protocol specifically designed for the monitoring and control of computer networks (although it can do other things as well). SNMP is "simple" because 1) It defines only four operations (Get, GetNext, Set, and Trap), which operate on data, rather than defining an endless set of procedural commands (INIT-SYS, RTRV-LOG, SET-DAT, etc.), 2) SNMP messages are small in size and contain only minimal necessary information, and 3) Management information defined by SNMP consists of simple data objects. SNMP is the recommended management protocol for TCP/IP networks.

SNMPv1

Simple Network Management Protocol, version 1. SNMPv1 is the first release of SNMP and the most widely used version of SNMP. SNMPv1 is currently defined by RFCs 1155, 1212, 1213, and 1157.

SNMPv2

Simple Network Management Protocol, version 2. Party-based SNMP with security. Also called SNMPv2p.

SNMPv2*

A combination of SNMPv2p and SNMPv2u. Pronounced "SNMPv2 star."

SNMPv2c

Community-based SNMPv2 without security. Defined by RFCs 1901, 1905, and 1906.

SNMPv2p   *see SNMPv2*

SNMPv2u

User-based SNMPv2 with security. Also called SNMPv2usec.

SNMPv3

Simple Network Management Protocol, version 3. A combination of SNMPv2* and SNMPv2u, and additional enhancements. SNMPv3 is currently under development by SNMPv3 Working Group of the IETF.

SNMP-managed node

Any network node that supports an SNMP agent and responds to SNMP requests. See *network element*.

SNMP message

An SNMP PDU with an SNMP preamble that contains authentication information. Any packet that contains as its payload an SNMP PDU. See *packet, Protocol Data Unit*.

SNMP Protocol Data Unit

A PDU used to store and convey SNMP information. See *Protocol Data Unit, SNMP message*.

SNMP protocol errors

Errors defined by SNMP that may occur during the processing of an SNMP request message. SNMPv1 lists the following errors: noError, tooBig, badValue, readOnly, noSuchName, and genErr.

SNMP service

The Win32 service that contains the Microsoft extendible agent and enables a Win32 system to support SNMP management. See *extendible agent, service, Service Control Manager*.

SNMP variable   *see MIB variable*

socket

A logical reference or connection to a network service. Sockets are an abstraction of the end-point of a network connection and are similar in concept to a file descriptor or window handle. Applications access the network by first opening a socket to a specific protocol service. The concept of sockets is used in all of networking and is not restricted to TCP/IP.

software

Code that is loaded from permanent storage and into volatile memory before it is executed, and that disappears from memory when the power is removed. See *firmware, RAM*.

stack   *see protocol stack*

subagent   *see extension agent*

subidentifier

The smallest component in an OID. Each subidentifier represents a unique node in the MIB tree. The OIDs "1.3.6.1" and "iso.org.dod.internet" each contain four subidentifiers. See *Object IDentifier.*

subnet *see subnetwork*

subnetwork
An addressable partition of an IP network, usually specified using the lower 16 bits of an IP address. Subnets are primarily used to control the amount of network traffic that is routed to a group of hosts.

subtree
A section of the MIB tree. The MIB tree is conceptually a collection of subtrees, with each subtree containing other subtrees or branches. See *branches, leaf node.*

subtype
An ASN.1 data type definition that restricts the range of values that may be stored by a MIB variable. A common subtype used in SNMP is DisplayString, which is an OCTET STRING that may only contain 0 to 255 octets.

system management
The policies, processes, and activities used to monitor, control, and maintain individual systems or groups of systems. System management is more concerned with the operation of devices as discrete units. Network management is more concerned with the operation of a device as only one small component influencing the operational status of an entire network. Compare *network management.*

table
A structure defined in the SMI used to store data in a two-dimensional array, or "tabular" format. In SNMP, a table is zero or more columnar MIB objects. See *columnar, tabular.*

tabular
Referring to a table or data stored in the form of a table. SNMP tables are columnar MIB objects that are stored in a tabular structure. See *columnar, table.*

TCP
Transport Control Protocol. The primary, connection-oriented transport protocol found in the TCP/IP protocol suite. See *TCP/IP.*

TCP/IP
Transfer Control Protocol/Internet Protocol. The term "TCP/IP" is a bit overloaded. It refers to the common pairing of a specific transport and network protocol to a suite (family, collec-

tion, toolkit, etc.) of related network protocols, and to any network that uses the TCP/IP protocol suite. See *Internet, TCP/IP protocol suite, UDP/IP.*

TCP/IP network
A network containing nodes that exchange data using communications protocols supported by the TCP/IP protocol suite. TCP/IP describes each network node as either a "router" or a "host." (OSI networks use the descriptions "intermediate system" and "end system.") See *host, internet, Internet, router, TCP/IP.*

TCP/IP protocol suite
The collection of protocols used to operate, support, and maintain a TCP/IP network. Also called the "Internet Protocol Suite." See *TCP/IP, TCP/IP network.*

telco
Telephone company.

telecom
Telecommunications.

thread
A single chain of execution started by a process. Threads allow a single process to perform multiple tasks concurrently by interleaving independent sets of executable instructions. A thread is sometimes called a "child process" or a "lightweight process" because it uses the same environment as its parent process and shares resources with its sibling threads.

threshold
A discrete boundary that when crossed causes an event to occur. A threshold can be physical (1100 feet in altitude, 60°F, -48 volts, or 5.16 pounds in weight), logical (if more than 50 packets are received and less than 10% of memory is free), or temporal (17 or more CRC errors per second). See *trap.*

throttling
The act of controlling the physical quantity of data moving across a communications link. Used in the terms "throttle-up" and "throttle-back" to indicate, respectively, an increase or decrease in the rate at which data is sent. In SNMP, throttling is used to control the rate at which an agent may send traps.

TimeTicks

An ASN.1 APPLICATION data type defined by SNMP. TimeTicks is typically a 32-bit integer that stores a value allowed only to increment within the range of 0 to 4294967295. A TimeTicks value is typically a time stamp recording elapsed time and is always interpreted in centiseconds.

TL1

Transaction Language 1. An ASCII-based system management protocol widely used in the United States for the management of telco devices. TL1 is derived from the Man-Machine Language (MML) described by CCITT standards Z.301 through Z.352; TL1 itself is described in the Bellcore manual FR-NWT-000439.

topology map

A graphical representation of a network depicted by the physical and logical interconnections of its nodes. A topology map shows the configuration and inventory of a network, and may also be used to indicate the operational status of each node.

transport layer

The fourth layer in the OSI reference model. The transport layer provides the reliable—or unreliable—transportation of data between network hosts. See *OSI reference model.*

trap

A message that is used as a notification that a predefined event has occurred. When an agent detects such an event, the agent sends a special message to indicate that the "trap has been sprung." See *Trap PDU.*

trap-directed polling

A model for collecting network management information based on polling specific managed objects as a response to the reception of specific trap messages. See *polling.*

Trap PDU

The section of an SNMP trap message used to store the header and variable binding information of a trap. See *trap.*

TRAP-TYPE

A SNMP construct used to define traps. Although a trap is always associated with a particular MIB branch, it is not an addressable object. Compare *OBJECT-TYPE.*

trouble ticket   *see problem report*

UDP

User Datagram Protocol. The primary datagram transport protocol of the   TCP/IP protocol suite. UDP is the transport mechanism used by several   TCP/IP protocols, including TFTP, SMTP, and SNMP.

UDP/IP

User Datagram Protocol/Internet Protocol. This term is used when it is necessary to explicitly indicate that a protocol uses the UDP transport service rather than TCP. SNMP uses UDP/IP, and some protocols may use either TCP/IP or UDP/IP (e.g., RPC). See *UDP.*

validation

The process of comparing new data to the attributes of an object to determine if the new data is acceptable. See *object attributes.*

varbinds   *see variable bindings*

variable bindings

A data structure containing the OID of a MIB object instance, the size and data type of the object, and the value (data) associated with the object. Every SNMP request and response message contains a list of one or more variable bindings. Also called "varbinds" for short.

vendor MIB   *see enterprise MIB*

volatile memory

Memory that loses its state when power is removed, such as conventional RAM. Also called "volatile storage." See *non-volatile memory.*

well-known ports

Port numbers reserved by IANA for well-known network services, such as UDP, FTP, and SNMP. Well-known port numbers are in the range of 0 to 1023.

Win16

The Microsoft Windows 16-bit operating system and API used by Windows 3.1 and Windows for Workgroups 3.1.

Win32

The Microsoft Windows 32-bit operating system and API used by Windows 95, Windows NT, and Windows CE.

WinSNMP

Windows-based Simple Network Management Protocol. A standard that promotes the development of SNMP-based network management applications running under the Microsoft Windows operating systems.

WinSock

The standard Windows network sockets interface. Any Windows application that needs to communicate across a network will use the WinSock API.

workstation

A generic term for a single-user, generic computer. This term is gradually replacing "PC" and "PC clone," which are now largely regarded as describing older, slower, and obsolete personal computers. A workstation typically has a very fast processor (100 MHz or better), a moderate amount of RAM (32 to 128Mb), high-fidelity audio, and high-resolution video capability. A modem and/or network interface controller are also becoming standard workstation peripherals.

Index

About the Author

James D. Murray started his computer career in 1981 on a Version 6 UNIX system running on a PDP-11/45 and programming in C. Over the years he has specialized in serial communications, image processing and analysis, UNIX and Windows NT systems programming, and telco network management. Currently he works for a telecommunications company developing network management stations and as a staff writer for O'Reilly & Associates. James is a coauthor of the O'Reilly book, *Encyclopedia of Graphics File Formats*, and maintains the Graphics File Formats FAQ. He lives in Southern California, has a degree in cultural anthropology, has studied computer science and both Western and non-Western music, and practices the Japanese martial arts of Aikido and Iaido (Japanese swordsmanship).

Colophon

The animal featured on the cover of *Windows NT SNMP* is a moose. The moose is the largest member of the deer family. A male (bull) moose can stand as high as 7.5 feet to the shoulder and weigh between 900 and 1400 pounds. A female (cow) moose can weigh between 600 and 800 pounds. They are surprisingly fast runners and excellent swimmers.

Moose are found in the northern woodlands and swamps of Asia, Europe, and North America. They eat soft wood, bark, branches, grass, evergreen tips, and aquatic plants such as water lilies. Their large upper lips are well suited to stripping leaves and branches off of trees, but their short necks make feeding from the ground difficult. In order to do so, they have to spread their long legs in a wide, awkward stance.

A moose will never be mistaken for another deer. Their elongated heads and short necks distinguish them from their cousins. Also unique to the moose are the wide, spoon-shaped antlers of the bulls. The antlers, the strongest among all the living deer, grow up to 6 feet across and weight as much as 90 pounds. They are shed every autumn and grown in the spring. Male moose also have a flap of skin hanging below their chins. As they age this flap grows into a beard.

Moose mating season is in the fall. Bull moose become extremely aggressive during this time. Mating battles between bulls are violent and occasionally fatal. Humans who wander too close to a bull moose during mating season are sometimes attacked. Gestation lasts for eight months, after which time it is not unusual for twins to be born. The calves stay with their mothers for nine to 12 months. Moose are fully grown at five years and have a life expectancy of 20 to 25 years.

The moose population has decreased because of the loss of deciduous forest and swamps, but it is making a comeback now.

Edie Freedman designed the cover of this book, using a 19th-century engraving from the Dover Pictorial Archive. The cover layout was produced with Quark XPress 3.3 using the ITC Garamond font.

The inside layout was designed by Nancy Priest and implemented in FrameMaker 5.0 by Mike Sierra. The text and heading fonts are ITC Garamond Light and Garamond Book. The illustrations that appear in the book were created in Macromedia Freehand 7 by Robert Romano. This colophon was written by Claire-marie Fisher O'Leary.

More Titles from O'Reilly

Windows NT Administration

Windows NT in a Nutshell

By Eric Pearce
1st Edition June 1997
364 pages, ISBN 1-56592-251-4

Anyone who installs Windows NT, creates a user, or adds a printer is an NT system administrator (whether they realize it or not). This book features a new tagged callout approach to documenting the 4.0 GUI as well as real-life examples of command usage and strategies for problem solving, with an emphasis on networking. Windows NT in a Nutshell will be as useful to the single-system home user as it will be to the administrator of a 1,000-node corporate network.

Windows NT User Administration

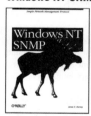

By Ashley J. Meggitt & Timothy D. Ritchey
1st Edition November 1997
218 pages, ISBN 1-56592-301-4

Many Windows NT books introduce you to a range of topics, but seldom do they give you enough information to master any one thing. This book (like other O'Reilly animal books) is different. *Windows NT User Administration* makes you an expert at creating users efficiently, controlling what they can do, limiting the damage they can cause, and monitoring their activities on your system. Don't simply react to problems; use the techniques in this book to anticipate and prevent them.

Windows NT SNMP

By James D. Murray
1st Edition January 1998 (est.)
488 pages (est.), Includes CD-ROM
ISBN 1-56592-338-3

This book describes the implementation of SNMP (the Simple Network Management Protocol) on Windows NT 3.51 and 4.0 (with a look ahead to NT 5.0) and Windows 95 systems. It covers SNMP and network basics and detailed information on developing SNMP management applications and extension agents. The book comes with a CD-ROM containing a wealth of additional information: standards documents, sample code from the book, and many third-party, SNMP-related software tools, libraries, and demos.

Essential Windows NT System Administration

By Æleen Frisch
1st Edition February 1998
486 pages, ISBN 1-56592-274-3

This book combines practical experience with technical expertise to help you manage Windows NT systems as productively as possible. It covers the standard utilities offered with the Windows NT operating system and from the Resource Kit, as well as important commercial and free third-party tools. By the author of O'Reilly's bestselling book, *Essential System Administration*.

Windows NT Backup & Restore

By Jody Leber
1st Edition April 1998 (est.)
250 pages (est.), ISBN 1-56592-272-7

Beginning with the need for a workable recovery policy and ways to translate that policy into requirements, *Windows NT Backup & Restore* presents the reader with practical guidelines for setting up an effective backup system in both small and large environments. It covers the native NT utilities as well as major third-party hardware and software.

Windows NT Server 4.0 for NetWare Administrators

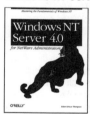

By Robert Bruce Thompson
1st Edition November 1997
756 pages, ISBN 1-56592-280-8

This book provides a fast-track means for experienced NetWare administrators to build on their knowledge and master the fundamentals of using the Microsoft Windows NT Server. The broad coverage of many aspects of Windows NT Server is balanced by a tightly focused approach of comparison, contrast, and differentiation between NetWare and NT features and methodologies.

Windows NT Desktop Reference

By AEleen Frisch
1st Edition January 1998
64 pages, ISBN 1-56592-437-1

A hip-pocket quick reference to Windows NT commands, as well as the most useful commands from the Resource Kits. Commands are arranged ingroups related to their purpose and function. Covers Windows NT 4.0.

O'REILLY™

TO ORDER: **800-998-9938** • *order@oreilly.com* • *http://www.oreilly.com/*
OUR PRODUCTS ARE AVAILABLE AT A BOOKSTORE OR SOFTWARE STORE NEAR YOU.
FOR INFORMATION: **800-998-9938** • **707-829-0515** • *info@oreilly.com*

Network Administration

Managing IP Networks with Cisco Routers

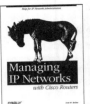

By Scott M. Ballew
1st Edition October 1997
352 pages, ISBN 1-56592-320-0

Managing IP Networks with Cisco Routers is a practical guide to setting up and maintaining a production network. It discusses how to select routing protocols and how to configure protcols to handle most common situations. It also discusses less esoteric but equally important issues like how to evaluate network equipment and vendors and how to set up a help desk. Although the book focuses on Cisco routers, and gives examples using Cisco's IOS, the principles discussed are common to all IP networks, regardless of the vendor you choose.

Topics covered include:

- Designing an IP network
- Evaluating equipment and vendors
- Selecting routing protocols
- Configuring common interior protocols (RIP, OSPF, EIGRP)
- Connecting to external networks, and configuring exterior protocols (BGP)
- Ongoing network management: troubleshooting and maintenance
- Security and privacy issues

Virtual Private Networks

Charlie Scott, Paul Wolfe & Mike Erwin
1st Edition February 1998 (est.)
184 pages (est.), ISBN 1-56592-319-7

Historically, only large companies could afford secure networks, which they created from expensive leased lines. Smaller folks had to make do with the relatively untrusted Internet. Nowadays, even large companies have to go outside their private nets, because so many people telecommute or log in while they're on the road. How do you provide a low-cost, secure electronic network for your organization?

The solution is a virtual private network: a collection of technologies that creates secure connections or "tunnels" over regular Internet lines—connections that can be easily used by anybody logging in from anywhere. This book tells you how to plan and build a VPN. It starts with general concerns like costs, configuration, and how a VPN fits in with other networking technologies like firewalls. It continues with detailed descriptions of how to install and use VPN technologies that are available for Windows NT and UNIX, such as PPTP and L2TP, the Altavista Tunnel, and the Cisco PIX Firewall.

sendmail, 2nd Edition

By Bryan Costales & Eric Allman
2nd Edition January 1997
1050 pages, ISBN 1-56592-222-0

This new edition of *sendmail* covers sendmail Version 8.8 from Berkeley and the standard versions available on most systems. It is far and away the most comprehensive book ever written on sendmail, the program that acts like a traffic cop in routing and delivering mail on UNIX-based networks. Although sendmail is used on almost every UNIX system, it's one of the last great uncharted territories—and most difficult utilities to learn—in UNIX system administration.

This book provides a complete sendmail tutorial, plus extensive reference material on every aspect of the program. Part One is a tutorial on understanding sendmail; Part Two covers the building, installation, and m4 configuration of sendmail; Part Three covers practical issues in sendmail administration; Part Four is a comprehensive reference section; and Part Five consists of appendices and a bibliography.

In this second edition an expanded tutorial demonstrates hub's *cf* file and *nullclient.mc*. Other new topics include the #error delivery agent, sendmail's exit values, MIME headers, and how to set up and use the user database, *mailertable*, and *smrsh*. Solution-oriented examples throughout the book help you solve your own sendmail problems. This new edition is cross-referenced with section numbers.

sendmail Desktop Reference

By Bryan Costales & Eric Allman
1st Edition March 1997
74 pages, ISBN 1-56592-278-6

This quick-reference guide provides a complete overview of the latest version of sendmail (V8.8), from command-line switches to configuration commands, from options declarations to macro definitions, and from m4 features to debugging switches—all packed into a convenient, carry-around booklet co-authored by the creator of sendmail. Includes extensive cross-references to *sendmail*, second edition.

DNS and BIND, 2nd Edition

By Paul Albitz & Cricket Liu
2nd Edition December 1996
438 pages, ISBN 1-56592-236-0

This book is a complete guide to the Internet's Domain Name System (DNS) and the Berkeley Internet Name Domain (BIND) software, the UNIX implementation of DNS. In this second edition, the authors continue to describe BIND version 4.8.3, which is included in most vendor implementations today. In addition, you'll find complete coverage of BIND 4.9.4, which in all probability will be adopted as the new standard in the near future.

In addition to covering the basic motivation behind DNS and how to set up the BIND software, this book covers many more advanced topics, including using DNS and BIND on Windows NT systems; how to become a "parent" (i.e., "delegate" the ability to assign names to someone else); how to use DNS to set up mail forwarding correctly; debugging and troubleshooting; and programming. Assumes a basic knowledge of system administration and network management.

Getting Connected: The Internet at 56K and Up

By Kevin Dowd
1st Edition June 1996
424 pages, ISBN 1-56592-154-2

A complete guide for businesses, schools, and other organizations who want to connect their computers to the Internet. This book covers everything you need to know to make informed decisions, from helping you figure out which services you really need to providing down-to-earth explanations and configuration instructions for telecommunication options at higher than modem speeds, such as frame relay, ISDN, and leased lines. Once you're online, it shows you how to set up basic Internet services, such as a World Wide Web server. Tackles issues for PC, Macintosh, and UNIX platforms.

Using & Managing PPP

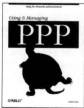

By Andrew Sun
1st Edition March 1998 (est.)
400 pages (est.), ISBN 1-56592-321-9

Covers all aspects of PPP, including setting up dial-in servers, debugging, and PPP options. Also contains overviews of related areas, like serial communications, DNS setup, and routing.

Networking Personal Computers with TCP/IP

By Craig Hunt
1st Edition July 1995
408 pages, ISBN 1-56592-123-2

This book offers practical information as well as detailed instructions for attaching PCs to a TCP/IP network and its UNIX servers. It discusses the challenges you'll face and offers general advice on how to deal with them, provides basic TCP/IP configuration information for some of the popular PC operating systems, covers advanced configuration topics and configuration of specific applications such as email, and includes a chapter on on integrating Netware with TCP/IP.

TCP/IP Network Administration, 2nd Edition

By Craig Hunt
2nd Edition December 1997
630 pages, ISBN 1-56592-322-7

TCP/IP Network Administration, 2nd Edition, is a complete guide to setting up and running a TCP/IP network for administrators of networks of systems or lone home systems that access the Internet. It starts with the fundamentals: what the protocols do and how they work, how addresses and routing are used to move data through the network, and how to set up your network connection.

Beyond basic setup, this new second edition discusses advanced routine protocols (RIPv2, OSPF, and BGP) and the *gated* software package that implements them. It contains a tutorial on configuring important network services, including PPP, SLIP, sendmail, Domain Name Service (DNS), BOOTP and DHCP configuration servers, some simple setups for NIS and NFS, and chapters on troubleshooting and security. In addition, this book is a command and syntax reference for several important packages including *pppd, dip, gated, named, dhcpd,* and *sendmail.*

Covers Linux, BSD, and System V TCP/IP implementations.

Perl

Perl Resource Kit—UNIX Edition

By Larry Wall, Nate Patwardhan, Ellen Siever,
David Futato & Brian Jepson
1st Edition November 1997
1812 pages, ISBN 1-56592-370-7

The *Perl Resource Kit—UNIX Edition* gives
you the most comprehensive collection of
Perl documentation and commercially
enhanced software tools available today.
Developed in association with Larry Wall,
the creator of Perl, it's the definitive Perl distribution for web-
masters, programmers, and system administrators.

The *Perl Resource Kit* provides:

* Over 1800 pages of tutorial and in-depth reference documentation for Perl utilities and extensions, in 4 volumes.
* A CD-ROM containing the complete Perl distribution, plus hundreds of freeware Perl extensions and utilities—a complete
  snapshot of the Comprehensive Perl Archive Network (CPAN)—
  as well as new software written by Larry Wall just for the Kit.

Perl Software Tools All on One Convenient CD-ROM
Experienced Perl hackers know when to create their own, and
when they can find what they need on CPAN. Now all the power
of CPAN—and more—is at your fingertips. *The Perl Resource Kit*
includes:

* A complete snapshot of CPAN, with an install program for
  Solaris and Linux that ensures that all necessary modules are
  installed together. Also includes an easy-to-use search tool
  and a web-aware interface that allows you to get the latest
  version of each module.
* A new Java/Perl interface that allows programmers to write
  Java classes with Perl implementations. This new tool was
  written specially for the Kit by Larry Wall.

Experience the power of Perl modules in areas such as CGI, web spi-
dering, database interfaces, managing mail and USENET news, user
interfaces, security, graphics, math and statistics, and much more.

Perl in a Nutshell

By Stephen Spainhour, Ellen Siever &
Nathan Patwardhan
1st Edition May 1998 (est.)
450 pages (est.), ISBN 1-56592-286-7

The perfect companion for working programmers, *Perl in a Nutshell* is a comprehensive reference guide to the world of Perl.
It containseverything you need to know for
all but the most abstruse Perl questions.This
wealth of information is packed into an efficient, extraordinarily
usable format.

Programming Perl, 2nd Edition

By Larry Wall, Tom Christiansen &
Randal L. Schwartz
2nd Edition September 1996
670 pages, ISBN 1-56592-149-6

Programming Perl, 2nd Edition, is the
authoritative guide to Perl version 5, the
scripting utility that has established itself
as the programming tool of choice for the
World Wide Web, UNIX system administra-
tion, and a vast range of other applications. Version 5 of Perl
includes object-oriented programming facilities. The book is
coauthored by Larry Wall, the creator of Perl.

Perl is a language for easily manipulating text, files, and processes. It provides a more concise and readable way to do many jobs
that were formerly accomplished (with difficulty) by programming with C or one of the shells. Perl is likely to be available
wherever you choose to work. And if it isn't, you can get it and
install it easily and free of charge.

This heavily revised second edition of *Programming Perl* contains a full explanation of the features in Perl version 5.003. Contents include:

* An introduction to Perl
* Explanations of the language and its syntax
* Perl functions
* Perl library modules
* The use of references in Perl
* How to use Perl's object-oriented features
* Invocation options for Perl itself, and also for the utilities
  that come with Perl
* Other oddments: debugging, common mistakes, efficiency,
  programming style, distribution and installation of Perl, Perl
  poetry, and so on.

Perl 5 Desktop Reference

By Johan Vromans
1st Edition February 1996
46 pages, ISBN 1-56592-187-9

This is the standard quick-reference guide for
the Perl programming language. It provides a
complete overview of the language, from variables to input and output, from flow control to
regular expressions, from functions to document formats—all packed into a convenient,
carry-around booklet. Updated to cover Perl version 5.003.

Perl

Learning Perl, 2nd Edition

By Randal L. Schwartz &
Tom Christiansen,
Foreword by Larry Wall
2nd Edition July 1997
302 pages, ISBN 1-56592-284-0

In this update of a bestseller, two leading Perl trainers teach you to use the most universal scripting language in the age of the World Wide Web. With a foreword by Larry Wall, the creator of Perl, this smooth, carefully paced book is the "official" guide for both formal (classroom) and informal learning. It is now current for Perl version 5.004.

Learning Perl is a hands-on tutorial designed to get you writing useful Perl scripts as quickly as possible. Exercises (with complete solutions) accompany each chapter. A lengthy, new chapter in this edition introduces you to CGI programming, while touching also on the use of library modules, references, and Perl's object-oriented constructs.

Perl is a language for easily manipulating text, files, and processes. It comes standard on most UNIX platforms and is available free of charge on all other important operating systems. Perl technical support is informally available—often within minutes—from a pool of experts who monitor a USENET newsgroup (*comp.lang.perl.misc*) with tens of thousands of readers.

Contents include:

* A quick tutorial stroll through Perl basics
* Systematic, topic-by-topic coverage of Perl's broad capabilities
* Lots of brief code examples
* Programming exercises for each topic, with fully worked-out answers
* How to execute system commands from your Perl program
* How to manage DBM databases using Perl
* An introduction to CGI programming for the Web

The Perl Cookbook

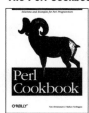

By Tom Christiansen & Nathan Torkington
1st Edition April 1998 (est.)
600 pages (est.), ISBN 1-56592-243-3

The Perl Cookbook is a collection of hundreds of problems and their solutions (with examples) for anyone programming in Perl. The topics range from beginner questions to techniques that even the most experienced Perl programmers might learn from.

Advanced Perl Programming

By Sriram Srinivasan
1st Edition August 1997
434 pages, ISBN 1-56592-220-4

This book covers complex techniques for managing production-ready Perl programs and explains methods for manipulating data and objects that may have looked like magic before. It gives you necessary background for dealing with networks, databases, and GUIs, and includes a discussion of internals to help you program more efficiently and embed Perl within C or C within Perl.

Learning Perl on Win32 Systems

By Randal L. Schwartz, Erik Olson & Tom Christiansen
1st Edition August 1997
306 pages, ISBN 1-56592-324-3

In this carefully paced course, leading Perl trainers and a Windows NT practitioner teach you to program in the language that promises to emerge as the scripting language of choice on NT. Based on the "llama" book, this book features tips for PC users and new, NT-specific examples, along with a foreword by Larry Wall, the creator of Perl, and Dick Hardt, the creator of Perl for Win32.

Mastering Regular Expressions

By Jeffrey E. F. Friedl
1st Edition January 1997
368 pages, ISBN 1-56592-257-3

Regular expressions, a powerful tool for manipulating text and data, are found in scripting languages, editors, programming environments, and specialized tools. In this book, author Jeffrey Friedl leads you through the steps of crafting a regular expression that gets the job done. He examines a variety of tools and uses them in an extensive array of examples, with a major focus on Perl.

How to stay in touch with O'Reilly

1. Visit Our Award-Winning Web Site

http://www.oreilly.com/

★ "Top 100 Sites on the Web" —*PC Magazine*
★ "Top 5% Web sites" —*Point Communications*
★ "3-Star site" —*The McKinley Group*

Our web site contains a library of comprehensiveproduct information (including book excerpts and tables of contents), downloadable software, background articles, interviews with technology leaders, links to relevant sites, book cover art, and more. File us in your Bookmarks or Hotlist!

2. Join Our Email Mailing Lists

New Product Releases
To receive automatic email with brief descriptions of all new O'Reilly products as they are released, send email to:
listproc@online.oreilly.com
Put the following information in the first line of your message (*not* in the Subject field):
subscribe oreilly-news

O'Reilly Events
If you'd also like us to send information about trade show events, special promotions, and other O'Reilly events, send email to:
listproc@online.oreilly.com
Put the following information in the first line of your message (*not* in the Subject field):
subscribe oreilly-events

3. Get Examples from Our Books via FTP

There are two ways to access an archive of example files from our books:

Regular FTP
- ftp to:
  ftp.oreilly.com
  (login: anonymous
  password: your email address)
- Point your web browser to:
  ftp://ftp.oreilly.com/

FTPMAIL
- Send an email message to:
  ftpmail@online.oreilly.com
  (Write "help" in the message body)

4. Contact Us via Email

order@oreilly.com
To place a book or software order online. Good for North American and international customers.

subscriptions@oreilly.com
To place an order for any of our newsletters or periodicals.

books@oreilly.com
General questions about any of our books.

software@oreilly.com
For general questions and product information about our software. Check out O'Reilly Software Online at **http://software.oreilly.com/** for software and technical support information. Registered O'Reilly software users send your questions to: **website-support@oreilly.com**

cs@oreilly.com
For answers to problems regarding your order or our products.

booktech@oreilly.com
For book content technical questions or corrections.

proposals@oreilly.com
To submit new book or software proposals to our editors and product managers.

international@oreilly.com
For information about our international distributors or translation queries. For a list of our distributors outside of North America check out:
http://www.oreilly.com/www/order/country.html

O'Reilly & Associates, Inc.
101 Morris Street, Sebastopol, CA 95472 USA
TEL   707-829-0515 or 800-998-9938
       (6am to 5pm PST)
FAX   707-829-0104

O'REILLY™

Titles from O'Reilly

Please note that upcoming titles are displayed in italic.

WEB PROGRAMMING
Apache: The Definitive Guide
Building Your Own Web Conferences
Building Your Own Website
CGI Programming for the World Wide Web
Designing for the Web
HTML: The Definitive Guide, 2nd Ed.
JavaScript: The Definitive Guide, 2nd Ed.
Learning Perl
Programming Perl, 2nd Ed.
Mastering Regular Expressions
WebMaster in a Nutshell
Web Security & Commerce
Web Client Programming with Perl
World Wide Web Journal

USING THE INTERNET
Smileys
The Future Does Not Compute
The Whole Internet User's Guide & Catalog
The Whole Internet for Win 95
Using Email Effectively
Bandits on the Information Superhighway

JAVA SERIES
Exploring Java
Java AWT Reference
Java Fundamental Classes Reference
Java in a Nutshell
Java Language Reference, 2nd Edition
Java Network Programming
Java Threads
Java Virtual Machine

SOFTWARE
WebSite™ 1.1
WebSite Professional™
Building Your Own Web Conferences
WebBoard™
PolyForm™
Statisphere™

SONGLINE GUIDES
NetActivism   NetResearch
Net Law   NetSuccess
NetLearning   NetTravel
Net Lessons

SYSTEM ADMINISTRATION
Building Internet Firewalls
Computer Crime: A Crimefighter's Handbook
Computer Security Basics
DNS and BIND, 2nd Ed.
Essential System Administration, 2nd Ed.
Getting Connected: The Internet at 56K and Up
Linux Network Administrator's Guide
Managing Internet Information Services
Managing NFS and NIS
Networking Personal Computers with TCP/IP
Practical UNIX & Internet Security, 2nd Ed.
PGP: Pretty Good Privacy
sendmail, 2nd Ed.
sendmail Desktop Reference
System Performance Tuning
TCP/IP Network Administration
termcap & terminfo
Using & Managing UUCP
Volume 8: X Window System Administrator's Guide
Web Security & Commerce

UNIX
Exploring Expect
Learning VBScript
Learning GNU Emacs, 2nd Ed.
Learning the bash Shell
Learning the Korn Shell
Learning the UNIX Operating System
Learning the vi Editor
Linux in a Nutshell
Making TeX Work
Linux Multimedia Guide
Running Linux, 2nd Ed.
SCO UNIX in a Nutshell
sed & awk, 2nd Edition
Tcl/Tk Tools
UNIX in a Nutshell: System V Edition
UNIX Power Tools
Using csh & tsch
When You Can't Find Your UNIX System Administrator
Writing GNU Emacs Extensions

WEB REVIEW STUDIO SERIES
Gif Animation Studio
Shockwave Studio

WINDOWS
Dictionary of PC Hardware and Data Communications Terms
Inside the Windows 95 Registry
Inside the Windows 95 File System
Windows Annoyances
Windows NT File System Internals
Windows NT in a Nutshell

PROGRAMMING
Advanced Oracle PL/SQL Programming
Applying RCS and SCCS
C++: The Core Language
Checking C Programs with lint
DCE Security Programming
Distributing Applications Across DCE & Windows NT
Encyclopedia of Graphics File Formats, 2nd Ed.
Guide to Writing DCE Applications
lex & yacc
Managing Projects with make
Mastering Oracle Power Objects
Oracle Design: The Definitive Guide
Oracle Performance Tuning, 2nd Ed.
Oracle PL/SQL Programming
Porting UNIX Software
POSIX Programmer's Guide
POSIX.4: Programming for the Real World
Power Programming with RPC
Practical C Programming
Practical C++ Programming
Programming Python
Programming with curses
Programming with GNU Software
Pthreads Programming
Software Portability with imake, 2nd Ed.
Understanding DCE
Understanding Japanese Information Processing
UNIX Systems Programming for SVR4

BERKELEY 4.4 SOFTWARE DISTRIBUTION
4.4BSD System Manager's Manual
4.4BSD User's Reference Manual
4.4BSD User's Supplementary Documents
4.4BSD Programmer's Reference Manual
4.4BSD Programmer's Supplementary Documents
X Programming
Vol. 0: X Protocol Reference Manual
Vol. 1: Xlib Programming Manual
Vol. 2: Xlib Reference Manual
Vol. 3M: X Window System User's Guide, Motif Edition
Vol. 4M: X Toolkit Intrinsics Programming Manual, Motif Edition
Vol. 5: X Toolkit Intrinsics Reference Manual
Vol. 6A: Motif Programming Manual
Vol. 6B: Motif Reference Manual
Vol. 6C: Motif Tools
Vol. 8 : X Window System Administrator's Guide
Programmer's Supplement for Release 6
X User Tools
The X Window System in a Nutshell

CAREER & BUSINESS
Building a Successful Software Business
The Computer User's Survival Guide
Love Your Job!
Electronic Publishing on CD-ROM

TRAVEL
Travelers' Tales: Brazil
Travelers' Tales: Food
Travelers' Tales: France
Travelers' Tales: Gutsy Women
Travelers' Tales: India
Travelers' Tales: Mexico
Travelers' Tales: Paris
Travelers' Tales: San Francisco
Travelers' Tales: Spain
Travelers' Tales: Thailand
Travelers' Tales: A Woman's World

O'REILLY™

TO ORDER: **800-998-9938** • **order@oreilly.com** • **http://www.oreilly.com/**
OUR PRODUCTS ARE AVAILABLE AT A BOOKSTORE OR SOFTWARE STORE NEAR YOU.
FOR INFORMATION: **800-998-9938** • **707-829-0515** • **info@oreilly.com**

International Distributors

UK, EUROPE, MIDDLE EAST AND NORTHERN AFRICA (EXCEPT FRANCE, GERMANY, SWITZERLAND, & AUSTRIA)

INQUIRIES
International Thomson Publishing Europe
Berkshire House
168-173 High Holborn
London WC1V 7AA
United Kingdom
Telephone: 44-171-497-1422
Fax: 44-171-497-1426
Email: itpint@itps.co.uk

ORDERS
International Thomson Publishing Services, Ltd.
Cheriton House, North Way
Andover, Hampshire SP10 5BE
United Kingdom
Telephone: 44-264-342-832 (UK)
Telephone: 44-264-342-806 (outside UK)
Fax: 44-264-364418 (UK)
Fax: 44-264-342761 (outside UK)
UK & Eire orders: itpuk@itps.co.uk
International orders: itpint@itps.co.uk

FRANCE

Editions Eyrolles
61 bd Saint-Germain
75240 Paris Cedex 05
France
Fax: 33-01-44-41-11-44

FRENCH LANGUAGE BOOKS
All countries except Canada
Telephone: 33-01-44-41-46-16
Email: geodif@eyrolles.com
English language books
Telephone: 33-01-44-41-11-87
Email: distribution@eyrolles.com

GERMANY, SWITZERLAND, AND AUSTRIA

INQUIRIES
O'Reilly Verlag
Balthasarstr. 81
D-50670 Köln
Germany
Telephone: 49-221-97-31-60-0
Fax: 49-221-97-31-60-8
Email: anfragen@oreilly.de

ORDERS
International Thomson Publishing
Königswinterer Straße 418
53227 Bonn, Germany
Telephone: 49-228-97024 0
Fax: 49-228-441342
Email: order@oreilly.de

JAPAN

O'Reilly Japan, Inc.
Kiyoshige Building 2F
12-Banchi, Sanei-cho
Shinjuku-ku
Tokyo 160-0008 Japan
Telephone: 81-3-3356-5227
Fax: 81-3-3356-5261
Email: kenji@oreilly.com

INDIA

Computer Bookshop (India) PVT. LTD.
190 Dr. D.N. Road, Fort
Bombay 400 001 India
Telephone: 91-22-207-0989
Fax: 91-22-262-3551
Email: cbsbom@giasbm01.vsnl.net.in

HONG KONG

City Discount Subscription Service Ltd.
Unit D, 3rd Floor, Yan's Tower
27 Wong Chuk Hang Road
Aberdeen, Hong Kong
Telephone: 852-2580-3539
Fax: 852-2580-6463
Email: citydis@ppn.com.hk

KOREA

Hanbit Media, Inc.
Sonyoung Bldg. 202
Yeksam-dong 736-36
Kangnam-ku
Seoul, Korea
Telephone: 822-554-9610
Fax: 822-556-0363
Email: hant93@chollian.dacom.co.kr

SINGAPORE, MALAYSIA, THAILAND

Addison Wesley Longman Singapore PTE Ltd.
25 First Lok Yang Road
Singapore 629734
Telephone: 65-268-2666
Fax: 65-268-7023
Email: daniel@longman.com.sg

PHILIPPINES

Mutual Books, Inc.
429-D Shaw Boulevard
Mandaluyong City, Metro
Manila, Philippines
Telephone: 632-725-7538
Fax: 632-721-3056
Email: mbikikog@mnl.sequel.net

CHINA

Ron's DataCom Co., Ltd.
79 Dongwu Avenue
Dongxihu District
Wuhan 430040
China
Telephone: 86-27-3892568
Fax: 86-27-3222108
Email: hongfeng@public.wh.hb.cn

ALL OTHER ASIAN COUNTRIES

O'Reilly & Associates, Inc.
101 Morris Street
Sebastopol, CA 95472 USA
Telephone: 707-829-0515
Fax: 707-829-0104
Email: order@oreilly.com

AUSTRALIA

WoodsLane Pty. Ltd.
7/5 Vuko Place, Warriewood NSW 2102
P.O. Box 935
Mona Vale NSW 2103
Australia
Telephone: 61-2-9970-5111
Fax: 61-2-9970-5002
Email: info@woodslane.com.au

NEW ZEALAND

Woodslane New Zealand Ltd.
21 Cooks Street (P.O. Box 575)
Waganui, New Zealand
Telephone: 64-6-347-6543
Fax: 64-6-345-4840
Email: info@woodslane.com.au

THE AMERICAS

McGraw-Hill Interamericana Editores, S.A. de C.V.
Cedro No. 512
Col. Atlampa 06450
Mexico, D.F.
Telephone: 52-5-541-3155
Fax: 52-5-541-4913
Email: mcgraw-hill@infosel.net.mx

SOUTH AFRICA

International Thomson Publishing South Africa
Building 18, Constantia Park
138 Sixteenth Road
P.O. Box 2459
Halfway House, 1685 South Africa
Telephone: 27-11-805-4819
Fax: 27-11-805-3648